WILFRED RHODES

by

Brian Croudy

Published by the Association of Cricket Statisticians and Historians, West Bridgford, Nottingham
2002
Typeset by Limlow Books
Printed by Tranters, Derby
ISBN: 1 902171 59 4

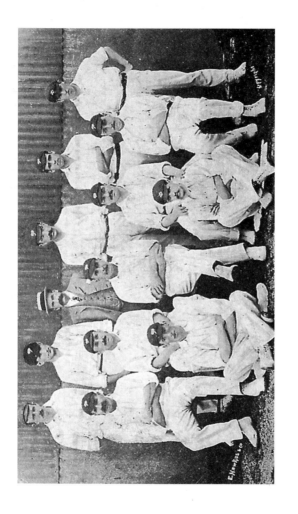

Yorkshire C.C.C.
Back: J.T.Newstead, J.W.Rothery, Mr.Hoyland, D.Denton, W.H.Wilkinson, W.E.Bates
Middle: D.Hunter, G.H.Hirst, Lord Hawke, S.Haigh, W.Rhodes
Front: H.Myers, C.H.Grimshaw

Foreword

Some few years ago when I took on the task of compiling Wilfred Rhodes career I felt quite competent to do so, and it is interesting to me that I have now compiled both Colin Blythe and Wilfred Rhodes, the two most outstanding slow left arm bowlers of that and any other era. Rhodes, of course, was the natural successor to both Edwin Peate and Robert Peel in the Yorkshire team and was to go on to take the most wickets any bowler has ever taken in a career, and is ever likely to take, while Colin Blythe, who might also have come close to that figure, given that it had been probable that he would continue after the Great War, was cut off in his prime. Apart from his bowling Rhodes went on to be a great opening batsman, which of course to some extent affected his bowling so who knows what total he might have reached had he not been so encumbered. I have always been of the opinion that Rhodes, having produced extraordinary bowling figures in his first few years, become bored with the ease of taking wickets and decided to try and become an equally accomplished batsmen. That he succeeded is history, and following the Great War he once more put more effort in to his bowling which had suffered by comparison.

Figures are very easy to compile given the time and inclination but it is not so easy to write an introduction to a Yorkshire person when not a Yorkshireman and I shied away from this particular task and instead asked Tony Woodhouse if he would write it for me. This he readily agreed to do. Two or three years later came the call to set the manuscript for publication but by this time Tony had found himself unable to do the task, so Mick Pope suggested Derek Hodgson. Derek produced the required couple of pages almost by return post, and I have to thank him very sincerely for his time and trouble. Tony Woodhouse had already contributed to the book by checking my century wicket partnerships up to the first war and for this I thank him kindly and also Brian Heald who checked the post First World War partnerships. Kit Bartlett as usual produced a seasonal list of items of interest as well as contributing to the Introduction with personal details of Rhodes's family which Derek wrote into his finished article. He also read the manuscript and unearthed some hidden errors. Others who have given help are Philip Bailey who never seems to me to go to bed and is always on the other end of the telephone, and he helped me by adding to my list of corrections to *Wisden*, of which there are a considerable number for Rhodes. Robert Brooke kindly checked out the Warwickshire scorebook for the match against Yorkshire at Edgbaston in 1905. The Warwickshire analysis was given as 57.5 overs, agreeing with the Yorkshire *Yearbook* and *Wisden* but the actual ball-by-ball figures added to 58.5 overs. I have used the figures which have thus far appeared in print. The usual publications have been consulted in compiling this book and are acknowledged below-

Wisden Cricketers' Almanack
The Cricketer
History of South African Cricket – M.W.Luckin
First Class Cricket in Australia – Volume 1 – Ray Webster
The British Library Newspaper section at Colindale
Test Cricket – Volume 1 - W.H.Frindall
Corrections to Wisden - the late Leslie Fielding

Introduction

by Derek Hodgson

Eighty years ago, which is very roughly, half the age of first-class cricket, Neville Cardus was unequivocal on one point : "[Rhodes] is the greatest of slow bowlers on all wickets". At that time (1920) he would have seen some of the 'giants' of the Golden age, including not only Rhodes but Briggs and Blythe, but as a school-boy, I am unsure whether he had been able to make comparisons with the South African googly bowlers and Australia's Arthur Mailey.

Cardus had then been three years with the *Manchester Guardian* and had seen and absorbed enough cricket to make such a pronouncement with some confidence. Wilfred had been playing since 1898 and had yet more glory to come. His prowess on English turf, whether wet, drying, baked hard or crumbling, was renowned. He had made this claim to world status in Australia in 1903/04 when his mastery of flight and length, bowling on bone-hard pitches in stifling heat, to the likes of Trumper, Duff and Noble, was more of a legend than a memory. Australian crowds, it is reported, would sing out as he strolled up to deliver "Dum...dum...de-dum" over after over.

Rhodes was, in the vernacular, the archetypal Yorkshireman. During his playing days he was taciturn, he conserved his cash and his breath and there are not too many photographs, in contrast to his great partner George Herbert Hirst, of his smile. There are stories to treasure.

In his later years it was alleged, by some iconoclast, that his power of spin had faded and that he won his wickets on reputation. Wilfred's reply was succinct. "If they think it's turning – it's turning". In the 1920s, when Yorkshire were officially captained by a series of well-meaning amateurs, mostly good club batsmen, the team was in fact directed by Wilfred and Emmott Robinson. On one occasion the captain, on the second morning, was about to put on his pads to go into bat at number seven, when Emmott interrupted him. "I wouldn't bother Major, if I were thee. Wilfred's set on declaring after the next over". Then there was the occasion, between overs in a tense, heated match between one of the great rivals, probably Lancashire, when Yorkshire's captain was advised to post himself at long-off. Puzzled, he departed, to be told later "Wilfred didn't think it were right that tha should have to listen to all that strong language".

Wilfred Rhodes was born at Moor Top, Kirkheaton, near Huddersfield, on 29th October 1877, the son of Alfred Rhodes, a miner, and Elizabeth Holliday. On leaving school at Hopton, he obtained a job in the engine sheds at Mirfield Station, his boyhood enclosing many hours of bowling against the door of a local barn, one side of the ball painted white so he could measure the amount of spin.

He followed George Hirst into the Kirkheaton team, for whom he played on Saturday afternoons after finishing work at 2 p.m., which often meant that he had to run to the ground in order to be there for the start. Then he rang the knocking off bell 30 minutes early on one of those afternoons and his railway career ended abruptly. By then it was clear that he was an outstanding cricketer and he sought to make his living from the game, first being employed as a professional at the Galashiels club. In the years 1896/97 he took 169 wickets at an average of less than eight. The president of Scotland's leading club. The Grange, advised Wilfred to return to England to further his career, advice that has never deterred the Scots from claiming they taught Wilfred all he knew.

Warwickshire might have recruited Rhodes firstly, the way into Yorkshire's first team being blocked by Bobby Peel but he returned home where the Yorkshire club had decided to allocate the young left-arm spinner to Sheffield United. After Peel had been sacked Rhodes and a Bradford spinner,

Albert Cordingley, were called in to join the party for the opening match of the 1898 season against the M.C.C. & Ground at Lord's. The story goes that Hawke, the Yorkshire captain, asked F.S.Jackson to take the two spinners to the nets, Jackson returning to recommend that Rhodes should play. Hawke later denied this, saying that Rhodes was always first choice. There is some suggestion that Yorkshire planned to play Cordingley in the next match versus Somerset at Bath. Rhodes took six wickets against a strong M.C.C. side, Cordingley was called home because of his mother's illness so Rhodes stayed in the side at Bath where, on a drying turf, he took 13 wickets for 24 and never looked back. The unlucky Cordingley eventually played for Sussex and settled into club cricket on the south coast where he is still fondly remembered.

If Wilfred was the greatest bowler of his time he was also no mean batsmen. He rose up the ranks from no 11 to no 1 for both Yorkshire and England and still holds the record, with Sir Jack Hobbs, for an opening partnership against Australia of 323 at Melbourne in 1911/12, he making 179 runs. He was no stylist, but a severely practical right-hander of sound defensive technique and endless patience. As Peter Thomas put it, Rhodes was a Test bowler who became a Test batsman and then, after the Great War, became a Test bowler again to fill the gaps. He did the double of 1000 runs and a 100 wickets in 16 of his 29 seasons, he played for England for more than 30 years, a record span, and in 1900 took 240 wickets for Yorkshire alone.

His later years were afflicted by blindness and there is a story of his being led into Headingley just after the last war, by his daughter, the crowd rising silently in tribute when word went round that the old man in the suit, shuffling along with his stick, his arm held, was Wilfred Rhodes. Cardus was to later write that a phrase he used in his essay "The Legendary Rhodes" was far too extravagant. Wilfred's career was compared with the 'surge and thunder of Odyssey'. It's an intriguing thought:- had Homer been a cricket writer what would he have made of this epic career.

1898

As it has been seen with the book I compiled on Colin Blythe, *Wisden* at this time was remarkably accurate with its talent spotting. "Beyond everything else, the feature of Yorkshire's season was the discovery of Wilfred Rhodes" it trumpeted. In his remarkable debut season Rhodes played no fewer than twenty-nine first-class matches for Yorkshire taking 142 wickets at 13.95. Nothing like it had been seen since A.G.Steel appeared 23 years earlier. As a natural successor to Peate and Peel he merged into the team as if to the 'manor born' and he never lost his place for the next thirty years except by the call of his country. In his first season he appeared for the Players v Gentlemen at Scarborough, where he opened the bowling with W.R.Cuttell, and for The Rest of England at Hastings. His total of 154 wickets is the highest number of wickets ever taken by a player on his debut season surpassing all the other ten players who took more than 100 wickets on their debut and is almost certainly never likely to be beaten. A modest beginning against the M.C.C. at Lord's was followed by 13-45 in the match against Somerset at Bath. He followed this five matches later with 12-70 against Surrey at Bradford and it was obvious that a high-class bowler had evolved. Other highlights of the season were 11-92 against Essex again at Bradford.

	Own Team Total	O	M	R	W		Opp Total	Ct
1. Yorkshire v MCC & Ground, Lord's, May 12, 13, 14 (Yorkshire won by 99 runs)								
b A.E.Trott	4	118	13	4	39	2	A.E.Trott b	135	1
							W.Chatterton st D.Hunter		
b A.E.Trott	16	185	22	12	24	4	A.Hearne b	69	
							W.Chatterton c D.Hunter		
							C.P.Foley b		
							J.S.R.Tufton st D.Hunter		
2. Yorkshire v Somerset, Bath, May 16, 17, 18 (Yorkshire won by 198 runs)								
c G.B.Nichols b E.J.Tyler	7	163	13.4	4	24	7	G.B.Nichols c D.Hunter	104	
							W.Trask b		
							S.M.J.Woods b		
							G.Fowler c D.Hunter		
							A.E.Newton st D.Hunter		
							E.J.Tyler b		
							D.J.Smith c D.Hunter		
not out	5	174-7d	13	6	21	6	E.Robson c S.Haigh	35	
							L.C.H.Palairet st D.Hunter		
							R.C.N.Palairet b		
							G.Fowler c E.Wainwright		
							E.J.Tyler b		
							D.J.Smith st D.Hunter		
3. Yorkshire v Gloucestershire, Bristol, May 19, (20), (21) (Match drawn)								
did not bat	-	263-3							
4. Yorkshire v Cambridge University, Fenner's, May 23, 24 (Yorkshire won by an innings and 22 runs)								
c A.E.Hind									
b C.R.Worthington	7	220	16.3	8	35	3	A.T.Coode lbw	67	1
							J.H.Stogdon c and b		
							H.H.B.Hawkins c D.Hunter		
			20.3	9	25	2	T.L.Taylor lbw	131	
							H.H.B.Hawkins c D.Hunter		
5. Yorkshire v Hampshire, Southampton, May 26, 27 (Yorkshire won by an innings and 79 runs)								
c W.Andrew b A.J.L.Hill	28	157	15	8	20	2	A.J.L.Hill c F.S.Jackson	42	1
							A.S.Webb c F.S.Jackson		
			7	3	10	1	V.A.Barton c J.T.Brown	36	
6. Yorkshire v Warwickshire, Headingley, May 30, 31, June 1 (Match drawn)								
c T.Forrester b S.Santall	0	112	49	20	69	5	H.W.Bainbridge b	218	
							Walter Quaife c G.H.Hirst		
							William Quaife lbw		
							A.C.S.Glover c E.Wainwright		
							T.Forrester b		
did not bat	-	85-0	4	0	14	0		50-5	

7. Yorkshire v Essex, Leyton, June 2, 3, 4 (Yorkshire won by three wickets)
```
   c C.P.McGahey b F.G.Bull   0   118      11   6    9   3   A.J.Turner  b              78      2
                                                                T.M.Russell  c and b
                                                                G.Tosetti  c and b
   did not bat                -   129-7    20   8   38   2   P.A.Perrin  st D.Hunter     168
                                                                C.P.McGahey  b
```

8. Yorkshire v Surrey, Bradford, June 6, 7, 8 (Yorkshire won by an innings and 121 runs)
```
   c D.L.A.Jephson
        b T.Richardson   13   297-9     30.3  12   46   5   T.W.Hayward  st D.Hunter    139
                                                               K.J.Key  c F.S.Jackson
                                                               A.E.Street  c J.Tunnicliffe
                                                               W.H.Lockwood  st D.Hunter
                                                               T.Richardson  c D.Denton
                                         19.1   9   24   7   R.Abel  c F.S.Jackson        37
                                                               D.L.A.Jephson  c J.T.Brown
                                                               A.E.Street  st D.Hunter
                                                               W.H.Lockwood  c D.Hunter
                                                               W.S.Lees  st D.Hunter
                                                               H.Wood  st D.Hunter
                                                               T.Richardson  c D.Hunter
```

9. Yorkshire v Hampshire, Huddersfield, June 9, 10 (Yorkshire won by an innings and 98 runs)
```
   b A.J.L.Hill        6   226     21   13   20   3   R.M.Poore  lbw               45
                                                         A.J.L..Hill  b
                                                         E.Tate  b
                                    18    7   35   4   A.S.Webb  lbw                83
                                                         W.C.Russell  c J.Tunnicliffe
                                                         C.Heseltine  b
                                                         H.Baldwin  c D.Denton
```

10. Yorkshire v Kent, Bramall Lane, June 13,14,15 (Yorkshire won by 129 runs)
```
   b F.Martin       4   289     14   7   28   0                                    218
   did not bat      -   229-3d    9   4   15   3   G.J.V.Weigall  b                171
                                                     F.Martin  c F.S.Jackson
                                                     F.H.Huish  c G.H.Hirst
```

11. Yorkshire v Middlesex, Lord's, June 16, 17, 18 (Yorkshire won by an innings and 9 runs)
```
   b J.T.Rawlin    78   445      9   2   18   1   G.MacGregor  lbw                118
                                28   7   61   1   A.E.Stoddart  c J.Tunnicliffe   318
```

12. Yorkshire v Nottinghamshire, Headingley, June 20, 21, 22 (Match drawn)
```
   b W.W.Henson    0   143     23   9   35   1   F.H.Guttridge  c D.Denton   215   1
   did not bat     -    56-6     4   1   13   0                              105-5d
```

13. Yorkshire v Leicestershire, Grace Road, Leicester, June 23, 24 (Yorkshire won by an innings and 266 runs)
```
   not out        4   449     20   9   33   5   A.E.Knight  c J.T.Brown        57
                                                  L.Brown  st J.Binns
                                                  A.D.Pougher  b
                                                  C.E.de Trafford  c F.S.Jackson
                                                  F.Geeson  st J.Binns
                              12.4   1   34   4   J.H.King  b                   126   2
                                                  C.E.de Trafford  c and b
                                                  F.Geeson  c and b
                                                  J.P.Whiteside  b
```

14. Yorkshire v Essex, Bradford, June 27, 28, 29 (Yorkshire won by an innings and 38 runs)
```
   not out       20   278     20.4   9   24   6   H.G.P.Owen  c G.H.Hirst        64
                                                    H.A.Carpenter  b
                                                    C.P.McGahey  b
                                                    A.P.Lucas  b
                                                    C.J.Kortright  c D.Denton
                                                    F.G.Bull  c J.T.Brown
                              46.1  26   68   5   P.A.Perrin  c G.H.Hirst        176
                                                    C.J.Kortright  c R.Moorhouse
                                                    T.M.Russell  c F.S.Jackson
                                                    F.G.Bull  lbw
                                                    H.I.Young  c R.Moorhouse
```

15. Yorkshire v Leicestershire, Dewsbury, June 30, July 1 (Yorkshire won by an innings and 24 runs)
```
   c F.Geeson b A.D.Pougher   3   178     30   16   25   5   C.J.B.Wood  st A.Bairstow    56
                                                               A.E.Knight  c A.Bairstow
                                                               A.D.Pougher  c E.Wainwright
                                                               R.Joyce  c G.H.Hirst
                                                               A.Woodcock  c F.W.Milligan
```

```
                        18    7   28   2   A.E.Knight  c A.Bairstow      98      1
                                              L.Brown  c E.Wainwright
16. Yorkshire v Sussex,  Bradford, July 4, 5, 6 (Yorkshire won by seven wickets)
    c F.Parris b C.H.G.Bland    13   282    36   11   77   3   F.W.Marlow  c A.Bairstow   189
                                                                 G.Brann  b
    did not bat              -   126-3   13    3   35   0   F.Parris  c J.T.Brown          218      1
17. Yorkshire v Lancashire, Bramall Lane, July 11, 12, 13 (Match drawn)
    c S.M.Tindall
            b W.B.Stoddart    33   316    24   10   47   2   J.T.Tyldesley c J.Tunnicliffe 288
                                                              W.B.Stoddart  c J.Tunnicliffe
    did not bat              -   253-2   16   13    6   1   C.R.Hartley c J.Tunnicliffe  140-5
18. Yorkshire v Kent, Maidstone, July 14, 15, 16 (Kent won by six wickets)
            b W.Wright        31   199    23    6   39   2   B.D.Bannon  c E.Wainwright  199
                                                              L.J.Le Fleming  c J.Tunnicliffe
    not out                   6   124    17    9   17   0                                 127-4
19. Yorkshire v Somerset, Scarborough, July 21, 22, 23 (Yorkshire won by six wickets)
    not out                  13   397    21    7   50   1   G.B.Nichols  b               208
    did not bat              -    54-4   21    9   45   3   G.B.Nichols  b               242
                                                              J.Daniell  b
                                                              E.J.Tyler  c J.Tunnicliffe
20. Yorkshire v Gloucestershire, Bramall Lane, July 25, 26 (Yorkshire won by an innings and 12 runs)
    c W.S.A.Brown b G.L.Jessop 1   331    30    8   71   6   C.O.H.Sewell  st D.Hunter   192
                                                              F.H.Bateman-Champain
                                                                          c J.Tunnicliffe
                                                              G.L.Jessop  st D.Hunter
                                                              W.McG Hemingway  c D.Denton
                                                              J.H.Board  c F.S.Jackson
                                                              F.G.Roberts  st D.Hunter
                                              17    6   42   2   G.L.Jessop  c J.Tunnicliffe  127
                                                              H.Wrathall  c E.Wainwright
21. Yorkshire v Derbyshire, Harrogate, July 28, 29, 30 (Match drawn)
            b J.W.Hancock      0   252    24    5   78   4   S.H.Evershed  c J.T.Brown    238
                                                              W.Sugg  c J.Tunnicliffe
                                                              A.Charlesworth  c F.W.Milligan
                                                              G.G.Walker  c G.H.Hirst
    not out                  67   321-9d  14    2   54   0                                 219-3
22. Yorkshire v Warwickshire, Edgbaston, August 1, 2, 3 (Match drawn)
    c A.F.A.Lilley b S.Santall  36   448    40   18   55   1   S.Santall  c J.Tunnicliffe  406
                                               4    0    9   0                             102-4
23. Yorkshire v Surrey, Kennington Oval, August 4, 5 (Surrey won by an innings and 272 runs)
    not out                   1    78    36    9   96   1   F.C.Holland  c J.T.Brown     536
    c C.Baldwin
            b W.H.Lockwood     4   186
24. Yorkshire v Nottinghamshire, Trent Bridge, August 8, 9, 10 (Match drawn)
    not out                  50   277    30   13   32   6   A.O.Jones  st D.Hunter        90
                                                              A.Shrewsbury  c and b
                                                              W.Gunn  b
                                                              W.Attewell  c G.H.Hirst
                                                              C.E.Dench  c G.H.Hirst
                                                              F.H.Guttridge  st D.Hunter
                                              19   12   26   1   A.O.Jones  b              90-1    1
25. Yorkshire v Lancashire, Old Trafford, August 11, 12 (Yorkshire won by ten wickets)
    lbw b J.Briggs            3   114    36   15   44   2   A.C.MacLaren  b              112
                                                              L.Radcliffe  hit wkt
    did not bat              -    63-0   17    9   19   2   A.C.MacLaren  c D.Hunter      64      1
                                                              C.R.Hartley  c S.Haigh
26. Yorkshire v Middlesex, Headingley, August 15, 16 (Middlesex won by eight wickets)
    c A.E.Trott b F.H.E.Cunliffe 20   142    23    3   52   1   C.M.Wells  c G.H.Hirst     128
            b A.E.Trott        0    45    7.4   2   24   1   P.F.Warner  c J.T.Brown       62-2
27. Yorkshire v Derbyshire, Chesterfield, August 18, 19, 20 (Yorkshire won by an innings and 387 runs)
    c W.Storer b G.G.Walker    6   662     1    1    0   1   A.P.Charlesworth  c S.Haigh  118
                                              29   13   47   3   L.G.Wright  st D.Hunter   157     2
                                                              W.Chatterton  c and b
                                                              W.Sugg  b
```

8

28. Yorkshire v Sussex, Hove, August 22, 23, 24 (Yorkshire won by 192 runs)

b E.H.Killick	20	428	19.4	7	42	2	P.H.Latham c S.Haigh	311	
							W.Humphreys c C.E.M.Wilson		
did not bat	-	166-7d	15	8	26	3	C.B.Fry b	91	2
							W.L.Murdoch b		
							C.H.G.Bland b		

29. Yorkshire v MCC & Ground, Scarborough, August 25, 26, (27) (Match drawn)

c J.H.Board b W.Attewell	5	225	26	7	59	5	H.A.Carpenter c J.T.Brown	269	
							W.Gunn b		
							H.B.Chinnery lbw		
							W.Attewell c J.T.Brown		
							J.H.Board c D.Denton		
did not bat	-	26-2							

30. Players v Gentlemen, Scarborough, August 29, 30, 31 (Gentlemen won by eight wickets)

c and b A.O.Jones	2	126	34	12	72	4	Lord Hawke st D.Hunter	208	
							H.B.Chinnery c A.Ward		
							G.L.Jessop c W.Storer		
							F.W.Milligan c G.R.Baker		
b A.O.Jones	21	169	9	3	17	0		90-2	

31. Yorkshire v Mr.C.I.Thornton's XI, Scarborough, September 1, 2, 3 (Match drawn)

c A.Ward b W.Attewell	0	228	37	15	55	0		316	
c W.Gunn b W.Attewell	11	289	-	-	-	-		136-5	1

32. Rest of England v A.E.Stoddart's XI, Hastings, September 5, 6, 7 (A.E.Stoddart's XI won by five wickets)

not out	2	236	23	6	64	4	E.Wainwright c W.Brockwell	261	1
							A.E.Stoddart c A.Shrewsbury		
							J.Briggs c W.G.Grace		
							J.H.Board c C.L.Townsend		
b T.Richardson	1	206	16	7	40	0		182-5	

33. Rest of England v Surrey and Sussex, Hastings, September 8, 9, 10 (Rest of England won by four wickets)

c F.W.Tate b T.Richardson	16	176	6	1	24	0		254	
did not bat	-	223-6	16.4	5	50	4	D.L.A.Jephson b	141	
							W.L.Murdoch b		
							F.W.Tate c J.H.Board		
							T.Richardson c G.L.Jessop		

SEASON'S AVERAGES

Batting and Fielding	M	I	NO	Runs	HS	Ave	100	50	Ct
Players v Gentlemen	1	2	0	23	21	11.50	-	-	-
Championship	26	30	8	472	78	21.45	-	3	14
Other Yorkshire matches	4	6	0	43	14	7.16	-	-	3
Other matches	2	3	1	19	16	9.50	-	-	1
Season	33	41	9	557	78	17.40	-	3	18

Bowling	O	M	R	W	BB	Ave	5i	10m
Players v Gentlemen	43	15	89	4	4-72	22.25	-	-
Championship	990	393	1745	126	7-24	13.84	11	3
Other Yorkshire matches	135.1	55	237	16	5-59	14.81	1	-
Other matches	61.4	19	178	8	4-50	22.25	-	-
Season (5-ball)	1230	482	2249	154	7-24	14.60	12	3

1899

Rhodes was head and shoulders above the other Yorkshire bowlers in his second season which saw him go from strength to strength. His performances for Yorkshire against Essex at Leyton in which he captured 15-56 including 9-28 in the first innings and 7-147 against Middlesex were rewarded by selection for the First Test Match at Trent Bridge against Australia, which was incidentally W.G.Grace's last appearance. In passing it is interesting to note that these two remarkable cricketers had a first-class career span between them of 65 years. Rhodes dismissed Monty Noble twice in this match. A feature of this season was a return of 9-24 for C.I.Thornton's England XI v The Australians who were dismissed for 83 which remained his best innings analysis. Trumper fell to him twice -

caught and stumped by William Storer behind the wicket. In the next match at Scarborough he had 7-56 against C.I.Thornton's XI.

	Own Team Total	O	M	R	W		Opp Total	Ct

34. Yorkshire v Worcestershire, Worcester, May 4, 5, 6 (Yorkshire won by 11 runs)

b E.G.Arnold	4 139	21	4	51	2	H.K.Foster c J.T.Brown, sen.	211	
						A.Bird c E.Wainwright		
c W.L.Foster b G.A.Wilson	1 205	13	2	45	2	H.K.Foster b	122	
						G.E.Bromley-Martin c J.Tunnicliffe		

35. Yorkshire v MCC & Ground, Lord's, May 8, 9, 10 (Yorkshire won by one wicket)

c A.Hearne b J.T.Hearne	0 177	21	6	45	1	A.Hearne c A.Bairstow	188	
b J.T.Hearne	1 197-9	24	10	51	1	J.T.Hearne c sub	185	

36. Yorkshire v Somerset, Bath, May 11, 12, 13 (Yorkshire won by an innings and 301 runs)

c A.E.Newton								
b G.B.Nichols	21 499	18	11	22	0		125	2
		9.4	5	11	5	S.M.J.Woods c Lord Hawke	73	
						A.E.Lewis b		
						A.E.Newton c D.Denton		
						E.J.Tyler c G.H.Hirst		
						G.C.Gill b		

37. Yorkshire v Gloucestershire, Bristol, May 15, 16, 17 (Yorkshire won by an innings and 196 runs)

c W.Troup b C.L.Townsend	6 314	14.4	5	16	6	W.Troup c E.Wainwright	44	
						H.Wrathall c S.Haigh		
						W.S.A.Brown b		
						E.L.Thomas b		
						W.H.Hale b		
						J.H.Board b		
		14	9	15	3	H.Wrathall b	74	
						C.L.Townsend b		
						G.H.Beloe c E.Wainwright		

38. Yorkshire v Cambridge University, Fenner's, May 18, 19, 20 (Yorkshire won by an innings and 83 runs)

c T.L.Taylor b E.R.Wilson	1 429	20	6	80	3	A.M.Sullivan c J.Tunnicliffe	246	
						E.R.Wilson b		
						E.F.Penn c J.Tunnicliffe		
		15	5	18	4	L.J.Moon b	100	
						J.H.Stogdon c A.Bairstow		
						T.L.Taylor c A.Bairstow		
						G.E.Winter c A.Bairstow		

39. Yorkshire v Australians, Bramall Lane, May (22), 23, (24) (Match drawn)

did not bat	- 83-3							

40. Yorkshire v Essex, Leyton, May 25, 26 (Yorkshire won by 241 runs)

lbw b W.Mead	3 172	15.2	6	28	9	H.G.P.Owen b	59	
						H.A.Carpenter b		
						P.A.Perrin b		
						C.P.McGahey b		
						A.J.Turner b		
						G.W.Ayres c E.Wainwright		
						T.M.Russell c G.H.Hirst		
						W.Reeves c D.Denton		
						F.G.Bull b		
b G.W.Ayres	8 192	16.3	4	28	6	H.A.Carpenter st D.Hunter	64	
						C.P.McGahey b		
						G.W.Ayres st D.Hunter		
						W.Reeves st D.Hunter		
						W.Mead b		
						F.G.Bull c F.S.Jackson		

41. Yorkshire v Middlesex, Lord's, May 29, 30, 31 (Middlesex won by an innings and 2 runs)

not out	18 203	65.1	20	147	7	P.F.Warner st D.Hunter	488	
						H.B.Hayman b		
						H.H.Cobb b		
						C.P.Foley c J.Tunnicliffe		
						A.E.Trott c G.H.Hirst		
						R.S.Lucas lbw		
						J.T.Hearne b		
b W.Roche	13 283							

42. ENGLAND v AUSTRALIA, Trent Bridge, June 1, 2, 3 (Match drawn)

c J.J.Kelly b E.Jones	6	193	35.2	13	58	4	M.A.Noble b	252
							F.J.Laver b
							W.P.Howell c T.W.Hayward
							E.Jones c C.B.Fry
did not bat	-	155-7	20	3	60	3	J.Darling b
							M.A.Noble lbw
							H.Trumble c K.S.Ranjitsinhji

43. Yorkshire v Essex, Bramall Lane, June 5, 6, 7 (Essex won by nine wickets)

not out	0	220	63	24	108	4	H.G.P.Owen c D.Hunter	368	
							C.P.McGahey c F.S.Jackson		
							J.H.Inns c Lord Hawke		
							W.Reeves c F.S.Jackson		
c W.Reeves b W.Mead	5	166	4.2	1	12	1	H.G.P.Owen c and b	19-1	1

44. Yorkshire v Derbyshire, Dewsbury, June 8, 9, 10 (Yorkshire won by nine wickets)

c J.Humphries b W.Bestwick	12	343	32	12	65	5	L.G.Wright b	203	
							T.A.Higson c D.Hunter		
							J.W.Hancock c L.Whitehead		
							J.H.Young c J.Tunnicliffe		
							J.Humphries c G.H.Hirst		
did not bat	-	33-1	14.2	4	50	4	J.W.Hancock c D.Hunter	171	3
							J.J.Hulme c E.Wainwright		
							J.H.Young c and b		
							W.Bestwick st D.Hunter		

45. ENGLAND v AUSTRALIA, Lord's, June 15, 16, 17 (Australia won by ten wickets)

b E.Jones	2	206	39	14	108	3	J.Worrall c T.W.Hayward	421
							J.Darling c K.S.Ranjitsinhji	
							M.A.Noble c A.F.A.Lilley	
c and b M.A.Noble	2	240	5	1	9	0		28-0

46. Yorkshire v Surrey, Headingley, June 19, 20, 21 (Match drawn)

not out	20	250	50	20	102	3	E.G.Hayes b	393
							H.B.Richardson c S.Haigh	
							W.S.Lees c S.Haigh	
b T.Richardson	0	209						

47. Yorkshire v Warwickshire, Scarborough, June 22, 23, 24 (Yorkshire won by 167 runs)

run out	25	184	21	6	45	0		121	2
not out	1	212	18	6	31	4	T.S.Fishwick b	108	
							A.F.A.Lilley c D.Hunter		
							H.W.Bainbridge b		
							A.C.S.Glover c E.Wainwright		

48. Yorkshire v Lancashire, Bramall Lane, June 26, 27, 28 (Lancashire won by 59 runs)

b A.W.Mold	3	115	31	2	91	4	A.C.MacLaren c F.Mitchell	203
							A.Ward hit wkt	
							J.Hallows c F.Mitchell	
							C.Smith c L.Whitehead	
c and b J.Briggs	3	186	38	16	50	4	A.Ward c J.Tunnicliffe	157
							J.T.Tyldesley b	
							F.H.Sugg c J.Tunnicliffe	
							W.R.Cuttell c F.Mitchell	

49. Yorkshire v Derbyshire, Derby, July 3, 4, 5 (Yorkshire won by an innings and 160 runs)

c C.J.B.Wood b J.J.Hulme	16	432	20	11	26	2	L.G.Wright b	78	
							W.Bestwick c J.Tunnicliffe		
				22	10	36	3	W.Sugg b	194	1
							S.H.Wood c F.Mitchell		
							J.J.Hulme c J.T.Brown		

50. Yorkshire v Sussex, Harrogate, July 6, 7, 8 (Match drawn)

c C.L.A.Smith									
b K.S.Ranjitsinhji	2	147	32	12	57	5	C.B.Fry c G.H.Hirst	149	1
							G.Brann b		
							E.H.Killick b		
							J.Vine c G.H.Hirst		
							F.W.Tate c C.E.M.Wilson		
not out	81	332-9d	30	5	101	2	G.Brann c C.E.M.Wilson	262-4	
							E.H.Killick c D.Hunter		

51. Players v Gentlemen, Lord's, July 10, 11, 12 (Gentlemen won by an innings and 59 runs)

not out   7 196   55 11 131 2 C.B.Fry b   480
K.S.Ranjitsinhji c T.W.Hayward
c A.C.MacLaren
    b C.L.Townsend 31 225

52. Yorkshire v Warwickshire, Edgbaston, July 13, 14, 15 (Yorkshire won by ten wickets)

c C.Charlesworth
    b E.F.Field 19 466   13 7 20 1 E.J.Diver b   143 1
not out   8 8-0   26 12 25 3 J.H.G.Devey c G.H.Hirst 329 1
S.J.Whitehead lbw
E.F.Field b

53. Yorkshire v Middlesex, Bradford, July 20, 21, 22 (Match drawn)

not out   0 575-7d 11.3 3 27 1 G.MacGregor c J.T.Brown 188 1
                      10   2 24 3 P.F.Warner b   87-3
L.J.Moon c D.Hunter
F.G.J.Ford c J.Tunnicliffe

54. Yorkshire v Kent, Headingley, July 24, 25, 26 (Yorkshire won by an innings and 30 runs)

c J.R.Mason b W.M.Bradley 10 367   35 16 36 4 W.L.Knowles c D.Denton 149 1
J.Le Fleming lbw
G.J.V.Weigall c D.Hunter
F.Martin b
                      24.1 12 29 3 R.N.R.Blaker c D.Hunter 188 2
F.Martin c and b
W.M.Bradley c and b

55. Yorkshire v Gloucestershire, Huddersfield, July 27, 28 (Yorkshire won by seven wickets)

c W.S.A.Brown b G.L.Jessop 2 102   4 1 15 1 W.Troup lbw   173 1
did not bat - 163-3   1 1 0 1 G.Romans c F.S.Jackson 91

56.Yorkshire v Nottinghamshire, Bradford, July 31, August 1, 2 (Match drawn)

c C.E.Dench b G.H.Chambers 4 562   41 13 108 1 A.O.Jones b   444
c A.O.Jones b P.Mason   4 120-9

57. Yorkshire v Lancashire, Old Trafford, August 3, 4, 5 (Match drawn)

b T.Lancaster   4 344   52 22 98 3 T.Lancaster c D.Hunter 450
C.Smith c J.Tunnicliffe
J.T.Tyldesley b
did not bat - 222-5

58. Yorkshire v Worcestershire, Bramall Lane, August 7, 8, 9 (Match drawn)

run out   2 268   31 16 32 3 G.E.Bromley-Martin
                                      c J.T.Brown 236
T.Straw c F.Mitchell
H.K.Foster c J.T.Brown
not out   8 265-7d 16 10 14 0   148-5

59. Yorkshire v Surrey, Kennington Oval, August 10, 11, 12 (Match drawn)

b T.Richardson 8 704   28 11 51 0   551-7

60. ENGLAND v AUSTRALIA, Kennington Oval, August 14, 15, 16 (Match drawn)

not out   8 576   25 2 79 0   352
                      22 8 27 3 V.T.Trumper c and b 254-5 1
S.E.Gregory b
C.E.McLeod b

61. Yorkshire v Nottinghamshire, Trent Bridge, August 17, 18, 19 (Yorkshire won by an innings and 42 runs)

b J.A.Dixon   38 391   40.2 14 74 3 W.Gunn b   257
A.Shrewsbury c F.Mitchell
T.G.Wass c D.Denton
                      25.3 14 38 8 J.A.Dixon st D.Hunter 92
J.R.Gunn b
A.O.Jones c F.S.Jackson
A.Shrewsbury c E.Smith
W.B.Goodacre c J.Tunnicliffe
G.J.Groves b
W.Attewell c E.Smith
T.G.Wass b

62. Yorkshire v Kent, Tonbridge, August 21, 22, 23 (Kent won by eight wickets)

b W.M.Bradley 0 164   46.4 19 90 3 H.C.Stewart b   369
F.H.Huish b
C.Blythe c J.Tunnicliffe
not out   10 325   15 4 27 1 S.H.Day st D.Hunter 124-2

```
63. Yorkshire v Sussex, Hove, August 24, 25, 26 (Match drawn)
    st H.R.Butt b W.Humphreys  0  341      41  22  64  6  C.B.Fry  c E.Smith            169
                                                          P.H.Latham  c E.Smith
                                                          G.Brann  lbw
                                                          K.S.Ranjitsinhji  c D.Hunter
                                                          A.Collins  b
    did not bat             -   53-1   58  26  112  3     W.Humphreys  c F.Mitchell
                                                          E.H.Killick  b               339
                                                          A.Collins  c D.Hunter
                                                          F.W.Tate  lbw

64. Yorkshire v MCC & Ground, Scarborough, August 28, 29, 30 (Match drawn)
    b W.Mead               0  237    38   9  111  5      F.L.Fane  c D.Denton           255   1
                                                         A.O.Jones  c S.Haigh
                                                         T.L.Taylor  c E.Wainwright
                                                         J.Carlin  c J.Tunnicliffe
                                                         H.D.G.Leveson-Gower  st D.Hunter
    did not bat            -  145-6d   -   -    -  -                                     49-5

65. Mr.C.I.Thornton's England XI v Australians, Scarborough, August 31 September 1, 2 (Match drawn)
    c and b H.Trumble      1  185    19    9  27  1      V.T.Trumper  c W.Storer         233   1
    did not bat            -   81-7  18.4  10  24  9      H.Trumble  c W.Storer           83
                                                         V.T.Trumper  st W.Storer
                                                         M.A.Noble  lbw
                                                         J.Darling  b
                                                         F.A.Iredale  b
                                                         S.E.Gregory  st W.Storer
                                                         F.J.Laver  c H.D.G.Leveson-Gower
                                                         J.J.Kelly  c F.S.Jackson
                                                         E.Jones  c F.Mitchell

66. Yorkshire v Mr.C.I.Thornton's XI, Scarborough, September 4, 5, 6 (Yorkshire won by 51 runs)
    not out               0  156    24.2  10  56  7      W.L.Foster  c F.S.Jackson      115
                                                         W.Gunn  c D.Hunter
                                                         W.Storer  st D.Hunter
                                                         A.E.Trott  c F.Mitchell
                                                         E.G.Wynyard  lbw
                                                         W.R.Cuttell  st D.Hunter
                                                         W.Attewell  c G.H.Hirst
    b A.E.Trott          14  302    27    4  91  3       R.E.Foster  st D.Hunter        292
                                                         H.D.G.Leveson-Gower  lbw
                                                         W.Attewell  b

67. Rest of England v Home Counties, Hastings, September 7, 8, 9 (Match drawn)
    c A.Hearne b H.I.Young 0  233   17    5  31  0                                      331   2
    did not bat           -  251-5  10    1  35  1       A.E.Stoddart  c F.Mitchell     212-6d  1
```

SEASON'S AVERAGES

Batting and Fielding	M	I	NO	Runs	HS	Ave	100	50	Ct
Test matches	3	4	1	18	8*	6.00	-	-	1
Players v Gentlemen	1	2	1	38	31	38.00	-	-	-
Championship	23	35	9	359	81*	13.80	-	1	17
Other Yorkshire matches	5	6	1	16	14	3.20	-	-	1
Other matches	2	2	0	1	1	0.50	-	-	4
Season	34	49	12	432	81*	11.67	-	1	23
Career	67	90	21	989	81*	14.33	-	4	41

Bowling	O	M	R	W	BB	Ave	5i	10m
Test matches	146.2	41	341	13	4-58	26.23	-	-
Players v Gentlemen	55	11	131	2	2-131	65.50	-	-
Championship	1083.1	420	2021	129	9-28	15.66	9	2
Other Yorkshire matches	169.2	50	452	24	7-56	18.83	2	1
Other matches	64.4	25	117	11	9-24	10.63	1	1
Season (5-ball)	1518.4	547	3062	179	9-24	17.10	12	4
Career (5-ball)	2748.4	1029	5311	333	9-24	15.94	24	7

1900

The adage that bowlers hunt better in pairs was never more than justified this year when Rhodes and Schofield Haigh carried all before them. For Yorkshire they dismissed 351 batsmen in County matches alone and 400 in all matches. Rhodes, the supreme artist, charmed the batsmen out while Haigh veritably frightened them out, his vicious break-back gaining many a wicket. While researching Haigh's career for a possible booklet some years ago it appeared to me that he was the finest exponent of dismissing 8, 9, 10 and 11 with unerring accuracy. In his first match against Worcestershire at Bradford Rhodes took 7-20 and he had 8-68 against Cambridge University at Fenner's. By the end of May he had already taken 59 wickets. In the 'Roses' match he had 8-43 and followed this with 7-46 against Essex at Leyton. Rhodes' 8-23 for Yorkshire against Hampshire at Hull came two matches later and proved to be his best analysis this year although he also took ten wickets in a match on five occasions.

	Own Team Total	O	M	R	W		Opp Total	Ct
68. Yorkshire v Worcestershire, Bradford, May 7 (Yorkshire won by an innings and 5 runs)								
c and b H.M.Bannister	0	99	13	6	16	4	H.K.Foster c J.Tunnicliffe	43
							E.G.Arnold c D.Hunter	
							A.W.Isaac st D.Hunter	
							H.M.Bannister b	
			11.1	4	20	7	J.Howard c J.Tunnicliffe	51
							E.G.Arnold st D.Hunter	
							F.L.Bowley st D.Hunter	
							A.W.Isaac c S.Haigh	
							A.Bird st D.Hunter	
							G.A.Wilson c D.Denton	
							T.Straw lbw	
69. Yorkshire v Kent, Catford, May 10, 11, 12 (Yorkshire won by 131 runs)								
b A.Hearne	1	163	13	4	35	0		112
c A.Hearne b W.M.Bradley	0	260	11.5	2	21	3	E.Humphreys c G.H.Hirst	180
							F.H.Huish c J.T.Brown	
							W.M.Bradley st D.Hunter	
70. Yorkshire v MCC & Ground, Lord's, May 14, 15, 16 (MCC & Ground won by 182 runs)								
c W.Storer b J.T.Hearne	24	187	26.5	6	76	6	A.Hearne lbw	346
							P.F.Warner b	
							G.J.Thompson b	
							H.I.Young c D.Hunter	
							J.T.Hearne c D.Denton	
							W.Mead c J.T.Brown, jun.	
b H.I.Young	16	289	29	7	85	3	H.A.Carpenter b	312
							C.O.H.Sewell b	
							A.Page lbw	
71. Yorkshire v Cambridge University, Fenner's, May 17, 18, 19 (Yorkshire won by an innings and 15 runs)								
st T.L.Taylor b A.E.Fernie	42	391	32	11	73	3	E.R.Wilson st D.Hunter	224
							S.H.Day c G.H.Hirst	
							T.L.Taylor lbw	
			28.1	9	68	8	E.R.Wilson c J.T.Brown, sen.	152
							J.Stanning c G.H.Hirst	
							S.H.Day st D.Hunter	
							E.M.Dowson b	
							T.L.Taylor c D.Hunter	
							J.Daniell c S.Haigh	
							A.E.Hind b	
							G.A.Scott b	
72. Yorkshire v Derbyshire, Bramall Lane, May 21, 22, (23) (Match drawn)								
c W.Storer b J.O'Connor	21	259-8d	31	11	72	7	H.Bagshaw b	175
							W.Chatterton b	
							F.A.Barrs b	
							H.S.Pink b	
							J.H.Young c E.Wainwright	
							J.J.Hulme c J.Tunnicliffe	
							W.Bestwick b	
			2	1	5	1	H.Bagshaw b	9-1

73. Yorkshire v Leicestershire, Huddersfield, May 24, 25, 26 (Yorkshire won by ten wickets)
```
    c A.D.Pougher b J.H.King   27  302      25  11  46  2  C.Agar  c D.Denton              262    1
                                                            F.Geeson  c E.Wainwright
    did not bat              -  61-0     24   8  52  6  A.D.Pougher  c E.Wainwright 100
                                                            H.Whitehead  st D.Hunter
                                                            J.H.King  c J.T.Brown, jun.
                                                            C.E.de Trafford  c J.T.Brown, jun.
                                                            C.Agar  b
                                                            F.Geeson  b
```
74. Yorkshire v Warwickshire, Headingley, May 28, 29, 30 (Match drawn)
```
    b S.Hargreave            31  359      33   3  81  3  C.Charlesworth
                                                              c E.Wainwright  228
                                                            S.Santall  b
                                                            E.J.Diver  c J.T.Brown, sen.
    did not bat             -  86-3      45  23  49  6  Walter Quaife  b             294
                                                            S.P.Kinneir  c D.Hunter
                                                            C.Charlesworth  c S.Haigh
                                                            T.S.Fishwick  c E.Smith
                                                            E.J.Diver  c S.Haigh
                                                            H.W.Bainbridge  b
```
75. Yorkshire v Middlesex, Lord's, May 31, June 1, 2 (Yorkshire won by six wickets)
```
    lbw b A.E.Trott          0  307      30   6  77  4  J.T.Rawlin  b               202
                                                            A.E.Trott  c E.Smith
                                                            G.MacGregor  c S.Haigh
                                                            R.S.Lucas  c J.Tunnicliffe
    did not bat             -  98-4      36   7  75  3  G.W.Beldam  lbw             202
                                                            R.W.Nicholls  c W.A.I.Washington
                                                            J.T.Hearne  c E.Wainwright
```
76. Yorkshire v Leicestershire, Grace Road, Leicester, June 7, 8, 9 (Yorkshire won by ten wickets)
```
    b H.Burgess             27  241    34.1  11  63  4  C.J.B.Wood  c J.Tunnicliffe  162    1
                                                            A.E.Knight  c and b
                                                            A.D.Pougher  b
                                                            C.E. de Trafford  c J.Tunnicliffe
    did not bat             -  15-0    17.2  10  15  2  H.Whitehead  c J.Tunnicliffe   93
                                                            A.Woodcock  lbw
```
77. Yorkshire v Lancashire, Bradford, June 11, 12, 13 (Match drawn)
```
    not out                  7  230      19   4  43  8  A.C.MacLaren  lbw             96
                                                            A.Ward  c G.H.Hirst
                                                            A.G.Paul  st D.Hunter
                                                            C.R.Hartley  st D.Hunter
                                                            W.R.Cuttell  c E.Smith
                                                            A.Eccles  c D.Denton
                                                            J.Holland  c J.Tunnicliffe
                                                            C.Smith  c D.Hunter
    did not bat             -  64-6d
```
78. Yorkshire v Essex, Leyton, June 14, 15 (Yorkshire won by six wickets)
```
    b C.J.Kortright          8  152      17   5  32  2  H.A.Carpenter  c S.Haigh     132
                                                            T.M.Russell  c D.Denton
    did not bat             -  102-4     19   4  46  7  C.P.McGahey  c D.Denton      120
                                                            P.A.Perrin  c E.Smith
                                                            C.J.Kortright  b
                                                            A.E.Russell  c J.T.Brown, jun.
                                                            W.Reeves  st D.Hunter
                                                            H.I.Young  c J.T.Brown, jun.
                                                            W.Mead  c J.Tunnicliffe
```
79. Yorkshire v Surrey, Bramall Lane, June 18, 19, 20 (Match drawn)
```
    not out                  8  195      39  12  83  3  W.Brockwell  c J.Tunnicliffe 242
                                                            E.G.Hayes  st D.Hunter
                                                            W.S.Lees  st D.Hunter
    did not bat             -  31-1    24.3   6  58  6  R.Abel  c D.Hunter           146
                                                            W.Brockwell  c J.Tunnicliffe
                                                            V.F.S.Crawford  st D.Hunter
                                                            T.W.Hayward  c D.Hunter
                                                            D.L.A.Jephson  b
                                                            W.S.Lees  c J.T.Brown, sen.
```

80. Yorkshire v Hampshire, Hull, June 21, 22, 23 (Yorkshire won by an innings and 271 runs)
```
b T.Soar              0   460      30.3  9  43  6   A.S.Webb  c J.T.Brown, sen.   128
                                                    E.M.Sprot  b
                                                    E.C.Lee  c J.Tunnicliffe
                                                    T.Soar  c G.H.Hirst
                                                    D.A.Steele  c J.Tunnicliffe
                                                    H.Baldwin  b
                                   12.5  5  23  8   C.Robson  b                    61   1
                                                    A.S.Webb  c D.Hunter
                                                    E.Newton  c J.Tunnicliffe
                                                    E.C.Lee  st D.Hunter
                                                    V.A.Barton  c E.Wainwright
                                                    T.Soar  c G.H.Hirst
                                                    C.Budden  c and b
                                                    G.Bull  b
```
81. Yorkshire v Derbyshire, Derby, June 25, 26 (Yorkshire won by an innings and 24 runs)
```
c J.Humphries b J.H.Young  53  195  20.4  6  32  7  L.G.Wright  c D.Hunter         69
                                                    H.Bagshaw  b
                                                    W.Storer  c D.Hunter
                                                    W.Sugg  c S.Haigh
                                                    J.H.Young  st D.Hunter
                                                    J.Humphries  b
                                                    W.Bestwick  c D.Denton
                                    21   5  45  4   A.E.Lawton  c D.Hunter        102   1
                                                    J.H.Young  c S.Haigh
                                                    J.Humphries  c H.Riley
                                                    W.Bestwick  c and b
```
82. Yorkshire v Somerset, Dewsbury, June 28, 29 (Yorkshire won by 140 runs)
```
lbw E.Robson           0   137     20    4  52  4   C.A.Bernard  c E.Smith        140
                                                    E.Robson  c W.A.I.Washington
                                                    B.Cranfield  c D.Denton
                                                    G.C.Gill  c W.A.I.Washington
b A.E.Lewis           14   191     11    3  22  4   C.A.Bernard  c Lord Hawke      48
                                                    W.Trask  st D.Hunter
                                                    E.Robson  c J.T.Brown
                                                    W.Hyman  c E.Wainwright
```
83. Yorkshire v Kent, Headingley, July 2, (3), 4 (Match drawn)
```
b C.Blythe             4   132     41   12 101  3   C.J.Burnup
                                                       c W.A.I.Washington 230
                                                    E.Humphreys  c D.Hunter
                                                    C.Blythe  c Lord Hawke
did not bat            -   51-3    13    5  16  0                              42-3d
```
84. Yorkshire v Nottinghamshire, Scarborough, July 5 ,6, 7 (Match drawn)
```
b J.Atkinson          23   311     31    7  83  3   J.A.Dixon  st D.Hunter        279
                                                    P.Mason  c S.Haigh
                                                    J.Carlin  c J.T.Brown, sen.
                                    9    6   8  1   A.O.Jones  c L.Whitehead      72-6
```
85. Yorkshire v Sussex, Bramall Lane, July 9, 10, 11 (Yorkshire won by an innings and 93 runs)
```
c C.B.Fry b K.S.Ranjitsinhji 79 489-9d 23  3  82  2  K.S.Ranjitsinhji
                                                        c J.Tunnicliffe          232
                                                    H.R.Butt  c J.Tunnicliffe
                                    28   4  59  7   C.B.Fry  c D.Hunter           164
                                                    A.E.Relf  c E.Smith
                                                    E.H.Killick  b
                                                    K.S.Ranjitsinhji  c S.Haigh
                                                    J.Vine  c L.Whitehead
                                                    H.R.Butt  st D.Hunter
                                                    C.H.G.Bland  c G.H.Hirst
```
86. Players v Gentlemen, Lord's, July 16, 17, 18 (Players won by two wickets)
```
not out                1   136     30    4  93  4   C.B.Fry  b                    297   1
                                                    D.L.A.Jephson  lbw
                                                    G.L.Jessop  c A.F.A.Lilley
                                                    S.M.J.Woods  c A.F.A.Lilley
not out                7   502-8   15    2  51  2   A.O.Jones  b                  339
                                                    C.L.Townsend  b
```

87. Yorkshire v Lancashire, Old Trafford, July 19, 20, 21 (Match drawn)
c W.R.Cuttell b J.Hallows   8   235   33   9   72   2   W.J.Hibbert b   228
                                                            J.T.Tyldesley c E.Wainwright
not out   2   146   -   -   -   -   20-2

88. Yorkshire v Gloucestershire, Bradford, July 23, 24, 25 (Yorkshire won by 40 runs)
not out   23   409   20.5 6   72   8   C.O.H.Sewell c Lord Hawke   269
                                                            W.S.A.Brown c D.Hunter
                                                            J.H.Board c C.Oyston
                                                            H.Wrathall c E.Wainwright
                                                            G.L.Jessop c Lord Hawke
                                                            F.H.Bateman-Champain c D.Hunter
                                                            A.H.G.Fargus st D.Hunter
                                                            A.J.Paish c D.Denton
not out   11   187   24.4 5 120   6   C.O.H.Sewell lbw   287
                                                            W.S.A.Brown c J.Tunnicliffe
                                                            H.Wrathall c S.Haigh
                                                            G.L.Jessop c J.Tunnicliffe
                                                            F.H.Bateman-Champain
                                                                             c T.L.Taylor
                                                            A.J.Paish b

89. Yorkshire v Surrey, Kennington Oval, July 26, 27, 28 (Match drawn)
not out   4   380   43 15   73   0   360
                                           13   7   26   4   R.Abel c G.H.Hirst   52
                                                            W.H.Lockwood lbw
                                                            T.W.Hayward lbw
                                                            W.S.Lees c E.Wainwright

90. Yorkshire v Nottinghamshire, Trent Bridge, July 30, 31, August 1 (Match drawn)
not out   4   270   41 17   74   1   C.E.Dench st A.Bairstow   335   1
did not bat   -   197-3

91. Yorkshire v Essex, Harrogate, August 2, (3), 4 (Yorkshire won by 96 runs)
c and b W.Mead   9   171   16.2 5   40   6   H.A.Carpenter c S.Haigh   65
                                                            C.P.McGahey c A.Bairstow
                                                            W.Reeves st A.Bairstow
                                                            J.H.Inns b
                                                            T.M.Russell c E.Wainwright
                                                            F.G.Bull c E.Smith
did not bat   -   42-1d   12.5 4   28   8   H.G.P.Owen st A.Bairstow   52
                                                            H.A.Carpenter st A.Bairstow
                                                            P.A.Perrin c G.H.Hirst
                                                            C.P.Buckenham b
                                                            W.Reeves st A.Bairstow
                                                            J.H.Inns c G.H.Hirst
                                                            T.M.Russell b
                                                            F.G.Bull b

92. Yorkshire v Warwickshire, Edgbaston, August (9), (10), 11 (Match drawn)
did not bat   - 158-2d   29.5 11   47   6   T.S.Fishwick st D.Hunter   84
                                                            S.P.Kinneir c E.Smith
                                                            William Quaife c S.Haigh
                                                            Walter Quaife lbw
                                                            E.J.Diver st D.Hunter
                                                            E.F.Field st D.Hunter
                                           12   7   13   3   J.H.G.Devey c J.Tunnicliffe 43-5   1
                                                            T.S.Fishwick c and b
                                                            A.F.A.Lilley b

93. Yorkshire v Middlesex, Headingley, August 13, 14, 15 (Yorkshire won by 63 runs)
c R.N.Douglas b A.E.Trott   6   235   38   8 102   4   C.M.Wells st D.Hunter   192
                                                            J.T.Rawlin c T.L.Taylor
                                                            A.E.Trott c E.Smith
                                                            R.W.Nicholls b
c J.Douglas b C.M.Wells   15   96   24 14   29   2   J.Douglas b   76
                                                            R.N.Douglas c Lord Hawke

94. Yorkshire v Gloucestershire, Cheltenham, August 16, 17 (Yorkshire won by an innings and 44 runs)
b G.L.Jessop   9   305   21.2 11   36   6   C.L.Townsend c E.Smith   101
                                                            A.G.Richardson c D.Denton
                                                            G.L.Jessop c D.Denton
                                                            J.H.Board c J.Tunnicliffe
                                                            W.S.A.Brown b
                                                            A.J.Paish b

```
              27.4   7   67   7   R.W.Rice  lbw                        160
                                  H.Wrathall  c Lord Hawke
                                  A.G.Richardson  c E.Wainwright
                                  G.L.Jessop  st D.Hunter
                                  W.S.A.Brown  c Lord Hawke
                                  F.N.Townsend  st D.Hunter
                                  A.H.C.Fargus  c E.Wainwright
```

95. Yorkshire v Somerset, Taunton, August 20, 21, 22 (Yorkshire won by an innings and 120 runs)
```
    did not bat       -  518-8d  33   9  104  3   A.E.Lewis  b              250
                                                  G.C.Gill  b
                                                  C.E.Dunlop  c T.L.Taylor
                                  26.1 10  59  6   C.A.Bernard  c J.Tunnicliffe  148
                                                  E.Robson  c J.Tunnicliffe
                                                  J.Daniell  st D.Hunter
                                                  G.C.Gill  b
                                                  C.E.Dunlop  c D.Hunter
                                                  E.J.Tyler  c L.Whitehead
```

96. Yorkshire v Sussex, Hove, August 23, 24, 25 (Match drawn)
```
    c and b F.W.Tate   6   214   42.3  7  115  7   A.E.Relf  c L.Whitehead  268
                                                  P.H.Latham  lbw
                                                  A.Collins  c D.Denton
                                                  F.H.Gresson  b
                                                  H.R.Butt  lbw
                                                  C.H.G.Bland  c G.H.Hirst
                                                  F.W.Tate  st D.Hunter
    did not bat        -   199-8
```

97. Yorkshire v MCC & Ground, Scarborough, August 27, 28, 29 (Yorkshire won by 272 runs)
```
    b G.J.Thompson    12   191   18   8   21  3   H.A.Carpenter  c Lord Hawke  99
                                                  E.T.Pereira  c T.L.Taylor
                                                  C.E.M.Wilson  b
    not out           51   285   20   4   54  4   W.L.Foster  c Lord Hawke  105
                                                  E.T.Pereira  b
                                                  H.B.Chinnery  b
                                                  H.D.G.Leveson-Gower
                                                          c L.Whitehead
```

98. Players v Gentlemen, Scarborough, August 30, 31, September 1 (Players won by an innings and 22 runs)
```
    c G.L.Jessop b E.Smith  40  457  23   3   68  2   Lord Hawke  c J.T.Brown  259
                                                  G.L.Jessop  st D.Hunter
                                     22   5   55  2   W.L.Foster  c H.I.Young  176
                                                  G.L.Jessop  c J.T.Brown
```

99. Yorkshire v Mr.C.I.Thornton's XI, Scarborough, September 3, 4, 5 (Yorkshire won by three wickets)
```
    c G.L.Jessop b R.E.Foster  16  336  17.3  3  53  5   G.L.Jessop  c J.Tunnicliffe  266
                                                  G.J.Thompson  c D.Denton
                                                  A.E.Trott  c E.Wainwright
                                                  J.H.Board  c G.H.Hirst
                                                  H.I.Young  b
    did not bat        -   208-7  30   4   92  2   H.D.G.Leveson-Gower
                                                          st D.Hunter  276
                                                  R.E.Foster  b
```

100. North v South, Hastings, September 6, 7, 8 (Match drawn)
```
    b D.L.A.Jephson    0   440   36   9  120  5   C.L.Townsend  c J.T.Brown  287
                                                  T.W.Hayward  st A.F.A.Lilley
                                                  D.L.A.Jephson  c J.T.Brown
                                                  A.E.Stoddart  c A.C.MacLaren
                                                  W.G.Grace  lbw
    did not bat        -   234-5d   9   5   9   0                      266-5   2
```

101. Rest of England v Surrey and Sussex, Hastings, September 10, 11, 12 (Match drawn)
```
    b K.S.Ranjitsinhji  16  355  18.2  7   55  3   E.H.Killick  b           359   2
                                                  H.R.Butt  st A.F.A.Lilley
                                                  F.W.Tate  c W.G.Grace
    did not bat        -   301-6d  29   7   98  3   R.Abel  c J.T.Brown  215-5
                                                  C.B.Fry  c W.G.Grace
                                                  T.W.Hayward  c E.F.Field
```

102. North v South, Lord's, September 13, 14, 15 (Match drawn)
```
    not out           30   405    4   2   3   0                          474
    c A.E.Stoddart
        b D.L.A.Jephson  0   130    -   -   -   -                        143-6
```

Batting and Fielding	M	I	NO	Runs	HS	Ave	100	50	Ct
Players v Gentlemen	2	3	2	48	40	48.00	-	-	1
North v South	2	3	1	30	30*	15.00	-	-	2
Championship	26	29	7	400	79	18.18	-	2	6
Other Yorkshire matches	4	6	1	161	51*	32.20	-	1	-
Other matches	1	1	0	16	16	16.00	-	-	2
Season	35	42	11	655	79	21.12	-	3	11
Career	102	132	32	1644	81*	16.44	-	7	52

Bowling	O	M	R	W	BB	Ave	5i	10m
Players v Gentlemen	90	14	267	10	4-93	26.70	-	-
North v South	49	16	132	5	5-120	26.40	1	-
Championship	1165.1	359	2532	206	8-23	12.29	20	6
Other Yorkshire matches	201.3	52	522	34	8-68	15.35	3	1
Other matches	47.2	14	153	6	3-55	25.50	-	-
Season (6-ball)	1553	455	3606	261	8-23	13.81	24	7
Career (6-ball)	1553	455 }	8917	594	9-24	15.01	48	14
(5-ball)	2748.4	1029 }						

1901

Rhodes again took over two hundred wickets and also scored his first century which came in a festival match at Scarborough. This year he had great success against the 'big hitters' of the day. His best analysis came in his second match: 14-141 (7-78 & 7-63) against Gloucestershire at Bristol. Gilbert Jessop, one of his 'rabbits', fell twice in this match. The next game against Somerset at Taunton gave him 12-182 (5-115 & 6-67) and saw Sammy Woods dismissed twice and his 13-96 against Leicestershire at Leicester gave him both C.J.B.Wood and A.E.Knight 'doubles'. Against Gloucestershire in the return match at Hull he dismissed Jessop twice more in taking 12-86 in 49.2 overs. Nonstop success this year saw him sign off with 8-55 against Kent in late August and 12-159 for the Players against the Gentlemen at Scarborough.

	Own Team Total	O	M	R	W		Opp Total	Ct
103. Yorkshire v MCC & Ground, Lord's, May 6, 7, 8 (Yorkshire won by six wickets)								
c A.Woodcock b A.E.Trott	1 305	30	12	51	3	E.G.Wynyard c L.Whitehead	241	1
						W.L.Murdoch lbw		
						H.A.Carpenter c D.Hunter		
did not bat	- 57-4	24.3	5	56	2	W.Mead hit wkt	120	
						A.Woodcock c F.Mitchell		
104. Yorkshire v Gloucestershire, Bristol, May 9, 10 (Yorkshire won by ten wickets)								
c T.Langdon b H.J.Huggins	24 224	21.2	2	78	7	C.O.H.Sewell c J.Tunnicliffe	150	
						G.L.Jessop c J.Tunnicliffe		
						W.H.Hale c T.L.Taylor		
						H.J.J.Hodgkins b		
						J.H.Board b		
						A.J.Paish b		
						F.G.Weaver c D.Denton		
did not bat	- 16-0	16	3	63	7	C.O.H.Sewell c J.Tunnicliffe	89	
						H.Wrathall hit wkt		
						G.L.Jessop c J.T.Brown		
						W.H.Hale c J.T.Brown		
						H.J.J.Hodgkins b		
						J.H.Board lbw		
						H.J.Huggins c S.Haigh		

105. Yorkshire v Somerset, Taunton, May 13, 14, 15 (Yorkshire won by one wicket)

b B.Cranfield 38 391 38.2 10 115 6 A.E.Lewis b 349 1
F.A.Philiips c Lord Hawke
S.M.J.Woods st D.Hunter
E.Robson c D.Denton
G.C.Gill b
W.L.Price c and b
not out 11 241-9 28 7 67 6 L.C.H.Palairet c and b 281 1
L.C.Braund lbw
S.M.J.Woods c J.Tunnicliffe
E.Robson c E.Wainwright
E.A.Grant c F.Mitchell
W.L.Price c S.Haigh

106. Yorkshire v Worcestershire, Dewsbury, May 16, 17, 18 (Yorkshire won by 90 runs)

c F.L.Bowley b G.A.Wilson 40 205 23 6 74 3 F.A.Pearson b 218
R.E.Foster b
R.D.Burrows c E.Wainwright
b R.D.Burrows 36 245 24.3 7 54 6 F.L.Bowley lbw 142 1
E.G.Arnold c J.Tunnicliffe
R.E.Foster c J.Tunnicliffe
G.F.Wheldon b
H.M.Bannister c J.Tunnicliffe
G.A.Wilson c and b

107. Yorkshire v Derbyshire, Huddersfield, May 20, 21 (Yorkshire won by an innings and 282 runs)

did not bat - 481-8d 9 5 23 1 H.Bagshaw b 106 1
9 6 14 0 93 1

108. Yorkshire v Lancashire, Old Trafford, May 27, 28 (Yorkshire won by nine wickets)

not out 2 134 24.1 7 67 5 J.T.Tyldesley c G.H.Hirst 133
A.Eccles c T.L.Taylor
W.R.Cuttell c E.B.Myers
C.R.Hartley c S.Haigh
C.Smith c S.Haigh
did not bat - 44-1 14 9 14 2 A.Eccles b 44 1
C.R.Hartley b

109. Yorkshire v Leicestershire, Aylestone Road, Leicester, May 30,31 (Yorkshire won by an innings and 128 runs)

st J.P.Whiteside b F.Geeson 6 348 15 5 41 6 C.J.B.Wood b 84 1
A.E.Knight c J.T.Brown
J.H.King b
H.Whitehead c S.Haigh
R.T.Crawford b
A.Woodcock c D.Denton
21 4 55 7 C.J.B.Wood c G.H.Hirst 136 1
A.E.Knight b
A.D.Pougher c J.Tunnicliffe
C.E.de Trafford c L.Whitehead
S.Coe b
F.Geeson c T.L.Taylor
J.P.Whiteside c D.Denton

110. Yorkshire v Hampshire, Bournemouth, June 3, 4 (Yorkshire won by an innings and 82 runs)

c C.Robson b J.G.Greig 10 365 14 5 32 4 V.A.Barton st J.Higgins 75
C.B.Llewellyn lbw
A.S.Webb c E.Wainwright
C.Heseltine c Lord Hawke
17 2 63 3 C.Robson b 208
D.A.Steele c E.Wainwright
C.Heseltine c T.L.Taylor

111. Yorkshire v Middlesex, Lord's, June 6, 7, 8 (Yorkshire won by seven wickets)

not out 41 398 26.2 9 53 8 G.W.Beldam c J.Tunnicliffe 168
L.J.Moon lbw
H.B.Chinnery b
A.E.Trott c G.H.Hirst
G.MacGregor b
J.Oliman st D.Hunter
J.T.Rawlin c J.Tunnicliffe
J.T.Hearne b

20

did not bat   -   54-3   36   11   81   4   H.B.Hayman   c S.Haigh   282   1
                                                      B.J.T.Bosanquet   c and b
                                                      H.B.Chinnery   c T.L.Taylor
                                                      A.E.Trott   c J.Tunnicliffe

112. Yorkshire v Surrey, Bradford, June 10, 11, 12 (Match drawn)
c R.Abel b T.Richardson   6   290   28   10   51   1   R.Abel   c J.Tunnicliffe   172
did not bat   -   157-7   45   13   135   3   W.Brockwell   c L.Whitehead   431-9d   2
                                                      E.G.Hayes   c J.T.Brown
                                                      V.F.S.Crawford   c F.Mitchell

113. Yorkshire v Warwickshire, Edgbaston, June 13, 14, 15 (Match drawn)
did not bat   -   401-5d   39   17   83   3   T.S.Fishwick   st D.Hunter   320
                                                      C.Charlesworth   c S.Haigh
                                                      A.C.S.Glover   c J.T.Brown

114. Yorkshire v Essex, Headingley, June 17, 18 (Yorkshire won by an innings and 60 runs)
b H.I.Young   21   252   25   13   33   4   C.P.McGahey   st D.Hunter   97
                                                      A.J.Turner   b
                                                      W.Reeves   st D.Hunter
                                                      H.I.Young   c D.Denton
                            18.5   5   45   6   P.A.Perrin   b   95   1
                                                      C.P.McGahey   c J.Tunnicliffe
                                                      A.J.Turner   c J.T.Brown
                                                      W.Reeves   lbw
                                                      T.M.Russell   st D.Hunter
                                                      W.Mead   c G.H.Hirst

115. Yorkshire v Nottinghamshire, Trent Bridge, June 20, 21 (Yorkshire won by an innings and 18 runs)
c T.G.Wass b A.W.Hallam   11   204   7.5   4   4   6   A.W.Hallam   c J.Tunnicliffe   13
                                                      W.Gunn   c D.Hunter
                                                      J.A.Dixon   c J.Tunnicliffe
                                                     J.Carlin   c J.Tunnicliffe
                                                      I.M.Harrison   c S.Haigh
                                                      T.G.Wass   st D.Hunter
                            22   4   53   1   J.A.Dixon   b   173

116. Yorkshire v Kent, Bramall Lane, June 24, 25, 26 (Yorkshire won by 212 runs)
b C.Blythe   17   201   26.1   9   60   5   K.S.Singh   c D.Hunter   218   1
                                                      J.R.Mason   c and b
                                                      F.Marchant   c D.Denton
not out   35   309   15.3   1   34   5   F.D.Browne   b   80
                                                      J.R.Mason   c F.Mitchell
                                                      A.Hearne   c E.Wainwright
                                                      F.Marchant   c J.Tunnicliffe
                                                      F.H.Huish   c T.L.Taylor

117. Yorkshire v Derbyshire, Glossop, June 27, 28, 29 (Yorkshire won by 245 runs)
b J.J.Hulme   1   213   19   13   24   3   H.Bagshaw   b   141
                                                      A.E.Lawton   b
                                                      S.H.Wood   c J.Tunnicliffe
did not bat   -   359-5d   23   10   60   4   H.Bagshaw   b   186
                                                      W.Storer   b
                                                      A.E.Lawton   c J.Tunnicliffe
                                                      W.Wilmot   c E.Wainwright

118. Yorkshire v Sussex, Bradford, July 1, (2), 3 (Yorkshire won by ten wickets)
not out   6   158   14.5   3   36   5   C.B.Fry   c J.Tunnicliffe   52
                                                      K.S.Ranjitsinhji   c J.Tunnicliffe
                                                      W.Newham   c J.Tunnicliffe
                                                      A.E.Relf   c G.H.Hirst
                                                      C.H.G.Bland   st D.Hunter
did not bat   -   50-0   27   12   57   3   J.Vine   c D.Hunter   155   1
                                                      W.Newham   c L.Whitehead
                                                      C.D.Fisher   lbw

119. Yorkshire v Leicestershire, Scarborough, July 4, 5, 6 (Yorkshire won by an innings and 247 runs)
c R.MacDonald b J.H.King   4   562   17   2   59   3   C.J.B.Wood   c F.Mitchell   103
                                                      S.Coe   b
                                                      A.E.Davis   b
                            31   10   46   6   C.E.de Trafford   c G.H.Hirst   212
                                                      A.E.Knight   c J.Tunnicliffe
                                                      R.MacDonald   c J.Tunnicliffe
                                                      R.T.Crawford   lbw
                                                      S.Coe   lbw
                                                      H.Whitehead   c J.Tunnicliffe

120. Players v Gentlemen, Lord's, July 8, 9, 10 (Players won by 221 runs)
```
    not out              2   394      11   2   27   0                                    245
    did not bat          -   256-6d   14   6   24   0                                    184
```

121. Yorkshire v Worcestershire, Worcester, July 11, 12, 13 (Yorkshire won by an innings and 212 runs)
```
    b F.A.Pearson       53   530    23.4   9   45   4   G.F.Wheldon  c J.Tunnicliffe  156
                                                        T.Straw  c J.Tunnicliffe
                                                        R.D.Burrows  c Lord Hawke
                                                        G.A.Wilson  c E.Wainwright
                                15   7   35   2   H.K.Foster  c G.H.Hirst           162    1
                                                        G.H.T.Simpson-Hayward  b
```

122. Yorkshire v Somerset, Headingley, July 15, 16, 17 (Somerset won by 279 runs)
```
    c A.E.Lewis b E.Robson   44   325     16   8   39   5   L.C.Braund  b                 87
                                                            A.E.Lewis  c J.Tunnicliffe
                                                            E.Robson  c D.Hunter
                                                            G.C.Gill  c D.Hunter
                                                            G.Burrington  c J.T.Brown
    st A.E.Newton b B.Cranfield  0   113   46.5  12  145   6   A.E.Lewis  b               630
                                                            V.T.Hill  c G.H.Hirst
                                                            E.Robson  c J.Tunnicliffe
                                                            G.C.Gill  st D.Hunter
                                                            A.E.Newton  c T.L.Taylor
                                                            G.Burrington  st D.Hunter
```

123. Yorkshire v Warwickshire, Bradford, July 18, 19, 20 (Match drawn)
```
    c A.F.A.Lilley
        b William Quaife   30   237    57.2  22  118   4   J.H.G.Devey  st D.Hunter     401    1
                                                            S.P.Kinneir  c and b
                                                            William Quaife  c D.Hunter
                                                            C.Charlesworth  st D.Hunter
    did not bat            -   281-2
```

124. Yorkshire v Nottinghamshire, Bramall Lane, July 22, 23 (Yorkshire won by an innings and 226 runs)
```
    c T.G.Wass b J.A.Dixon   9   528     6   2   25   0                                  151
                                        17   2   63   3   A.O.Jones  c D.Denton         151
                                                            J.Iremonger  b
                                                            J.Carlin  b
```

125. Yorkshire v Gloucestershire, Hull, July 29, 30 (Yorkshire won by 55 runs)
```
    b G.L.Jessop           8   186    20.2  12   20   7   T.Langdon  c D.Hunter          70
                                                            G.L.Jessop  st D.Hunter
                                                            J.H.Board  c D.Denton
                                                            J.A.Healing  b
                                                            T.H.Fowler  c G.H.Hirst
                                                            J.Wilkinson  b
                                                            F.G.Roberts  b
    c H.Wrathall b F.G.Roberts  3  123    29   9   66   5   H.Wrathall  c J.Tunnicliffe 184    1
                                                            S.A.P.Kitcat  c G.H.Hirst
                                                            G.L.Jessop  st D.Hunter
                                                            T.H.Fowler  st D.Hunter
                                                            J.Wilkinson  b
```

126. Yorkshire v South Africans, Harrogate, August 1, 2, 3 (Yorkshire won by 151 runs)
```
    c A.Reid b J.H.Sinclair   3   215    11.4   3   38   3   J.H.Sinclair  c D.Denton   193
                                                            R.Graham  c D.Denton
                                                            J.J.Kotze  c E.Smith
    b J.J.Kotze              35   369     30   12   53   3   L.J.Tancred  c and b        240    2
                                                            A.Reid  c T.L.Taylor
                                                            J.H.Sinclair  c and b
```

127. Yorkshire v Lancashire, Headingley, August 5, 6, 7 (Match drawn)
```
    c W.R.Cuttell b J.Hallows   1   319   66.2  36   85   3   J.T.Tyldesley  c J.Tunnicliffe 413
                                                            E.E.Steel  c L.Whitehead
                                                            C.Smith  c Lord Hawke
    did not bat            -   175-5
```

128. Yorkshire v Hampshire, Harrogate, August 8, 9 (Yorkshire won by an innings and 81 runs)
```
    not out               26   439    23.4   9   51   3   A.S.Webb  c J.Tunnicliffe     204
                                                            H.G.Bignell  c J.Hunter
                                                            D.A.Steele  c J.Tunnicliffe
                                22   8   51   5   J.G.Greig  c F.Mitchell             154
                                                            C.Robson  c E.Smith
                                                            V.A.Barton  c J.Tunnicliffe
                                                            G.B.Raikes  c J.Tunnicliffe
                                                            C.B.Llewellyn  c J.T.Brown
```

129. Yorkshire v Middlesex, Bramall Lane, August 12, 13, (14) (Match drawn)
c and b B.J.T.Bosanquet   7   363   12   4   23   1   J.Douglas st D.Hunter   62-3

130. Yorkshire v Essex, Leyton, August 15, 16 (Yorkshire won by an innings and 33 runs)
not out   9   104   8   0   17   2   W.Reeves c D.Denton   30
                                         T.M.Russell c T.L.Taylor
                   10   2   20   4   C.P.McGahey lbw   41   1
                                         G.Tosetti c and b
                                         W.Reeves st D.Hunter
                                         W.Mead st D.Hunter

131. Yorkshire v Sussex, Hove, August 19, 20, 21 (Match drawn)
b E.H.Killick   7   92   46   11   97   0   560-5d
did not bat   -   107-0

132. Yorkshire v Kent, Canterbury, August 22, 23, 24 (Yorkshire won by 247 runs)
c F.H.Huish b J.R.Mason   11   251   31.4   11   55   8   C.J.Burnup c J.Tunnicliffe   206   1
                                         E.W.Dillon b
                                         A.Hearne c D.Hunter
                                         J.R.Mason c G.H.Hirst
                                         R.N.R.Blaker b
                                         E.Humphreys st D.Hunter
                                         F.H.Huish c and b
                                         W.M.Bradley c J.Tunnicliffe
c A.Hearne b C.Blythe   5   265   9   1   35   3   E.W.Dillon c D.Hunter   63   1
                                         S.H.Day lbw
                                         F.H.Huish c and b

133. Yorkshire v MCC & Ground, Scarborough, August 26, 27, 28 (Yorkshire won by an inning and 49 runs)
b W.O.Holloway   105   376   18.1   3   47   6   G.J.V.Weigall c J.Tunnicliffe 149
                                         H.D.G.Leveson-Gower st D.Hunter
                                         J.Burns c J.Tunnicliffe
                                         H.J.Stevenson b
                                         H.I.Young c T.L.Taylor
                                         W.Mead st D.Hunter
                   7   1   31   0   178

134. Under 30 v Over 30, Scarborough, August 29, 30, 31 (Under 30 won by an innings and 146 runs)
not out   5   480-8d   18.2   4   38   3   J.Tunnicliffe b   94   1
                                         W.R.Cuttell c L.C.Braund
                                         W.Mead b
                   18   5   52   3   A.Ward c L.C.Braund   240
                                         W.R.Cuttell c G.H.Hirst
                                         Lord Hawke c A.O.Jones

135. Yorkshire v Mr.C.I.Thornton's XI, Scarborough, September 2, 3, 4 (Match drawn)
c and b L.C.Braund   17   302   25   6   100   2   G.J.Thompson
                                                  c E.Wainwright   321
                                         C.Heseltine c T.L.Taylor
not out   23   240-8   20   6   66   3   A.O.Jones c J.Tunnicliffe   303-5d
                                         L.C.Braund st D.Hunter
                                         J.T.Tyldesley c L.Whitehead

136. Yorkshire v An England XI, Hastings, September 5, 6, 7 (Match drawn)
c A.F.A.Lilley b J.R.Mason   36   214   42   15   92   5   A.O.Jones c J.Tunnicliffe   306
                                         J.R.Mason c D.Hunter
                                         K.S.Ranjitsinhji c E.Wainwright
                                         G.L.Jessop c G.H.Hirst
                                         W.G.Grace st D.Hunter
not out   17   303-6d   -   -   -   -   141-2

137. Players v Gentlemen, Hastings, September 9, 10, 11 (Match drawn)
not out   6   238   36.2   10   132   6   A.O.Jones c J.T.Tyldesley   406
                                         T.L.Taylor c G.H.Hirst
                                         G.L.Jessop c T.W.Hayward
                                         E.Smith c T.W.Hayward
                                         K.O.Goldie b
                                         E.A.Halliwell c J.T.Brown
did not bat   -   177-3   12   4   27   6   A.O.Jones c A.F.A.Lilley   59
                                         J.R.Mason c D.Denton
                                         T.L.Taylor st A.F.A.Lilley
                                         G.L.Jessop st A.F.A.Lilley
                                         E.Smith c E.H.Killick
                                         J.H.Sinclair c J.T.Brown

138. Yorkshire v Rest of England, Lord's, September 12, 13, 14 (Rest of England won by an innings and 115 runs)

c and b J.H.Sinclair	26	229		43	6	179	3	P.F.Warner c E.Wainwright	526
								G.W.Beldam c J.Tunnicliffe	
c and b A.E.Trott	15	182						C.B.Fry c G.H.Hirst	

139. Yorkshire v Surrey (non-Championship), Kennington Oval, September 16, (17), 18 (Match drawn)

not out	41	254		42.3	15	110	6	E.G.Hayes b	309
								T.W.Hayward c D.Denton	
								F.C.Holland c J.Tunnicliffe	
								W.Brockwell c D.Denton	
								F.Stedman c D.Denton	
								T.Richardson c G.H.Hirst	
				6	1	10	1	T.W.Hayward lbw	17-4

SEASON'S AVERAGES

Batting and Fielding	M	I	NO	Runs	HS	Ave	100	50	Ct
Players v Gentlemen	2	2	2	8	6*	-	-	-	-
Championship	27	31	7	522	53	21.75	-	1	20
Other Yorkshire matches	7	11	3	319	105	39.87	1	-	3
Other matches	1	1	1	5	5*	-	-	-	1
Season	37	45	13	854	105	26.68	1	1	24
Career	139	177	45	2498	105	18.92	1	8	76

Bowling	O	M	R	W	BB	Ave	5i	10m
Players v Gentlemen	73.2	22	210	12	6-27	17.50	2	1
Championship	1155.4	389	2664	196	8-53	13.59	20	8
Other Yorkshire matches	299.5	85	833	37	6-47	22.51	3	-
Other matches	36.2	9	90	6	3-38	15.00	-	-
Season (6-ball)	1565.1	505	3797	251	8-53	15.12	25	9
Career (6-ball)	3118.1	960 ⎱	12714	845	9-24	15.04	73	23
(5-ball)	2748.4	1029 ⎰						

1902

For the third consecutive season Rhodes dismissed over two hundred batsmen to give him one thousand wickets in five seasons. The summer was dominated by the Australians under Joe Darling and Rhodes played in all five Test matches including the Oval game where he and George Hirst scored the fifteen runs for the tenth wicket to win the game. He took 22 wickets in the series at an average of 15.27, having a best performance of 7-17 in the First Test at Edgbaston where he and Hirst dismissed Australia for 36 in less than one and a half hours - their lowest score in all Test matches up to this day. On the county circuit he was devastating once more. In mid July he took 12-195 against Essex again at Bradford. Gloucestershire suffered at Leeds two matches later, 12-58 in 29 overs, and he got Jessop once again and in the return at Cheltenham three weeks later 10-60 (Jessop twice). After this he was below his best and had no other really outstanding analysis but his reputation was intact.

	Own Team Total	O	M	R	W		Opp Total	Ct

140. Yorkshire v MCC & Ground, Lord's, May 5, 6 (Yorkshire won by an innings and 71 runs)

c C.Heseltine b J.T.Hearne	0	196	11	5	15	6	G.J.Thompson c D.Hunter	27
							J.H.King b	
							A.E.Relf c D.Denton	
							A.W.F.Somerset st D.Hunter	
							C.Heseltine st D.Hunter	
							J.T.Hearne c J.Tunnicliffe	
			11	2	35	3	G.J.Thompson c W.Ringrose	98
							A.E.Relf c E.Haigh	
							C.C.T.Doll st D.Hunter	

141. Yorkshire v Essex, Leyton, May (8), (9), 10 (Match drawn)
did not bat   - 171-3   30   12   44   4   H.G.P.Owen   c F.S.Jackson   89
                                                 C.P.McGahey   c Lord Hawke
                                                 A.E.Russell   c J.Tunnicliffe
                                                 C.P.Buckenham   c J.Tunnicliffe

142. Yorkshire v Sussex, Headingley, May 12, 13, 14 (Match drawn)
b C.H.G.Bland   25   302   34   7   89   1   J.Vine   c D.Denton   232
did not bat   - 182-5d   7   1   22   0   126-3

143. Yorkshire v Leicestershire, Huddersfield, May 15, (16), 17 (Match drawn)
not out   3   323-6d   27   5   82   4   J.H.King   b   228   2
                                                   A.E.Knight   b
                                                   S.Coe   c and b
                                                   F.Geeson   c J.T.Brown, sen.
                             4.3   3   4   0   10-1

144. Yorkshire v Lancashire, Bramall Lane, May 19, 20 (Yorkshire won by an innings and 22 runs)
not out   17   148   26   14   29   3   A.C.MacLaren   lbw   72
                                                   J.Hallows   b
                                                   W.R.Cuttell   c Lord Hawke
                             13   4   25   4   A.C.MacLaren   st D.Hunter   54
                                                   J.T.Tyldesley   c J.T.Brown, sen.
                                                   A.Eccles   b
                                                   E.E.Steel   st D.Hunter

145. Yorkshire v Cambridge University, Fenner's, May 22, 23, 24 (Match drawn)
c E.R.Wilson b L.T.Driffield   7   219-8d   14   5   44   3   E.R.Wilson   c G.E.Lowe   126
                                                   H.C.McDonell   b
                                                   L.T.Driffield   c H.Rudston
st C.E.Winter b E.M.Dowson 11   64-3d   14   6   29   0   85-7

146. Yorkshire v Kent, Bradford, May 26, 27 (Yorkshire won by an innings and 108 runs)
c James Seymour b C.Blythe 2   337   23   9   42   6   C.J.Burnup   lbw   100
                                                   A.Hearne   lbw
                                                   J.R.Mason   st D.Hunter
                                                   P.C.Baker   b
                                                   S.J.Croft   b
                                                   H.R.Murrell   b
                             18   5   39   2   E.Humphreys   c J.Tunnicliffe 129
                                                   James Seymour   c Lord Hawke

147. ENGLAND v AUSTRALIA, Edgbaston, May 29, 30, 31 (Match drawn)
not out   38   376-9d   11   3   17   7   R.A.Duff   c G.L.Jessop   36
                                                   J.Darling   c G.L.Jessop
                                                   M.A.Noble   st A.F.A.Lilley
                                                   W.W.Armstrong   c A.F.A.Lilley
                                                   A.J.Y.Hopkins   c A.F.A.Lilley
                                                   E.Jones   c F.S.Jackson
                                                   W.P.Howell   c C.B.Fry
                             10   5   9   1   V.T.Trumper   c L.C.Braund   46-2

148. Yorkshire v Australians, Headingley, June 2, 3 (Yorkshire won by five wickets)
c V.T.Trumper
   b W.P.Howell   12   107   13   1   43   2   C.Hill   c J.T.Brown. sen.   131
                                                   E.Jones   c S.Haigh
did not bat   - 50-5   -   -   -   -   23

149. Yorkshire v Derbyshire, Chesterfield, June 5, 6, 7 (Match drawn)
b W.Bestwick   0   150   -   -   -   -   64   1
c J.J.Hulme b A.E.Lawton   5   309   7   3   11   1   L.G.Wright   c D.Hunter   24-3

150. Yorkshire v Middlesex, Bradford, June 9, 10 (Yorkshire won by an innings and 22 runs)
c G.F.S.Griffin b A.E.Trott   3   175   22   11   24   7   B.J.T.Bosanquet   c D.Hunter   73
                                                   G.W.Beldam   c J.Tunnicliffe
                                                   A.E.Trott   c G.H.Hirst
                                                   C.P.Foley   c Lord Hawke
                                                   G.F.S.Griffin   c D.Denton
                                                   G.MacGregor   b
                                                   J.T.Rawlin   b
                             16   3   32   3   G.W.Beldam   c J.Tunnicliffe   80
                                                   R.O.Schwarz   hit wkt
                                                   J.T.Hearne   c T.L.Taylor

151. ENGLAND v AUSTRALIA, Lord's, June 12, (13), (14) (Match drawn)
                                     -   -   -   -   102-2

152. Yorkshire v Somerset, Bramall Lane, June 16, (17), 18 (Somerset won by 34 runs)
      b L.C.Braund   5   74   26   10   39   4   L.C.Braund c and b   86   1
                                                               S.M.J.Woods lbw
                                                               A.E.Lewis c S.Haigh
                                                               F.M.Lee c D.Denton
      c and b L.C.Braund   5   84   12   0   44   1   S.M.J.Woods c G.H.Hirst   106

153. Yorkshire v Warwickshire, Edgbaston, June 19, (20), 21 (Yorkshire won by an innings and 63 runs)
      not out   16   208   26   7   41   4   J.H.G.Devey b   100
                                                               William Quaife b
                                                               A.F.A.Lilley b
                                                               C.Charlesworth c L.Whitehead
                                    17.3   9   16   4   J.H.G.Devey b   45
                                                               William Quaife b
                                                               J.F.Byrne c D.Hunter
                                                               F.Moorhouse st D.Hunter

154. Yorkshire v Australians, Bradford, June 23, 24 (Australians won by 44 runs)
      b J.V.Saunders   0   77   11   2   49   5   V.T.Trumper c G.H.Hirst   106   1
                                                               C.Hill c E.Wainwright
                                                               S.E.Gregory lbw
                                                               M.A.Noble c and b
                                                               J.J.Kelly c J.Tunnicliffe
      run out   5   72   18   8   22   4   V.T.Trumper c D.Hunter   87   2
                                                               M.A.Noble c and b
                                                               J.J.Kelly b
                                                               H.Trumble c D.Hunter

155. Yorkshire v Nottinghamshire, Hull, June 26, 27, 28 (Yorkshire won by 227 runs)
      c and b G.Anthony   4   184   16   4   45   3   A.Shrewsbury b   155
                                                               G.Anthony c D.Denton
                                                               T.W.Oates c J.Tunnicliffe
      c T.W.Oates b J.R.Gunn 13   346   23   6   40   3   W.B.Goodacre st D.Hunter 148
                                                               J.A.Dixon c D.Hunter
                                                               G.Anthony b

156. Yorkshire v Surrey, Headingley, June 30, July 1, 2 (Yorkshire won by an innings and 102 runs)
      c and b D.L.A.Jephson   0   362-8d 29   7   76   5   W.H.Lockwood b   188
                                                               T.W.Hayward b
                                                               W.Brockwell c D.Denton
                                                               V.F.S.Crawford c J.Tunnicliffe
                                                               T.Richardson lbw
                                    22   15   17   2   D.L.A.Jephson c D.Hunter   72
                                                               V.F.S.Crawford lbw

157. ENGLAND v AUSTRALIA, Bramall Lane, July 3, 4, 5 (Australia won by 143 runs)
      not out   7   145   13   3   33   1   M.A.Noble c L.C.Braund   194   1
      not out   7   195   17.1 3   63   5   R.A.Duff c G.H.Hirst   289
                                                               W.W.Armstrong b
                                                               J.J.Kelly c G.H.Hirst
                                                               H.Trumble b
                                                               J.V.Saunders b

158. Players v Gentlemen, Lord's, July 7, 8, 9 (Players won by an innings and 68 runs)
      c E.M.Dowson b T.C.Ross 19 444   10   3   15   0   187   1
                                     3   1   6   0   189

159. Yorkshire v Sussex, Hove, July 10, 11, 12 (Match drawn)
      not out   92   372   47   20   83   1   A.E.Relf b   455   1
      did not bat   -   84-6

160. Yorkshire v Essex, Bradford, July 14, 15, 16 (Yorkshire won by an innings and 30 runs)
      c G.Tosetti
           b C.P.Buckenham   27   504   32   4 123   7   P.A.Perrin st D.Hunter   281
                                                               C.J.Kortright lbw
                                                               E.H.D.Sewell c Lord Hawke
                                                               G.Tosetti c D.Denton
                                                               C.P.Buckenham lbw
                                                               T.M.Russell c J.T.Brown, sen.
                                                               H.I.Young c S.Haigh
                                    31   0   72   5   H.G.P.Owen st D.Hunter   193
                                                               P.A.Perrin b
                                                               C.P.McGahey lbw
                                                               C.J.Kortright c D.Hunter
                                                               E.H.D.Sewell c S.Haigh

161. Yorkshire v Nottinghamshire, Trent Bridge, July 17, 18, 19 (Match drawn)
```
b A.W.Hallam          10  497      33   5   91   5   J.Iremonger  c S.Haigh        328
                                                     J.A.Dixon  c G.H.Hirst
                                                     J.R.Gunn  st J.Higgins
                                                     W.B.Goodacre  c J.Tunnicliffe
                                                     G.Anthony  b
                      24  11  39   0                                               255-2
```
162. Yorkshire v Gloucestershire, Headingley, July 21, 22, 23 (Yorkshire won by an innings and 91 runs)
```
c T.Langdon b E.J.Spry   0  253    10   1   22   5   T.Langdon
                                                     c W.A.I.Washington    46
                                                     J.H.Board  c J.Tunnicliffe
                                                     G.L.Jessop  c D.Denton
                                                     H.J.Huggins  c W.A.I.Washington
                                                     J.Wilkinson  b
                         19   8   36   7   H.Wrathall  c J.Tunnicliffe   116
                                                     T.Langdon  b
                                                     W.H.Rowlands  c D.Hunter
                                                     H.J.Huggins  c G.H.Hirst
                                                     L.D.Brownlee  b
                                                     E.J.Spry  c J.Tunnicliffe
                                                     J.Wilkinson  c J.Tunnicliffe
```
163. ENGLAND v AUSTRALIA, Old Trafford, July 24, 25, 26 (Australia won by 3 runs)
```
c and b H.Trumble      5  262     25   3  104   4   V.T.Trumper  c A.F.A.Lilley  299    2
                                                    M.A.Noble  c and b
                                                    S.E.Gregory  c A.C.MacLaren
                                                    J.Darling  c A.C.MacLaren
not out                4  120   14.4   5   26   3   J.Darling  c L.C.H.Palairet    86
                                                    W.W.Armstrong  b
                                                    J.V.Saunders  c J.T.Tyldesley
```
164. Yorkshire v Warwickshire, Bramall Lane, July 28, 29, 30 (Yorkshire won by 100 runs)
```
b E.F.Field            0  135     37  15   62   3   S.P.Kinneir  b                207
                                                    C.Charlesworth  c D.Denton
                                                    William Quaife  c D.Hunter
c A.F.A.Lilley
 b S.Hargreave        32  270   22.3   9   33   6   J.H.G.Devey  b                 98    1
                                                    T.S.Fishwick  lbw
                                                    A.F.A.Lilley  c and b
                                                    S.Santall  c G.H.Hirst
                                                    F.Moorhouse  st D.Hunter
                                                    E.F.Field  b
```
165. Yorkshire v Surrey, Kennington Oval, July 31 August 1, 2 (Match drawn)
```
not out               18  470     37  12  116   2   H.D.G.Leveson-Gower
                                                    c J.Tunnicliffe   359
                                                    F.Stedman  c D.Hunter
did not bat            -  363-3
```
166. Yorkshire v Lancashire, Old Trafford, August 4, 5, (6) (Match drawn)
```
did not bat            -  499-5     42  10   85   3   A.C.MacLaren  st D.Hunter  243
                                                     J.Hallows  b
                                                     W.Findlay  c F.S.Jackson
```
167. ENGLAND v AUSTRALIA, Kennington Oval, August 11, 12, 13 (England won by one wicket)
```
not out                0  183     28   9   46   0                               324    1
not out                6  263     22   7   38   1   J.V.Saunders  c J.T.Tyldesley
```
168. Yorkshire v Gloucestershire, Cheltenham, August 14, 15 (Yorkshire won by an innings and 102 runs)
```
c F.G.Roberts b E.J.Spry  4  261   17.3   9   26   4   R.W.Rice  c D.Hunter     104
                                                       T.Langdon  c W.A.I.Washington
                                                       G.L.Jessop  c J.Tunnicliffe
                                                       W.Troup  c L.Whitehead
                          15   4   34   6   R.W.Rice  lbw                         55
                                                       C.L.Townsend  b
                                                       T.Langdon  c G.H.Hirst
                                                       G.L.Jessop  st D.Hunter
                                                       W.Troup  c J.Tunnicliffe
                                                       F.H.Bateman-Champain  b
```

169. Yorkshire v Somerset, Taunton, August (18), (19), 20 (Match drawn)
```
   b E.Robson            0   129     18    5   32   6   L.C.H.Palairet st D.Hunter   104    1
                                                        L.C.Braund  c L.Whitehead
                                                        V.T.Hill  b
                                                        F.A.Phillips  c E.Smith
                                                        H.Martyn  c L.Whitehead
                                                        A.E.Lewis  c J.Tunnicliffe
   did not bat            -    63-1
```

170. Yorkshire v Middlesex, Lord's, August 21, 22 (Yorkshire won by four wickets)
```
   b B.J.T.Bosanquet     0   125    26.5   10   47   4   R.N.Douglas  c G.H.Hirst      99
                                                        B.J.T.Bosanquet  c J.Tunnicliffe
                                                        C.M.Wells  c J.T.Brown, sen.
                                                        G.MacGregor  c J.Tunnicliffe
   did not bat           -    68-6    25.2   10   34   3   G.MacGregor  c D.Hunter      93
                                                        R.O.Schwarz  c J.Tunnicliffe
                                                        J.T.Hearne  c D.Hunter
```

171. Yorkshire v Kent, Catford, August 25, 26 (Yorkshire won by nine wickets)
```
   lbw b E.Humphreys    18    97    14.5    4   26   8   C.J.Burnup  c E.Smith         71
                                                        E.W.Dillon  b
                                                        A.Hearne  c S.Haigh
                                                        James Seymour  c W.A.I.Washington
                                                        J.R.Mason  st D.Hunter
                                                        C.H.B.Marsham  b
                                                        R.N.R.Blaker  c L.Whitehead
                                                        C.Blythe  c Lord Hawke
   did not bat           -    78-1    25.4   11   26   4   A.Hearne  c S.Haigh         100
                                                        S.H.Day  c D.Hunter
                                                        R.N.R.Blaker  b
                                                        C.Blythe  c J.Tunnicliffe
```

172. Yorkshire v MCC & Ground, Scarborough, August 28, 29 (MCC & Ground won by 26 runs)
```
   c G.J.V.Weigall
         b L.C.Braund     0   161     15    6   42   2   A.O.Jones  lbw              161
                                                        E.R.Wilson  lbw
   b L.C.Braund            1    74    18.5    3   49   6   W.Findlay  b               100
                                                        A.O.Jones  lbw
                                                        L.C.Braund  st D.Hunter
                                                        H.A.Carpenter  lbw
                                                        E.R.Wilson  lbw
                                                        G.J.Thompson  b
```

173. Players v Gentlemen, Scarborough, September 1, 2, 3 (Match drawn)
```
   c R.E.Foster b C.J.Burnup   14   314   38.4   13   71   5   C.J.Burnup  c D.Hunter   303    1
                                                        W.Findlay  c and b
                                                        R.E.Foster  c J.Tunnicliffe
                                                        E.Smith  b
                                                        Lord Hawke  st D.Hunter
   not out               19   250-8d   9.5    4   11   3   A.O.Jones  b               133-7
                                                        F.S.Jackson  c J.T.Brown, sen.
                                                        T.L.Taylor  b
```

174. Mr.C.I.Thornton's XI v Australians, Scarborough, September 4, 5, 6 (Match drawn)
```
   c R.A.Duff b H.Trumble   0   198     36    6   95   4   V.T.Trumper  lbw           247
                                                        R.A.Duff  lbw
                                                        W.W.Armstrong  b
                                                        H.Trumble  b
   not out               25   202-9d    7    1   34   0                              120-4
```

175. Yorkshire v Rest of England, Lord's, September (11), 12, 13 (Match drawn)
```
   b S.Hargreave          0   204     22    7   42   3   C.J.Burnup  c and b          193    1
                                                        P.F.Warner  st D.Hunter
                                                        A.E.Trott  b
   did not bat           -    60-1
```

176. Players of England v Australians, Kennington Oval, September 15, 16, 17 (Match drawn)
```
   not out               11   356    36.4    3  115   5   V.T.Trumper  c and b         414    2
                                                        M.A.Noble  b
                                                        R.A.Duff  c T.W.Hayward
                                                        H.Trumble  b
                                                        J.J.Kelly  b
   did not bat           -   117-3
```

SEASON'S AVERAGES

Batting and Fielding	M	I	NO	Runs	HS	Ave	100	50	Ct
Test matches	5	7	6	67	38*	67.00	-	-	4
Players v Gentlemen	2	3	1	52	19*	26.00	-	-	2
Championship	22	24	5	299	92*	15.73	-	1	7
Other Yorkshire matches	6	9	0	36	12	4.00	-	-	4
Other matches	2	3	2	36	25*	36.00	-	-	2
Season	37	46	14	490	92*	15.31	-	1	19
Career	176	223	59	2988	105	18.29	1	9	95

Bowling	O	M	R	W	BB	Ave	5i	10m
Test matches	140.5	38	336	22	7-17	15.27	2	-
Players v Gentlemen	61.3	21	103	8	5-71	12.87	1	-
Championship	876.4	291	1748	140	8-26	12.18	12	5
Other Yorkshire matches	147.5	45	370	34	6-15	10.88	3	-
Other matches	79.4	10	244	9	5-115	27.11	1	-
Season (6-ball)	1306.3	405	2801	213	8-26	13.15	19	5
Career (6-ball)	4424.4	1365 ⎱	15515	1058	9-24	14.66	92	28
(5-ball)	2748.4	1029 ⎰						

1903

Rhodes just missed out on another 200 wicket tally, taking 193 wickets including four totals of ten or more in a match. He completed the 'double' for the first of sixteen occasions and made his highest score to date, 98 against the M.C.C. on the Nursery ground at Lord's. He decimated Worcestershire at Worcester with his best performance of the season taking 14-211 in 94.4 overs but Yorkshire failed to win the match. In July he had the extraordinary analysis of 5 wickets for 4 runs against Worcestershire at Huddersfield. In consecutive matches at the end of July he took 23 wickets: 10-81 at the Oval, not one of his favourite venues - the pitches were too true - and 13-152 against Lancashire at Bradford. At the Hastings festival in September he had another good return, 13-118 against the cream of England's batsmen dismissing Tom Hayward and Ranjitsinhji twice in the match and also getting 'W.G.' On his form in these early seasons he was an automatic choice for the M.C.C. tour of Australia in the winter.

	Own Team	O	M	R	W		Opp	Ct
	Total						Total	

177. Yorkshire v MCC & Ground, Nursery Ground, Lord's, May (11), (12), 13 (Match drawn)

not out	98 184	5	1	9	1	L.C.Braund b	133	

178. Yorkshire v Essex, Leyton, May 14, 15, 16 (Yorkshire won by 261 runs)

c E.H.D.Sewell b W.Mead	24 240	6.5	0	22	3	C.J.Kortright c G.H.Hirst	96	
						H.I.Young c J.Tunnicliffe		
						W.Mead b		
b W.Mead	16 189	-	-	-	-		72	

179. Yorkshire v Gloucestershire, Bristol, May 18, 19 (Yorkshire won by an innings and 142 runs)

b E.J.Spry	42 313	31	15	39	4	H.Wrathall lbw	101	1
						W.H.Hale c D.Hunter		
						J.H.Board b		
						A.J.Paish lbw		
		16	5	34	4	T.H.Fowler c and b	70	1
						H.Wrathall c J.Tunnicliffe		
						W.H.Rowlands st D.Hunter		
						F.G.Roberts c J.Tunnicliffe		

180. Yorkshire v Somerset, Taunton, May 21, 22 (Somerset won by six wickets)

c L.C.Braund b E.Robson	0 147	29	5	71	3	S.M.J.Woods b	256	
						P.R.Johnson c W.H.Wilkinson		
						F.M.Lee b		
c A.E.Newton b L.C.Braund	33 190	8	2	20	1	P.R.Johnson c D.Denton	82-4	1

181. Yorkshire v Worcestershire, Worcester, May 25, 26, 27 (Match drawn)
```
   c A.W.Isaac b R.D.Burrows  42   518      46   17   87   8   J.E.Nichols  c D.Hunter       278
                                                              F.L.Bowley  lbw
                                                              E.G.Arnold  b
                                                              G.F.Wheldon  b
                                                              F.H.Hunt  b
                                                              R.S.Brinton  c D.Hunter
                                                              A.Bird  b
                                                              R.D.Burrows  c W.H.Wilkinson
                                          48.4  13  124   6   F.L.Bowley
                                                                  c W.H.Wilkinson       381      1
                                                              E.G.Arnold  c J.Tunnicliffe
                                                              G.F.Wheldon  c and b
                                                              A.W.Isaac  c D.Hunter
                                                              R.D.Burrows  b
                                                              G.A.Wilson  c D.Denton
```

182. Yorkshire v Cambridge University, Fenner's, May 28, 29, 30 (Yorkshire won by five wickets)
```
   lbw b E.M.Dowson        5   291      27   16   26   2   C.H.M.Ebden  c and b         262      1
                                                              E.W.Mann  c W.H.Wilkinson
   b E.M.Dowson           31   159-5   26.1   7   84   5   R.T.Godsell  c D.Denton       184
                                                              E.W.Mann  lbw
                                                              F.B.Wilson  c D.Denton
                                                              R.P.Keigwin  c H.Myers
                                                              G.Howard-Smith  c L.Whitehead
```

183. Yorkshire v Lancashire, Old Trafford, June 1, 2, 3 (Match drawn)
```
   c A.C.MacLaren b W.Brearley 8  360    41   15   78   2   R.H.Spooner  b               230
                                                              J.T.Tyldesley  b
   b W.Brearley           18   215      29   11   57   0                                 254-3
```

184. Yorkshire v Middlesex, Lord's, June 4, 5, 6 (Middlesex won by nine wickets)
```
   lbw b J.T.Hearne        4   157      45    8  101   0                                 349
   b J.H.Hunt              8   240       8    1   24   0                                 49-1
```

185. Yorkshire v Sussex, Bradford, June 8, 9, 10 (Sussex won by an innings and 180 runs)
```
   b G.R.Cox               0   120      57   12  135   2   A.E.Relf  c F.S.Jackson       558-8d
                                                              C.L.A.Smith  c F.S.Jackson
   lbw b F.W.Tate          2   258
```

186. Yorkshire v Warwickshire, Edgbaston, June 11, 12, (13) (Match drawn)
```
   c C.Charlesworth
        b R.Moorhouse     46   261      43   21   62   4   S.P.Kinneir  c W.Ringrose     198      1
                                                              R.Moorhouse  c D.Hunter
                                                              J.F.Byrne  c S.Haigh
                                                              A.C.S.Glover  c J.T.Brown
   did not bat              -   67-4
```

187. Yorkshire v Cambridge University, Bramall Lane, June 15, 16 (Yorkshire won by 206 runs)
```
   c E.W.Mann b R.P.Keigwin  7  210    18    6   40   4   R.T.Godsell  b                75
                                                              E.W.Mann  c W.H.Wilkinson
                                                              K.R.B.Fry  b
                                                              R.P.Keigwin  b
   b F.B.Roberts           7   110      11    5   15   3   E.W.Mann  c D.Hunter          39
                                                              F.B.Wilson  c R.W.Frank
                                                              P.R.May  st D.Hunter
```

188. Yorkshire v Derbyshire, Derby, June 18, 19, 20 (Yorkshire won by seven wickets)
```
   b A.Warren             69   184      11    4   16   0                                 133
   did not bat             -   145-3    14    3   33   1   L.G.Wright  c D.Denton        194
```

189. Yorkshire v Kent, Headingley, June 22, 23 (Yorkshire won by an innings and 130 runs)
```
   c F.H.Huish b A.Fielder  2  315       5    2   11   1   E.Humphreys  c J.Tunnicliffe  66
                                          8    4   11   0                                119
```

190. Yorkshire v Nottinghamshire, Trent Bridge, June 25, 26, 27 (Yorkshire won by an innings and 63 runs)
```
   c G.Gunn b A.W.Hallam  63   364    29.3  11   40   7   J.Iremonger  c J.Tunnicliffe  132
                                                              W.Gunn  lbw
                                                              G.Anthony  c G.H.Hirst
                                                              H.W.Dexter  c S.Haigh
                                                              J.Hardstaff, sen.  c D.Hunter
                                                              A.W.Hallam  c G.H.Hirst
                                                              B.W.Taylor  st D.Hunter
                                          25    9   32   2   G.Gunn  b                    169
                                                              A.O.Jones  lbw
```

191. Yorkshire v Surrey, Bramall Lane, June 29, 30, July 1 (Surrey won by 145 runs)
```
     b W.H.Lockwood        2   182      35   10   70   2   W.H.Lockwood  b              280    1
                                                             E.H.L.Nice  c and b
     b T.Richardson         0   122      16    5   29   4   E.H.L.Nice  b              169    1
                                                             H.P.Clode  b
                                                             H.Strudwick  st D.Hunter
                                                             T.Richardson  c W.H.Wilkinson
```
192. Yorkshire v Leicestershire, Dewsbury, July 2, 3 (Yorkshire won by an innings and 280 runs)
```
     not out               79   562      10    4   20   1   R.T.Crawford  b            164
                                         16    5   41   2   H.Whitehead  c D.Hunter    118
                                                             J.H.Brown  b
```
193. Players v Gentlemen, Kennington Oval, July 9, 10, 11 (Gentlemen won by 54 runs)
```
     run out                7   188      21    4   55   2   G.H.T.Simpson-Hayward
                                                               c A.E.Trott  311          2
                                                             C.Robson  c H.Strudwick
     lbw
       b G.H.T.Simpson-Hayward 18  240   13    7   18   1   L.O.S.Poidevin  c A.E.Trott  171
```
194. Yorkshire v Somerset, Bradford, July 13, 14, 15 (Match drawn)
```
     not out               24   417-6d   33   13   49   4   L.C.Braund  c F.Smith      118
                                                             E.Robson  c G.H.Hirst
                                                             F.M.Lee  c Lord Hawke
                                                             J.Daniell  c J.Tunnicliffe
                                         22    8   31   3   L.C.Braund  c G.H.Hirst    71-7
                                                             P.R.Johnson  c J.Tunnicliffe
                                                             W.C.Hedley  c Lord Hawke
```
195. Yorkshire v Worcestershire, Huddersfield, July (16), 17, 18 (Match drawn)
```
     did not bat            -   76-1d     9    6    4   5   H.K.Foster  c G.H.Hirst     24
                                                             E.G.Arnold  st D.Hunter
                                                             W.S.Caldwell  c D.Hunter
                                                             G.W.Gaukrodger  c J.Tunnicliffe
                                                             G.A.Wilson  c W.H.Wilkinson
                                         21   16    8   3   G.F.Wheldon  st D.Hunter   27-6   1
                                                             G.W.Gaukrodger  c G.H.Hirst
                                                             A.W.Isaac  c and b
```
196. Yorkshire v Nottinghamshire, Headingley, July 20, 21, 22 (Yorkshire won by 164 runs)
```
     not out               51   339      33    9   57   5   A.O.Jones  c J.Tunnicliffe  202   1
                                                             J.R.Gunn  c D.Denton
                                                             G.Gunn  st D.Hunter
                                                             G.Anthony  b
                                                             T.W.Oates  b
     c A.O.Jones b J.R.Gunn  3   90-6d  10.3    2   27   2   J.R.Gunn  c D.Denton        63
                                                             A.W.Hallam  c D.Denton
```
197. Yorkshire v Warwickshire, Hull, July 23, 24, 25 (Yorkshire won by 69 runs)
```
     c C.Charlesworth
       b R.Moorhouse       13   217      30   15   35   2   F.R.Loveitt  b             147
                                                             S.P.Kinneir  c J.T.Brown
     c S.P.Kinneir b S.Hargreave 7  140  18    9   22   1   C.Charlesworth  c J.T.Brown 141
```
198. Yorkshire v Gloucestershire, Bramall Lane, July 27, 28, 29 (Yorkshire won by an innings and 183 runs)
```
     c H.Wrathall b G.L.Jessop  9  284   9.1   3   18   2   L.D.Brownlee  c and b        65    1
                                                             J.H.Board  c G.H.Hirst
                                        10.5   4   20   5   G.L.Jessop  c W.Ringrose    36
                                                             T.Langdon  lbw
                                                             R.W.Rice  b
                                                             F.E.Thomas  c F.T.Asquith
                                                             H.J.Huggins  c J.T.Brown
```
199. Yorkshire v Surrey, Kennington Oval, July 30, 31 (Yorkshire won by an innings and 97 runs)
```
     c W.H.Lockwood
       b W.C.Smith          5   254      17    3   43   4   E.G.Hayes  c J.T.Brown      84    1
                                                             W.S.Lees  c D.Denton
                                                             W.C.Smith  c J.Tunnicliffe
                                                             H.Strudwick  c Lord Hawke
                                         12    1   38   6   T.W.Hayward  b             73
                                                             H.S.Bush  c L.Whitehead
                                                             L.Walker  b
                                                             W.S.Lees  st D.Hunter
                                                             J.H.Moulder  b
                                                             W.C.Smith  b
```

200. Yorkshire v Lancashire, Bradford, August 3, 4, 5 (Yorkshire won by five wickets)
```
    b S.F.Barnes          30   238     34.4  6   91   5   W.Findlay lbw                233
                                                          A.H.Hornby c D.Hunter
                                                          J.Sharp c D.Denton
                                                          J.S.Heap b
                                                          W.R.Cuttell c D.Denton
    not out               13   164-5   30    8   61   8   R.H.Spooner c L.Whitehead  168
                                                          J.T.Tyldesley b
                                                          W.Findlay lbw
                                                          H.G.Garnett c D.Denton
                                                          A.Eccles b
                                                          A.H.Hornby c J.Tunnicliffe
                                                          J.S.Heap c G.H.Hirst
                                                          W.R.Cuttell c J.Tunnicliffe
```

201. Yorkshire v Leicestershire, Aylestone Road, Leicester, August 6, 7, 8 (Yorkshire won by ten wickets)
```
    b W.W.Odell           72   415     28    7   77   1   J.H.King b                   322
    did not bat            -   15-0    8     1   26   3   C.E.de Trafford c J.T.Brown  106
                                                          J.H.King b
                                                          H.Whitehead c Lord Hawke
```

202. Yorkshire v Middlesex, Headingley, August 10, 11, 12 (Yorkshire won by 230 runs)
```
    b J.T.Hearne          13   253     22.3  7   37   6   E.A.Beldam c J.Tunnicliffe    79
                                                          G.W.Beldam lbw
                                                          B.J.T.Bosanquet c G.H.Hirst
                                                          C.M.Wells c D.Hunter
                                                          A.E.Trott c E.Smith
                                                          J.T.Rawlin st D.Hunter
    not out                0   233-6d  35   12   57   2   P.F.Warner b                 177
                                                          A.E.Trott c J.Tunnicliffe
```

203. Yorkshire v Derbyshire, Harrogate, August 13, (14), (15) (Match drawn)
```
    c A.Warren
        b S.W.A.Cadman    28   220     9     3   10   1   W.Storer c S.Haigh           53-3
```

204. Yorkshire v Essex, Bramall Lane, August 17, (18), 19 (Match drawn)
```
    b H.I.Young            5   115     17    4   54   4   E.H.D.Sewell c D.Denton      106
                                                          P.A.Perrin c Lord Hawke
                                                          R.P.Keigwin c D.Hunter
                                                          W.Mead c D.Denton
    did not bat            -   76-3d   9     2   21   5   E.H.D.Sewell lbw             36-8
                                                          C.P.McGahey lbw
                                                          C.J.Kortright c S.Haigh
                                                          J.W.H.T.Douglas c S.Haigh
                                                          C.P.Buckenham lbw
```

205. Yorkshire v Kent, Canterbury, August 20, (21), 22 (Match drawn)
```
    c R.N.R.Blaker b A.Hearne  2   79  28    4   91   4   A.Hearne c E.Smith          181-7d  1
                                                          R.N.R.Blaker c and b
                                                          James Seymour c S.Haigh
                                                          E.W.Dillon b
    not out                7   51-8
```

206. Yorkshire v Sussex, Hove, August 24, 25, 26 (Sussex won by four wickets)
```
    c and b F.W.Tate       0   72      33    8   60   5   J.Vine c E.Smith             132
                                                          E.H.Killick b
                                                          K.S.Ranjitsinhji c J.Tunnicliffe
                                                          A.E.Relf st D.Hunter
                                                          H.R.Butt c E.Smith
    b F.W.Tate            11   96      4     0   11   0                                37-6
```

207. Yorkshire v MCC, Scarborough, August 27, 28, 29 (Yorkshire won by an innings and 16 runs)
```
    b G.J.Thompson         0   331-9d  12.4  5   24   6   A.E.Relf c J.T.Brown         100
                                                          G.J.V.Weigall c E.Smith
                                                          J.C.Hartley b
                                                          L.Whitehead c S.Haigh
                                                          H.D.G.Leveson-Gower b
                                                          F.A.Tarrant b
                                   18    3   54   2   A.E.Relf lbw                 215
                                                          G.R.Cox st D.Hunter
```

208. Players v Gentlemen, Scarborough, August 31, September 1, 2 (Players won by an innings and 8 runs)
```
    c B.J.T.Bosanquet
        b E.Smith         82   444     13.3  2   31   2   E.Smith c and b              200  1
                                                          C.Headlam c D.Hunter
                                     21    3   41   1   W.L.Foster b                 236
```

209. Yorkshire v Mr.C.I.Thornton's XI, Scarborough, September 3, 4, (5) (Match drawn)

c B.J.T.Bosanquet
   b F.A.Tarrant   13   183   30   7   63   3   J.R.Gunn b   189
                                              G.J.Thompson c G.H.Hirst
                                              C.Headlam b
not out   35   187-4

210. Lancashire and Yorkshire v Rest of England, Hastings, September 7, 8, 9 (Lancashire and Yorkshire won by 87 runs)

lbw b W.W.Odell   31   255   32   12   72   6   T.W.Hayward lbw   173   2
                                              G.W.Beldam c and b
                                              K.S.Ranjtisinhji c Lord Hawke
                                                 A.O.Jones c and b
                                                W.G.Grace b
                                                W.W.Odell c J.T.Tyldesley
did not bat   -   125-4d   22   6   46   7   T.W.Hayward c D.Denton   120
                                              J.Vine c D.Hunter
                                              K.S.Ranjitsinhji c A.Eccles
                                              L.C.Braund c W.R.Cuttell
                                              A.E.Relf c E.Smith
                                              W.W.Odell c Lord Hawke
                                              H.Strudwick c J.T.Tyldesley

211. Players v Gentlemen, Hastings, September 10, 11, 12 (Match drawn)

not out   16   352-6d   16   2   45   1   Lord Hawke c T.W.Hayward 172-7

212. Rest of England v Middlesex, Kennington Oval, September 14, 15, 16 (Match drawn)

b J.T.Hearne   36   184   14   5   27   0   230   2
did not bat   -   229-5   16   1   58   4   P.F.Warner c E.G.Arnold   254-8d
                                              J.Douglas c G.H.Hirst
                                              B.J.T.Bosanquet lbw
                                              J.H.Hunt st H.Strudwick

SEASON'S AVERAGES

Batting and Fielding	M	I	NO	Runs	HS	Ave	100	50	Ct
Players v Gentlemen	3	4	1	123	82	41.00	-	1	3
Championship	26	37	6	751	79	24.22	-	5	12
Other Yorkshire matches	5	8	2	196	98*	32.66	-	1	1
Other matches	2	2	0	67	36	33.50	-	-	4
Season	36	51	9	1137	98*	27.07	-	7	20
Career	212	274	68	4125	105	20.02	1	16	115

Bowling	O	M	R	W	BB	Ave	5i	10m
Players v Gentlemen	84.3	18	190	7	27.14	2-31	-	-
Championship	1061.4	333	2105	143	14.72	8-61	12	3
Other Yorkshire matches	147.5	50	315	26	12.11	6-24	2	-
Other matches	84	24	203	17	11.94	7-46	2	1
Season (6-ball)	1378	425	2813	193	14.57	8-61	16	4
Career (6-ball)	5802.4	1790 ⎫ 18328		1251	14.65	9-24	108	32
(5-ball)	2748.4	1029 ⎭						

1903/04 - MCC in Australia

Rhodes made the first of his overseas tours this winter when he was selected for the first Test playing side deemed the M.C.C. Previously all tours had been private ventures led by a plethora of players and entrepreneurs. He found the Australian wickets to his liking and in the second Test at Melbourne took 15-124 to help England win by 185 runs. He also captured 31 wickets in the series which was won by England by three Tests to two. Outside the Tests he had the greatest successes on the Melbourne wickets which he found much to his liking. He had 8-84 against Victoria in the first game in November, then came the second Test and he followed this with 11-68 (which included 6-5 in the second innings) when Victoria were put out for 15 runs. He never achieved that amount of success on any other ground during the tour.

213. MCC v South Australia, Adelaide, November 7, 9, 10, 11 (Match drawn)

did not bat	- 483-8d	11	2	27	1	F.T.Hack b	172	1
		41	11	78	2	F.T.Hack c T.W.Hayward	343-7	
						J.C.Reedham c L.C.Braund		

214. MCC v Victoria, Melbourne, November 13, 14, 16 (MCC won by an innings and 71 runs)

not out	2 443-8d	20.2	8	26	5	G.H.S.Trott st H.Strudwick	162	
						W.W.Armstrong b		
						B.J.Tuckwell c B.J.T.Bosanquet		
						F.B.Collins lbw		
						J.V.Saunders c B.J.T.Bosanquet		
		40	15	58	3	W.Bruce c B.J.T.Bosanquet	210	1
						G.H.S.Trott c and b		
						W.W.Armstrong c T.W.Hayward		

215. MCC v New South Wales, Sydney, November 20, 21, 23 (MCC won by an innings and 10 runs)

not out	0 319	17	2	55	6	V.T.Trumper st A.F.A.Lilley	108	1
						A.J.Y.Hopkins c L.C.Braund		
						S.E.Gregory lbw		
						J.J.Kelly c J.T.Tyldesley		
						W.P.Howell c E.G.Arnold		
						C.W.Gregory st A.F.A.Lilley		
		7	2	17	0		201	

216. MCC v Queensland, Brisbane, November 27, 28, 29 (MCC won by six wickets)

c R.MacDonald b T.Byrnes	6 215	10	0	38	1	W.T.Evans c R.E.Foster	242	
did not bat	- 119-4	5	1	6	0		91	1

217. ENGLAND v AUSTRALIA, Sydney, December 11, 12, 14, 15, 16, 17 (England won by five wickets)

not out	40 577	17.2	3	41	2	F.J.Laver lbw	285	
						J.J.Kelly c L.C.Braund		
did not bat	- 194-5	40.2	10	94	5	R.A.Duff c A.E.Relf	485	
						W.W.Armstrong c B.J.T.Bosanquet		
						A.J.Y.Hopkins c E.G.Arnold		
						S.E.Gregory c A.F.A.Lilley		
						F.J.Laver c A.E.Relf		

218. ENGLAND v AUSTRALIA, Melbourne, January 1, 2, 4, 5 (England won by 185 runs)

lbw b H.Trumble	2 315	15.2	3	56	7	R.A.Duff st A.F.A.Lilley	122	1
						V.T.Trumper c J.T.Tyldesley		
						M.A.Noble c sub (H.Strudwick)		
						S.E.Gregory c G.H.Hirst		
						H.Trumble c sub (H.Strudwick)		
						W.W.Armstrong c L.C.Braund		
						W.P.Howell c A.Fielder		
lbw b H.Trumble	9 103	15	0	68	8	R.A.Duff c L.C.Braund	111	2
						V.T.Trumper c A.E.Relf		
						C.Hill c A.E.Relf		
						A.J.Y.Hopkins c and b		
						H.Trumble c L.C.Braund		
						W.W.Armstrong c T.W.Hayward		
						J.J.Kelly c A.F.A.Lilley		
						W.P.Howell c G.H.Hirst		

219. ENGLAND v AUSTRALIA, Adelaide, January 15, 16, 18, 19, 20 (Australia won by 216 runs)

c W.W.Armstrong b C.E.McLeod	9 245	14	3	45	1	W.W.Armstrong lbw	388	
run out	8 278	21	4	46	1	V.T.Trumper lbw	351	1

220. MCC v Tasmania, Hobart, January 25, 26 (Match drawn)

not out	6 185	31	13	52	2	E.A.C.Windsor c E.G.Arnold	191	1
						C.J.Eady b		
did not bat	- 354-4d	-	-	-	-		63-1	

221. MCC v Tasmania, Launceston, January 29, 30 (Match drawn)

run out	39 353	9	2	33	0		141	
		11	4	21	0		259-3	1

222. MCC v Victoria, Melbourne, February 5, (6), 8, 9 (MCC won by eight wickets)

b F.J.Laver	5 248	30	6	62	6	P.A.McAlister b	299	
						W.W.Armstrong lbw		
						F.J.Laver c R.E.Foster		
						W.J.Scott c E.G.Arnold		
						W.Carkeek c G.H.Hirst		
						H.J.Fry c P.F.Warner		

did not bat   - 68-2   6.1 3   6 5 P.A.McAlister st H.Strudwick 15   1
W.W.Armstrong c H.Strudwick
G.H.S.Trott c E.G.Arnold
F.J.Laver b
H.J.Fry c B.J.T.Bosanquet

223. MCC v New South Wales, Sydney, February 12, 13, 15 (MCC won by 278 runs)
not out   2 190   19 7 50 3 A.J.Y.Hopkins b   232
A.J.Bowden b
A.Cotter b
not out   49 461   10 3 20 0   141   2

224. ENGLAND v AUSTRALIA, Sydney, February 26, 27, (29), March 1, 2, 3 (England won by 157 runs)
st J.J.Kelly b M.A.Noble   10 249   11 3 33 4 P.A.McAlister c E.G.Arnold 131
C.E.McLeod b
S.E.Gregory c R.E.Foster
H.Trumble c A.F.A.Lilley
c P.A.McAlister b A.Cotter 29 210   11 7 12 0   171

225. ENGLAND v AUSTRALIA, Melbourne, March 5, 7, 8 (Australia won by 218 runs)
c D.R.A.Gehrs b A.Cotter   3   61   12 1 41 1 C.Hill c L.C.Braund   247   1
not out   16 101   15 2 52 2 R.A.Duff c P.F.Warner   133
M.A.Noble st A.F.A.Lilley

226. MCC v South Australia, Adelaide, March 12, 14, 15 (MCC won by nine wickets)
b H.J.Hill   4 154   5 0 18 0   259
did not bat   - 184-1   -   -   -   -   77

SEASON'S AVERAGES

Batting and Fielding	M	I	NO	Runs	HS	Ave	100	50	Ct
Test matches	5	9	2	126	40*	18.00	-	-	5
Other matches	9	9	5	113	49*	28.25	-	-	9
Tour	14	18	7	239	49*	21.72	-	-	14
Career	226	292	75	4364	105	20.11	1	16	129

Bowling	O	M	R	W	BB	Ave	5i	10m
Test matches	172	36	488	31	8-68	15.74	3	1
Other matches	272.3	79	567	34	6-55	16.67	4	1
Tour (6-ball)	444.3	115	1055	65	8-68	16.23	7	2
Career (6-ball)	6247.1	1905 ⎱	19383	1316	9-24	14.72	115	34
(5-ball)	2748.4	1029 ⎰						

1904

Yorkshire came a poor second to Lancashire in the Championship this year. An unprecedented decision of a match being declared void was occasioned by the pitch being tampered with at Harrogate against Kent which deprived Rhodes of another seven wickets and Haigh of a hat-trick which he accomplished bowling slow leg-breaks, dismissing Hubble, Fairservice and Blythe. As if to show he was becoming a genuine all-rounder Rhodes' batting improved out of all recognition and he made over 1500 runs with a highest score of 196 against Worcestershire at Worcester. His bowling fell off slightly - which is not surprising - but he still took 131 wickets. It wasn't until the Essex match at Leyton in June that he had 5-68 in each innings for 10-136 in the match. He quickly followed this with 10-39 in 23 overs against Hampshire at Headingley and 12-128 against Warwickshire at Edgbaston in the next match. After this he fell away a little but all told had a satisfactory season.

	Own Team Total	O	M	R	W		Opp Total	Ct
227. MCC Australian Team v Rest of England, Lord's, May 9, (10), 11 (Match drawn)
b S.Hargreave   0 300   31 13 62 3 William Quaife
c A.F.A.Lilley   247
D.Denton c P.F.Warner
A.C.MacLaren c R.E.Foster
did not bat   - 34-1

228. Yorkshire v Cambridge University, Fenner's, May 12, 13 (Yorkshire won by an innings and 118 runs)
```
not out                      85   405     12    4   18   0                                          93        1
                              -    -     -    -                                       194       1
```
229. Yorkshire v Leicestershire, Bradford, May 16, 17, 18 (Match drawn)
```
c R.T.Crawford
  b W.W.Odell     16   321     17    7   33   2   J.H.King  b                        196       1
                                                  J.P.Whiteside  c J.Tunnicliffe
c J.H.King b G.C.Gill     0   259-9d    30    7   77   3   H.Whitehead  c sub        230-6
                                                  J.H.King  lbw
                                                  R.T.Crawford  b
```
230. Yorkshire v Oxford University, The Parks, May 19, 20, (21) (Match drawn)
```
c W.S.Bird b G.T.Branston    8   426    32.4   2   129   4   J.E.Raphael  c D.Denton     374
                                                  F.Weatherby  c D.Hunter
                                                  L.D.Brownlee  c F.Mitchell
                                                  R.C.W.Burn  b
```
231. Yorkshire v Lancashire, Old Trafford, May 23, 24, (25) (Match drawn)
```
not out                     94   293    21    5   64   0                             273
did not bat                  -    34-3
```
232. Yorkshire v Derbyshire, Derby, May 26, (27), 28 (Match drawn)
```
c and b A.Warren            29   237    16    6   37   2   G.R.Gregory  b             126       1
                                                  A.Warren  c F.S.Jackson
did not bat                  -    25-3
```
233. Yorkshire v Worcestershire, Bramall Lane, May 30, (31) June 1 (Match drawn)
```
c W.B.Burns b A.Bird        10    88    42   16   61   5   H.KFoster  b               192
                                                  E.G.Arnold  c C.H.Grimshaw
                                                  G.F.Wheldon  c C.H.Grimshaw
                                                  R.D.Burrows  c W.Ringrose
                                                  A.Bird  st D.Hunter
                                      9    5   15   2   F.L.Bowley  c J.Tunnicliffe   46-5
                                                  E.G.Arnold  b
```
234. Yorkshire v Middlesex, Lord's, June 2, 3, 4 (Middlesex won by 77 runs)
```
b A.E.Trott                  5    72    30   11   51   1   C.P.Foley  c J.Tunnicliffe  214      1
c B.J.T.Bosanquet
  b J.T.Hearne     24   160     7    0   33   1   L.J.Moon  c F.S.Jackson            95
```
235. Yorkshire v Surrey, Bradford, June 6, 7, 8 (Yorkshire won by 297 runs)
```
lbw b W.C.Smith             21   139     2    0    2   1   H.D.G.Leveson-Gower  b     127      1
c H.Strudwick b W.S.Lees   107   398-7d  11    2   22   1   W.C.Smith  c W.Ringrose   113
```
236. Yorkshire v Nottinghamshire, Trent Bridge, June 9, 10, 11 (Yorkshire won by ten wickets)
```
b T.G.Wass                  35   452    17    4   54   0                             352
did not bat                  -    12-0   13.1   7   12   4   J.R.Gunn  b              111       3
                                                  G.Anthony  c and b
                                                  J.Hardstaff, sen.  lbw
                                                  A.W.Hallam  c and b
```
237. Yorkshire v Sussex, Bramall Lane, June 13, 14, 15 (Match drawn)
```
c K.S.Ranjitsinhji b G.R.Cox25   220    35    5   91   2   C.B.Fry  c J.Tunnicliffe   440-9d
                                                  J.Vine  c J.Tunnicliffe
did not bat                  -    218-2
```
238. Yorkshire v Worcestershire, Worcester, June 16, 17, 18 (Match drawn)
```
c G.E.Bromley-Martin
  b F.A.Pearson   196   447    12    3   21   0                             211
                                31    9   54   0                             456-8
```
239. Yorkshire v Essex, Leyton, June 20, 21, 22 (Yorkshire won by nine wickets)
```
b C.P.Buckenham              6   369    21    3   68   5   F.L.Fane  c J.Tunnicliffe  207
                                                  P.A.Perrin  lbw
                                                  C.P.McGahey  c J.Tunnicliffe
                                                  F.H.Gillingham  c D.Hunter
                                                  B.Tremlin  b
did not bat                  -    58-1  32.3  13   68   5   F.L.Fane  c E.Wainwright   217
                                                  G.Tosetti  b
                                                  W.Reeves  c E.Wainwright
                                                  C.P.Buckenham  c D.Hunter
                                                  T.M.Russell  c J.Tunnicliffe
```
240. Yorkshire v Somerset, Hull, June 23, 24, 25 (Yorkshire won by seven wickets)
```
b A.E.Lewis                 15   328    30    8   71   0                             302
did not bat                  -    152-3  17    6   26   2   L.C.Braund  c and b       176       1
                                                  P.R.Johnson  lbw
```

241. Yorkshire v Hampshire, Headingley, June 27, 28 (Yorkshire won by 370 runs)
c E.B.Frederick
    b H.V.Hesketh-Prichard 3 194   16 7 27 6 A.C.Johnston b   62
    A.S.Webb b
    E.M.Sprot c W.H.Wilkinson
    J.Stone st D.Hunter
    F.H.Bacon c W.H.Wilkinson
    T.Langford c S.Haigh
c C.B.Llewellyn
    b H.V.Hesketh-Prichard 41 274   7 3 12 4 E.M.Sprot lbw   36
    J.Stone c D.Hunter
    T.H.K.Dashwood c D.Hunter
    M.W.Hayter c W.H.Wilkinson

242. Yorkshire v Warwickshire, Edgbaston, June 30, July 1, 2 (Yorkshire won by an innings and 4 runs)
c J.F.Byrne b S.Hargreave 4 419   41 18 95 6 T.S.Fishwick c D.Hunter 307   1
    A.C.S.Glover c and b
    J.F.Byrne c E.Wainwright
    A.F.A.Lilley lbw
    C.Charlesworth b
    A.E.M.Whittle c E.Wainwright
    16 7 33 6 S.P.Kinneir b   108
    A.C.S.Glover c G.H.Hirst
    William Quaife c H.Myers
    C.Charlesworth c D.Denton
    A.E.M.Whittle c G.H.Hirst
    F.Moorhouse b

243. Players v Gentlemen, Lord's, July 4, 5, 6 (Gentlemen won by two wickets)
c M.W.Payne
    b B.J.T.Bosanquet 50 327   3 0 8 0   171
    b F.S.Jackson 31 255   13 3 32 0   412-8

244. Yorkshire v Hampshire, Portsmouth, July 11, 12, 13 (Yorkshire won by an innings and 18 runs)
c sub b A.J.L.Hill 98 549   27 8 68 2 E.M.Sprot st D.Hunter 331
    T.A.Chignell b
    14 1 43 2 A.S.Webb c J.Tunnicliffe 200
    E.M.Sprot c H.Wilkinson

245. Yorkshire v Kent, Tunbridge Wells, July 14, 15, 16 (Match drawn)
c James Seymour
    b J.R.Mason 36 241   45 15 73 1 James Seymour c D.Denton 419
    b E.Humphreys 0 492   - - - -   151-3

246. Yorkshire v Surrey, Kennington Oval, July 18, 19, 20 (Match drawn)
b E.H.L.Nice 3 162   34 10 70 3 T.W.Hayward c D.Hunter 349
    A.Baker b
    E.G.Hayes c H.Wilkinson
b E.H.L.Nice 14 492-5d   7 1 13 0   131-3   1

247. Yorkshire v Gloucestershire, Dewsbury, July 21, 22, 23 (Match drawn)
c H.J.Huggins
    b E.G.Dennett 46 279   3 1 5 1 F.E.Thomas c F.S.Jackson 186   2
did not bat - 47-1   21 7 66 2 J.H.Board c H.Myers 343
    T.Langdon c W.Ringrose

248. Yorkshire v Nottinghamshire, Bradford, July 25, 26, 27 (Match drawn)
c J.W.Day b J.R.Gunn 0 229   17 3 50 3 G.Gunn lbw   194
    J.Hardstaff, sen. c J.Tunnicliffe
    V.H.Cartwright c D.Denton
did not bat - 9-1

249. Yorkshire v South Africans, Hull, July 28, 29, (30) (Match drawn)
lbw b J.Middleton 31 370   27 14 54 1 W.A.Shalders c D.Hunter 148   1
    22 8 29 2 L.J.Tancred b 158-8
    C.M.H.Hathorn c D.Hunter

250. Yorkshire v Lancashire, Bradford, August 1, 2, 3 (Match drawn)
lbw b A.Kermode 1 403   17 9 19 0   173
    18 6 42 1 L.O.S.Poidevin c D.Hunter 163-3

251. Yorkshire v Leicestershire, Aylestone Road, Leicester, August 4, 5, 6 (Match drawn)
c V.F.S.Crawford b G.C.Gill 10 414   30 5 84 5 C.E.de Trafford c D.Denton 310
    J.H.King b
    G.C.Gill c D.Denton
    T.C.Allsopp b
    J.P.Whiteside c D.Hunter

did not bat   -   147-3d   19   8   30   2   C.E.de Trafford c and b   94-7   1
                                                     C.J.B.Wood c D.Hunter

252. Yorkshire v Middlesex, Bramall Lane, August 8, 9, 10 (Match drawn)
c A.E.Trott b R.E.More   76   309   27   2   116   2   B.J.T.Bosanquet c E.Smith   488
                                                     P.F.Warner b
b J.T.Hearne   10   369-9d   9   1   38   1   E.A.Beldam st D.Hunter   89-2

253. Yorkshire v Warwickshire, Huddersfield, August 11, 12, 13 (Warwickshire won by 6 runs)
lbw b S.Hargreave   9   116   6   1   9   1   S.Hargreave c D.Denton   164
c A.F.A.Lilley c E.F.Field   8   124   13   2   42   4   C.Charlesworth c J.Tunnicliffe 82   2
                                                     J.F.Byrne b
                                                     A.E.M.Whittle c and b
                                                     S.Santall c J.Tunnicliffe

254. Yorkshire v Essex, Headingley, August 15, 16, (17) (Match drawn)
c P.A.Perrin b C.P.McGahey 58   379   23   8   59   1   C.P.McGahey c J.Tunnicliffe 204
                              15.3   7   12   4   P.A.Perrin lbw   118-6
                                                     C.P.McGahey c J.Tunnicliffe
                                                     F.H.Gillingham c D.Hunter
                                                     A.J.Turner b

255. Yorkshire v Sussex, Hove, August 18, 19, 20 (Match drawn)
b G.R.Cox   8   292   56   23   92   1   J.Vine c J.Tunnicliffe   377
did not bat   -   86-3

256. Yorkshire v Gloucestershire, Cheltenham, August 22, 23, 24 (Match drawn)
c and b G.Pepall   25   148   15.4   1   40   6   H.Wrathall lbw   84
                                                     G.L.Jessop lbw
                                                     F.H.Bateman-Champain c S.Haigh
                                                     L.D.Brownlee c J.Tunnicliffe
                                                     G.Pepall c J.Tunnicliffe
                                                     H.J.Huggins c sub
b G.E.Dennett   0   147

257. Yorkshire v Somerset, Taunton, August 25, 26, 27 (Yorkshire won by an innings and 152 runs)
not out   49   472-7d   2.4   1   3   2   H.Martyn c J.Tunnicliffe   109
                                                     B.Cranfield c D.Hunter
                             24   4   69   2   L.C.H.Palairet c E.Smith   211   1
                                                    S.M.J.Woods c I.Grimshaw

258. Yorkshire v MCC & Ground, Scarborough, August 29, 30, 31 (Match drawn)
c H.D.G.Leveson-Gower
       b R.H.Spooner   26   475   11   2   31   0   234
                                 20   2   81   1   J.H.King lbw   471-8

259. Yorkshire v South Africans, Scarborough, September 1, 2, 3 (Match drawn)
b G.C.White   19   387   14   5   41   4   C.M.H.Hathorn
                                                        c J.Tunnicliffe   102
                                                    F.Mitchell c G.H.Hirst
                                                    J.H.Sinclair c D.Denton
                                                    R.O.Schwarz c J.Tunnicliffe
                               35   12   73   2   L.J.Tancred c J.Tunnicliffe 232-5
                                                    G.C.White c D.Denton

260. North v South, Scarborough, September 5, 6, 7 (Match drawn)
c A.E.Relf b G.J.Thompson   9   241   15   3   47   3   G.J.Thompson st D.Hunter   246   1
                                                    F.H.Huish c J.Tunnicliffe
                                                   C.Blythe c H.Wilkinson
not out   74   331-9d   -   -   -   -   42-1

261. North v South, Hastings, September (8), 9, 10 (North won by ten wickets)
c T.W.Hayward
       b J.T.Hearne   93   319   6   0   26   0   110   1
did not bat   -   33-0   21.1   3   88   5   A.Hearne c A.F.A.Lilley   240
                                                    S.H.Day lbw
                                                    L.C.Braund st A.F.A.Lilley
                                                   G.W.Beldam c D.Denton
                                                    M.W.Payne b

262. Rest of England v Lancashire, Kennington Oval, September 12, 13, (14), 15 (Match drawn)
run out   29   235   10   1   17   2   R.H.Spooner b   177   1
                                                    L.O.S.Poidevin c and b
did not bat   -   156-4d   7   3   23   0   106-5

SEASON'S AVERAGES

Batting and Fielding	M	I	NO	Runs	HS	Ave	100	50	Ct
Players v Gentlemen	1	2	0	81	50	40.50	-	1	-
North v South	2	3	1	176	93	88.00	-	2	2
Championship	26	35	2	1082	196	32.78	2	4	16
Other Yorkshire matches	5	5	1	169	85*	42.25	-	1	3
Other matches	2	2	0	29	29	14.50	-	-	1
Season	36	47	4	1537	196	35.74	2	8	22
Career	262	339	79	5901	196	22.69	3	24	151

Bowling	O	M	R	W	BB	Ave	5i	10m
Players v Gentlemen	16	3	40	0	-	-	-	-
North v South	42.1	6	161	8	5-88	20.12	1	-
Championship	917.3	276	2070	104	6-27	19.90	8	3
Other Yorkshire matches	173.4	49	456	14	4-41	32.57	-	-
Other matches	48	17	102	5	3-66	20.40	-	-
Season (6-ball)	1197.2	351	2829	131	6-27	21.59	9	3
Career (6-ball)	7444.3	2256 } 22212		1447	9-24	15.35	124	37
(5-ball)	2748.4	1029 }						

1905

Rhodes continued the improvement with his batting and made his first double century, 201 against Somerset at Taunton, and 108 against the same opponents at Harrogate. He increased his wicket total to 182 at 16.95. He played in four Tests against the Australians missing out on one through injury. This being Jackson's year - never losing the toss in all the five Tests - it is not surprising that England won the series although Rhodes had a poor return of only ten wickets. In the Championship he was 'par excellence'. Forty-seven wickets in May contained 8-60 against Warwickshire at Edgbaston and he also had 6-87 against Worcestershire at Worcester. A quiet June culminated with 10-74 against Warwickshire at Dewsbury and he had 8-119 for the Players at Lord's in July. He ran riot in August with 9-115 in the 'Roses' match at Sheffield, 10-115 against Surrey at Headingley, 10-145 against Middlesex at Bradford and 11-158 against the Rest of England in September at the Oval. All told he was, as *Wisden* said, challenging Hirst as the best all-round man in England.

	Own Team Total	O	M	R	W		Opp Total	Ct
263. Yorkshire v Somerset, Taunton, May 1, 2, 3 (Yorkshire won by an innings and 224 runs)								
c E.Robson b F.P.Hardy	201 549-9d	25	9	42	3	A.E.Lewis b	98	
						L.C.Braund b		
						S.M.J.Woods c H.Myers		
		17.3	4	59	4	L.C.Braund b	227	2
						S.M.J.Woods lbw		
						H.S.Burrington c I.Grimshaw		
						B.Cranfield b		
264. Yorkshire v Gloucestershire, Bristol, May 8, 9 (Yorkshire won by an innings and 55 runs)								
c J.H.Board b E.G.Dennett	6 338	19.2	6	36	5	E.E.Barnett b	96	
						G.L.Jessop b		
						F.E.Thomas b		
						H.J.Huggins c D.Hunter		
						F.G.Roberts c I.Grimshaw		
		16	4	59	2	W.H.Hale c D.Hunter	187	1
						J.H.Board lbw		
265. Yorkshire v Worcestershire, Worcester, May 11, 12, 13 (Yorkshire won by 65 runs)								
b E.G.Arnold	12 225	-	-	-	-		97	2
b J.A.Cuffe	4 232	52.5	21	87	6	F.L.Bowley c G.H.Hirst	295	
						F.A.Pearson st D.Hunter		
						J.A.Cuffe c D.Hunter		
						W.B.Burns c J.Tunnicliffe		
						R.D.Burrows c D.Hunter		
						G.A.Wilson c D.Denton		

266. Yorkshire v Derbyshire, Bradford, May 15, 16 (Yorkshire won by an innings and 61 runs)
     b A.Warren   0   289   4   2   4   0   108   1
                                       15.1   5   43   4   L.G.Wright c J.Tunnicliffe 120   2
                                                               E.M.Ashcroft c D.Hunter
                                                               A.Morton c J.Tunnicliffe
                                                               W.Bestwick c D.Denton

267. Yorkshire v Leicestershire, Aylestone Road, Leicester, May 18, 19, 20 (Match drawn)
     c A.E.Davis b G.C.Gill   11   515   41.2 16   82   4   A.E.Knight c J.Tunnicliffe 419
                                                               G.C.Gill st D.Hunter
                                                               A.E.Davis c J.Tunnicliffe
                                                               W.W.Odell st D.Hunter
                                       23   13   22   3   C.E.de Trafford
                                                               c H.Wilkinson 121-7
                                                               V.F.S.Crawford lbw
                                                               R.T.Crawford b

268. Yorkshire v Australians, Bramall Lane, May 22, 23, 24 (Australians won by 174 runs)
     b A.Cotter   0   197   21   1   84   3   R.A.Duff b   322
                                                               J.Darling c J.Tunnicliffe
                                                               C.E.McLeod c J.Tunnicliffe
     c M.A.Noble b F.J.Laver 22   78   12   3   29   3   M.A.Noble lbw   127   1
                                                               S.E.Gregory b
                                                               W.P.Howell b

269. Yorkshire v Warwickshire, Edgbaston, May 25, 26 27 (Match drawn)
     c F.Moorhouse b S.Santall 14   361   57.5 21   90   8   J.F.Byrne c C.H.Grimshaw   313   2
                                                               S.P.Kinneir c J.Tunnicliffe
                                                               J.H.G.Devey lbw
                                                               A.F.A.Lilley c and b
                                                               J.W.Smith b
                                                               A.E.M.Whittle c D.Hunter
                                                               S.Santall c D.Hunter
                                                               S.Hargreave c D.Denton
                                       10   3   33   0   238-4   1

270. ENGLAND v AUSTRALIA, Trent Bridge, May 29, 30, 31 (England won by 213 runs)
     c M.A.Noble b F.J.Laver 29   196   18   6   37   1   W.W.Armstrong
                                                               st A.F.A.Lilley 221
     not out   39   426-5d   30   8   58   1   A.Cotter b   188

27.. Yorkshire v Middlesex, Lord's June 1, 2, 3 (Yorkshire won by seven wickets)
     b J.H.Hunt   25   275   21   6   55   2   E.Field c F.S.Jackson   145
                                                               G.Crosdale st D.Hunter
     not out   7   103-3   27   7   59   2   P.F.Warner lbw   232   1
                                                               B.J.T.Bosanquet c S.Haigh

272. Yorkshire v Australians, Bradford, June 5, 6, 7 (Match drawn)
     b M.A.Noble   70   324   19   5   45   1   J.J.Kelly b   208
     not out   13   266-4d   19   5   38   1   C.Hill c D.Hunter   187

273. Yorkshire v Cambridge University, Fenner's, June 8, 9 (Yorkshire won by an innings and 43 runs)
     c H.C.McDonell
           b G.G.Napier   46   243   14   4   16   6   R.A.Young b   39
                                                               C.H.Eyre c C.H.Grimshaw
                                                               E.W.Mann c J.Tunnicliffe
                                                               W.P.Harrison lbw
                                                               R.P.Keigwin lbw
                                                               M.W.Payne b
                                       22   4   69   1   M.W.Payne c D.Denton   161   1

274. Yorkshire v Lancashire, Old Trafford, June 12, 13, 14 (Lancashire won by an innings and 52 runs)
     c W.Findlay b W.Brearley 17   133   31   6   70   0   399
     c L.O.S.Poidevin
           b A.Kermode   65   214

275. ENGLAND v AUSTRALIA, Lord's, June 15, 16, (17) (Match drawn)
     b A.J.Y.Hopkins   15   282   16.1   1   70   3   R.A.Duff c A.F.A.Lilley   181
                                                               S.E.Gregory c A.O.Jones
                                                               J.J.Kelly lbw
     did not bat   -   151-5

276. Yorkshire v Nottinghamshire, Bramall Lane, June 19, 20, 21 (Yorkshire won by 127 runs)
     c J.R.Gunn b T.G.Wass   1   61   15   1   43   2   J.Iremonger c D.Denton   122
                                                               J.R.Gunn b

c T.W.Oates b T.G.Wass   0   227   14   7   15   4   J.Iremonger b   39
                                                        J.Hardstaff, sen. b
                                                        A.O.Jones lbw
                                                        H.Staunton c D.Denton

277. Yorkshire v Warwickshire, Dewsbury, June 22, 23 (Yorkshire won by 66 runs)
  b S.Santall   54 153   30   9   48   5   J.H.G.Devey c D.Hunter   138   1
                                                        William Quaife b
                                                        T.S.Fishwick st D.Hunter
                                                        C.S.Baker c F.S.Jackson
                                                        S.Santall st D.Hunter
  c F.R.Loveitt b S.Santall 7 108 13   4   26   5   J.H.G.Devey lbw   57   1
                                                        F.R.Loveitt lbw
                                                        A.F.A.Lilley lbw
                                                        T.S.Fishwick c J.Tunnicliffe
                                                        S.Hargreave c D.Denton

278. Yorkshire v Sussex, Headingley, June 26, 27, 28 (Match drawn)
  b G.R.Cox   16 295   44   8   102 3   C.B.Fry st D.Hunter   294
                                                        E.H.Killick b
                                                        A.L.Gorringe c D.Hunter
  not out   10 243-7   8   0   25   0   77-3

279. Yorkshire v Kent, Hull, June 29, 30 (Kent won by six wickets)
  c James Seymour b C.Blythe 0 77 16   7   28   1   A.Hearne lbw   124
  b C.Blythe   50 162   3   1   13   0   116-4

280. Yorkshire v Somerset, Harrogate, July 6, 7 (Yorkshire won by an innings and 149 runs)
  c L.C.Braund b B.Cranfield 108 474 - -   -   -   125   1
                                    16.2 4   31   4   E.Robson c D.Hunter   200
                                                        B.Cranfield b
                                                        A.E.Bailey c G.Deyes
                                                        J.Bucknell c S.Haigh

281. Players v Gentlemen, Lord's, July 10, 11, 12 (Players won by 149 runs)
  b W.Brearley   22 356   19   2   48   3   C.B.Fry b   185
                                                        F.S.Jackson b
                                                        W.H.B.Evans b
  did not bat   - 293-4d   33   12 71   5   F.S.Jackson b   315
                                                        W.H.B.Evans c G.H.Hirst
                                                        B.J.T.Bosanquet c S.Haigh
                                                        G.L.Jessop lbw
                                                        H.V.Hesketh-Prichard b

282. Yorkshire v Kent, Tunbridge Wells, July 13, 14 (Yorkshire won by eight wickets)
  c C.H.B.Marsham
      b J.R.Mason   53 239   -   -   -   -   142   1
  did not bat   - 81-2   16   7   40   1   E.W.Dillon b   174   1

283. Yorkshire v Hampshire, Bournemouth, July 17, 18 (Yorkshire won by an innings and 167 runs)
  c W.H.B.Evans b H.Baldwin 48 491   -   -   -   172   1
                                     6   0   24   0   152   1

284. Yorkshire v Surrey, Kennington Oval, July 20, 21, 22 (Yorkshire won by an innings and 108 runs)
  c J.B.Hobbs b N.A.Knox 0 442   2.2 0   5   2   E.G.Hayes c D.Denton   116   1
                                                        N.A.Knox b
                                     24   8   41   2   W.S.Lees c H.Rudston   218   1
                                                        N.A.Knox b

285. ENGLAND v AUSTRALIA, Old Trafford, July 24, 25, 26 (England won by an innings and 80 runs)
  not out   27 446   5.5 1   25   2   W.W.Armstrong b   197   1
                                                        F.J.Laver b
                                     11.3 3   36   3   V.T.Trumper lbw   169   4
                                                        D.R.A.Gehrs c and b
                                                        C.E.McLeod c E.G.Arnold

286. Yorkshire v Nottinghamshire, Trent Bridge, July 27, 28 (Yorkshire won by an innings and 55 runs)
  c T.W.Oates
      b J.H.Pennington 9 343   11.3 3   34   5   G.Gunn b   114   2
                                                        J.Hardstaff, sen. c W.Ringrose
                                                        G.V.Chambers c D.Denton
                                                        A.W.Hallam st D.Hunter
                                                        J.H.Pennington c E.Smith
                                     21   6   57   3   R.E.Hemingway c S.Haigh 174   1
                                                        G.T.Branston c D.Denton
                                                        G.V.Chambers c H.Myers

287. Yorkshire v Gloucestershire, Bradford, July 31, August 1, 2 (Yorkshire won by an innings and 118 runs)
    c C.L.Townsend
      b W.S.A.Brown   40   504-7d   8.4   0   32   2   E.G.Dennett c S.Haigh   245
                                                         F.A.Watts b
                                      11   3   41   3   J.H.Board c J.Tunnicliffe   141
                                                         E.Spry c G.H.Hirst
                                                         F.A.Watts b

288. Yorkshire v Hampshire, Hull, August (3), 4, (5) (Match drawn)
    did not bat   -   303-4d   13   5   23   0   88-3

289. Yorkshire v Lancashire, Bramall Lane, August 7, 8, 9 (Yorkshire won by 44 runs)
    c H.G.Garnett b W.Brearley 2   76   22   3   66   5   A.C.MacLaren st D.Hunter   177
                                                           R.H.Spooner b
                                                           J.T.Tyldesley c G.H.Hirst
                                                           H.G.Garnett lbw
                                                           A.Kermode b
    c A.C.MacLaren
      b W.Brearley 74   285   21.4   6   49   4   L.O.S.Poidevin st D.Hunter   140   2
                                                         H.G.Garnett c and b
                                                         J.Hallows c and b
                                                         W.Brearley c E.Smith

290. Yorkshire v Surrey, Headingley, August 10, 11 (Yorkshire won by five wickets)
    not out   59   231   26.2   3   73   6   T.W.Hayward c D.Hunter   171   2
                                                         F.C.Holland c and b
                                                         J.E.Raphael c D.Hunter
                                                         J.B.Hobbs c and b
                                                         W.S.Lees st D.Hunter
                                                         N.A.Knox st D.Hunter
    c and b N.A.Knox   0   33-5   14.2   2   42   4   F.C.Holland st D.Hunter   91
                                                         J.B.Hobbs c W.H.Wilkinson
                                                         Lord Dalmeny b
                                                         W.S.Lees c E.Smith

291. ENGLAND v AUSTRALIA, Kennington Oval, August 14, 15, 16 (Match drawn)
    b A.Cotter   36   430-7d   21   2   59   0   363   1
    did not bat   -   261-6d   8   0   29   0   124-4

292. Yorkshire v Essex, Huddersfield, August 17, 18, 19 (Yorkshire won by an innings and 193 runs)
    c C.P.Buckenham
      b C.P.McGahey 66   423-6d   3   1   6   0   172   3
                                    8.2   4   9   6   P.A.Perrin c D.Denton   58
                                                         W.Reeves hit wkt
                                                         R.P.Keigwin c G.H.Hirst
                                                         E.J.O'Connor b
                                                         C.E.Benham b
                                                         A.E.Russell lbw

293. Yorkshire v Middlesex, Bradford, August 21, 22, 23 (Match drawn)
    c C.M.Wells b J.T.Hearne 21   281   26   5   100   3   B.J.T.Bosanquet c E.Smith   285   1
                                                            G.MacGregor c J.Tunnicliffe
                                                            A.R.Litteljohn c D.Denton
    did not bat   -   59-0   16   3   45   7   P.F.Warner c D.Hunter   87   1
                                                         J.Douglas st D.Hunter
                                                         F.A.Tarrant c F.S.Jackson
                                                         B.J.T.Bosanquet c and b
                                                         C.M.Wells st D.Hunter
                                                         G.MacGregor c I.Grimshaw
                                                         A.R.Litteljohn c H.Myers

294. Yorkshire v Essex, Leyton, August 24, 25, 26 (Match drawn)
    b J.W.H.T.Douglas   2   98   29.4   2   107   2   C.P.McGahey b   521   1
                                                         A.E.Russell b
    b C.P.Buckenham   6   227-7

295. Yorkshire v Sussex, Hove, August 28, 29, 30 (Match drawn)
    not out   79   203   25.4   6   71   4   J.Vine lbw   137   1
                                                         C.B.Fry b
                                                         E.H.Killick c Lord Hawke
                                                         K.O.Goldie c H.Myers
    c K.O.Goldie b G.R.Cox 50   154-5d   16   1   49   0   119-1

296. Yorkshire v MCC & Ground, Scarborough, August 31, September 1 (Yorkshire won by three wickets)

b W.Mead	6	110	15	3	53	6	C.E.de Trafford c D.Denton 108

J.H.King c H.Myers
J.E.Raphael c Lord Hawke
C.L.Townsend c F.S.Jackson
W.Findlay c J.Tunnicliffe
H.D.G.Leveson-Gower c D.Hunter

not out	22	97-7	-	-	-	-	98

297. North v South, Scarborough, September 4, 5, (6) (Match drawn)

c G.R.Cox

b B.J.T.Bosanquet	56	418	28	6	88	4	J.E.Raphael c D.Hunter 215

F.A.Tarrant st D.Hunter
G.J.Thompson c J.T.Tyldesley
G.R.Cox c J.T.Tyldesley

did not bat	- 125-2

298. Mr.C.I.Thornton's England XI v Australians, Scarborough, September 7, 8, 9 (Match drawn)

b F.J.Laver	4	282	27	2	86	2	V.T.Trumper lbw 392

J.Darling c D.Denton

did not bat	- 176-5

299. Yorkshire v Rest of England, Kennington Oval, September 14, 15, 16 (Yorkshire won by 65 runs)

c T.W.Hayward

b J.N.Crawford	15	190	34.1	7	99	6	L.G.Wright b 172	

J.T.Tyldesley b
A.F.A.Lilley c S.Haigh
J.N.Crawford c H.Myers
E.G.Arnold c E.Smith
W.S.Lees c J.W.Rothery

b C.Blythe	42	213	25	3	59	5	T.W.Hayward st D.Hunter 166	1

E.G.Hayes c and b
J.T.Tyldesley b
J.N.Crawford b
W.S.Lees st D.Hunter

SEASON'S AVERAGES

Batting and Fielding	M	I	NO	Runs	HS	Ave	100	50	Ct
Test matches	4	5	2	146	39*	48.66	-	-	6
Players v Gentlemen	1	1	0	22	22	22.00	-	-	-
North v South	1	1	0	56	56	56.00	-	1	-
Championship	25	35	4	1117	201	36.03	2	9	35
Other Yorkshire matches	5	9	2	236	70	33.71	-	1	3
Other matches	1	1	0	4	4 .	4.00	-	-	-
Season	37	52	8	1581	201	35.93	2	11	44
Career	299	391	87	7482	201	24.61	5	35	195

Bowling	O	M	R	W	BB	Ave	5i	10m
Test matches	110.3	21	314	10	3-36	31.40	-	-
Players v Gentlemen	52	14	119	8	5-71	14.87	1	-
North v South	28	6	88	4	4-88	22.00	-	-
Championship	842.5	232	1986	126	8-90	15.76	10	3
Other Yorkshire matches	181.1	35	492	32	6-16	15.37	4	1
Other matches	27	2	86	2	2-86	43.00	-	-
Season (6-ball)	1241.3	310	3085	182	8-90	16.95	15	4
Career (6-ball)	8686	2566 } 25297		1629	9-24	15.52	139	41
(5-ball)	2748.4	1029 }						

1906

Rhodes had by his standards a very ordinary year although he played in thirty-six matches in the season - all bar three for Yorkshire - and made 1618 runs, his wicket tally falling to 128 this being his lowest total for nine seasons. *Wisden* put this down to improvement as a batsmen and stated that 'his great advancement as a batsman did not compensate for his marked decline as a bowler'. Although still as deadly on a bad wicket batsmen did not fear him anymore on a good one and the fact that he took ten wickets in a match only once and had a best analysis of 6-90 against Sussex at Hove highlights the problem. He had trouble with his action and tried to copy John Gunn, who gave the ball an extraordinary amount of height, towards the end of the season without much luck. His batting however remained consistent and he scored the most runs to date. Three centuries were obtained all for Yorkshire, 119 against Leicestershire at Leicester, 115* against Somerset at Bath and 109 against the M.C.C. & Ground at Scarborough.

	Own Team Total	O	M	R	W		Opp Total	Ct
300. Yorkshire v MCC & Ground, Lord's, May 7, 8, 9 (MCC & Ground won by 40 runs)								
c F.H.Huish b A.E.E.Vogler	0 132	17	5	51	4	G.L.Jessop b	218	1
						C.B.W.Magnay c and b		
						C.P.Buckenham c J.Tunnicliffe		
						F.H.Huish c J.W.Rothery		
b W.Mead	52 288	24	2	118	5	J.Hardstaff, sen.		
						c J.Tunnicliffe	242	
						A.E.E.Vogler b		
						G.L.Jessop lbw		
						E.G.Wynyard c D.Denton		
						F.H.Liebenrood lbw		
301. Yorkshire v Hampshire, Southampton, May 10, 11, 12 (Yorkshire won by seven wickets)								
c E.M.C.Ede b J.R.Badcock	1 421	11.5	2	25	1	F.J.Hopkins c G.H.Hirst	198	
did not bat	- 58-3	34.2	8	63	3	D.V.Norbury c A.Dolphin	277	
						J.R.Badcock c C.H.Grimshaw		
						E.M.C.Ede c S.Haigh		
302. Yorkshire v Cambridge University, Fenner's, May 14, 15, 16 (Cambridge University won by 305 runs)								
c R.P.Keigwin b P.R.May	3 119	20	1	81	1	P.R.May c J.W.Rothery	312	1
c C.H.Eyre b P.R.May	4 51	16	5	34	2	C.C.Page c J.Tunnicliffe	163	1
						F.H.Mugliston c J.Tunnicliffe		
303. Yorkshire v Kent, Catford, May 17, 18, 19 (Yorkshire won by 119 runs)								
c F.H.Huish b A.Fielder	7 229	11	1	54	2	A.Hearne lbw	178	1
						E.Humphreys st A.Dolphin		
lbw b C.Blythe	10 137	19	7	27	2	A.P.Day c J.W.Rothery	69	
						F.H.Huish c J.W.Rothery		
304. Yorkshire v Leicestershire, Headingley, May 21, 22 (Yorkshire won by an innings and 103 runs)								
c H.Whitehead b W.W.Odell	38 244	8	2	16	3	C.J.B.Wood c H.Myers	34	1
						J.H.King c H.Myers		
						G.C.Gill st A.Dolphin		
		10	2	33	1	V.F.S.Crawford lbw	107	
305. Yorkshire v Warwickshire, Edgbaston, May 24, 25, (26) (Match drawn)								
st A.F.A.Lilley								
b C.Charlesworth	24 190	23	4	54	2	A.F.A.Lilley c S.Haigh	133	
						C.S.Baker b		
		-	-	-	-		114-5	1
306. Yorkshire v Worcestershire, Stourbridge, May 28, 29, 30 (Yorkshire won by nine wickets)								
b R.D.Burrows	51 254						141	1
did not bat	- 73-1						185	1
307. Yorkshire v Oxford University, The Parks, May 31, June 1, 2 (Yorkshire won by an innings and 106 runs)								
c sub b R.G.Barnes	0 358-9	-	-	-	-		168	
		7	1	21	0		84	
308. Yorkshire v Lancashire, Bradford, June 4, 5 (Yorkshire won by six wickets)								
lbw b F.Harry	20 177	7	1	12	0		67	
did not bat	- 42-4	11	3	18	2	J.T.Tyldesley c D.Denton	151	
						L.O.S.Poidevin c G.H.Hirst		
309. Yorkshire v Derbyshire, Chesterfield, June 7, 8, 9 (Yorkshire won by 33 runs)								
c and b S.W.A.Cadman	43 130	7	4	9	0		169	
c J.Humphries								
c S.W.A.Cadman	20 243	15	3	41	1	C.A.Ollivierre		
						c W.H.Wilkinson	171	
310. Yorkshire v Hampshire, Bramall Lane, June 11, 12, 13 (Yorkshire won by three wickets)								
b J.R.Badcock	0 201	-	-	-	-		138	

44

c T.Langford
    b R.H.Mornement 7 165-7   30.3 13 65 4 C.P.Mead c and b   225   2
                                                    C.B.Llewellyn b
                                                    A.Stone b
                                                  J.R.Badcock c J.W.Rothery

311. Yorkshire v Middlesex, Lord's, June 14, 15, 16 (Yorkshire won by 281 runs)
    c and b G.W.Beldam 10 329   22 4 29 2 A.E.Trott c J.Tunnicliffe 161
                                                J.H.Hunt c H.Myers
    run out   76 255-5d 23 8 25 2 M.W.Payne c C.A.Midgley 142
                                                J.H.Hunt c S.Haigh

312. Yorkshire v Essex, Bradford, June 18, 19 (Yorkshire won by nine wickets)
    lbw b W.Mead   53 315   11 1 25 3 H.A.Carpenter b   117   1
                                                C.P.McGahey lbw
                                                W.M.Turner st D.Hunter
    did not bat   - 7-1   16.3 6 69 2 P.A.Perrin lbw   204
                                                W.Reeves st D.Hunter

313. Yorkshire v Nottinghamshire, Trent Bridge, June 21, 22, 23 (Match drawn)
    b J.R.Gunn   83 266   37.2 9 95 6 T.W.Oates lbw   253
                                                J.R.Gunn c H.Myers
                                                A.O.Jones b
                                                J.Hardstaff, sen. b
                                                W.E.G.Payton c D.Hunter
                                                T.G.Wass b
    c J.Iremonger b J.R.Gunn 4 256-6d 6 1 17 0   137-3

314. Yorkshire v Kent, Bramall Lane, June 25, 26, 27 (Match drawn)
    b A.Fielder   80 287   27 7 91 1 K.L.Hutchings c D.Denton 292
    c James Seymour
        b A.Fielder 10 257   13 4 29 0   189-7   1

315. Yorkshire v Essex, Leyton, June 28, 29, 30 (Match drawn)
    c H.A.Carpenter
        b C.P.Buckenham 13 138   17 0 72 2 W.M.Turner c J.Tunnicliffe 231
                                                W.Reeves b
    c and b C.P.McGahey 14 141-3 10 0 30 2 H.A.Carpenter c D.Hunter 204-7d 1
                                                C.P.Buckenham c J.Tunnicliffe

316. Yorkshire v Gloucestershire, Headingley, July (2), 3, 4 (Match drawn)
    b H.J.Huggins   58 232   20.4 4 62 5 H.Wrathall c J.Tunnicliffe 151
                                                T.Langdon c G.H.Hirst
                                                L.D.Brownlee c J.Tunnicliffe
                                                E.G.Dennett b
                                                P.T.Mills c H.Myers
    b E.G.Dennett   33 78-8d 11 1 30 1 T.Langdon lbw   91-6

317. Yorkshire v Nottinghamshire, Dewsbury, July 5, 6 (Nottinghamshire won by 25 runs)
    c T.W.Oates b J.R.Gunn 16 151   -   -   - -   74   2
    c T.W.Oates b T.G.Wass 11 68   9 2 21 0   170

318. Players v Gentlemen, Lord's, July 9, 10, 11 (Gentlemen won by 45 runs)
    c B.J.T.Bosanquet
        b N.A.Knox 1 199   11 3 28 0   167
    c B.J.T.Boasanquet
        b W.Brearley 19 244   5 2 6 0   321   1

319. Yorkshire v Sussex, Hove, July 12, 13, 14 (Yorkshire won by six wickets)
    c R.R.Relf
        b J.E.B.B.P.Q.C.Dwyer 1 357   24 4 94 5 A.E.Relf c G.H.Hirst 282   1
                                                R.R.Relf c D.Denton
                                                H.L.Simms st D.Hunter
                                                John Seymour c G.H.Hirst
                                                J.E.B.B.P.Q.C.Dwyer c W.H.Wilkinson
    run out   9 122-4 26 3 90 6 J.Vine c W.H.Wilkinson 194   2
                                                A.E.Relf c D.Denton
                                                R.R.Relf st D.Hunter
                                                G.R.Cox c and b
                                                G.Leach c T.L.Taylor
                                                John Seymour b

320. Yorkshire v Derbyshire, Bramall Lane, July 16, 17, 18 (Yorkshire won by ten wickets)
    b A.Warren   21 239   8.4 2 30 2 L.G.Wright c G.Deyes 113
                                                W.Bestwick c D.Denton
    not out   6 9-0   11 0 30 2 E.Needham c W.H.Wilkinson 134   1
                                                A.Hogg c S.Haigh

321. Yorkshire v Somerset, Huddersfield, July 19, 20, 21 (Yorkshire won by an innings and 6 runs)
c A.E.Lewis b F.P.Hardy   93 417   5   0   25 1 F.M.Lee c A.Farrar   172   2
                            14   3   28 0   239   1

322. Yorkshire v Sussex, Bradford, July 23, 24, 25 (Match drawn)
c R.R.Relf b A.E.Relf   19 212   18   0   86 2 R.R.Relf c T.L.Taylor   340
                                            C.L.A.Smith c Lord Hawke
b A.E.Relf   13 250   -   -   - -   45-5   1

323. Yorkshire v Surrey, Kennington Oval, July 26, 27, 28 (Surrey won by nine wickets)
c E.G.Hayes b N.A.Knox 15 186 19.1 3   77 2 P.R.May c J.W.Rothery   387   1
                                          H.Strudwick c and b
b P.R.May   53 297   2   0   10 0   97-1

324. Yorkshire v Worcestershire, Hull, July 30, 31 (Yorkshire won by an innings and 10 runs)
b G.A.Wilson   9 271   -   -   - -   25   1
                              20   2   53 1 F.L.Bowley lbw   236   1

325. Yorkshire v West Indians, Harrogate, August 2, 3, 4 (West Indians won by 262 runs)
c L.S.Constantine
        b S.G.Smith 1   50   15   2   39 1 O.H.Layne c T.L.Taylor   270
hit wkt b S.G.Smith   13 263   17   4   41 2 L.S.Constantine c D.Denton 305-6d
                                          S.G.Smith c A.Dolphin

326. Yorkshire v Lancashire, Old Trafford, August 6, 7, 8 (Yorkshire won by 107 runs)
b H.Dean   8 291   19   2   62 2 J.T.Tyldesley b   280
                                          W.Findlay lbw
c J.T.Tyldesley
        b A.Kermode 12 193   16   3   49 5 A.C.MacLaren hit wkt   97   3
                                          L.O.S.Poidevin c and b
                                          J.Sharp c J.Tunnicliffe
                                          F.Harry c E.Smith
                                          W.Findlay c and b

327. Yorkshire v Leicestershire, Aylestone Road, Leicester, August 9, 10, 11 (Match drawn)
c H.Whitehead
        b C.J.B.Wood 119 483   28   0 102 2 A.E.Knight c J.Tunnicliffe 425
                                          V.F.S.Crawford c C.H.Hardisty
                              13   0   50 1 A.E.Knight st D.Hunter   169-5   1

328. Yorkshire v Middlesex, Headingley, August 13, 14, 15 (Match drawn)
c and b F.A.Tarrant   28 144   15   3   53 0   276
not out   3 4-0   -   -   - -   23-4d   1

329. Yorkshire v Warwickshire, Harrogate, August 16, 17, 18 (Yorkshire won by an innings and 91 runs)
b S.Hargreave   0 255-8d   -   -   - -   79
                            17   2   40 5 T.S.Fishwick lbw   85   1
                                          C.Charlesworth c G.H.Hirst
                                          William Quaife b
                                          S.P.Kinneir c and b
                                          A.F.A.Lilley c J.W.Rothery

330. Yorkshire v Surrey, Bramall Lane, August 20, 21, 22 (Yorkshire won by 102 runs)
b N.A.Knox   6 144   16   3   44 3 E.G.Hayes c J.Tunnicliffe 154
                                          J.N.Crawford c E.Smith
                                          Lord Dalmeny c E.Smith
c F.C.Holland b W.S.Lees 94 225   -   -   - -   113   1

331. Yorkshire v Gloucestershire, Bristol, August 23, 24, 25 (Gloucestershire won by 1 run)
c J.H.Board b E.G.Dennett 9 159   4   2   5 0   164   1
c F.H.Bateman-Champain
        b E.G.Dennett 52 232   18   7   34 2 F.H.Bateman-Champain
                                                       c H.Myers 228
                                          F.B.Roberts lbw

332. Yorkshire v Somerset, Bath, August 27, 28, 29 (Yorkshire won by 389 runs)
c P.R.Johnson b A.E.Bailey 64 368   14   4   28 3 P.R.Johnson b   125
                                          F.A.Phillips lbw
                                          H.S.Poyntz c G.H.Hirst
not out   115 280-1   10   1   34 0   134   1

333. Yorkshire v MCC & Ground, Scarborough, August 30, 31, September 1 (Yorkshire won by five wickets)
c L.C.Braund b A.E.E.Vogler 5 292   24.3 3 102 4 R.H.Spooner b   346
                                          F.L.Fane c J.Tunnicliffe
                                          M.W.Payne b
                                          G.G.Napier c H.Myers

c H.D.G.Leveson-Gower
    b L.C.Braund 109 287-5   6   0   56   3 A.C.MacLaren
                                              c C.H.Hardisty   232-8d   1
                                  E.G.Wynyard c W.Ringrose
                                  G.J.Thompson c H.Myers

334. North v South, Scarborough, September 3, 4, 5 (North won by an innings and 71 runs)
    b G.G.Napier   45   590   13   2   61   3 K.L.Hutchings
                                            c A.C.MacLaren 204
                                  A.E.Relf lbw
                                  G.J.Thompson st D.Hunter
                        29.4   4 124   5 J.W.H.T.Douglas
                                            c R.H.Spooner 315
                                  A.E.Relf st D.Hunter
                                  G.J.Thompson c D.Hunter
                                  M.W.Payne c D.Hunter
                                  G.G.Napier hit wkt

335. Players v Gentlemen, Scarborough, September 6, 7, 8 (Match drawn)
    c M.W.Payne
      b J.W.H.T.Douglas 19 324   21.1   0 122   4 F.L.Fane c H.Myers   387
                                            J.W.H.T.Douglas c G.H.Hirst
                                          H.D.G.Leveson-Gower c J.Tunnicliffe
                                          N.A.Knox c G.J.Thompson
    c H.K.Foster
      b J.W.H.T.Douglas 3 374-6d   13   1   57   3 R.H.Spooner c T.W.Hayward 208-6
                                          E.G.Wynyard c E.G.Hayes
                                          M.W.Payne st D.Hunter

336. Rest of England v Kent, Kennington Oval, September 10, 11, 12, 13 (Rest of England won by 251 runs)
    b A.Fielder   15   392   10   0   41   0   365   2
    c James Seymour b C.Blythe 1 344-8d   1   1   0   0   120

SEASON'S AVERAGES

Batting and Fielding	M	I	NO	Runs	HS	Ave	100	50	Ct
Players v Gentlemen	2	4	0	42	19	10.50	-	-	1
North v South	1	1	0	45	45	45.00	-	-	-
Championship	28	46	3	1431	119	33.27	2	11	32
Other Yorkshire matches	5	9	0	187	109	20.77	1	1	4
Other matches	1	2	0	16	15	8.00	-	-	2
Season	37	62	3	1721	119	29.16	3	12	39
Career	336	453	90	9203	201	25.35	8	47	234

Bowling	O	M	R	W	BB	Ave	5i	10m
Players v Gentlemen	50.1	6	213	7	4-122	30.42	-	-
North v South	42.4	6	185	8	5-124	23.12	1	-
Championship	729	141	2036	91	6-90	22.37	6	1
Other Yorkshire matches	146.3	23	543	22	5-118	24.68	1	-
Other matches	11	1	41	0	-	-	-	-
Season (6-ball)	979.2	177	3018	128	6-90	23.57	8	1
Career (6-ball)	9665.2	2743 ⎫ 28315	1757	9-24	16.11	147	42	
(5-ball)	2748.4	1029 ⎭						

1907

Yorkshire finished in third place in the Championship behind Nottinghamshire (Champions) and Worcestershire. Three men were head and shoulders above all others in the Yorkshire team, Hirst, Haigh and Rhodes taking 359 wickets between them. Rhodes was much more the bowler of earlier days but although he bowled consistently well in the early part of the season the Test honours went to Colin Blythe who played in all three matches. The South Africans with their plethora of 'googly' bowlers failed to live up to their form in South Africa in 1905/06 and had a disappointing Test series, although their county form was excellent. With 1055 runs and 177 wickets Rhodes once more completed the 'double' and his best match aggregate was 12-130 against Somerset at Taunton followed by 11-138 in the 'Roses' match at Headingley. He took 55 wickets in May and 42 in August.

	Own Team Total	O	M	R	W		Opp Total	Ct

337. Yorkshire v Gentlemen of Ireland, Bray, May 2, 3, 4 (Yorkshire won by an innings and 1 run)

	Own Team Total	O	M	R	W		Opp Total	Ct
b E.J.Donovan	10 292	21	6	47	4	J.M.Magee b	102	
						R.H.Lambert c D.Hunter		
						T.C.Ross c G.H.Hirst		
						G.W.F.Kelly c S.Haigh		
		10	5	17	0		189	1

338. Yorkshire v MCC & Ground, Lord's, May 6, (7), 8 (Match drawn)

	Own Team Total	O	M	R	W		Opp Total	Ct
b F.A.Tarrant	0 142	14.4	2	47	4	P.F.Warner c D.Denton	134	
						J.Hardstaff, sen. b		
						A.E.Relf c J.Tunnicliffe		
						A.Fielder c S.Haigh		
c S.J.Snooke b A.E.Trott	0 83-9							

339. Yorkshire v Somerset, Taunton, May 9, 10, 11 (Yorkshire won by nine wickets)

	Own Team Total	O	M	R	W		Opp Total	Ct
lbw b A.E.Bailey	0 181	27.2	7	61	6	L.C.Braund b	110	
						A.E.Lewis c D.Hunter		
						S.M.J.Woods c D.Denton		
						G.W.Hodgkinson c S.Haigh		
						A.E.Newton lbw		
						A.E.Bailey b		
did not bat	- 44-1	26.1	2	69	6	A.E.Lewis c D.Denton	113	
						W.Montgomery c W.H.Wilkinson		
						G.W.Hodgkinson c B.B.Wilson		
						A.E.Newton c B.B.Wilson		
						A.E.M.Whittle b		
						A.E.Bailey st D.Hunter		

340. Yorkshire v Gloucestershire, Bristol, May 13, 14, 15 (Yorkshire won by three wickets)

	Own Team Total	O	M	R	W		Opp Total	Ct
c and b E.G.Dennett	12 126	25	10	45	3	J.H.Board c G.H.Hirst	145	
						G.L.Jessop b		
						A.E.Winstone b		
c J.H.Board b E.G.Dennett	16 138-7	20	1	72	5	R.T.Godsell st D.Hunter	115	
						G.L.Jessop c D.Denton		
						H.J.Huggins st D.Hunter		
						A.E.Winstone b		
						E.J.Spry b		

341. Yorkshire v Worcestershire, Worcester, May 16, 17, 18 (Worcestershire won by 54 runs)

	Own Team Total	O	M	R	W		Opp Total	Ct
c H.K.Foster b J.A.Cuffe	6 119	26	4	78	4	H.K.Foster b	292	
						W.B.Burns c D.Hunter		
						R.S.Swalwell b		
						A.W.Isaac c S.Haigh		
c W.B.Burns b J.A.Cuffe	0 258	23.3	4	58	5	F.L.Pearson	139	·1
						J.A.Cuffe c D.Hunter		
						R.S.Swalwell c and b		
						G.W.Gaukrodger c J.Tunnicliffe		
						R.D.Burrows c W.H.Wilkinson		

342. Yorkshire v Lancashire, Old Trafford, May 20, 21, 22 (Match drawn)

	Own Team Total	O	M	R	W		Opp Total	Ct
b W.Cook	68 248	23	5	61	3	J.T.Tyldesley st D.Hunter	275	
						J.Sharp b		
						E.L.Wright c J.Tunnicliffe		
		20	10	46	6	J.W.H.Makepeace c and b	109	1
						J.S.Heap b		
						J.Sharp b		
						E.L.Wright c J.W.Rothery		
						W.Cook c J.Tunnicliffe		
						A.Kermode c H.S.Kaye		

343. Yorkshire v Hampshire, Bradford, May (27), 28, 29 (Match drawn)

	Own Team Total	O	M	R	W		Opp Total	Ct
c C.P.Mead b H.G.Smoker	25 112	29.1	4	101	6	C.P.Mead c and b	209	1
						C.B.Llewellyn b		
						M.F.D.Wood st D.Hunter		
						J.R.Badcock c D.Denton		
						F.H.Bacon b		
						J.A.Newman lbw		
		8	2	15	3	C.B.Llewellyn c and b	45-6	1
						M.F.D.Wood c C.H.Hardisty		
						J.R.Badcock c J.Tunnicliffe		

48

344. Yorkshire v Nottinghamshire, Trent Bridge, May 30, (31), June (1) (Match drawn)
did not bat   -   47-1

345. Yorkshire v Kent, Headingley, June 3, 4, (5) (Match drawn)
c H.T.W.Hardinge
   b A.Fielder   0   150   11   3   20   3   F.E.Woolley c H.Myers   78   1
                                                  K.L.Hutchings c D.Hunter
                                                  W.J.Fairservice b
not out   18   65-4

346. Yorkshire v Cambridge University, Fenner's, June 6, 7, 8 (Yorkshire won by an innings and 26 runs)
   b C.F.Lyttelton   7   207   22   4   37   3   R.E.H.Bailey c G.H.Hirst   109   2
                                                  M.B.Elderton c D.Hunter
                                                  H.J.Goodwin lbw
                              20   4   42   4   C.C.G.Wright st D.Hunter   72
                                                  J.N.Buchanan st D.Hunter
                                                  C.Palmer b
                                                  M.B.Elderton b

347. Yorkshire v Surrey, Bradford, June 10, 11, (12) (Match drawn)
c J.N.Crawford b W.S.Lees 18   134   20   4   72   4   J.B.Hobbs lbw   144   1
                                                  A.Baker c and b
                                                  Lord Dalmeny c D.Denton
                                                  N.A.Knox c D.Denton
c A.Marshal b N.A.Knox   0   158-9

348. Yorkshire v Middlesex, Lord's, June 13, 14, (15) (Match drawn)
lbw b F.A.Tarrant   11   163   39   5   97   5   F.A.Tarrant c D.Hunter   244   1
                                                  G.W.Beldam c J.Tunnicliffe
                                                  R.V.Buxton c and b
                                                  C.C.Page hit wkt
                                                  A.E.Trott c D.Denton
                              4   2   2   0   57-2

349. Yorkshire v Sussex, Bramall Lane, June 17, 18, 19 (Sussex won by 65 runs)
b J.E.B.B.P.Q.C. Dwyer   7   181   34   4   76   5   J.Vine b   223
                                                  E.H.Killick b
                                                  C.L.A.Smith c J.Tunnicliffe
                                                  G.R.Cox b
                                                  J.E.B.B.P.Q.C.Dwyer c H.S.Kaye
c and b G.R.Cox   19   87   13.3   2   52   2   E.H.Killick b   110
                                                  H.R.Butt b

350. Yorkshire v Essex, Dewsbury, June 20, 21, 22 (Yorkshire won by five wickets)
b C.P.Buckenham   30   160   27   5   50   4   J.W.H.T.Douglas   142
                                                  C.P.McGahey c S.Haigh
                                                  C.J.Kortright c J.W.Rothery
                                                  C.P.Buckenham c H.S.Kaye
b J.W.H.T.Douglas   19   95-5   18.3   4   34   2   C.E.Benham c D.Denton   109
                                                  W.Mead c S.Haigh

351. Yorkshire v Somerset, Headingley, June 24, 25, 26 (Yorkshire won by an innings and 45 runs)
run out   40   260-7d   13   3   41   1   L.C.H.Palairet
                                                  c W.H.Wilkinson   93   1
                              11   2   29   0   122   1

352. Yorkshire v Leicestershire, Aylestone Road, Leicester, June 27, 28, 29 (Match drawn)
run out   112   515   30.1   10   65   2   W.E.Astill c G.H.Hirst   249
                                                  J.Shields b
                              16   4   49   2   A.E.Knight c J.Tunnicliffe   270-7
                                                  W.W.Odell c S.Haigh

353. Players v Gentlemen, Lord's, July 8, 9, (10) (Match drawn)
b W.Brearley   2   278   1   0   1   1   G.MacGregor b   160
b W.Brearley   6   138   -   -   -   -   41-2

354. Yorkshire v Essex, Leyton, July 11, 12 (Yorkshire won by an innings and 32 runs)
c C.P.Buckenham b W.Mead 24   310   23   7   44   4   P.A.Perrin c A.Dolphin   69
                                                  J.W.H.T.Douglas c J.Tunnicliffe
                                                  E.J.Freeman c A.Dolphin
                                                  W.Reeves b
                              33   6   80   4   F.L.Fane c J.Tunnicliffe   209   1
                                                  C.P.McGahey c A.Dolphin
                                                  E.J.Freeman c and b
                                                  C.E.Benham b

355. Yorkshire v South Africans, Bradford, July 15, 16 (South Africans won by five wickets)
   c W.A.Shalders b G.C.White 24   150   12   3   23   2   G.A.Faulkner c G.H.Hirst   148
                                                             G.C.White b
   b R.O.Schwarz   3   113   4   0   18   1   G.A.Faulkner c D.Hunter   116-5

356. Yorkshire v Gloucestershire, Harrogate, July 18, 19 (Yorkshire won by 38 runs)
   c T.Langdon b P.T.Mills   69   130   11   5   22   1   C.L.Townsend c S.Haigh   133
   b E.G.Dennett   13   236   11.1   3   40   3   F.M.Luce c J.Tunnicliffe   195
                                                            P.T.Mills c J.Tunnicliffe
                                                            E.G.Dennett b

357. Yorkshire v Warwickshire, Bramall Lane, July 22, 23 (Yorkshire won by ten wickets)
   c T.S.Fishwick b S.Santall   20   140   25   6   48   2   G.Weldrick b   107
                                                              C.S.Baker b
   did not bat   -   15-0   -   -   -   -   47

358. Yorkshire v Derbyshire, Glossop, July 25, 26 (Yorkshire won by an innings and 130 runs)
   c S.W.A.Cadman
          b F.C.Bracey   0   246   10   1   22   6   C.A.Ollivierre c W.E.Bates   44
                                                          I.Dearnaley c D.Denton
                                                          H.Cooper c J.Tunnicliffe
                                                          S.W.A.Cadman c J.W.Rothery
                                                          R.B.Rickman c J.Tunnicliffe
                                                          J.Humphries c J.Tunnicliffe
                                          14.3   0   49   2   J.Humphries c D.Denton   72   1
                                                          G.Green b

359. Yorkshire v Leicestershire, Hull, August 1, 2 (Yorkshire won by ten wickets)
   c H.Whitehead b W.W.Odell   1   114   8   4   10   2   W.W.Odell c W.E.Bates   60
                                                            W.E.Benskin b
   did not bat   -   1-0   10   3   15   3   H.Whitehead lbw   54
                                                            A.G.Hazlerigg c E.Smith
                                                            W.E.Benskin c J.W.Rothery

360. Yorkshire v Lancashire, Headingley, August 5, 6, 7 (Yorkshire won by nine wickets)
   b A.Kermode   69   183   28   8   71   6   R.H.Spooner c J.Tunnicliffe   136
                                                  J.T.Tyldesley lbw
                                                  H.D.Stanning c W.E.Bates
                                                  H.Dean b
                                                  L.W.Cook lbw
                                                  A.Kermode c E.Smith
   did not bat   -   133-1   27.3   4   67   5   R.H.Spooner lbw   179
                                                  J.T.Tyldesley st D.Hunter
                                                  F.Harry b
                                                  H.Dean c D.Denton
                                                  A.Kermode c W.E.Bates

361. Yorkshire v Warwickshire, Edgbaston, August 8, 9, 10 (Match drawn)
   b S.Hargreave   37   407   52.3   15   132   6   C.Charlesworth
                                                           c J.Tunnicliffe   343
                                                      William Quaife lbw
                                                      J.F.Byrne c J.Tunnicliffe
                                                      F.G.Stephens b
                                                      S.Santall c A.Dolphin
                                                      F.Moorhouse c D.Denton
   did not bat   -   65-2   -   -   -   -   200-4d

362. Yorkshire v Middlesex, Bramall Lane, August 12, 13 (Yorkshire won by seven wickets)
   c and b C.M.Wells   66   248   17   6   30   1   J.Douglas c D.Hunter   173   1
   did not bat   -   20-3   8   2   20   1   M.W.Payne c D.Hunter   91

363. Yorkshire v Surrey, Kennington Oval, August 15, 16, 17 (Match drawn)
   b J.N.Crawford   5   162   25   4   92   2   T.W.Hayward c W.E.Bates   294
                                                 J.B.Hobbs b
   did not bat   -   221-3   19   2   74   3   T.W.Hayward b   206-5d
                                                 E.G.Hayes c D.Hunter
                                                 Lord Dalmeny c W.E.Bates

364. Yorkshire v Kent, Canterbury, August 22, 23, 24 (Match drawn)
   c James Seymour b C.Blythe 3   147   18   1   56   2   F.E.Woolley b   209   1
                                                            K.L.Hutchings b
   c E.Humphreys b J.R.Mason 95   278   14   4   21   1   E.Humphreys c G.H.Hirst   66-4

365. Yorkshire v Sussex, Hove, August 26, 27, 28 (Yorkshire won by five wickets)
   c and b J.Vine   24   273   10   3   23   1   C.B.Fry c J.Tunnicliffe   186

c G.Leach b G.R.Cox   16 131-5   20   2   63   4 K.O.Goldie lbw   215

c G.Leach b G.R.Cox	16	131-5	20	2	63	4	K.O.Goldie lbw	215
							A.E.Relf b	
							H.L.Simms b	
							G.R.Cox lbw	

366. Yorkshire v Hampshire, Bournemouth, August 29, 30, 31 (Match drawn)

c H.A.W.Bowell b J.R.Badcock	18	301	22	4	103	2	W.N.White c and b	361
							J.R.Badcock c D.Denton	1
c H.W.Persse b C.B.Llewellyn	29	130-4	21.2	9	39	3	C.B.Llewellyn c W.H.Wilkinson	221-8d
							J.R.Badcock b	
							T.Langford b	

367. Yorkshire v MCC & Ground, Scarborough, September 2, 3, 4 (MCC & Ground won by 44 runs)

c G.R.Cox b A.Fielder	7	63	7.4	1	16	4	K.L.Hutchings c W.H.Wilkinson	93
							G.R.Cox st D.Hunter	1
							H.D.G.Leveson-Gower c W.H.Wilkinson	
							G.G.Napier st D.Hunter	
b A.Fielder	13	154	10	2	26	1	K.L.Hutchings lbw	168

368. North v South, Scarborough, September 5, 6 (North won by seven wickets)

c W.S.Bird b G.G.Napier	0	153	9	1	19	6	T.W.Hayward c J.Tunnicliffe	108
							F.L.Fane c D.Hunter	1
							W.S.Bird b	
							Lord Dalmeny c J.T.Tyldesley	
							G.R.Cox c D.Hunter	
							G.G.Napier c J.Tunnicliffe	
b G.Cox	12	102-3	15.3	3	29	2	J.B.Hobbs c D.Denton	142
							N.A.Knox c G.H.Hirst	

369. Mr.C.I.Thornton's England XI v South Africans, Scarborough, September 9, 10, 11 (Match drawn)

run out	81	397	20	2	74	3	J.J.Kotze hit wkt	319
							S.J.Snooke c R.H.Spooner	1
							G.C.White b	
did not bat	-	232-2	15	2	47	1	A.W.Nourse b	192-5

SEASON'S AVERAGES

Batting and Fielding	M	I	NO	Runs	HS	Ave	100	50	Ct
Players v Gentlemen	1	2	0	8	6	4.00	-	-	-
North v South	1	2	0	12	12	6.00	-	-	1
Championship	25	34	1	890	112	26.96	1	5	14
Other Yorkshire matches	5	8	0	64	24	8.00	-	-	4
Other matches	1	1	0	81	81	81.00	-	1	1
Season	33	47	1	1055	112	22.93	1	6	20
Career	369	500	91	10258	201	25.08	9	53	254

Bowling	O	M	R	W	BB	Ave	5i	10m
Players v Gentlemen	1	0	1	1	1-1	1.00	-	-
North v South	24.3	4	48	8	6-19	6.00	1	-
Championship	893.2	196	2314	141	6-22	18.41	12	2
Other Yorkshire matches	121.2	27	273	23	4-20	11.86	-	-
Other matches	35	4	121	4	3-74	30.25	-	-
Season (6-ball)	1075.1	231	2757	177	6-22	15.57	13	2
Career (6-ball)	10740.3	2974 ⎱	31072	1934	9-24	16.06	160	44
(5-ball)	2748.4	1029 ⎰						

1907/08 - MCC in Australia

Rhodes was an automatic choice for his second tour of Australia but in truth he did not perform well on the tour. In all Test matches he took only seven wickets at over 60 runs a wicket and made one fifty at Sydney in the Fifth Test, England losing the series 4-1. Apart from the Tests he did not fare too badly making 105 against a Victoria XI at Melbourne and 119 against Tasmania at Hobart.

	Own Team Total	O	M	R	W		Opp Total	Ct

370. MCC v Western Australia, Perth, October 26, 28, 29 (MCC won by an innings and 134 runs)
not out | 32 | 402 | 17 | 9 | 16 | 1 | A.H.Christian b | 152 |
| | | 0.4 | 0 | 4 | 2 | W.W.Hogue c J.Humphries | 116 |
| | | | | | | E.Jones b | |

371. MCC v South Australia, Adelaide, November 9, 11, 12, 13 (MCC won by an innings and 183 runs)
not out | 11 | 660-8d | 16 | 4 | 44 | 1 | C.Hill c J.Humphries | 343 |
| | | - | - | - | - | | 134 |

372. MCC v Victoria, Melbourne, November 15, 16, 18, 19, 20 (Match drawn)
not out | 27 | 198 | - | - | - | - | | 233 |
c F.A.Tarrant
b J.V.Saunders | 40 | 422-9 | 20 | 0 | 78 | 1 | F.A.Tarrant c K.L.Hutchings | 463 | 1

373. MCC v New South Wales, Sydney, November 22, 23, 25 (MCC won by 408 runs)
c A.J.Y.Hopkins b A.Cotter | 28 | 304 | | | | | | 101 |
b F.B.Johnson | 50 | 301 | | | | | | 96 |

374. MCC v Queensland, Brisbane, November 30, December 2 (MCC won by an innings and 44 runs)
not out | 70 | 308 | - | - | - | - | | 78 |
| | | 21 | 5 | 58 | 3 | J.S.Redgrave lbw | 186 | 2
| | | | | | | M.M.F.Dunn b | |
| | | | | | | W.T.Evans b | |

375. MCC v Australian XI, Brisbane, December 6, 7, (9) (Match drawn)
b C.G.Macartney | 8 | 223 | 8 | 1 | 29 | 0 | | 299 | 1
| | | 3 | 0 | 3 | 0 | | 110-2 |

376. ENGLAND v AUSTRALIA, Sydney, December 13, 14, 16, 17, (18), 19 (Australia won by two wickets)
run out | 1 | 273 | 5 | 2 | 13 | 1 | V.S.Ransford c L.C.Braund | 300 |
c P.A.McAlister
b C.G.Macartney | 29 | 300 | 7 | 3 | 13 | 0 | | 275-8 |

377. MCC v Victorian XI, South Melbourne, December 21, 23, 24 (Match drawn)
not out | 105 | 503-9d | 40 | 9 | 90 | 3 | T.S.Warne c G.Gunn | 488 |
| | | | | | | C.McKenzie b | |
| | | | | | | W.W.Armstrong c E.G.Hayes | |

378. ENGLAND v AUSTRALIA, Melbourne, January 1, 2, 3, 4, 6, 7 (England won by one wicket)
b J.V.Saunders | 32 | 382 | 11 | 0 | 37 | 1 | M.A.Noble c L.C.Braund | 266 |
run out | 15 | 282-9 | 16 | 6 | 38 | 0 | | 397 |

379. ENGLAND v AUSTRALIA, Adelaide, January 10, 11, 13, 14, 15, 16 (Australia won by 245 runs)
c H.Carter
b J.D.A.O'Connor | 38 | 363 | 15 | 5 | 35 | 0 | | 285 |
c W.W.Armstrong
b J.D.A.O'Connor | 9 | 183 | 27 | 9 | 81 | 0 | | 506 | 1

380. MCC v Tasmania, Launceston, January 18, 20, 21 (MCC won by 120 runs)
not out | 7 | 321 | 11 | 2 | 27 | 0 | | 276 |
not out | 8 | 249 | 3 | 1 | 6 | 0 | | 174 | 1

381. MCC v Tasmania, Hobart, January 24, 25, 27 (Match drawn)
c G.D.Paton
b E.A.C.Windsor | 119 | 455 | - | - | - | - | | 113 |
| | | 22 | 10 | 29 | 3 | C.W.B.Martin b | 317-8 | 1
| | | | | | | C.J.Eady c K.L.Hutchings | |
| | | | | | | E.J.K.Burn c and b | |

382. ENGLAND v AUSTRALIA, Melbourne, February 7, 8, 10, 11 (Australia won by 308 runs)
c P.A.McAlister
b J.V.Saunders | 0 | 105 | 5 | 0 | 21 | 0 | | 214 |
c H.Carter b J.D.A.O'Connor | 2 | 186 | 24 | 5 | 66 | 1 | V.S.Ransford c J.Humphries | 385 |

383. MCC v New South Wales, Sydney, February 14, 15, 17, 18, 19, (20) (Match drawn)
c E.F.Waddy b L.A.Minnett | 45 | 298 | 20 | 3 | 63 | 0 | | 368 | 1
c A.Diamond
b C.G.Macartney | 53 | 456 | 40 | 11 | 73 | 5 | A.Diamond c E.G.Hayes | 375-9 |
						A.J.Y.Hopkins st R.A.Young	
						E.F.Waddy c R.A.Young	
						A.J.Bowden c E.G.Hayes	
						P.A.Newton c J.Hardstaff, sen.	

384. ENGLAND v AUSTRALIA, Sydney, February 21, 22, 24, 25, 26, 27 (Australia won by 49 runs)
c M.A.Noble
    b W.W.Armstrong   10 281   10   5   15 0   137
    b M.A.Noble   69 229   37.4 7 102 4 M.A.Noble lbw   422
                                           V.T.Trumper c G.Gunn
                                         H.Carter c J.B.Hobbs
                                         J.V.Saunders c R.A.Young

385. MCC v South Australia, Adelaide, March 2, 3, 4 (Match drawn)
    not out   78 404   10   2   33 1 R.E.Mayne st R.A.Young 445
    c C.Hill b N.Claxton 39 134-4

386. MCC v Western Australia, Perth, March 13, 14, 16 (Match drawn)
    b A.H.Christian   4 362-7d 23 8 56 2 O.H.Kelly c K.L.Hutchings 256
                                      L.Gouly b
                          15   1   39 2 S.H.D.Rowe c A.O.Jones 265-7
                                      G.B.Moysey c A.O.Jones

SEASON'S AVERAGES

Batting and Fielding	M	I	NO	Runs	HS	Ave	100	50	Ct
Test matches	5	10	0	205	69	20.50	-	1	1
Other matches	12	17	8	724	119	80.44	2	4	7
Tour	17	27	8	929	119	48.89	2	5	8
Career	3786	527	99	11187	201	26.13	11	58	262

Bowling	O	M	R	W	BB	Ave	5i	10m
Test matches	157.4	42	421	7	4-102	60.14	-	-
Other matches	269.4	66	648	24	5-73	27.00	1	-
Tour (6-ball)	427.2	108	1069	31	5-73	34.48	1	-
Career (6-ball)	11167.5	3082 } 32141		1965	9-24	16.35	161	44
(5-ball)	2748.4	1029 }						

1908

Rhodes, on his return to England, put his disappointments behind him and enjoyed a competent season for Yorkshire helping them to win the Championship again, the sixth time since he made his debut. Good performances with the ball were 6-17 against Leicestershire at Leicester and 6-33 against Nottinghamshire at Headingley but he did not take ten wickets in a match all summer. With the bat he made 146 against Worcestershire at Sheffield, 140 against Northamptonshire at Huddersfield and 122 against Leicestershire at Harrogate.

	Own Team Total	O	M	R	W		Opp Total	Ct

387. Yorkshire v Northamptonshire, Northampton, May 7, 8 (Yorkshire won by an innings and 314 runs)
    b R.W.R.Hawtin   40 356-8d   27
                                                    15

388. Yorkshire v MCC, Lord's, May 11, 12, 13 (Yorkshire won by an innnings and 10 runs)
    b J.T.Hearne   40 216   10   4   18 1 F.A.Tarrant lbw   111
                            8.1 2   13 2 M.C.Bird st D.Hunter 95
                                         J.T.Hearne st D.Hunter

389. Yorkshire v Cambridge University, Fenner's, May 14, 15, 16 (Yorkshire won by an innings and 133 runs)
    b C.Reunert   45 298   13   3   26 2 R.E.H.Bailey b   109
                                         E.Olivier c sub
                          8   3   21 2 F.H.Mugliston c D.Denton 56
                                         C.Reunert c W.H.Wilkinson

390. Yorkshire v Kent, Bradford, May 18, 19 (Yorkshire won by nine wickets)
    b W.J.Fairservice   45 101   6   3   16 1 C.H.B.Marsham b   77
    c James Seymour b C.Blythe 6 25-1   -   -   -   -   46

391. Yorkshire v Essex, Leyton, May 21, 22, 23 (Match drawn)
    c W.F.O.Faviell
        b C.P.Buckenham 1 188   20   4   42 2 J.W.H.T.Douglas
                                              c W.H.Wilkinson   226
                                          P.A.Perrin lbw

b H.I.Young　　　　　　　33　210-4　　20　6　39　1　C.P.McGahey　c H.Myers　226-9d

392. Yorkshire v Surrey, Headingley, May 25, 26 (Yorkshire won by seven wickets)
　　b W.C.Smith　　　　　　12　113　　　　　　　　　　　　　　　　90
　　b J.N.Crawford　　　　　11　48-3　　　　　　　　　　　　　　69

393. Yorkshire v Derbyshire, Chesterfield, May 28, 29, 30 (Yorkshire won by 196 runs)
　　c J.Humphries b W.Bestwick 11　190　　-　　-　　-　　-　　　　　102
　　b A.E.Lawton　　　　　28　352-5d　16　5　51　2　A.Morton　c W.E.Bates　244
　　　　　　　　　　　　　　　　　　　　　　　　　　　S.W.A.Cadman　c D.Denton

394. Yorkshire v Warwickshire, Edgbaston, June 1, 2, 3 (Match drawn)
　　b C.S.Baker　　　　　　81　339　　13　8　8　0　　　　　　　121
　　　　　　　　　　　　　　　　　　　　6　2　16　0　　　　　　　166-5

395. Yorkshire v Worcestershire, Worcester, June 4, 5, 6 (Yorkshire won by 69 runs)
　　c E.W.Bale b J.A.Cuffe　39　130　　23　10　32　2　F.A.Pearson　b　197
　　　　　　　　　　　　　　　　　　　　　　　　　　　E.G.Arnold　c D.Hunter
　　run out　　　　　　　　0　228　　7　1　16　0　　　　　　　92

396. Yorkshire v Lancashire, Bramall Lane, June 8, 9, 10 (Yorkshire won by 193 runs)
　　b W.Brearley　　　　　4　209　　5　2　17　0　　　　　　　129
　　c J.W.H.Makepeace
　　　　　b W.Brearley　24　210　　11.2　3　30　4　J.T.Tyldesley　b　97
　　　　　　　　　　　　　　　　　　　　　　　　　　　C.R.Hartley　c D.Denton
　　　　　　　　　　　　　　　　　　　　　　　　　　　W.A.Worsley　c sub
　　　　　　　　　　　　　　　　　　　　　　　　　　　H.Dean　c I.Grimshaw

397. Yorkshire v Leicestershire, Aylestone Road, Leicester, June 11, 12 (Yorkshire won by an innings and 321 runs)
　　c J.Shields b W.E.Astill　50　437　　15　7　17　6　C.J.B.Wood　c D.Hunter　58
　　　　　　　　　　　　　　　　　　　　　　　　　　　H.Whitehead　c J.T.Newstead
　　　　　　　　　　　　　　　　　　　　　　　　　　　J.H.King　c D.Denton
　　　　　　　　　　　　　　　　　　　　　　　　　　　S.Coe　c D.Denton
　　　　　　　　　　　　　　　　　　　　　　　　　　　J.Burgess　c W.E.Bates
　　　　　　　　　　　　　　　　　　　　　　　　　　　W.E.Astill　st D.Hunter
　　　　　　　　　　　　　　　　　　　　10　3　20　2　S.Coe　c A.W.Lupton　58
　　　　　　　　　　　　　　　　　　　　　　　　　　　T.Jayes　c G.H.Hirst

398. Yorkshire v Northamptonshire, Huddersfield, June 15, 16, (17) (Match drawn)
　　c G.J.Thompson b W.Wells 140　347　　28　9　58　4　W.East　c C.H.Grimshaw　196
　　　　　　　　　　　　　　　　　　　　　　　　　　　W.Wells　c C.H.Grimshaw
　　　　　　　　　　　　　　　　　　　　　　　　　　　M.Cox　lbw
　　　　　　　　　　　　　　　　　　　　　　　　　　　W.A.Buswell　c C.H.Hardisty

399. Yorkshire v Middlesex, Lord's, June 18, 19 (Yorkshire won by three wickets)
　　b F.A.Tarrant　　　　　3　157　　15　3　59　4　L.J.Moon　lbw　　130
　　　　　　　　　　　　　　　　　　　　　　　　　　　E.S.Litteljohn　c D.Hunter
　　　　　　　　　　　　　　　　　　　　　　　　　　　C.C.Page　st D.Hunter
　　　　　　　　　　　　　　　　　　　　　　　　　　　A.E.Trott　c G.H.Hirst
　　b J.H.Hunt　　　　　　40　127-7　14.1　4　30　2　P.F.Warner　b　153　1
　　　　　　　　　　　　　　　　　　　　　　　　　　　A.E.Trott　lbw

400. Yorkshire v Warwickshire, Bradford, June 22, 23, 24 (Yorkshire won by three wickets)
　　run out　　　　　　　　18　239　　17　1　43　1　F.Moorhouse　b　294
　　c S.P.Kinneir b E.F.Field　13　216-7　25　9　36　3　C.S.Baker　c J.T.Newstead　159
　　　　　　　　　　　　　　　　　　　　　　　　　　　C.Charlesworth　lbw
　　　　　　　　　　　　　　　　　　　　　　　　　　　S.Hargreave　c W.E.Bates

401. Yorkshire v Nottinghamshire, Trent Bridge, June 25, 26, 27 (Match drawn)
　　c G.T.Branston b B.W.Taylor 2　179　　31　11　46　2　W.E.G.Payton　c D.Hunter　207
　　　　　　　　　　　　　　　　　　　　　　　　　　　c C.C.James　c H.Myers
　　c A.O.Jones b B.W.Taylor　39　374-6d　12　1　36　2　A.O.Jones　c J.T.Newstead　66-4
　　　　　　　　　　　　　　　　　　　　　　　　　　　J.Hardstaff, sen.　c D.Denton

402. Yorkshire v Somerset, Dewsbury, June 29, 30 (Yorkshire won by eight wickets)
　　lbw b B.Cranfield　　　2　240　　13　3　28　0　　　　　　　160
　　did not bat　　　　　　-　53-2　　17　7　27　3　E.S.M.Poyntz　lbw　132
　　　　　　　　　　　　　　　　　　　　　　　　　　　A.E.M.Whittle　c W.H.Wilkinson
　　　　　　　　　　　　　　　　　　　　　　　　　　　J.Daniell　lbw

403. Players v Gentlemen, Lord's, July 2, 3 (Players won by seven wickets)
　　b J.W.H.T.Douglas　　15　339　　-　　-　　-　　*　　　　　217
　　did not bat　　　　　　-　55-3　　5　2　10　1　P.F.Warner　lbw　176　1

404. Yorkshire v Kent, Dover, July 6, 7, 8 (Match drawn)
　　c E.W.Dillon b C.Blythe　40　401　　26　8　38　1　F.H.Huish　b　242　1
　　c James Seymour b A.Fielder　0　90-3

405. Yorkshire v Sussex, Huddersfield, July 9, 10, 11 (Match drawn)
c A.E.Relf b J.H.Vincett   53   164   18   5   57   2   R.R.Relf   c W.E.Bates   290
                                         J.W.W.Nason   c W.E.Bates

406. Yorkshire v Nottinghamshire, Headingley, July 13, 14, 15 (Yorkshire won by 140 runs)
c A.O.Jones b T.G.Wass   23   189   8   1   22   1   A.O.Jones   c W.H.Wilkinson   113
c E.B.Alletson
    b A.W.Hallam   10   132   18   7   33   6   J.Iremonger   lbw   68
                                           J.Hardstaff, sen. b
                                           A.O.Jones   c Lord Hawke
                                           T.W.Oates   c D.Denton
                                           A.W.Hallam   c G.H.Hirst
                                           T.G.Wass   c W.H.Wilkinson

407. Yorkshire v Essex, Hull, July 16, (17), (18) (Match drawn)
                         17   6   24   1   C.P.McGahey   c Lord Hawke   42-3

408. Yorkshire v Gloucestershire, Bramall Lane, July 20, 21 (Yorkshire won by an innings and 95 runs)
b A.E.Dipper   95   340   11   3   37   0   153
                         13.5   4   26   2   J.H.Board   b   92
                                           T.H.Toogood   c W.E.Bates

409. Yorkshire v Leicestershire, Harrogate, July 23, 24, 25 (Match drawn)
b T.Jayes   122   325   35.2   10   82   3   A.E.Knight   c G.H.Hirst   309
                                           J.Shields   lbw
                                           W.E.Astill   c S.Haigh
not out   38   69-0

410. Yorkshire v Derbyshire, Headingley, July 27, 28, 29 (Yorkshire won by an innings and 131 runs)
b W.Bestwick   5   394-8d   6   3   10   0   127
                           21   7   54   2   C.B.Sherwin   c C.H.Hardisty   136
                                           H.F.Purdy   c D.Hunter

411. Yorkshire v Lancashire, Old Trafford, August 1, 3, 4 (Yorkshire won by 190 runs)
c A.C.MacLaren
    b W.Brearley   3   206   9   5   11   3   L.O.S.Poidevin   c D.Hunter   144
                                           A.C.MacLaren   b
                                           K.G.MacLeod   b
c A.C.MacLaren
    b R.Whitehead   39   243   -   -   -   -   115

412. Yorkshire v All Ireland, Dublin, August 6, 7 (Yorkshire won by ten wickets)
c H.H.Corley b T.C.Ross   13   202   5   2   11   4   G.A.Morrow   c J.W.Rothery   49   2
                                           F.H.Browning   c M.W.Booth
                                           T.C.Ross   c and b
                                           H.H.Corley   lbw
did not bat   -   17-0   22   5   77   5   G.J.Meldon   c W.E.Bates   168
                                           G.A.Morrow   c M.W.Booth
                                           F.H.Browning   c C.H.Hardisty
                                           W.Harrington   c M.W.Booth
                                           W.H.Napper   c W.H.Wilkinson

413. Yorkshire v Middlesex, Bradford, August 10, 11, 12 (Match drawn)
c L.J.Moon c J.T.Hearne   34   279   18.4   6   49   5   F.A.Tarrant   c J.W.Rothery   164
                                           W.Harrington   c J.T.Newstead
                                           S.G.Etherington   c W.H.Wilkinson
                                           C.M.Wells   c S.Haigh
                                           F.A.H.Henley   lbw
c and b F.A.Tarrant   30   153-1d   11   1   43   2   P.F.Warner   c C.H.Hardisty   232-8
                                           C.C.Page   c H.Watson

414. Yorkshire v Surrey, Kennington Oval, August 13, 14, 15 (Yorkshire won by seven wickets)
c E.G.Hayes b J.W.Hitch   33   162   4   3   1   0   117   1
c E.G.Hayes b J.W.Hitch   17   135-3   15   1   58   2   A.Marshal   c Lord Hawke   177
                                           W.S.Lees   c sub

415. Yorkshire v Worcestershire, Bramall Lane, August 17, 18, (19) (Match drawn)
c R.D.Burrows
    b E.G.Arnold   146   378   24-1

416. Yorkshire v Gloucestershire, Cheltenham, August 20, 21, 22 (Yorkshire won by 182 runs)
b C.W.L.Parker   8   219   3.5   2   6   2   F.B.Roberts   c W.E.Bates   83   1
                                           E.J.Spry   st H.Watson
lbw b E.G.Dennett   12   222   17   6   38   1   G.L.Jessop   b   176

417. Yorkshire v Somerset, Taunton, August 24, 25, 26 (Match drawn)
```
     c J.Daniell b W.T.Greswell   7   210      9   2   20   3   L.C.Braund   c H.Myers           101    1
                                                                A.E.M.Whittle   c J.T.Newstead
                                                                E.Robson   c S.Haigh
     b E.Robson                  55   240-6d   7   1   19   1   L.C.Braund   c H.Myers            64-3
```

418. Yorkshire v MCC, Scarborough, August 31, September 1, 2 (Match drawn)
```
     c W.S.Bird b G.G.Napier     14   325     18   5   36   5   R.H.Spooner   c H.Myers          271    1
                                                                W.S.Bird   b
                                                                H.D.G.Leveson-Gower   c S.Haigh
                                                                C.P.Buckenham   c G.H.Hirst
                                                                G.G.Napier   c and b
     b J.W.H.T.Douglas           14   208-5d   3   2   4    0                                     72-0
```

419. MCC Australian Team v An England XI, Hastings, September 3, (4), 5 (Match drawn)
```
     b E.G.Arnold                23   107     32   5   78   5   S.H.Day   lbw                     161
                                                                G.L.Jessop   c E.Humphreys
                                                                F.H.Gillingham   b
                                                                K.S.Ranjitsinhji   st J.Humphries
                                                                J.R.Mason   lbw
     not out                      0   41-3    12   0   54   4   C.B.Fry   hit wkt                  87-7d  1
                                                                P.F.Warner   st J.Humphries
                                                                G.L.Jessop   c J.N.Crawford
                                                                A.E.Relf   b
```

420. MCC Australian Team v Lord Londesborough's England XI, Scarborough, September 7, 8, 9 (Match drawn)
```
     c B.J.T.Bosanquet
       b F.A.Tarrant              3   238     24   8   54   1   B.J.T.Bosanquet
                                                                     c K.L.Hutchings             408-6d  1
     not out                      2   106-4
```

421. MCC Australian Team v Mr.J.Bamford's XI, Scarborough, September 10, 11, 12 (MCC Australian Team won by nine wickets)
```
     lbw b A.Marshal             33   201     23.5  7   63   2   J.W.Rothery   c G.Gunn           180    1
                                                                 A.F.A.Lilley   lbw
     not out                     23   60-1     9    1   14   2   J.Vine   lbw                      80
                                                                 A.Marshal   c J.Hardstaff, sen.
```

422. Yorkshire v Rest of England, Kennington Oval, September 14, 15, 16, 17 (Match drawn)
```
     c T.W.Hayward
       b C.P.Buckenham           27   264     18    1   81   1   T.W.Hayward   st H.Watson        483-7d
     b E.F.Field                  9   170-2
```

SEASON'S AVERAGES

Batting and Fielding	M	I	NO	Runs	HS	Ave	100	50	Ct
Players v Gentlemen	1	1	0	15	15	15.00	-	-	1
Championship	27	43	1	1412	146	33.61	3	5	5
Other Yorkshire matches	5	7	0	162	45	23.14	-	-	3
Other matches	3	6	3	84	33	28.00	-	-	3
Season	36	57	4	1673	146	31.56	3	5	12
Career	422	584	103	12860	201	26.73	14	63	274

Bowling	O	M	R	W	BB	Ave	5i	10m
Players v Gentlemen	5	2	10	1	1-10	10.00	-	-
Championship	593.1	183	1295	78	6-17	16.60	3	-
Other Yorkshire matches	105.1	27	287	22	5-36	13.04	2	-
Other matches	100.5	21	263	14	5-78	18.78	1	-
Season (6-ball)	804.1	233	1855	115	6-17	16.13	6	-
Career (6-ball)	11972	3315 ⎫	33996	2080	9-24	16.34	167	44
(5-ball)	2748.4	1029 ⎭						

1909

Rhodes had an exceptional season and notwithstanding his bowling skills he was picked for the Fifth Test against Australia at the Oval for his batting alone. He took eleven wickets in four games of the series (seven fewer than Blythe took in the first two matches) but in the Fifth Test he made 66 and 54 respectively going in first wicket down after Jessop had hurt his back. On the county scene he took 12-115 against Leicestershire at Dewsbury and 13-108 in the 'Roses' match at Bradford. But his batting also excelled and he made five three figure scores, the highest was 199 against Sussex at Hove. He also made 118 against Essex at Headingley, 108 v Australians at Sheffield, 101 twice, against Kent at Huddersfield and the M.C.C. at Scarborough.

	Own Team Total	O	M	R	W		Opp Total	Ct

423. Yorkshire v Derbyshire, Derby, May 3, 4, 5 (Yorkshire won by an innings and 127 runs)

	Own Team Total	O	M	R	W	Opp	Opp Total	Ct
c J.Humphries b A.Morton	19	381	9.5	4	17	3	L.Oliver b	112
							A.Warren b	
							W.Bestwick b	
			2	0	6	0		142

424. Yorkshire v Northamptonshire, Hull, May 6, 7, 8 (Match drawn)

b G.J.Thompson	9	363	17	2	57	0		253
b S.G.Smith	38	132-5d	8	5	5	0		116-5

425. Yorkshire v Somerset, Bath, May 10, 11, 12 (Match drawn)

c L.C.Braund b F.D.H.Joy	16	368	29	3	109	6	L.C.Braund c and b	286	1
							F.P.Hardy b		
							A.E.Lewis c S.Haigh		
							H.F.Montgomery c C.H.Hardisty		
							S.M.J.Woods b		
							W.T.Greswell st H.Watson		
did not bat	-	62-1	24	7	43	1	H.Chidgey c C.H.Hardisty	243-6d	1

426. Yorkshire v Worcestershire, Worcester, May 13, 14, 15 (Worcestershire won by 12 runs)

c W.H. Hickton b W.B.Burns	0	289	6	4	3	0		203
c H.K.Foster b E.G.Arnold	8	133	11	3	15	1	W.B.Burns b	231

427. Yorkshire v Essex, Headingley, May 17, 18, 19 (Yorkshire won by an innings and 88 runs)

c P.A.Perrin b C.P.Buckenham	114	292	5	3	9	0		90
			3	1	5	0		114

428. Yorkshire v Northamptonshire, Northampton, May 20, 22, 23 (Yorkshire won by eight wickets)

b S.G.Smith	17	253	9	3	15	1	C.Thorp lbw	138	1
not out	55	113-2	21	5	64	1	C.J.T.Pool b	227	1

429. Yorkshire v Somerset, Bradford, May 24, (25), 26 (Match drawn)

c E.S.M.Poyntz b E.Robson	48	345-9d	3	1	7	0		21-1

430. ENGLAND v AUSTRALIA, Edgbaston, May 27, 28, 29 (England won by ten wickets)

not out	15	121	-	-	-	-		74	1
did not bat	-	105-0	1	0	8	0		151	1

431. Yorkshire v Lancashire, Old Trafford, May 31 June 1, 2 (Yorkshire won by 65 runs)

c W.Worsley b W.Brearley	0	133	8	4	14	0		89
b W.Huddleston	16	78	-	-	-	-		57

432. Yorkshire v Warwickshire, Edgbaston, June 3, 4, 5 (Match drawn)

c S.P.Kinneir b C.Charlesworth	45	500	48	17	83	7	C.Charlesworth c D.Hunter	376	1
							S.P.Kinneir c G.H.Hirst		
							C.S.Baker c and b		
							William Quaife c J.T.Newstead		
							A.F.A.Lilley c D.Hunter		
							R.G.Pridmore st D.Hunter		
							S.Hargreave c J.W.Rothery		
did not bat	-	89-2							

433. Yorkshire v Kent, Huddersfield, June 7, 8, 9 (Kent won by seven wickets)

b A.Fielder	11	69	20	4	71	1	C.Blythe c D.Hunter	319
c E.W.Dillon b A.Fielder	101	364	5	0	30	1	K.L.Hutchings c W.E.Bates	115-3

434. Yorkshire v Middlesex, Lord's, June 10, 11, (12) (Match drawn)

c A.E.Trott b J.T.Hearne	28	112-4	15	5	36	6	E.H.Hendren st D.Hunter	161
							W.P.Robertson b	
							H.R.Murrell c W.E.Bates	
							J.W.Hearne c J.T.Newstead	
							G.L.Hebden c G.H.Hirst	
							J.H.Hunt b	

435. Yorkshire v Leicestershire, Dewsbury, June 17, 18, 19 (Yorkshire won by an innings and 21 runs)
```
c and b T.Jayes        11   410      22.5  6   68  6   A.E.Knight  c G.H.Hirst        235
                                                       C.J.B.Wood  c J.T.Newstead
                                                       J.H.King  c J.W.Rothery
                                                       S.Coe  c S.Haigh
                                                       T.Jayes  b
                                                       J.Shields  lbw
                       19.1  4   47  6   J.H.King  c and b                 154      2
                                                       S.Coe  c J.W.Rothery
                                                       V.F.S.Crawford  c J.T.Newstead
                                                       T.Jayes  c D.Hunter
                                                       W.Shipman  c and b
                                                       A.G.Hazlerigg  c W.H.Wilkinson
```

436. Yorkshire v Australians, Bradford, June 21, (22), 23 (Match drawn)
```
c and b F.J.Laver      42   299      12   3   45  2   W.Bardsley  b                  77-3
                                                       M.A.Noble  c J.W.Rothery
```

437. Lancashire and Yorkshire v Australians, Old Trafford, June (24), (25), 26, (Match drawn)
```
not out                 4   15-2     18   0   61  3   V.S.Ransford  lbw             217-6d
                                                       V.T.Trumper  c A.H.Hornby
                                                       C.G.Macartney  c D.Hunter
```

438. Yorkshire v Surrey, Bramall Lane, June 28, 29, 30 (Yorkshire won by 51 runs)
```
c E.G.Hayes b W.C.Smith  1   125      6   1   24  0                                 62
b W.C.Smith             22   91      5.3   2   12  2   J.N.Crawford
                                                         c W.H.Wilkinson            103
                                                       T.Rushby  b
```

439. ENGLAND v AUSTRALIA, Headingley, July 1, 2, 3 (Australia won by 126 runs)
```
c H.Carter b F.J.Laver  12   182      8   2   38  4   W.Bardsley  hit wkt            188
                                                       C.G.Macartney  c C.B.Fry
                                                       A.Cotter  b
                                                       H.Carter  lbw
c W.W.Armstrong
   b C.G.Macartney      16   87      19   3   44  2   W.W.Armstrong  b               207      1
                                                       A.Cotter  c A.C.MacLaren
```

440. Yorkshire v Nottinghamshire, Bradford, July 5, 6, 7 (Yorkshire won by four wickets)
```
c and b T.G.Wass       98   228      25.5  3   87  7   A.O.Jones  c G.H.Hirst        157
                                                       J.Iremonger  lbw
                                                       J.Hardstaff, sen.  st D.Hunter
                                                       W.E.G.Payton  b
                                                       J.R.Gunn  c J.T.Newstead
                                                       E.B.Alletson  c H.Myers
                                                       A.W.Hallam  c D.Denton
lbw b A.W.Hallam        6   45-6     16   7   32  1   J.Iremonger  c G.H.Hirst       115      1
```

441. Yorkshire v Leicestershire, Aylestone Road, Leicester, July 8, 9 (Yorkshire won by three wickets)
```
b T.Jayes              11   182      24   8   57  6   C.J.B.Wood  lbw                154      2
                                                       J.H.King  c and b
                                                       H.Whitehead  c J.T.Newstead
                                                       S.Coe  b
                                                       W.E.Astill  c J.T.Newstead
                                                       A.G.Hazlerigg  c S.Haigh
b T.Jayes              21   97-7     26   7   41  3   C.J.B.Wood  c D.Hunter         122
                                                       W.E.Astill  st D.Hunter
                                                       A.W.Shipman  c B.B.Wilson
```

442. Players v Gentlemen, Lord's, July 12, 13, 14 (Players won by 200 runs)
```
not out                61   214      3   0   8   1   H.K.Foster  b                   76
did not bat             -   204-5d   9   1   24  1   K.G.MacLeod  lbw               142
```

443. Yorkshire v Nottinghamshire, Trent Bridge, July 15, 16, 17 (Match drawn)
```
b A.W.Hallam           59   331-9d   28.4 10  48  3   J.Hardstaff, sen.  c S.Haigh   188
                                                       A.W.Hallam  c S.Haigh
                                                       T.G.Wass  c W.E.Bates
b A.W.Hallam           21   111-4d   10   3   18  2   G.Gunn  b                       82-2
                                                       J.Hardstaff, sen.  c D.Denton
```

444. Yorkshire v Australians, Bramall Lane, July 19, 20, 21 (Match drawn)
```
c S.E.Gregory b A.Cotter 100  346    16   0   46  3   M.A.Noble  c J.T.Newstead      267
                                                       S.E.Gregory  c J.T.Newstead
                                                       F.J.Laver  c G.H.Hirst
b A.J.Y.Hopkins        45   172-7d   3   0   7   0                                   53-0
```

445. Yorkshire v Warwickshire, Headingley, July 22, 23, 24 (Yorkshire won by five wickets)
c S.Hargreave b S.Santall   49   315   32.1   10   59   6   C.Charlesworth c S.Haigh   199
                                                                        William Quaife c G.H.Hirst
                                                                        J.E.Windridge c D.Denton
                                                                        S.Santall lbw
                                                                        S.Hargreave c D.Denton
                                                                        E.F.Field c G.H.Hirst
c F.R.Foster b S.Santall   20   76-5   28   5   84   3   C.Charlesworth c S.Haigh   191
                                                                        William Quaife c J.T.Newstead
                                                                        F.R.Foster b

446. ENGLAND v AUSTRALIA, Old Trafford, July 26, 27, 28 (Match drawn)
c H.Carter b F.J.Laver   5   119   -   -   -   -   147
not our   0   108-3   25   0   83   5   V.T.Trumper c J.T.Tyldesley   279
                                                                        W.W.Armstrong lbw
                                                                        A.J.Y.Hopkins c S.F.Barnes
                                                                        C.G.Macartney b
                                                                        A.Cotter c A.C.MacLaren

447. Yorkshire and Lancashire v Australians, Hull, July 29, (30), (31) (Match drawn)
not out   75   261-4

448. Yorkshire v Lancashire, Bradford, August 2, 3, 4 (Yorkshire won by 100 runs)
c K.G.MacLeod
   b W.Huddleston   24   159   16.4   2   68   7   R.H.Spooner c and b   120   1
                                                                        A.Hartley c J.W.Rothery
                                                                        J.Sharp st D.Hunter
                                                                        J.W.H.Makepeace b
                                                                        A.H.Hornby c S.Haigh
                                                                        W.Huddleston b
                                                                        W.Brearley c S.Haigh
c K.G.MacLeod b J.S.Heap 25   146   16   4   40   6   A.Hartley b   85   1
                                                                        J.W.H.Makepeace c W.E.Bates
                                                                        J.S.Heap c and b
                                                                        K.G.MacLeod c J.T.Newstead
                                                                        W.Brearley c S.Haigh
                                                                        W.A.Worsley c B.B.Wilson

449. ENGLAND v AUSTRALIA, Kennington Oval, August 9, 10, 11 (Match drawn)
c H.Carter c A.Cotter   66   352   12   3   34   0   325   3
st H.Carter
   b W.W.Armstrong   54   104-3   14   1   35   0   339-5d

450. Yorkshire v Derbyshire, Bramall Lane, August 12, 13, 14 (Yorkshire won by five wickets)
c S.W.A.Cadman b A.Warren 0   293   8   2   26   2   R.Sale b   108   1
                                                                        J.Chapman b
c J.Humphries b W.Bestwick 6   63-5   34.1   8   69   3   A.Morton c and b   247   3
                                                                        R.Sale b
                                                                        W.Bestwick c and b

451. Yorkshire v Middlesex, Headingley, August 16, 17, (18) (Match drawn)
run out   49   131   3   0   8   0   176
not out   0   5-0   14   2   29   2   P.F.Warner c J.T.Newstead   181   1
                                                                        J.Douglas c J.T.Newstead

452. Yorkshire v Surrey, Kennington Oval, August 19, 20, 21 (Surrey won by 86 runs)
b W.S.Lees   5   223   11   0   53   1   A.Marshal c S.Haigh   273
b W.C.Smith   0   26   10   3   21   4   A.Marshal c A.Drake   62   1
                                                                        M.C.Bird b
                                                                        W.E.Davis lbw
                                                                        H.Strudwick b

453. Yorkshire v Kent, Dover, August 23, (24), (25) (Match drawn)
b F.E.Woolley   53   100-1

454. Yorkshire v Essex, Leyton, August 26, 27, 28 (Yorkshire won by 151 runs)
b W.Reeves   27   155   11   2   27   3   H.A.Carpenter c W.E.Bates   114
                                                                        C.A.G.Russell st D.Hunter
                                                                        C.P.Buckenham c A.Drake

c H.A.Carpenter
   b C.P.Buckenham   35   211   23   9   29   6   J.W.H.T.Douglas
                                                                                 c W.E.Bates   101
                                                                        C.P.McGahey c D.Denton
                                                                        F.H.Gillingham c S.Haigh
                                                                        H.A.Carpenter c D.Hunter
                                                                        E.J.Freeman c S.Haigh
                                                                        C.A.G.Russell c S.Haigh

455. Yorkshire v Sussex, Hove, August 30, 31, September 1 (Match drawn)
```
    b R.R.Relf              199   377      36    7   99   0                              307
    c H.R.Butt b R.R.Relf    84   210-4
```
456. Yorkshire v MCC, Scarborough, September 2, 3, 4 (Match drawn)
```
    c and b A.E.Relf        101   203      16    8   18   3   K.L.Hutchings  lbw        124
                                                             A.E.Relf  c J.T.Newstead
                                                             W.S.Bird  lbw
    c A.E.Relf b W.B.Burns   16   116-4     8    0   42   0                             298-7d
```
457. Players v Gentlemen, Scarborough, September 6, (7), 8 (Match drawn)
```
    c W.S.Bird b W.T.Greswell 36  201       4    0   17   4   R.O.Schwarz  c A.E.Relf    137
                                                             W.S.Bird  st D.Hunter
                                                             D.W.Carr  st D.Hunter
                                                             H.D.G.Leveson-Gower  c D.Hunter
```
458. Lord Londesborough's XI v Australians, Scarborough, September 9, 10, 11 (Lord Londesborough's XI won
by 133 runs)
```
    c M.A.Noble b F.J.Laver   4   129      9.4   1   29   4   V.S.Ransford
                                                                c K.L.Hutchings   113
                                                             W.W.Armstrong  b
                                                             A.Cotter  c G.J.Thompson
                                                             H.Carter  b
    b A.J.Y.Hopkins           5   276      6.4   0   30   2   A.J.Y.Hopkins  b          159
                                                             A.Cotter  c D.Hunter
```
459. Rest of England v Kent, Kennington Oval, September (13), 14, 15, (16) Match drawn)
```
    c J.R.Mason b D.W.Carr   78   327       8    2   24   0                             151
                                           10    5   13   0                             132-3
```

SEASON'S AVERAGES

Batting and Fielding	M	I	NO	Runs	HS	Ave	100	50	Ct
Test matches	4	7	2	168	66	33.60	-	2	6
Players v Gentlemen	2	2	1	97	61*	97.00	-	1	-
Championship	24	40	2	1351	199	35.55	3	5	19
Other Yorkshire matches	3	5	0	312	108	62.40	2	-	-
Other matches	4	5	2	166	78	55.33	-	2	-
Season	37	59	7	2094	199	40.26	5	10	25
Career	459	643	110	14954	201	28.05	19	73	299

Bowling	O	M	R	W	BB	Ave	5i	10m
Test matches	79	9	242	11	5-83	22.00	1	-
Players v Gentlemen	16	1	49	6	4-17	8.16	-	-
Championship	670.5	176	1635	107	7-68	15.28	11	2
Other Yorkshire matches	55	11	158	8	3-18	19.75	-	-
Other matches	52.2	8	157	9	4-29	17.44	-	-
Season (6-ball)	873.1	205	2241	141	7-68	15.89	12	2
Career (6-ball)	12845.1	3520 ⎫	36237	2221	9-24	16.31	179	46
(5-ball)	2748.4	1029 ⎭						

1909/10 - MCC in South Africa

Rhodes' first trip to South Africa was under the captaincy of H.D.G.Leveson-Gower. Although playing in all five Test matches he had an extremely disappointing tour and took only two wickets in the Tests. Perhaps the matting wickets did not suit him. Naturally his batting took the forefront and he made over five hundred runs in first-class matches on the tour.

	Own Team Total	O	M	R	W		Opp Total	Ct
460. MCC v Western Province, Cape Town, December 4, 6 (MCC won by an innings and 133 runs)								
c E.B.Lundie b W.H.Short	10 351	-	-	-			67	
		9	1	28	1	M.Bisset c H.Strudwick	151	

461. MCC v Transvaal, Johannesburg, December 27, 28, 29, 30 (Transvaal won by 308 runs)
    b S.J.Snooke   27 196   14   1   39 2 A.E.E.Vogler c H.Strudwick 260
                                                            T.Campbell c M.C.Bird
    c C.E.Floquet b G.C.White 30 177   18   3   67 1 T.Campbell lbw   421-9d

462. ENGLAND v SOUTH AFRICA, Johannesburg, January 1, 3, 4, 5 (South Africa won by 19 runs)
    b A.E.E.Vogler   66 310   9   1   34 1 A.W.Nourse
                                                            c H.D.G.Leveson-Gower 208
    c A.W.Nourse
      b A.E.E.Vogler 2 224   9   3   25 0   345   2

463. MCC v Natal, Durban, January 8, 9, 10 (Match drawn)
    lbw b A.W.Nourse   64 331   18.5 4   43 5 H.W.Taylor c F.E.Woolley 250
                                                A.W.Nourse c M.C.Bird
                                              c O.C.Pearse c F.E.Woolley
                                              L.D.Dalton c D.Denton
                                              S.V.Samuelson c G.J.Thompson
                              23   8   34 2 W.K.Thomson c F.E.Woolley162
                                              G.C.Collins b

464. MCC v Natal, Pietermaritzburg, January 14, 15, 17, 18 (MCC won by nine wickets)
    c H.W.Taylor
      b S.V.Samuelson 1 229   -   -   - -   50
    did not bat   - 26-1   22   8   34 4 O.C.Pearse
                                                c G.H.T.Simpson-Hayward 203
                                              C.D.Saville c H.Strudwick
                                              D.Taylor, jun. b
                                              C.D.Robinson c C.Blythe

465. ENGLAND v SOUTH AFRICA, Durban, January 21, 22, 24, 25, 26 (South Africa won by 95 runs)
    c R.O.Schwarz
      b A.E.E.Vogler 44 199   5   1   11 0   199
    c G.C.White b J.H.Sinclair 17 252   19   6   43 0   347   2

466. MCC v Border, East London, January 29, 31, February 1 (Match drawn)
    st C.H.Johnson
      b G.P.D.Hartigan   35 137   144
    c C.H.Johnson b G.Preston 24 159-6   151

467. MCC v Eastern Province, Port Elizabeth, February 11, 12 (MCC won by an innings and 139 runs)
    c H.B.Londt b J.G.Paterson 31 263   45
                                                                   79

468. MCC v Transvaal, Johannesburg, February 18, 19, 21 (MCC won by 50 runs)
    b A.E.E.Vogler   45 291   12   1   43 2 J.W.Zulch lbw   270   1
                                              J.H.Moulder c F.L.Fane
    b A.E.E.Vogler   6 271   -   -   - -   242

469. MCC v Transvaal, Pretoria, February 22, (23), (24) (Match drawn)
                           29   5 100 2 L.A.Stricker c E.G.Wynyard 371-3   1
                                              N.V.Lindsay c D.Denton

470. ENGLAND v SOUTH AFRICA, Johannesburg, February 26, 28 March 1, 2, 3 (England won by three wickets)
    c G.A.Faulkner
      b A.E.E.Vogler 14 322   1   0   4 1 A.E.E.Vogler c F.E.Woolley 305   2
    c S.J.Snooke b G.A.Faulkner 1 221-7   4   1   6 0   237

471. ENGLAND v SOUTH AFRICA, Cape Town, March 7, 8, 9 (South Africa won by four wickets)
    c G.A.Faulkner b S.J.Snooke 0 203   -   -   - -   207   1
    b S.J.Snooke   5 178   3   2   2 0   175-6 1

472. ENGLAND v SOUTH AFRICA, Cape Town, March 11, 12, 14, 15 (England won by nine wickets)
    b A.W.Nourse   77 417   -   -   - -   103   2
    not out   0 16-1   7   0   22 0   327

SEASON'S AVERAGES

Batting and Fielding	M	I	NO	Runs	HS	Ave	100	50	Ct
Test matches	5	10	1	226	77	25.11	-	2	10
Other matches	8	10	0	273	64	27.30	-	1	2
Tour	13	20	1	499	77	26.26	-	3	12
Career	472	663	111	15453	201	27.99	19	76	311

Bowling	O	M	R	W	BB	Ave	5i	10m
Test matches	57	14	147	2	1-4	73.50	-	-
Other matches	145.5	31	388	19	5-43	20.42	1	-
Tour (6-ball)	202.5	45	535	21	5-43	25.47	1	-
Career (6-ball)	13048	3565 ⎱ 36772		2242	9-24	16.40	180	46
(5-ball)	2748.4	1029 ⎰						

1910

Rhodes had quite an ordinary season by his standards and perhaps his tour of the Union had taken its toll. Although his batting was consistent it was also quite ordinary and he made just the one century, 111 against Sussex at Hove. For the first time in his career Rhodes failed to take one hundred wickets. He had more bad days than good but had a marvellous match against Surrey at Bradford. Apart from innings of 2 and 88 not out, the second quite a fine effort, he also took 11-72. An amazing analysis against Derbyshire at Bradford gave him cause for celebration. In 4.4 overs he took 5 wickets for 5 runs as Yorkshire dismissed their opponents for 75 and 62, winning by an innings and 111 runs.

	Own	Team Total	O	M	R	W		Opp Total	Ct
473. Yorkshire v Northamptonshire, Northampton, May 9, 10, 11 (Yorkshire won by 145 runs)									
c W.H.Denton b W.East	41	104	-	-	-	-		61	1
c J.S.Denton b W.Wells	17	215	11.2	5	11	1	W.Wells c B.B.Wilson	113	1
474. Yorkshire v MCC, Lord's, May 12, 13 (Yorkshire won by 63 runs)									
lbw b F.A.Tarrant	47	216	18	5	45	4	F.A.Tarrant c H.Myers	157	1
							J.W.H.T.Douglas c J.W.Rothery		
							G.J.Thompson st H.Watson		
							A.C.G.Luther c B.B.Wilson		
b G.J.Thompson	10	100	11	1	33	2	G.J.Thompson c S.Haigh	96	
							J.R.C.Gannon c E.J.Radcliffe		
475. Yorkshire v Lancashire, Headingley, May 16, 17, (18) (Match drawn)									
b W.Brearley	15	152	20	1	68	1	A.Hartley lbw	229	
st W.A.Worsley b H.Dean	7	40-2	-	-	-	-		61	
476. Yorkshire v Leicestershire, Aylestone Road, Leicester, May (19), 21 (Match drawn)									
not out	38	51-1							
477. Yorkshire v Somerset, Bramall Lane, May 23, 24 (Yorkshire won by six wickets)									
c E.S.M.Poyntz b A.E.Lewis	13	178	7.2	3	16	2	L.C.Braund c H.Watson	153	
							J.C.White b		
lbw b A.E.Lewis	7	94-4	2	0	9	0		116	
478. Yorkshire v Derbyshire, Chesterfield, May 26, 27 (Yorkshire won by an innings and 142 runs)									
b A.Warren	13	378-5d	3	1	8	1	J.Chapman c G.H.Hirst	82	
			17	8	37	3	S.W.A.Cadman b	154	
							A.Warren c D.Denton		
							F.H.Taylor b		
479. Yorkshire v Hampshire, Bradford, May 30, 31 June 1 (Match drawn)									
c J.Stone b C.B.Llewellyn	1	194	18	3	45	1	E.M.Sprot c W.H.Wilkinson	180	
b J.A.Newman	19	232	1	1	0	1	A.C.Johnston c H.Watson	65-4	
480. Yorkshire v Nottinghamshire, Trent Bridge, June 2, 3, 4 (Match drawn)									
c and b A.W.Hallam	37	290	1	0	13	0		136	
c A.O.Jones b T.G.Wass	19	200-8d	15	3	59	1	A.O.Jones c S.Haigh	317-6	
481. Yorkshire v Kent, Dewsbury, June 6, 7, 8 (Kent won by eight wickets)									
b A.Fielder	2	81	19	6	37	1	James Seymour b	308	
c James Seymour									
b W.J.Fairservice	39	292	7	1	23	2	E.W.Dillon c W.H.Wilkinson	67-2	1
							E.Humphreys c and b		
482. Yorkshire v Essex, Leyton, June 9, (10), 11 (Essex won by ten wickets)									
not out	85	152	19	4	54	1	K.L.Gibson c G.H.Hirst	277	
b B.Tremlin	23	130	-	-	-	-		6-0	
483. Yorkshire v Middlesex, Lord's, June 16, 17, 18 (Yorkshire won by two wickets)									
b R.E.More	62	231	10	1	33	0		240	

b E.Mignon 8 331-8 23.1 4 57 5 J.W.Hearne c D.Denton 321
J.Wormald c A.Dolphin
R.E.More c H.Myers
E.Mignon b
J.T.Hearne b

484. Yorkshire v Northamptonshire, Bramall Lane, June 20, 21, 22 (Northamptonshire won by five wickets)
b G.J.Thompson 56 288 13 3 37 1 John Seymour b 237
b G.J.Thompson 0 132 19 6 41 3 G.A.T.Vials b 184-5
S.G.Smith c D.Denton
W.East lbw

485. Yorkshire v Warwickshire, Edgbaston, June 23, 24, 25 (Match drawn)
c H.J.Goodwin b E.F.Field 27 125 65
c E.J.Smith b E.F.Field 17 137-6d 51-2

486. Yorkshire v Worcestershire, Headingley, June 27, 28 (Yorkshire won by 109 runs)
c R.D.Burrows
b F.A.Pearson 41 194 20 3 54 3 F.L.Bowley c H.Myers 139
E.G.Arnold c M.W.Booth
R.E. Turner c M.W.Booth
c W.H.Taylor b R.D.Burrows 0 104 - - - - 50 1

487. Yorkshire v Surrey, Bradford, July 4, 5 (Yorkshire won by five wickets)
c M.C.Bird b W.C.Smith 2 89 11.2 1 34 5 C.T.A.Wilkinson c A.Turner 158
W.J.Abel st A.Dolphin
W.E.Davis b
W.C.Smith b
W.S.Lees c A.Drake
not out 88 158-5 16.2 6 38 6 T.W.Hayward lbw 87
E.G.Hayes st A.Dolphin
M.C.Bird b
C.T.A.Wilkinson b
W.J.Abel b
W.S.Lees c D.Denton

488. Players v Gentlemen, Kennington Oval, July 7, 8, 9 (Players won by 79 runs)
b F.R.Foster 40 237 11 4 23 0 193
c and b P.R. Le Couteur 10 192 2 0 15 1 F.R.Foster b 157 2

489. Players v Gentlemen, Lord's, July 11, 12 (Players won by ten wickets)
b F.R.Foster 30 209 - - - - 114 1
did not bat - 4-0 1 1 0 0 95

490. Yorkshire v Warwickshire, Huddersfield, July 14, 15, 16 (Yorkshire won by 172 runs)
b W.C.Hands 63 387 18.3 1 45 4 C.Charlesworth c A.Dolphin 319
William Quaife c M.W.Booth
F.E.Taylor c A.Drake
E.F.Field b
b S.Santall 12 197-7d 8 3 13 3 William Quaife b 93
F.E.Taylor b
E.F.Field c G.H.Hirst

491. Yorkshire v Nottinghamshire, Bramall Lane, July 18, 19, 20 (Match drawn)
c A.O.Jones b C.C.Clifton 20 441-8d 8 1 25 0 212
7 1 33 0 154-3

492. Yorkshire v Kent, Maidstone, July 21, 22, 23 (Kent won by 178 runs)
c A.P.Day b F.E.Woolley 0 120 10.5 0 43 5 A.P.Day b 203
J.C.Hubble b
F.H.Huish c G.H.Hirst
P.E.Morfee st A.Dolphin
H.J.B.Preston c H.Myers
b C.Blythe 21 78 10 2 25 1 C.Blythe c M.W.Booth 173

493. Yorkshire v Derbyshire, Bradford, July 25, 26 (Yorkshire won by an innings and 101 runs)
c L.Oliver b A.Morton 23 238 - - - - 75
4.4 2 5 5 F.A.Newton c A.Turner 62
J.Chapman c A.Turner
S.W.A.Cadman st A.Dolphin
L.Oliver c M.W.Booth
J.Humphries c A.Drake

494. Yorkshire v Sussex, Hull, July 28, 29, 30 (Yorkshire won by four wickets)
b J.H.Vincett 23 239 8 1 18 0 196
c J.W.W.Nason b J.Vine 67 153-6 18 5 45 3 R.B.Heygate c H.Myers 192
A.E.Relf c A.Drake
H.P.Chaplin c A.Dolphin

495. Yorkshire v Lancashire, Old Trafford, August 1, 2, 3 (Lancashire won by an innings and 111 runs)
```
    b W.Brearley              4   103      24   5   56   1   J.S.Heap  b                        395-5d   1
    c J.T.Tyldesley b J.S.Heap  34   181
```

496. Yorkshire v Worcestershire, Worcester, August 4, 5, 6 (Match drawn)
```
    c E.G.Arnold
          b R.D.Burrows   87   412                                                             299
    did not bat            -   234-4d                                                           251-5
```

497. Yorkshire v Leicestershire, Headingley, August 8, 9, 10 (Leicestershire won by 259 runs)
```
    b W.Shipman               2   130     20.3   6   37   3   T.Jayes  c B.B.Wilson             278      1
                                                             W.Shipman  c W.H.Wilkinson
                                                             J.Shields  c A.Dolphin
    c V.F.S.Crawford b T.Jayes 10   145    20   5   45   2   H.Whitehead  b                      256-5d
                                                             R.T.Turner  c W.E.Bates
```

498. Yorkshire v Surrey, Kennington Oval, August 11, 12, (13) (Match drawn)
```
    c T.W.Hayward b E.G.Hayes 19   266     28   7   98   3   T.W.Hayward  c D.Denton           437
                                                             H.S.Bush  c W.H.Wilkinson
                                                             A.Ducat  lbw
    nor out                   5   7-0
```

499. Yorkshire v Middlesex, Bramall Lane, August 15, 16, 17 (Middlesex won by 123 runs)
```
    c E.L.Kidd b J.T.Hearne   25   199      -    -    -   -                                     72       1
    b J.T.Hearne              0   61      24.5   7   73   5   F.A.Tarrant  lbw                   311
                                                             C.V.Baker  lbw
                                                             F.T.Mann  c M.W.Booth
                                                             E.L.Kidd  c G.H.Hirst
                                                             H.R.Murrell  b
```

500. Yorkshire v Essex, Harrogate, August 18, 19, 20 (Match drawn)
```
    c A.E.Russell
          b C.P.Buckenham  16   233      19   5   49   0                                        272
                             -   -    -    -                                                     26-2
```

501. Yorkshire v Hampshire, Portsmouth, August 22, 23, 24 (Yorkshire won by 6 runs)
```
    c and b J.A.Newman       40   116      -    -    -   -                                      133
    c J.Stone b J.A.Newman    4   256     25   6   61   4   A.C.Johnston  c S.Haigh            233      1
                                                             W.N.White  c E.J.Radcliffe
                                                             W.H.B.Evans  lbw
                                                             J.A.Newman  c M.W.Booth
```

502. Yorkshire v Sussex, Hove, August 25, 26, 27 (Match drawn)
```
    c R.B.Heygate
          b E.H.Killick   111   314      15   4   39   0                                        240
    did not bat            -   133-3d     -    -    -   -                                        67-2
```

503. Yorkshire v Somerset, Taunton, August (29), 30, 31 (Match drawn)
```
    c O.M.Samson b F.D.H.Joy 10   196                                                           59
    c E.J.Leat b F.D.H.Joy    9   48-3d                                                         25-3    1
```

504. Yorkshire v MCC, Scarborough, September 1, 2, 3 (Match drawn)
```
    b A.E.Relf              16   289     23.1   3   77   4   K.L.Hutchings  lbw                  287      1
                                                             F.L.Fane  b
                                                             G.J.Thompson  c G.N.Bayes
                                                             C.P.Buckenham  lbw
                                       15   3   50   0                                           103-1
```

505. Players v Gentlemen, Scarborough, September 5, 6, 7 (Match drawn)
```
    b W.B.Burns             1   321       7   0   32   0                                        248      2
    b J.W.H.T.Douglas      19   236       -    -    -   -                                        179-4
```

506. MCC South African Team v Lord Londesborough's XI, Scarborough, September 8, 9, 10 (Lord Londesborough's XI won by 97 runs)
```
    lbw b F.R.Foster        2   174       -    -    -   -                                        175
    b W.B.Burns             8   120       2   0   12   0                                        216      1
```

SEASON'S AVERAGES

Batting and Fielding	M	I	NO	Runs	HS	Ave	100	50	Ct
Players v Gentlemen	3	5	0	100	40	20.00	-	-	5
Championship	28	49	4	1282	111	28.48	1	7	9
Other Yorkshire matches	2	3	0	73	47	24.33	-	-	2
Other matches	1	2	0	10	8	5.00	-	-	1
Season	34	59	4	1465	111	26.63	1	7	17
Career	506	722	115	16918	201	27.87	20	83	328

Bowling	O	M	R	W	BB	Ave	5i	10m
Players v Gentlemen	21	5	70	1	1-15	70.00	-	-
Championship	522.5	121	1384	77	6-38	17.97	6	1
Other Yorkshire matches	67.1	12	205	10	4-45	20.50	-	-
Other matches	2	0	12	0	-	-	-	-
Season (6-ball)	613	138	1671	88	6-38	18.98	6	1
Career (6-ball)	13661	3703 ⎱ 38443		2330	9-24	16.49	186	47
(5-ball)	2748.4	1029 ⎰						

1911

Rhodes made 2,261 runs, including four centuries: 125 against Sussex at Hove, 121 for England against The Rest at Lord's and two in a match for the first time, 128 and 115 for Yorkshire v M.C.C. at Scarborough. It was the second time he had made over two thousand runs and more than made up for his disappointing summer in 1910. He also took more wickets, 117, which included 8-92 against Northamptonshire at Northampton. He had 7-16 against Derbyshire at Derby, 6-59 against Cambridge University at Fenner's, 6-141 against Northamptonshire at Dewsbury and 6-29 (11-83 in the match) against Surrey at Headingley. This was altogether a far happier time and he was selected to visit Australia in the winter where he struck up such an admirable partnership with Jack Hobbs. He was given the match against Lancashire at Bramall Lane for his benefit and although the takings were only £750 a collection was made on his behalf and he was later given £2,200.

	Own	Team Total	O	M	R	W		Opp Total	Ct
507. Yorkshire v MCC, Lord's, May 8, 9, 10 (Yorkshire won by 45 runs)									
b A.E.Relf	59	265	14.2	5	29	1	K.O.Goldie c G.H.Hirst	345	
lbw b F.A.Tarrant	42	338	6	0	39	0		213	
508. Yorkshire v Essex, Leyton, May 11, 12, 13 (Essex won by 131 runs)									
c H.A.Carpenter b J.W.H.T.Douglas	21	215	4	0	9	0		208	1
c H.A.Carpenter b W.Mead	17	119	14.3	3	43	3	J.W.H.T.Douglas c G.H.Hirst	257	
							H.A.Carpenter st A.Dolphin		
							W.Mead c M.W.Booth		
509. Yorkshire v Derbyshire, Bramall Lane, May 15, 16 (Yorkshire won by an innings and 47 runs)									
c E.Needham b A.Warren	100	250	-	-	-	-		61	
			9	3	17	0		142	
510. Yorkshire v Somerset, Taunton, May 18, 19, 20 (Yorkshire won by 272 runs)									
c L.C.Braund b A.E.Lewis	25	178	2	0	6	0		138	1
b J.J.Bridges	32	393-7d	12.2	2	34	4	C.G.Deane c S.Haigh	161	
							J.Daniell c D.Denton		
							A.E.Lewis st A.Dolphin		
							A.E.Newton c M.W.Booth		
511. Yorkshire v Worcestershire, Worcester, May 22, 23, 24 (Yorkshire won by ten wickets)									
c E.W.Bale b A.J.Conway	45	535	-	-	-	-		113	
did not bat	-	19-0	47	13	109	2	F.A.Pearson c and b	440	1
							H.K.Foster c J.T.Newstead		
512. Yorkshire v Derbyshire, Chesterfield, May 25, 26, 27 (Yorkshire won by an innings and 75 runs)									
b A.Morton	18	401-4d	12	2	41	2	A.Morton b	215	1
							A.Wickstead b		
			13.5	4	16	7	S.W.A.Cadman b	111	1
							A.Morton lbw		
							A.Wickstead c H.Watson		
							L.Oliver c and b		
							H.F.D.Jelf c H.Watson		
							C.F.Root c G.H.Hirst		
							A.Warren c R.H.Radcliffe		
513. Yorkshire v Somerset, Headingley, May 29, 30 (Yorkshire won by ten wickets)									
c J.Daniell b J.F.Bridges	43	219	7.1	1	15	3	E.S.M.Poyntz lbw	130	
							W.H.Taylor c		
							J.J.Bridges c A.Drake		
not out	6	18-0	2	0	7	0		106	

514. Yorkshire v Cambridge University, Fenner's, June 1, 2, 3 (Cambridge University won by 69 runs)
 c E.G.Forbes-Adam
          b J.F.Ireland   1   157   20   5 49 3 J.F.Ireland c A.Drake   220   2
                                                            E.G.Forbes-Adam c A.Dolphin
                                                            M.J.Susskind b
 c S.H.Saville b J.F.Ireland 10 200   20   2 59 6 S.H.Saville c E.J.Radcliffe 206
                                                            M.Falcon c J.T.Newstead
                                                            H.E.W.Prest c J.T.Newstead
                                                            M.J.Susskind c A.Drake
                                                            J.H.Bruce-Lockhart c E.J.Radcliffe
                                                            H.Grierson c G.W.Bayes

515. Yorkshire v Lancashire, Old Trafford, June 5, 6, 7 (Yorkshire won by 159 runs)
    b W.Brearley   15 199   7   2 24 0   224
    b H.Dean   18 376-8d 17   3 44 1 W.K.Tyldesley b   192   1

516. Yorkshire v Warwickshire, Edgbaston, June 8, 9, 10 (Yorkshire won by four wickets)
    b E.F.Field   47 347   19   2 58 1 G.W.Stephens c A.Dolphin 317   1
    b F.R.Foster   18 217-6   8   1 25 0   245

517. Yorkshire v Leicestershire, Bradford, June 12, 13, 14 (Yorkshire won by five wickets)
  c H.Whitehead b F.M.Joyce 92 334   16.3 3 47 3 S.Coe c G.H.Hirst   309
                                                            W.Shipman c B.B.Wilson
                                                            J.Shields c A.Dolphin
  c C.J.B.Wood b J.H.King 38 272-5   12   2 58 1 A.Mounteney c D.Denton 296

518. Yorkshire v Middlesex, Lord's, June 15, 16, 17 (Middlesex won by nine wickets)
  c E.H.Hendren b J.T.Hearne 2 354   42   7 132 3 J.W.Hearne c and b   425   2
                                                            H.R.Murrell c A.Dolphin
                                                             D.R.Osborne b
  c sub b F.A.Tarrant   24 104   5   1 12 1 P.F.Warner c E.Oldroyd   34-1

519. Yorkshire v Kent, Bramall Lane, June 19, 20, 21 (Match drawn)
  c James Seymour b A.P.Day 95 286   17   6 39 1 James Seymour c A.Dolphin 324
  b A.Fielder   6 144-4 12.5 2 42 1 E.W.Dillon c and b   282-6d 1

520. Yorkshire v Northamptonshire, Dewsbury, June 22, 23, (24) (Match drawn)
  not out   37 88-3   44.4 2 141 6 John Seymour st A.Dolphin 401   1
                                                            G.J.Thompson c and b
                                                            R.A.Haywood c H.E.Hartington
                                                            R.N.Beasley c J.T.Newstead
                                                            W.Wells b
                                                            W.A.Buswell c G.H.Hirst

521. Yorkshire v Surrey, Headingley, June 26, 27 (Surrey won by four wickets)
  lbw b T.Rushby   23   87   15   6 29 6 T.W.Hayward c D.Denton 103
                                                             E.G.Hayes lbw
                                                            M.C.Bird c S.Haigh
                                                            W.E.Davis st A.Dolphin
                                                            W.A.Spring st A.Dolphin
                                                            H.Strudwick b
  lbw b W.C.Smith   29 181   26   6 54 5 T.W.Hayward st A.Dolphin 166-6
                                                            J.B.Hobbs st A.Dolphin
                                                            E.G.Hayes c M.W.Booth
                                                            M.C.Bird b
                                                           W.E.Davis c G.H.Hirst

522. England v The Rest, Lord's, June 29, 30, July 1 (England won by ten wickets)
  b J.W.Hearne   121 393   -   -   - -   173   1
  did not bat   -   1-0   8   1 31 0   220

523. Yorkshire v Worcestershire, Bradford, July 3, 4 (Yorkshire won by nine wickets)
  c J.A.Cuffe b R.D.Burrows 92 265   9   1 35 0   165
  not out   41 81-1   25   4 88 2 E.G.Arnold c D.Denton 178
                                                             W.H.Taylor lbw

524. Players v Gentlemen, Kennington Oval, July 6, 7, 8 (Match drawn)
  b W.Brearley   24 388   11   1 46 1 J.W.H.T.Douglas
                                                                  c J.Iremonger   406
  not out   18 138-5   11   2 39 3 P.F.Warner c F.A.Tarrant 190-6d
                                                             I.P.F.Campbell st H.Strudwick
                                                            A.P.Day c J.T.Tyldesley

525. Players v Gentlemen, Lord's, July 10, 11, 12 (Gentlemen won by 106 runs)
  b F.R.Foster   20 201   10   0 52 0   352
  c J.W.H.T.Douglas
        b F.R.Foster   11 292   4   0 18 1 F.R.Foster b   271-9d

526. Yorkshire v Hampshire, Huddersfield, July 13, 14, 15 (Yorkshire won by ten wickets)
    c A.S.Kennedy b D.M.Evans 35   355   -   -   -   -   142
    did not bat   -   22-0   12   3   17   0   234

527. Yorkshire v Essex, Bramall Lane, July 17, 18, 19 (Match drawn)
    b J.W.H.T.Douglas   27   270   43   4 124   2   J.W.H.T.Douglas
                                                             st A.Dolphin   392
                                                             P.Campbell b

    c H.A.Carpenter
       b B.Tremlin   61   333-7d   -   -   -   -   78-2

528. Yorkshire v Northamptonshire, Northampton, July 20, 21, 22 (Northamptonshire won by 44 runs)
    b W.East   11   250   38   10   92   8   John Seymour st A.Dolphin 316
                                                             W.H.Denton c M.W.Booth
                                                             R.A.Haywood c M.W.Booth
                                                             G.J.Thompson c G.H.Hirst
                                                             H.S.Snell c G.H.Hirst
                                                             G.A.T.Vials c D.Denton
                                                             W.Wells c M.W.Booth
                                                             W.A.Buswell c A.Dolphin
    c John Seymour
       b G.J.Thompson   15   140   18   6   47   6   John Seymour c G.H.Hirst   118
                                                             R.A.Haywood c M.W.Booth
                                                             G.J.Thompson c G.H.Hirst
                                                             G.A.T.Vials c sub
                                                             W.East hit wkt
                                                             W.Wells c D.Denton

529. Yorkshire v Sussex, Headingley, July 24, 25, 26 (Yorkshire won by 281 runs)
    c A.E.Relf b G.Leach   20   225   1   0   2   1   N.J.Holloway st A.Dolphin 102   1
    c G.R.Cox b A.E.Relf   125   282   18   5   43   2   C.L.A.Smith c A.Drake   124
                                                             G.R.Cox c G.H.Hirst

530. Yorkshire v Warwickshire, Harrogate, July 27, 28, 29 (Warwickshire won by 198 runs)
    b F.R.Foster   7   310   23.1   3   92   3   E.J.Smith c W.E.Bates   341   1
                                                             S.Santall b
                                                             E.F.Field b
    c F.R.Foster b E.F.Field   4   58   6   1   34   0   225   3

531. Yorkshire v Nottinghamshire, Hull, July 31 August 1, 2 (Yorkshire won by 225 runs)
    c G.Gunn b J.Iremonger   25   269   -   -   -   -   146
    b W.Riley   55   293-6d 12.4   1   39   1   W.E.G.Payton c D.Denton   191

532. Yorkshire v Lancashire, Bramall Lane, August 7, 8, 9 (Match drawn)
    b W.Brearley   36   281   23   6   57   4   R.H.Spooner b   167
                                                             J.T.Tyldesley b
                                                             J.Sharp lbw
                                                             K.G.MacLeod b
    c J.S.Heap b W.Brearley   22   183-6 31.5   4 109   4   R.H.Spooner c A.Drake   364   1
                                                             J.T.Tyldesley c G.H.Hirst
                                                             H.G.Garnett c S.Haigh
                                                             H.Dean b

533. Yorkshire v Leicestershire, Aylestone Road, Leicester, August 10, 11, 12 (Leicestershire won by an innings
     and 20 runs)
    c and b W.Shipman   0   153   14   4   30   0   220   1
    c J.Shields b W.Shipman   0   47

534. Yorkshire v Middlesex, Bradford, August 14, 15, 16 (Match drawn)
    c F.A.Tarrant b E.Mignon   39   218   23.5   2 107   3   H.R.Murrell b   378
                                                             F.T.Mann c A.Drake
                                                             E.Mignon lbw
    lbw b J.W.Hearne   17   280-9 11   1   24   0   261-5d

535. Yorkshire v Surrey, Kennington Oval, August 17, 18, 19 (Match drawn)
    c M.C.Bird b W.C.Smith   91   372   22.4   2 115   4   T.W.Hayward c D.Denton   540
                                                             I.P.F.Campbell c G.H.Hirst
                                                             E.G.Goatly c A.Drake
                                                             T.Rushby b
    b J.W.Hitch   1   158-7

536. Yorkshire v Hampshire, Portsmouth, August 21, 22, 23 (Hampshire won by six wickets)
    c E.M.Sprot b W.Mead   55   169   10   2   38   2   G.Brown st A.Dolphin   191
                                                             H.C.McDonell lbw
    b A.S.Kennedy   7   158   7   0   29   0   137-4

537. Yorkshire v Kent, Canterbury, August 24, 25, 26 (Kent won by ten wickets)

lbw b C.Blythe	13	75	10	5	21	0			151	1
c James Seymour b C.Blythe	37	79	-	-	-	-			4-0	

538. Yorkshire v Sussex, Hastings, August 28, 29, 30 (Yorkshire won by an innings and 32 runs)

lbw b G.R.Cox	19	522-7d	20	5	71	1	H.P.Chaplin c M.W.Booth	278	
			13	1	44	0		212	

539. Yorkshire v MCC, Scarborough, August 31, September 1, 2 (Match drawn)

c G.L.Jessop b M.Falcon	128	387	6.2	1	23	1	G.J.Thompson st A.Dolphin	274
c W.S.Bird								
b G.J.Thompson	115	225-6d	9	0	68	1	J.Hardstaff, sen. c G.H.Hirst	334-7	1

540. Players v Gentlemen, Scarborough, September 4, 5, 6 (Match drawn)

c P.R. Le Couteur								
b M.Falcon	13	432	9	1	27	1	M.Falcon c G.H.Hirst	290	1
lbw b J.W.H.T.Douglas	8	181-5d	4	1	9	1	G.L.Jessop b	195-6

541. MCC Australian Team v Lord Londesborough's XI, Scarborough, September 7, 8, 9 (Match drawn)

b E.F.Field	0	190	8	2	35	1	K.L.Hutchings lbw	301	1
c W.S.Bird b E.F.Field	85	333-5	5	1	19	0		258-7d

542. England v Warwickshire, Kennington Oval, September 11, 12, 13, 14 (England XI won by an innings and 365 runs)

not out	0	631-5d	-	-	-	-		129	
			10.3	5	14	4	E.J.Smith lbw	137	1
							William Quaife c F.E.Woolley		
							S.Santall b		
							E.F.Field c C.P.Mead		

SEASON'S AVERAGES

Batting and Fielding	M	I	NO	Runs	HS	Ave	100	50	Ct
Players v Gentlemen	3	6	1	94	24	18.80	-	-	1
Championship	27	48	3	1606	125	35.68	2	7	20
Other Yorkshire matches	3	6	0	355	128	59.16	2	1	3
Other matches	3	4	1	206	121	68.66	1	1	3
Season	36	64	5	2261	128	38.32	5	9	27
Career	542	786	120	19179	201	28.79	25	92	355

Bowling	O	M	R	W	BB	Ave	5i	10m
Players v Gentlemen	49	5	191	7	3-39	27.28	-	-
Championship	758	141	2260	93	8-92	24.30	6	2
Other Yorkshire matches	75.4	13	267	12	6-59	22.25	1	-
Other matches	31.3	9	99	5	4-14	19.80	-	-
Season (6-ball)	914.1	168	2817	117	8-92	24.07	7	2
Career (6-ball)	14575.1	3871 }	41260	2447	9-24	16.86	193	49
(5-ball)	2748.4	1029 }						

1911/12 - MCC in Australia

The tour to Australia brought out Rhodes as a first-rate opening batsman and he and Hobbs made a start to their wonderful career together. His bowling deteriorated to such an extent that he failed to take a wicket in all matches and only sent down 62 overs. He had only four single figure innings on the tour and scored three consecutive hundreds, 179 in the Fourth Test at Melbourne in an opening partnership of 323 with Jack Hobbs which is still the highest partnership for this wicket against Australia. He followed this in the next match against New South Wales at Sydney with 119 and 109.

	Own Team Total	O	M	R	W		Opp Total	Ct
543. MCC v South Australia, Adelaide, November 10, 11, 13, 14 (MCC won by an innings and 194 runs)								
b W.J.Whitty	7	563	-	-	-	-	141	2
			5	1	10	0	228	
544. MCC v Victoria, Melbourne, November 17, 18, 20, 21, 22 (MCC won by 49 runs)								
lbw b F.J.Laver	28	318					274	1
lbw b W.W.Armstrong	66	234					229	

545. MCC v New South Wales, Sydney, November 24, (25), 27, (28) (Match drawn)
c A.Cotter b H.V.Hordern   15 238   198

546. MCC v Queensland, Brisbane, December 1, 2, 4 (MCC won by seven wickets)
not out   64 275   290   1
b J.W.McLaren   26 140-3   124

547. MCC v Australian XI, Brisbane, December 8, 9, 11 (Match drawn)
c J.N.Crawford
    b J.W.McLaren   0 267   10   2   45 0   347
b W.W.Armstrong   34 279-4

548. ENGLAND v AUSTRALIA, Sydney, December 15, 16, 18, 19, 20, 21 (Australia won by 146 runs)
c C.Hill b H.V.Hordern   41 318   8   0   26 0   447
c V.T.Trumper
    b H.V.Hordern   0 291   3   1   4 0   308   1

549. ENGLAND v AUSTRALIA, Melbourne, December 30, January 1, 2, 3 (England won by eight wickets)
c V.T.Trumper b A.Cotter   61 265   -   -   -   -   184
c H.Carter b A.Cotter   28 219-2   2   1   3 0   299

550. ENGLAND v AUSTRALIA, Adelaide, January 12, 13, 15, 16, 17 (England won by seven wickets)
lbw b A.Cotter   59 501   -   -   -   -   133   1
not out   57 112-3   1   0   6 0   476

551. MCC v Tasmania, Launceston, January 23, 24, 25 (MCC won by eight wickets)
c T.H.Elliott
    b M.S.McKenzie   14 332   11   2   40 0   217
not out   13 56-2   -   -   -   -   165

552. MCC v Tasmania, Hobart, January 26, 27, 29 (MCC won by an innings and 95 runs)
b C.W.B.Martin   102 574-4d   124
                                            355   2

553. MCC v Victoria, Melbourne, February 2, 3, 5, 6 (MCC won by eight wickets)
c W.W.Armstrong
    b W.J.Scott   16 467   -   -   -   -   195
not out   22 43-2   7   0   31 0   314

554. ENGLAND v AUSTRALIA, Melbourne, February 9, 10, 12, 13 (England won by an innings and 225 runs)
c H.Carter b R.B.Minnett 179 589   2   1   1 0   191   2
                                            173

555. MCC v New South Wales, Sydney, February 16, 17, 19, 20 (MCC won by eight wickets)
c C.Kelleway b G.R.Hazlitt 119 315   -   -   -   -   106
c H.L.Collins b C.Kelleway 109 195-2   11   1   45 0   403

556. ENGLAND v AUSTRALIA, Sydney, February 23, 24, (26), 27, 28, (29), March 1 (England won by 70 runs)
b C.G.Macartney   8 324   -   -   -   -   176
lbw b W.W.Armstrong   30 214   2   0   17 0   292   1

SEASON'S AVERAGES

Batting and Fielding	M	I	NO	Runs	HS	Ave	100	50	Ct
Test matches	5	9	1	463	179	57.87	1	3	5
Other matches	9	15	3	635	119	52.91	3	2	6
Tour	14	24	4	1098	179	54.90	4	5	11
Career	556	810	124	20277	201	29.55	29	97	366

Bowling		O	M	R	W	BB	Ave	5i	10m
Test maches		18	3	57	0	-	-	-	-
Other matches		44	6	177	0	-	-	-	-
Tour	(6-ball)	62	9	234	0	-	-	-	-
Career	(6-ball)	14637.1	3880 ⎱	41494	2447	9-24	16.95	193	49
	(5-ball)	2748.4	1029 ⎰						

1912

Rhodes opened the innings with Hobbs and played in all six Test matches in a disappointing year when the triangular series of Test matches was an abject failure mostly because of abnormally bad weather and the poor form shown by the South Africans who were on a 'hiding to nothing' whatever the weather. At least it can be said that it was the forerunner of the very successful triangular tournaments which started some seventy years later. Although in county matches Rhodes was a good second to David Denton, whose form outshone any of his previous years, he was indebted to two big innings as the rest were somewhat mediocre. He made 176 against Nottinghamshire at Harrogate and 107 against Leicestershire at Bradford. He was well down the bowling list this year taking only 37 wickets for Yorkshire.

	Own Team Total	O	M	R	W		Opp Total	Ct
557. England v The Rest, Kennington Oval, May 6, 7, 8 (England won by an innings and 13 runs)								
c James Seymour								
b W.C.Smith	12 352	5	1	14	1	J.W.H.T.Douglas lbw	119	1
		3	0	15	0		220	
558. Yorkshire v Leicestershire, Aylestone Road, Leicester, May 9, 10, 11 (Yorkshire won by nine wickets)								
c A.W.Shipman b W.E.Astill	78 344	4	2	3	1	J.H.King c G.H.Hirst	143	
not out	67 117-1	13	3	45	2	H.Whitehead c G.H.Hirst	317	1
						W.Shipman st A.Dolphin		
559. Yorkshire v Hampshire, Bramall Lane, May 13, 14, 15, (Match drawn)								
b J.A.Newman	46 471	-	-	-	-		80	
		18	8	35	0		260-4	
560. Yorkshire v South Africans, Huddersfield, May 16, 17, 18 (Match drawn)								
c C.P.Carter b S.J.Pegler	3 317	5	0	31	2	R.Beaumont b	170	
						S.J.Pegler c A.Drake		
not out	7 10-1	29	2	102	6	H.W.Taylor c J.Tasker	288	
						A.W.Nourse b		
						G.C.White c M.W.Booth		
						R.O.Schwarz lbw		
						R.Beaumont b		
						T.A.Ward b		
561. Yorkshire v Kent, Headingley, May (20), 21, (22) (Match drawn)								
c F.E.Woolley b C.Blythe	8 96	9	0	29	0		103-2	
562. MCC Australian XI v The Rest, Lord's, May 23, 24, 25 (MCC Australian XI won by an innings and 10 runs)								
c H.Strudwick								
b E.Humphreys	55 509						237	
							262	1
563. Yorkshire v Lancashire, Bradford, May 27, 28 (Yorkshire won by ten wickets)								
c P.M.Fairclough								
b W.Huddleston	107 226	3	0	8	0		76	1
not out	2 17-0	18	4	49	2	J.T.Tyldesley b	165	
						J.Sharp c S.Haigh		
564. Yorkshire v Somerset, Dewsbury, May 30, (31), June 1 (Match drawn)								
c W.T.Greswell b E.Robson	14 146						73	
c L.C.L.Sutton b E.Robson	16 111-8d						45-3	
565. Yorkshire v Essex, Huddersfield, June (6), 7, 8 (Match drawn)								
b C.P.Buckenham	20 242	14	2	27	1	W.Reeves c J.Tasker	103	
566. ENGLAND v SOUTH AFRICA, Lord's, June 10, 11, 12 (England won by an innings and 62 runs)								
b A.W.Nourse	36 337						58	
							217	
567. Yorkshire v Middlesex, Lord's, June 13, 14, 15 (Middlesex won by four wickets)								
c J.T.Hearne b F.A.Tarrant	25 157	12	0	38	2	E.H.Hendren b	185	
						R.Anson b		
c and b A.R.Litteljohn	84 166	4	0	23	0		139-6	
568. Yorkshire v Gloucestershire, Headingley, June 17, 18, 19 (Yorkshire won by 74 runs)								
c A.E.Dipper b C.W.L.Parker	2 82	-	-	-	-		68	1
c E.G.Dennett b G.L.Jessop	12 170	14.4	3	39	2	C.W.L.Parker hit wkt	110	
						A.E.North c B.B.Wilson		
569. Yorkshire v Nottinghamshire, Trent Bridge, June 20, 21, 22 (Yorkshire won by five wickets)								
c T.W.Oates b A.O.Jones	11 145	8.4	1	23	2	W.Riley b	261	
						T.G.Wass c A.Drake		
c T.W.Oates b J.Iremonger	4 249-5	-	-	-	-		132	1

70

570. ENGLAND v AUSTRALIA, Lord's, June 24, 25, 26 (Match drawn)
   c W.Carkeek b C.Kelleway 59 310-7d   19.2 5 59 3 C.Kelleway b   282
                                                      W.Bardsley lbw
                                                      G.R.Hazlitt b

571. Yorkshire v Warwickshire, Edgbaston, June 27, 28, (29) (Match drawn)
   c C.S.Baker
      b William Quaife 25 451-4d   21 3 54 2 S.P.Kinneir c A.Drake 183
                                             S.Santall lbw
                                 3 2 1 0   63-3

572. Yorkshire v Australians, Bramall Lane, July 1, (2), 3 (Match drawn)
   b W.J.Whitty   14 280   6.2 0 35 1 W.J.Whitty c M.W.Booth 299   2
                                   - - - -   3-0

573. Yorkshire v Worcestershire, Dewsbury, July 4, 5, 6 (Yorkshire won by 214 runs)
   c E.W.Bale b F.Chester 22 129   -   -   -   -   85
   c F.Chester b J.A.Cuffe 42 345-9d 20.5 4 50 4 F.L.Bowley lbw   175   1
                                              E.G.Arnold c M.W.Booth
                                              A.T.Cliff c S.Haigh
                                              R.D.Burrows c and b

574. ENGLAND v SOUTH AFRICA, Headingley, July 8, 9, 10 (England won by 174 runs)
   c and b S.J.Pegler   7 242   -   -   -   -   147
   b S.J.Pegler   10 238   4 1 14 0   159

575. Players v Gentlemen, Kennington Oval, July 11, 12, 13 (Match drawn)
   c F.R.Foster b H.L.Simms 39 378   366   1
   c D.C.Robinson
      b H.L.Simms   15 136-5   245-7d

576. Yorkshire v Leicestershire, Bramall Lane, July 15, 16, 17 (Yorkshire won by eight wickets)
   b W.E.Astill   29 350   11 3 23 2 W.N.Riley lbw   140   2
                                           C.A.Boden c A.Drake
   c J.Shields b W.E.Astill 3 115-2   24 10 42 3 J.H.King b   324
                                           C.A.Boden b
                                           J.Shields c A.Dolphin

577. Players v Gentlemen, Lord's, July 18, 19, 20 (Match drawn)
   b H.L.Simms   43 311   -   -   -   -   242
   b M.Falcon   42 181   0.2 0   0 1 K.S.Ranjitsinhji st E.J.Smith 159-6

578. Yorkshire v Surrey, Kennington Oval, July 22, 23, 24 (Match drawn)
   b J.W.Hitch   2 233   9 0 31 1 I.P.F.Campbell lbw 267   2
   lbw b J.W.Hitch   33 229-6d   1 0   5 0   93-1

579. Yorkshire v Hampshire, Southampton, July 25, 26, 27 (Yorkshire won by nine wickets)
   c C.P.Mead b A.S.Kennedy 0 492   12 1 48 2 J.A.Newman c E.Oldroyd 441   1
                                             W.V.Jephson b
   not out   18 45-1   -   -   -   -   95   1

580. ENGLAND v AUSTRALIA, Old Trafford, July 29, 30, (31) (Match drawn)
   b W.J.Whitty   92 203   14-0

581. Yorkshire v Warwickshire, Hull, August (1), (2), 3 (Match drawn)
   b E.J.Smith b F.R.Foster 16 88   59   1
                                                    64-3

582. Yorkshire v Lancashire, Old Trafford, August 5, 6, 7 (Match drawn)
   b H.Dean   13 103   12 2 38 0   347   1
   lbw b H.Dean   8 105-7

583. Yorkshire v Essex, Leyton, August 8, 9, 10 (Yorkshire won by ten wickets)
   lbw b C.P.Buckenham   29 278   7 1 24 1 F.H.Gillingham b   129
   not out   18 40-0   3 2 12 0   187

584. ENGLAND v SOUTH AFRICA, Kennington Oval, August 12, 13 (England won by ten wickets)
   b G.A.Faulkner   0 176   95   1
   did not bat   - 14-0   93

585. Yorkshire v Nottinghamshire, Harrogate, August 15, 16, 17 (Yorkshire won by an innings and 102 runs)
   c T.W.Oates b J.Iremonger 176 389   23.3 6 68 5 J.Hardstaff, sen. lbw 161
                                             W.E.G.Payton lbw
                                           A.O.Jones c A.Drake
                                           T.W.Oates c R.Kilner
                                           T.G.Wass c A.Drake
                            4 3 7 0   126   2

586. ENGLAND v AUSTRALIA, Kennington Oval, August 19, 20, 21, 22 (England won by 244 runs)
   b R.B.Minnett   49 245   -   -   -   -   111   2

b W.J.Whitty   4 175   2 1 1 0   65

587. Yorkshire v Somerset, Taunton, August 26, 27, 28 (Yorkshire won by an innings and 136 runs)

		O	M	R	W		Opp Total	Ct
c H.S.R.Critchley-Salmonson b E.Robson	16 330	2.1	0	6	2	J.Daniell lbw W.T.Greswell b	69	
		17	2	52	3	E.Robson c E.Oldroyd H.S.R. Critchley-Salmonson lbw W.T.Greswell c S.Haigh	125	1

588. Yorkshire v Sussex, Hove, August 29, (30), 31 (Match drawn)

		O	M	R	W	Opp Total	Ct
c G.R.Cox b A.E.Relf	19 141	4	0	28	0	154-8	1

589. Yorkshire v MCC, Scarborough, September 2, (3), 4 (Match drawn)

		Opp Total	Ct
·b J.W.H.T.Douglas	2 124	153	1
c G.L.Jessop b M.Falcon	9 79-7	84	

590. Lord Londesborough's XI v Australians, Scarborough, September 5, 6, 7 (Match drawn)

		O	M	R	W	Opp Total	Ct
c C.Kelleway b G.R.Hazlitt	51 294	20	4	46	2	R.E.Mayne c M.C.Bird R.B.Minnett lbw 203	1
c and b G.R.Hazlitt	28 131-5d	4	0	15	0	138-0	

591. Lord Londesborough's XI v South Africans, Scarborough, September 9, (10), (11) (Match drawn)

		Opp Total	Ct
b S.J.Pegler	4 63-4	100	1

592. C.B.Fry's XI v Australians, Bray, September 12, 13, 14 (C.B.Fry's XI won by eight wickets)

		Opp Total
c W.Carkeek b G.R.Hazlitt	12 280	72
b W.J.Whitty	9 97-2	304

593. Yorkshire v Rest of England, Kennington Oval, September 16, 17, 18 (Rest of England won by an innings and 122 runs)

		O	M	R	W	Opp Total
lbw b F.A.Tarrant	23 167	7	0	25	0	367
b J.W.H.T.Douglas	7 78					

SEASON'S AVERAGES

Batting and Fielding	M	I	NO	Runs	HS	Ave	100	50	Ct
Test matches	6	8	0	257	92	32.12	-	2	3
Players v Gentlemen	2	4	0	139	43	34.75	-	-	1
Championship	20	32	4	965	176	34.46	2	3	17
Other Yorkshire matches	4	7	1	65	23	10.83	-	-	4
Other matches	5	7	0	171	55	24.42	-	2	4
Season	37	58	5	1597	176	30.13	2	7	29
Career	593	868	129	21874	201	29.59	31	104	395

Bowling	O	M	R	W	BB	Ave	5i	10m
Test matches	25.2	7	74	3	3-59	24.66	-	-
Players v Gentlemen	0.2	0	0	1	1-0	0.00	-	-
Championship	292.5	62	808	37	5-68	21.83	1	-
Other Yorkshire matches	47.2	2	193	9	6-102	21.44	1	-
Other matches	32	5	90	3	2-46	30.00	-	-
Season (6-ball)	397.5	76	1165	53	6-102	21.98	2	-
Career (6-ball)	15035	3956 }	42659	2500	9-24	17.06	195	49
(5-ball)	2748.4	1029 }						

1913

Rhodes had an excellent season this year with the bat scoring nearly two thousand runs with four centuries. For Yorkshire he made over 1,500 runs with three centuries. He made another against Cambridge University. Taking 62 wickets as against 37 in 1912, he recalled memories of his greater years. His best bowling was against Northamptonshire at Headingley when he took 7-45.

	Own Team Total	O	M	R	W	Opp Total	Ct
594. Yorkshire v Lancashire, Old Trafford, May 12, 13 (Lancashire won by an innings and 3 runs)							
c J.Sharp b J.S.Heap	14 74					130	
lbw b H.Dean	9 53						

595. Yorkshire v Gloucestershire, Bristol, May 15, 16, 17 (Yorkshire won by 230 runs)
lbw b E.G.Dennett   9   271   14   5   31   0   210   1
lbw b E.G.Dennett   110   369-5d   34.4   7   98   4   D.C.Robinson b   200
           A.E.Dipper b
           A.K.G.White c G.H.Hirst
           E.G.Dennett c W.E.Bates

596. Yorkshire v Somerset, Bath, May 19, 20 (Yorkshire won by an innings and 132 runs)
c M.P.Bajana b E.Robson   28   289   90
           67

597. Yorkshire v Worcestershire, Worcester, May 22, 23, 24 (Yorkshire won by six wickets)
b R.D.Burrows   11   294   12   5   14   1   E.W.Bale c A.Dolphin   201   1
b R.D.Burrows   8   87-4   17   6   45   1   F.A.Pearson lbw   178

598. Yorkshire v Sussex, Bramall Lane, May 26, 27 (Yorkshire won by eight wickets)
c G.B.Street b J.Vine   59   317   0.4   0   3   1   G.B.Street lbw   135
not out   17   53-2   9.4   1   40   1   J.H.Vincett c D.Denton   233

599. Yorkshire v Cambridge University, Fenner's, May 29, 30, 31 (Match drawn)
c H.G.H.Mulholland
       b J.White 102   266   37.5   13   98   7   B.S.Cumberlege
                    st A.Dolphin   340   1
           S.H.Saville b
           R.B.Lagden c A.Drake
           H.G.H.Mulholland b
           E.L.Kidd c J.Tasker
           A.H.Lang c A.Dolphin
           J.H.Naumann c A.Dolphin
c B.S.Cumberlege
       b S.H.Saville 39   361-7d   12   6   14   3   R.B.Lagden c and b   184-6   1
           H.G.H.Mulholland b
           A.H.Lang c T.J.D.Birtles

600. Yorkshire v Kent, Bradford, June 2, 3, 4 (Match drawn)
c J.C.Hubble b A.Fielder   17   217   10   0   55   3   J.C.Hubble c M.W.Booth   251
           E.W.Dillon c A.Dolphin
           W.A.Powell b
c F.H.Huish b A.Fielder   4   192-4   21   4   42   0   275   1

601. Yorkshire v Nottinghamshire, Trent Bridge, June 5, 6, 7 (Match drawn)
run out   19   447   23   6   55   0   331   1
c T.W.Oates b J.Iremonger   0   112-3d   5   0   18   1   E.B.Alletson c M.W.Booth   129-3

602. Yorkshire v Leicestershire, Headingley, June 9, 10 (Yorkshire won by an innings and 108 runs)
lbw b G.Geary   18   300   2   1   8   0   95   1
           12   5   12   0   97

603. Yorkshire v Essex, Leyton, June 12, 13, 14 (Yorkshire won by seven wickets)
c G.B.Davies
     b C.P.Buckenham   2   271   19   13   15   0   233
b J.W.H.T.Douglas   97   216-3   16   4   37   2   E.J.Freeman lbw   252   1
           C.P.Buckenham c G.H.Hirst

604. Yorkshire v Worcestershire, Huddersfield, June 16, 17, 18 (Yorkshire won by 213 runs)
lbw b W.B.Burns   40   235   5   2   6   0   169
c F.L.Bowley b F.Chester   41   215-7d   23.4   11   24   4   F.A.Pearson c sub   68
           R.S.Swalwell c G.H.Hirst
           W.B.Burns c B.B.Wilson
           E.G.Arnold lbw

605. Yorkshire v Middlesex, Lord's, June 19, 20, 21 (Match drawn)
c N.E.Haig b E.Mignon   12   280   31   12   53   2   F.A.Tarrant b   262
           E.L.Kidd lbw
b F.A.Tarrant   57   234   12   4   23   0   186-6

606. Yorkshire v Warwickshire, Bramall Lane, June 23, 24, 25 (Yorkshire won by 89 runs)
b F.R.Foster   9   254   17   6   29   1   F.R.Foster b   152   2
c J.H.Parsons b S.Santall   13   195   13   2   48   1   F.R.Foster c R.Kilner   208   2

607. Yorkshire v Northamptonshire, Northampton, June 26, 27, 28 (Match drawn)
c J.V.Murdin b S.G.Smith 110   333   24   9   44   3   John Seymour b   305   1
           F.I.Walden lbw
           T.Thorpe lbw
run out   41   141-3   13   4   46   1   G.J.Thompson lbw   254-7d   1

608. Yorkshire v Somerset, Bradford, June 30, July 1, 2 (Yorkshire won by an innings and 25 runs)
st H.Chidgey b J.C.White   56   298   -   -   -   -   149   1

                                      3.2   0   16   1   J.C.White b   124   2
609. Yorkshire v Leicestershire, Aylestone Road, Leicester, July 3, 4, 5 (Yorkshire won by 190 runs)
    c A.W.Shipman b G.Geary 152   405   1   0   1   1   W.N.Riley b   168
    lbw b J.H.King   37   142-6d 24   5   85   3   A.Mounteney c M.W.Booth   189   2
                                                            A.W.Shipman c D.Denton
                                                            G.Geary c R.Kilner

610. Yorkshire v Northamptonshire, Headingley, June 7, 8, 9 (Northamptonshire won by 20 runs)
    c W.A.Buswell
        b G.J.Thompson   2   107   15.1   4   45   7   S.G.Smith c G.H.Hirst   145
                                                            G.J.Thompson st A.Dolphin
                                                            J.S.Denton lbw
                                                            John Seymour b
                                                            F.I.Walden lbw
                                                            E.Freeman c M.W.Booth
                                                            V.S.Murdin c B.B.Wilson
    b S.G.Smith   21   212   17   4   67   2   John Seymour c D.Denton   194   1
                                                            F.I.Walden lbw

611. Yorkshire v Lancashire, Liverpool, July 10, 11, 12 (Lancashire won by three wickets)
    lbw b H.Dean   58   177   11   2   35   5   W.K.Tyldesley st A.Dolphin   92
                                                            G.E.Tyldesley c P.Holmes
                                                            K.G.MacLeod c D.Denton
                                                            R.Whitehead c T.J.D.Birtles
                                                            W.Huddleston c G.W.Bayes
    c W.Huddleston b H.Dean   0   73   16.4   5   43   3   J.T.Tyldesley c G.H.Hirst   159-7 1
                                                            G.E.Tyldesley lbw
                                                            J.S.Heap c T.J.D.Birtles

612. Players v Gentlemen, Lord's, July 14, (15), 16 (Players won by seven wickets)
    run out   49   212   232
    b H.L.Simms   25   126-3   102

613. Yorkshire v Kent, Tunbridge Wells, July 17, (18), (19) (Match drawn)
    c James Seymour
        b F.E.Woolley   21   100   13.4   3   42   5   H.T.W.Hardinge
                                                               st A.Dolphin   135
                                                            F.E.Woolley c B.B.Wilson
                                                            J.C.Hubble c T.J.D.Birtles
                                                            F.H.Huish b
                                                            W.J.Fairservice b

614. Yorkshire v Gloucestershire, Bramall Lane, July 21, 22 (Gloucestershire won by 2 runs)
    b C.W.L.Parker   2   172   6.4   2   23   1   E.G.Dennett c and b   157   1
    c J.H.Board b T.H.Gange   2   107   9   1   41   1   J.W.W.Nason b   124

615. Yorkshire v Nottinghamshire, Dewsbury, July 24, 25, 26 (Yorkshire won by five wickets)
    lbw b W.Riley   25   309   23.4   7   66   4   J.R.Gunn c sub   285
                                                            E.B.Alletson c T.J.Birtles
                                                            G.O.Gauld lbw
                                                            T.G.Wass c D.Denton
    c G.Gunn b T.G.Wass   0   153-5 13   3   68   3   W.Walker lbw   176
                                                            J.Iremonger c A.Drake
                                                            T.W.Oates c M.W.Booth

616. Yorkshire v Surrey, Hull, July 28, 29, 30 (Surrey won by 57 runs)
    b J.W.Hitch   38   158   3   2   8   0   131
    c W.A.Spring b J.W.Hitch   8   182   4   3   5   0   266

617. Yorkshire v Hampshire, Harrogate, July 31, August 1, 2 (Yorkshire won by 182 runs)
    lbw b J.A.Newman   19   382   14   2   29   1   C.H.Abercrombie
                                                               c M.W.Booth   262   2
    c J.Stone b G.Brown   6   291   15   3   44   3   J.Stone lbw   229
                                                            C.H.Abercrombie c B.B.Wilson
                                                            W.V.Jephson b

618. Yorkshire v Lancashire, Headingley, August 4, 5, 6 (Yorkshire won by three wickets)
    c J.T.Tyldesley
        b R.Whitehead   13   249   15   2   33   1   F.R.R.Brooke b   275   1
    c F.R.R.Brooke b H.Dean   12   220-7   -   -   -   -   190

619. Yorkshire v Warwickshire, Edgbaston, August 7, 8, 9 (Match drawn)
    c F.R.Foster b P.Jeeves   50   369   19   4   59   0   336
    not out   37   64-2   4   0   18   0   142-5d

620. Yorkshire v Middlesex, Bramall Lane, August 11, 12, 13 (Yorkshire won by three wickets)
    b J.W.Hearne   36   245   11   2   24   0   247

not out	86	183-7	3	0	11	0		180

621. Yorkshire v Surrey, Kennington Oval, August 14, 15, 16 (Yorkshire won by an innings and 19 runs)

lbw b W.C.Smith	90	409-9d	6	1	20	0		177
			13	4	33	3	E.G.Hayes lbw	213
							E.G.Goatly hit wkt	
							A.W.Spring st A.Dolphin	

622. Yorkshire v Essex, Bradford, August 18, 19, 20 (Yorkshire won by an innings and 48 runs)

b J.W.H.T.Douglas	5	512-9d	7	1	16	0	115
			15	4	34	0	349

623. Yorkshire v An England XI, Harrogate, August 21, 22, 23 (Match drawn)

c L.C.Braund b S.J.Pegler	9	337	11	2	41	0		106
			13	2	27	1	J.H.King lbw	196-8

624. Yorkshire v Hampshire, Bournemouth, August 25, 26, 27 (Match drawn)

lbw b G.Brown	1	249	9	5	9	0	315
not out	66	148-6	4	0	17	0	200-7d

625. Yorkshire v Sussex, Hastings, August 28, 29, (30) (Match drawn)

b N.J.Holloway	1	374	40-2

626. Yorkshire v MCC, Scarborough, September (1), 2, 3 (Match drawn)

lbw b G.A.Faulkner	35	138		124
lbw b J.W.H.T.Douglas	31	169-8d		98	1

627. Players v Gentlemen, Scarborough, September 4, 5, 6 (Gentlemen won by 6 runs)

b J.W.H.T.Douglas	11	270	-	-	-	-		266
c W.S.Bird								
b J.W.H.T.Douglas	22	245	10	4	29	3	J.R.Mason c J.B.Hobbs	255	1
							G.L.Jessop c J.W.Hearne	
							J.W.H.T.Douglas c and b	

628. Lord Londesborough's XI v Kent, Scarborough, September 8, 9, 10 (Lord Londesborough's XI won by 337 runs)

c J.R.Mason b D.W.Carr	19	328	1.2	0	9	2	J.C.Hubble lbw	109
							D.W.Carr b	
c J.R.Mason b A.Fielder	6	220	-	-	-	-		102	1

629. Kent and Yorkshire v Rest of England, Kennington Oval, September 15, 16, 17 (Rest of England won by an innings and 45 runs)

lbw b S.F.Barnes	17	154	7	0	26	0	266
c J.W.Hitch b S.F.Barnes	9	67					

SEASON'S AVERAGES

Batting and Fielding	M	I	NO	Runs	HS	Ave	100	50	Ct
Players v Gentlemen	2	4	0	107	49	26.75	-	-	1
Championship	28	49	4	1531	152	34.02	3	8	24
Other Yorkshire matches	4	7	0	274	102	39.14	1	1	4
Other matches	2	4	0	51	19	12.75	-	-	1
Season	36	64	4	1963	152	32.71	4	9	30
Career	629	932	133	23837	201	29.83	35	113	425

Bowling	O	M	R	W	BB	Ave	5i	10m
Players v Gentlemen	10	4	29	3	3-29	9.66	-	-
Championship	603.1	169	1560	62	7-45	25.16	2	-
Other Yorkshire matches	101.3	30	258	19	7-98	13.57	2	1
Other matches	8.2	0	35	2	2-9	17.50	-	-
Season (6-ball)	723	203	1882	86	7-45	21.88	4	1
Career (6-ball)	15758	4159 ⎱ 44541		2586	9-24	17.22	199	50
(5-ball)	2748.4	1029 ⎰						

1913/14 - MCC in South Africa

Rhodes' second tour of South Africa saw him retain his reputation as an opening batsman. It was mainly the bowling of S.F.Barnes, who on the matting wickets was almost unplayable, that enabled England to win the series by a comfortable margin. Rhodes contributed with the bat making 152 in the

Second Test at Johannesburg. In this match he added 141 with A.E.Relf for the first wicket and 152 with C.P.Mead for the third. Although not really needed in the Tests when he took only six wickets, his bowling in the other first-class matches proved as accurate and hostile as ever taking 25 wickets.

		Own Team Total	O	M	R	W		Opp Total	Ct

630. MCC v Western Province, Cape Town, November 8, 10, 11 (Match drawn)
| run out | | 3 | 199 | 6 | 1 | 16 | 0 | | 376 | |
| b J.M.Blanckenberg | | 0 | 330 | | | | | | | |

631. MCC v Cape Province, Port Elizabeth, November 21, 22 (MCC won by an innings and 167 runs)
b N.O.Norton		5	385	15	2	54	4	F.W.Porter lbw	158	1
								P.T.Lewis lbw		
								N.O.Norton c J.W.Hearne		
								J.M.Blanckenberg c J.B.Hobbs		
		-	-	-	-				60	1

632. MCC v Border, East London, November 29, December 1, 2 (MCC won by an innings and 132 runs)
| lbw b G.D.Cross | | 20 | 356-8d | 12 | 3 | 28 | 1 | R.Oosthuizen c and b | 121 | 1 |
| | | | | 6 | 2 | 13 | 0 | | 103 | 2 |

633. MCC v Border, Kingwilliamstown, December 3, 4 (Match drawn)
b P.J.McDonagh		38	204	8	4	14	1	K.A.Gordon c J.B.Hobbs	126	
b G.D.Cross		29	163-4	7	0	27	4	R.H.Randell		
								c J.W.H.T.Douglas	159-6	1
								S.G.Fuller c L.H.Tennyson		
								W.O.S.Beauchamp c F.E.Woolley		
								K.A.Gordon c and b		

634. MCC v Natal, Pietermaritzburg, December 8, 9, 10 (Match drawn)
| lbw b A.W.Nourse | | 14 | 219-7 | 1 | 0 | 5 | 1 | J.L.Cox c M.W.Booth | 124 | |
| | | | | - | - | - | - | | 69-0 | |

635. ENGLAND v SOUTH AFRICA, Durban, December 13, 15, 16, 17 (England won by an innings and 157 runs)
| c G.L.Tapscott b J.L.Cox | | 18 | 450 | 7 | 0 | 26 | 0 | | 182 | |
| | | | | - | - | - | - | | 111 | 1 |

636. MCC v Transvaal, Johannesburg, December 20, 22, 23 (MCC won by an innings and 29 runs)
c C.Newberry										
b F.L. Le Roux		31	427-8d	19	5	59	3	J.W.Zulch c F.E.Woolley	202	
								L.J.Tancred st E.J.Smith		
								M.J.Susskind c J.B.Hobbs		
				7	0	30	0		196	

637. ENGLAND v SOUTH AFRICA, Johannesburg, December 26, 27, 29, 30 (England won by an innings and 12 runs)
| c and b J.M.Blanckenberg | 152 | 403 | 13 | 5 | 23 | 1 | G.P.D.Hartigan c E.J.Smith | 160 | 1 |
| | | | | 9 | 2 | 20 | 0 | | 231 | 2 |

638. ENGLAND v SOUTH AFRICA, Johannesburg, January 1, 2, 3, 5 (England won by 91 runs)
| lbw b H.W.Taylor | | 35 | 238 | 3.5 | 1 | 9 | 1 | C.Newberry c J.W.Hearne | 151 | 2 |
| c T.A.Ward b H.W.Taylor | | 0 | 308 | 6 | 1 | 17 | 0 | | 304 | |

639. MCC v Transvaal, Pretoria, January 9, 10, (12) (Match drawn)
| c E.B.Lundie b F.L.Le Roux | 1 | 330 | 4 | 0 | 24 | 0 | | 245 | 1 |
| | | | | - | - | - | - | | 21-2 | |

640. MCC v Transvaal, Vogelfontein, January 14, 15 (Match drawn)
| did not bat | | - | 350-4d | 2.4 | 1 | 7 | 2 | C.Lamb c and b | 170 | 1 |
| | | | | | | | | J.G.Milton st H.Strudwick | | |

641. MCC v Orange River Colony, Bloemfontein, January 23, 24, 26 (MCC won by an innings and 374 runs)
| c W.Love b N.V.Lindsay | 68 | 565-8d | 4 | 0 | 24 | 0 | | 117 | 3 |
| | | | | - | - | - | - | | 74 | 1 |

642. MCC v Transvaal, Johannesburg, January 30, 31, February 2 (Match drawn)
b F.L. Le Roux		62	386	11	1	39	1	T.A.Ward c and b	347	2
not out		76	211-0d	16	1	46	3	T.A.Ward c M.C.Bird	145-6	
								R.Beaumont c M.C.Bird		
								D.J.Meintjes c J.B.Hobbs		

643. MCC v Natal, Durban, February 7, 9, 10 (Natal won by four wickets)
| b C.P.Carter | | 7 | 132 | | | | | | 153 | 2 |
| c A.W.Nourse b C.P.Carter | 28 | 235 | | | | | | 216-6 | |

644. ENGLAND v SOUTH AFRICA, Durban, February 14, 16, 17, 18 (Match drawn)

lbw b C.P.Carter	22	163	14	5	33	3	P.A.M.Hands st H.Strudwick	170	1
							C.Newberry b		
							J.M.Blanckenberg		
							c J.W.H.T.Douglas		
lbw b C.P.Carter	35	154-5	26	6	53	1	A.W.Nourse		
							c L.H.Tennyson	305-9d	1

645. ENGLAND v SOUTH AFRICA, Port Elizabeth, February 27, 28 March 2, 3 (England won by ten wickets)

b C.P.Carter	27	411	-	-	- -			193	
not out	0	11-0	10	4	14	0		228	2

646. MCC v Western Province, Cape Town, March 7, 9, 10 (Match drawn)

b J.M.Blanckenberg	25	322	10	1	30	1	E.A.Budgen c A.E.Relf	210	2
not out	35	177-4d	23	8	51	4	R.R.Luyt c J.W.Hearne	178	1
							A.V.C.Bisset c sub		
							J.M.Blanckenberg		
							c J.W.H.T.Douglas		
							E.A.Budgen hit wkt		

SEASON'S AVERAGES

Batting and Fielding	M	I	NO	Runs	HS	Ave	100	50	Ct
Test matches	5	8	1	289	152	41.28	1	-	10
Other matches	12	16	2	442	76*	31.57	-	3	19
Tour	17	24	3	731	152	34.80	1	3	29
Career	646	956	136	24568	201	29.96	36	116	454

Bowling	O	M	R	W	BB	Ave	5i	10m
Test matches	88.5	24	195	6	3-33	32.50	-	-
Other matches	151.4	29	467	25	4-57	18.68	-	-
Tour (6-ball)	240.3	53	662	31	4-57	21.35	-	-
Career (6-ball)	15998.3	4212 ⎱	45302	2617	9-24	17.27	199	50
(5-ball)	2748.4	1029 ⎰						

1914

In the last season before the war in which Rhodes' great rival, Colin Blythe, lost his life, Yorkshire were severely handicapped by the demise of Hirst as a bowler. It fell on Booth, Drake and Rhodes to carry the team and Wilfred certainly rose to the occasion. In taking 110 wickets in county matches alone he produced better bowling than for some time, his best analyses being 7-19 at Headingley against Derbyshire, 6-109 against Surrey at Bradford and 6-68 against Middlesex at Bramall Lane. All told he took 118 wickets at 18.27 each. He made two centuries: 113 against Sussex at Bradford and 105* against Lancashire at Hull – a match outside the County Championship.

	Own Team Total	O	M	R	W		Opp Total	Ct
647. Yorkshire v Northamptonshire, Northampton, May 9, 10 (Yorkshire won by an innings and 156 runs)								
c S.G.Smith b C.N.Woolley 25	378	7	4	7	0		117	
		12.1	3	46	3	S.F.Smith b	105	1
						D.Hardy b		
						W.A.Buswell c D.C.F.Burton		
648. Yorkshire v MCC, Lord's, May 13, 14 (Yorkshire won by an innings and 119 runs)								
b A.Fielder 41	292	-	-	- -			39	
		11	1	39	0		134	1
649. Yorkshire v Essex, Leyton, May 16, 18, 19 (Yorkshire won by an innings and 41 runs)								
c G.M.Louden								
b J.W.H.T.Douglas 20	441	11.5	2	35	1	H.M.Hills b	259	2
		8.1	5	8	1	H.M.Hills c A.Drake	141	1
650. Yorkshire v Hampshire, Southampton, May 20, 21, 22 (Match drawn)								
b E.R.Remnant 24	232	27	6	75	3	E.R.Remnant b	416	
						J.A.Newman c R.Kilner		
						G.C.Harrison st A.Dolphin		
c W.H.Livsey b G.Brown 28	426-4d	12	4	23	1	J.A.Newman c A.Dolphin	77-3	1

651. Yorkshire v Surrey, Bradford, May 25, 26, 27 (Surrey won by 28 runs)
```
b J.W.Hitch             89  284     24  0  109  6  T.W.Hayward b               317
                                                   E.G.Hayes lbw
                                                   H.S.Harrison c A.Dolphin
                                                   A.Ducat b
                                                   C.T.A.Wilkinson c D.Denton
                                                   H.Strudwick c D.C.F.Burton
c P.G.H.Fender b T.Rushby  0  194   24  3  56   5  J.B.Hobbs c D.Denton        189
                                                   H.S.Harrison b
                                                   P.G.H.Fender lbw
                                                   J.W.Hitch c T.J.D.Birtles
                                                   W.C.Smith c D.Denton
```

652. Yorkshire v Cambridge University, Fenner's, May 28, 29 (Yorkshire won by an innings and 6 runs)
```
b E.C.Baker              3  296    9.4  0  39   3  J.S.F.Morrison c A.W.White  131
                                                   L.C.Leggat c A.Drake
                                                   E.C.Baker c M.W.Booth
                         8.2  0  39   3  G.B.Davies b                          159
                                                   J.White c D.C.F.Burton
                                                   E.C.Baker c G.H.Hirst
```

653. Yorkshire v Lancashire, Bramall Lane, June 1, 2, 3 (Match drawn)
```
c W.Huddleston b J.Sharp  53  381   36  4  112  4  J.Sharp c G.H.Hirst         370      3
                                                   G.E.Tyldesley c G.H.Hirst
                                                   J.S.Heap c and b
                                                   W.Huddleston c sub
not out                   0  299-4d  10  3  12  1  J.W.H.Makepeace
                                                       c M.W.Booth              130-2
```

654. Yorkshire v Leicestershire, Aylestone Road, Leicester, June 4, 5, 6 (Match drawn)
```
lbw b G.Geary            10  225   20.1  5  47   2  W.Brown c and b             241      1
                                                    A.Skelding b
lbw b G.Geary            15  132-8d  11  6  9   1  A.Mounteney c A.W.White      34-2
```

655. Yorkshire v Derbyshire, Headingley, June 8, 9, 10 (Yorkshire won by an innings and 5 runs)
```
b F.C.Bracey             21  252-9d  14.3  7  12  1  J.Gladwin c D.Denton       157      1
                                     15.5  7  19  7  L.Oliver lbw                90      1
                                                     A.Morton c and b
                                                     G.Curgenven c A.Drake
                                                     A.G.Slater c M.W.Booth
                                                     G.Beet c M.W.Booth
                                                     J.Bowden lbw
                                                     H.Wild st A.Dolphin
```

656. Yorkshire v Middlesex, Lord's, June 11, 12, 13 (Match drawn)
```
st H.R.Murrell b J.W.Hearne 56  179   29    7  73  1  J.W.Hearne b              277      1
c F.A.Tarrant b J.T.Hearne  41  123-4  30.2  10  35  4  P.F.Warner b             172      1
                                                       F.T.Mann c A.Drake
                                                       E.H.Hendren lbw
                                                       J.T.Hearne b
```

657. Yorkshire v Warwickshire, Dewsbury, June 15, 16, 17 (Match drawn)
```
lbw b P.Jeeves           66  262    42  12  116  4  S.P.Kinneir lbw            424-8d   1
                                                    C.Charlesworth c E.Oldroyd
                                                    F.R.Foster b
                                                    P.Jeeves c A.W.White
c J.H.Parsons b H.Howell  75  345-9d  4   0  17   2  F.R.Foster b                85-4
                                                    P.Jeeves c A.Dolphin
```

658. Yorkshire v Kent, Tonbridge, June 18, 19, 20 (Kent won by an innings and 149 runs)
```
c F.H.Huish b A.P.Day     5  227   41.3  13  93  5  E.Humphreys c G.H.Hirst    493      2
                                                    James Seymour b
                                                    L.H.W.Troughton b
                                                    W.J.Fairservice c and b
                                                    A.Fielder c and b
b W.J.Fairservice        17  117
```

659. MCC South African Team v Rest of England, Lord's, June 22, 23, 24 (Rest of England won by an innings
and 189 runs)
```
c A.Dolphin b J.W.Hitch   0  94    16  5  37   1  A.P.Day c M.C.Bird          467
c G.H.Hirst b W.C.Smith  52  184
```

660. Yorkshire v Nottinghamshire, Trent Bridge, June 25, 26, 27 (Match drawn)
```
lbw b F.Barratt           2  199   12  1  44   2  P.J.S.Pearson-Gregory
                                                      st A.Dolphin            213      1
                                                  F.Barratt c R.Kilner
```

c P.J.S.Pearson-Gregory
  b J.Hardstaff, sen. 66 214-6   28.4 7 128 2 G.Gunn lbw   431   2
                                                  P.J.S.Pearson-Gregory c A.Dolphin

661. Yorkshire v Essex, Headingley, June 29, 30, July 1 (Match drawn)
  lbw b C.P.Buckenham   3 150   9 0 34 1 P.A.Perrin c and b   215   1
  b C.P.Buckenham   11 313   3.2 1   3 1 W.Reeves c B.B.Wilson   139-7

662. Yorkshire v Hampshire, Hull, July 2, (3), 4 (Match drawn)
  c E.R.Remnant
    b A.S.Kennedy   11 152   16 4 27 0   103   1
  b A.S.Kennedy   7 142-4d 6 3   5 1 E.R.Remnant c and b   79-7   2

663. Yorkshire v Kent, Bramall Lane, July 6, 7 (Kent won by five wickets)
  c F.E.Woolley
    b W.J.Fairservice   2 101   7 3 27 1 E.Humphreys lbw   126   1
  c A.Fielder b C.Blythe 16 100   1.4 0   7 0   77-5

664. Yorkshire v Northamptonshire, Huddersfield, July 9, 10, 11 (Yorkshire won by an innings and 8 runs)
  lbw b S.G.Smith   59 346   -   -   - -   146   4
                              25.1 8 68 4 W.Wells b   192   1
                                         F.I.Walden c A.W.White
                                         W.A.Buswell c G.H.Hirst
                                         J.V.Murdin c M.W.Booth

665. Yorkshire v Derbyshire, Chesterfield, July 16, 17, 18 (Yorkshire won by an innings and 48 runs)
  c and b J.Horsley   39 297   23.2 8 54 4 L.Oliver lbw   181   1
                                         J.Bowden c and b
                                         G.Curgenven b
                                         R.R.C.Baggallay st A.Dolphin
                            7.4 2 12 4 A.Morton c A.Dolphin   68   1
                                         J.Bowden c A.Dolphin
                                         S.W.A.Cadman lbw
                                         J.Horsley lbw

666. Yorkshire v Nottinghamshire, Headingley, July 20, 21, 22 (Yorkshire won by 97 runs)
  b J.Iremonger   16 75   9 4 18 2 J.Iremonger c A.Dolphin 161   1
                                         W.E.G.Payton lbw
  c and b F.Barratt   2 286   23 9 33 4 G.M.Lee c R.Kilner   103
                                         J.Hardstaff, sen. st A.Dolphin
                                         J.R.Gunn c P.Holmes
                                         J.Iremonger lbw

667. Yorkshire v Lancashire (non-Championship), Hull, July 23, 24, 25 (Match drawn)
  not out   105 329   20 8 38 1 G.E.Tyldesley b   259
                         -   -   - -   9-1

668. Yorkshire v Somerset, Bramall Lane, July 27, 28 (Yorkshire won by an innings and 155 runs)
  c E.S.M.Poyntz
    b A.D.E.Rippon   43 372   -   -   - -   90
                              1   0   4 1 J.J.Bridges c R.Kilner 127

669. Yorkshire v Gloucestershire, Harrogate, July 30, 31 (Yorkshire won by an innings and 118 runs)
  b E.G.Dennett   38 449   13 6 28 0   185
                             1 1   0 0   146

670. Yorkshire v Lancashire, Old Trafford, August 3, 4, 5 (Yorkshire won by ten wickets)
  lbw b J.S.Heap   25 190   28 6 56 3 G.E.Tyldesley lbw   162
                                         W.Huddleston lbw
                                         C.H.Parkin b
  did not bat   - 56-0   15 5 30 4 G.E.Tyldesley c A.Drake   83
                                         H.G.Garnett c R.Kilner
                                         J.S.Heap lbw
                                         C.H.Parkin b

671. Yorkshire v Warwickshire, Edgbaston, August 6, 7 (Yorkshire won by 163 runs)
  b H.Howell   14 243   9 3 25 3 C.S.Baker c E.R.Wilson 110
                                         E.J.Smith c E.R.Wilson
                                         P.Jeeves c A.Dolphin
  c and b S.Santall   1 126   11.5 3 16 3 J.H.Parsons c A.Dolphin 96
                                         E.J.Smith c D.Denton
                                         H.Howell b

672. Yorkshire v Middlesex, Bramall Lane, August 10, 11, 12 (Yorkshire won by two wickets)

c and b H.W.Lee   9   345   24   6   68   6   J.W.Hearne lbw   175
                                          E.H.Hendren lbw
                                          E.L.Kidd lbw
                                          C.A.Saville b
                                          H.R.Murrell lbw
                                          J.T.Hearne st A.Dolphin
run out   7   89-8   27   6   60   1   E.L.Kidd c G.H.Hirst   255   1

673. Yorkshire v Surrey, Lord's, August 13, 14, 15 (Surrey won by an innings and 30 runs)

b P.G.H.Fender   29   204   38.5   6   134   2   T.W.Hayward c B.B.Wilson 549-6d
                                          P.G.H.Fender b
b J.W.Hitch   2   315

674. Yorkshire v Sussex, Bradford, August 17, 18, 19 (Yorkshire won by an innings and 183 runs)

c H.L.Wilson b J.H.Vincett 113   443   12.4   5   13   4   A.E.Relf lbw   111
                                          M.W.Tate c M.W.Booth
                                          G.Leach c G.H.Crawford
                                          G.B.Street c A.Dolphin
                          10   1   24   2   E.H.Bowley lbw   149
                                          H.L.Wilson c M.W.Booth

675. Yorkshire v Gloucestershire, Bristol, August 24, 25 (Yorkshire won by an innings and 227 runs)

b B.Cranfield   27   405   94   1
                                                     84

676. Yorkshire v Somerset, Weston-super-Mare, August 27, 28 (Yorkshire won by 140 runs)

c and b
    B.de la C.Hylton-Stewart 1   162   44   1
lbw b E.Robson   25   112   90

677. Yorkshire v Sussex, Hove, August 31, September 1, 2 (Match drawn)

c N.J.Holloway b J.Vine   54   461   32   1   143   3   H.L.Wilson c E.Oldroyd   405
                                          G.R.Cox lbw
                                          N.J.Holloway c A.Dolphin
c G.B.Street b J.H.Vincett   9   123-6

SEASON'S AVERAGES

Batting and Fielding	M	I	NO	Runs	HS	Ave	100	50	Ct
Championship	27	44	1	1176	113	27.34	1	8	35
Other Yorkshire matches	3	3	1	149	105*	74.50	1	-	1
Other matches	1	2	0	52	52	26.00	-	1	-
Season	31	49	2	1377	113	29.29	2	9	36
Career	677	1005	138	25945	201	29.92	38	125	490

Bowling	O	M	R	W	BB	Ave	5i	10m
Championship	775.4	200	1965	110	7-19	17.86	5	1
Other Yorkshire matches	49	9	155	7	3-39	22.14	-	-
Other matches	16	5	37	1	1-37	37.00	-	-
Season (6-ball)	840.4	214	2157	118	7-19	18.27	5	1
Career (6-ball)	16839.1	4426 ⎫	47360	2735	9-24	17.31	204	51
(5-ball)	2748.4	1029 ⎭						

1919

After spending the war working at a munitions factory and playing on Saturday afternoons for various league clubs Rhodes returned to the first-class game fully fit and refreshed. Reduced to two days the County Championship was won by Yorkshire but the performance was, perhaps, slightly devalued by the playing conditions. All told he took 164 wickets at 14.42 and stood first amongst the wicket-takers. This included a match analysis of 11-52 in the opening match against Gloucestershire at Gloucester and he also had 8-44 in the second innings against Warwickshire at Bradford. He had not bowled so well perhaps since his first four seasons and his length and spin off the wickets showed him to great advantage. Owing to his efforts in an ordinary bowling eleven his batting seemed secondary and he made only one century, 135 against Hampshire at Dewsbury.

	Own Team Total	O	M	R	W		Opp Total	Ct

678. Yorkshire v Gloucestershire, Gloucester, May 26, 27 (Yorkshire won by an innings and 63 runs)

	Own Team Total	O	M	R	W		Opp Total	Ct
c C.W.L.Parker								
b A.E.Dipper	72 277	15.4	5	47	7	A.K.G.White st A.Dolphin	125	
						A.E.Dipper c G.H.Hirst		
						W.H.Rowlands b		
						E.B.T.Studd c W.E.Blackburne		
						F.G.Robinson b		
						C.W.L.Parker c H.M.Claughton		
						W.Jeffries st A.Dolphin		
		3.3	1	5	4	F.J.Seabrook b	89	
						A.W.Barrow c P.Holmes		
						C.W.L.Parker c D.Denton		
						W.Jeffries st A.Dolphin		

679. Yorkshire v MCC, Lord's, May 29, 30, 31 (Match drawn)

	Own Team Total	O	M	R	W		Opp Total	Ct
b H.Watson	7 120	31	4	113	0		488	1
lbw b H.Watson	11 528-8d	1.4	0	2	1	J.W.Hearne lbw	38-3	

680. Yorkshire v Cambridge University, Fenner's, June 2, 3 (Match drawn)

	Own Team Total	O	M	R	W		Opp Total	Ct
c F.S.G.Calthorpe								
b A.E.R.Gilligan	7 383	25	7	50	2	J.C.W.MacBryan		
						c A.Dolphin	170	1
						J.S.F.Morrison c H.Sutcliffe		
not out	38 80-0	26	8	40	1	C.P.Johnstone lbw	300	

681. Yorkshire v Essex, Leyton, June 4, 5 (Match drawn)

	Own Team Total	O	M	R	W		Opp Total	Ct
c C.A.G.Russell b B.Tremlin	5 348	30	7	72	0		354	1
		-	-	-	-		55-1	

682. Yorkshire v Lancashire, Old Trafford, June 9, 10 (Lancashire won by 140 runs)

	Own Team Total	O	M	R	W		Opp Total	Ct
c C.H.Parkin b H.Dean	37 232	24.5	4	74	5	J.T.Tyldesley c G.H.Hirst	319	
						C.Hallows b		
						H.Dean c G.H.Hirst		
						C.H.Parkin c G.H.Hirst		
						C.S.Marriott c R.Kilner		
c J.C.H.L.Hollins								
b C.H.Parkin	7 153	23.5	8	49	4	J.W.H.Makepeace		
						c W.E.Blackburne	206-9d	1
						J.D.Tyldesley st A.Dolphin		
						R.A.Boddington c P.Holmes		
						C.H.Parkin st A.Dolphin		

683. Yorkshire v Warwickshire, Edgbaston, June 13, 14 (Yorkshire won by an innings and 63 runs)

	Own Team Total	O	M	R	W		Opp Total	Ct
c A.F.Lane b H.L.Benjamin	35 371-8d	6.3	0	16	5	S.H.Bates st A.Dolphin	115	
						A.F.Lane st A.Dolphin		
						H.L.Benjamin b		
						H.Austin c E.Robinson		
						H.Howell c P.Holmes		
		29	10	63	4	S.H.Bates c P.Holmes	193	
						C.Charlesworth lbw		
						William Quaife c D.C.F.Burton		
						H.Austin lbw		

684. Yorkshire v A.I.F., Bramall Lane, June 16, 17, 18 (A.I.F. won by one wicket)

	Own Team Total	O	M	R	W		Opp Total	Ct
c C.B.Willis b C.S.Winning	90 224	25	6	69	4	H.L.Collins c A.Dolphin	265	
						A.W.Lampard c R.Kilner		
						W.S.Stirling b		
						J.M.Gregory c H.Sutcliffe		
c W.L.Trennery								
b J.M.Gregory	5 210	17	6	37	2	W.S.Stirling lbw	170-9	
						E.A.Bull c R.Kilner		

685. Yorkshire v Derbyshire, Bradford, June 20, 21 (Yorkshire won by ten wickets)

	Own Team Total	O	M	R	W		Opp Total	Ct
c G.Beet b W.Bestwick	6 221	3	0	5	0		74	
not out	11 26-0	18.5	9	23	3	G.Beet c A.Dolphin	172	1
						J.Horsley st A.Dolphin		
						L.E.Flint c A.C.Williams		

686. Yorkshire v Nottinghamshire, Bramall Lane, June 27, 28 (Nottinghamshire won by six wickets)
c G.Gunn b F.Barratt   0   112   21.5   7   74   7   G.Gunn b   236   3
                                                                  J.Hardstaff, sen. c and b
                                                                  W.E.G.Payton lbw
                                                                  W.A.Flint c and b
                                                                  F.Barratt c N.Kilner
                                                                  T.L.Richmond c A.Dolphin
                                                                  B.Flint c and b
b F.Barratt   1   238   14   4   40   1   G.M.Lee st A.Dolphin   117-4

687. Yorkshire v Kent, Headingley, June 30, July 1 (Match drawn)
lbw b W.J.Fairservice   0   64   26.4   10   35   5   James Seymour b   169
                                                                  F.E.Woolley lbw
                                                                  G.de L.Hough st A.Dolphin
                                                                  W.J.Fairservice b
                                                                  A.P.Freeman b
did not bat   -   8-0

688. Yorkshire v Derbyshire, Chesterfield, July 2, (3) (Match drawn)
not out   82   251-6   12   4   16   1   A.Morton lbw   87

689. Yorkshire v Nottinghamshire, Trent Bridge, July 4, 5 (Match drawn)
b T.L.Richmond   39   232   36   10   83   3   G.Gunn b   197   1
                                                                  F.Barratt c D.C.F.Burton
                                                                  T.W.Oates c A.Dolphin
                                            28   11   27   4   G.Gunn c E.Smith (Ossett)   74-4
                                                                  G.M.Lee c A.Dolphin
                                                                  J.R.Gunn st A.Dolphin
                                                                  A.W.Carr c E.Smith (Ossett)

690. Yorkshire v Essex, Hull, July 7, 8 (Yorkshire won by an innings and 58 runs)
not out   47   241   13.2   9   8   3   E.J.Freeman lbw   106
                                                                  B.J.Strutton c G.H.Hirst
                                                                  F.J.Scoulding c R.Kilner
                                            7.1   3   22   2   B.Tremlin c H.Sutcliffe   77
                                                                  B.J.Strutton b

691. Yorkshire v Hampshire, Dewsbury, July 11, 12 (Yorkshire won by an innings and 143 runs)
c A.S.Kennedy
   b G.N.Bignell   135 401-8d   -   -   -   -   82
                                            24   4   66   6   B.G.von B.Melle
                                                                      c A.Waddington   176
                                                                  G.Brown b
                                                                  L.H.Tennyson st A.Dolphin
                                                                  A.S.Kennedy st A.Dolphin
                                                                  T.O.Jameson c E.Robinson
                                                                  L.G.Black c D.Denton

692. Yorkshire v Northamptonshire, Bramall Lane, July 14, 15 (Yorkshire won by 74 runs)
c W.A.Buswell b W.Wells 4   85   11   3   19   4   C.N.Woolley lbw   149   2
                                                                  W.Wells c E.Robinson
                                                                  L.J.Davies c and b
                                                                  B.Wright b
lbw b W.Wells   15   273   9   2   29   4   F.I.Walden b   135   2
                                                                  L.J.Davies st T.H.Hoyle
                                                                  W.A.Buswell lbw
                                                                  B.Wright c and b

693. Yorkshire v Leicestershire, Huddersfield, July 18, 19 (Match drawn)
c sub b A.Skelding   5   215   23   9   35   0   223   1
not out   78   314-6d   13   7   11   1   G.B.F.Rudd lbw   127-4

694. Yorkshire v Surrey, Bradford, July 21, 22 (Yorkshire won by ten wickets)
b T.Rushby   16   264   20   6   50   4   A.Ducat lbw   143
                                                                  A.Sandham b
                                                                  J.W.Hitch lbw
                                                                  E.C.Kirk st A.Dolphin
did not bat   -   25-0   23   9   50   3   J.B.Hobbs c H.Sutcliffe   145
                                                                  A.E.R.Gilligan c E.Robinson
                                                                  H.Strudwick st A.Dolphin

695. Yorkshire v Northamptonshire, Northampton, July 23, 24 (Yorkshire won by an innings and 196 runs)
not out   36   380-3d   20   5   34   4   C.N.Woolley b   72
                                                                  M.Cox b
                                                                  W.Wells lbw
                                                                  L.J.Davies c A.Dolphin

```
                                    20   6  33  6  C.N.Woolley lbw                112    3
                                                    R.A.Haywood b
                                                    John Seymour b
                                                    L.E.Holland c and b
                                                    W.Wells lbw
                                                    W.A.Buswell c and b
```

696. Yorkshire v Gloucestershire, Headingley, July 25, 26 (Yorkshire won by an innings and 125 runs)

```
c F.G.Robinson b F.E.Ellis   0  448-4d  22  13  32  2  P.F.C.Williams c P.Holmes  121
                                                        B.S.Bloodworth c E.Robinson
                                        16.1  6  57  2  P.G.Robinson b             202    2
                                                        F.G.Robinson c P.Holmes
```

697. Yorkshire v Sussex, Harrogate, August 1, 2 (Sussex won by five wickets)

```
c G.R.Cox b A.E.Relf   65  187  20  3  46  5  V.W.C.Jupp c G.Wilson        271
                                              A.E.Relf c R.Kilner
                                              G.R.Cox lbw
                                              M.W.Tate lbw
                                              A.H.H.Gilligan c H.Sutcliffe
b M.W.Tate              8  228   8  3  19  0                               145-5
```

698. Yorkshire v Lancashire, Bramall Lane, August 4, 5 (Match drawn)

```
not out                16  317-5  17.2  7  31  4  J.D.Tyldesley lbw        124
                                                  R.K.Tyldesley lbw
                                                  R.A.Boddington b
                                                  C.H.Parkin lbw
                                  23  8  47  0                            271-6
```

699. Yorkshire v Leicestershire, Aylestone Road, Leicester, August 8, 9 (Yorkshire won by an innings and 126 runs)

```
c T.E.Sidwell
  b W.E.Benskin  69  423   5  2   6  1  J.S.Curtis c A.Waddington  161
                          9  3  18  0                             136
```

700. Yorkshire v Surrey, Kennington Oval, August 11, 12 (Match drawn)

```
c H.Strudwick b J.W.Hitch  0  243  16.3  3  62  4  J.N.Crawford c R.Kilner     324
                                                   C.T.A.Wilkinson c A.Dolphin
                                                   J.W.Hitch b
                                                   H.Strudwick lbw
not out                    4  110-4  10  1  30  0                          189-4d  1
```

701. Yorkshire v Middlesex, Headingley, August 15, 16 (Yorkshire won by 187 runs)

```
b C.H.Gunasekara   8  190    24.1  5  80  5  H.W.Lee b                208
                                             E.H.Hendren lbw
                                             F.T.Mann lbw
                                             G.T.S.Stevens c H.Sutcliffe
                                             W.F.Lord b
st H.R.Murrell b J.W.Hearne  0  358-8d  18.3  2  42  5  E.H.Hendren c and b       153    2
                                                        G.T.S.Stevens c E.R.Wilson
                                                        C.H.Gunasekara st A.Dolphin
                                                        E.Martin b
                                                        H.R.Murrell c P.Holmes
```

702. Yorkshire v Warwickshire, Bradford, August 18, 19 (Yorkshire won by an innings and 91 runs)

```
c R.L.Holdsworth
  b G.A.Rotherham  56  381   9.2  1  31  2  R.L.Holdsworth
                                             c A.Waddington          183    1
                                           H.Howell lbw
                          12.2  1  44  8  C.Charlesworth
                                             c A.Waddington          107
                                           William Quaife c A.Waddington
                                           E.F.Waddy c E.Robinson
                                           R.L.Holdsworth c A.Dolphin
                                           F.S.G.Calthorpe c D.Denton
                                           G.A.Rotherham c A.Dolphin
                                           H.Howell c P.Holmes
                                           E.F.Field st A.Dolphin
```

703. Yorkshire v Middlesex, Lord's, August 21, 22 (Match drawn)

```
b N.E.Haig     0  187   21  2  56  4  P.F.Warner lbw             128
                                      J.W.Hearne b
                                      G.A.Fairbairn b
                                      H.R.Murrell c R.Kilner
did not bat    -  279-3d  21  4  45  1  N.E.Haig c H.Sutcliffe   234-8   1
```

704. Yorkshire v Kent, Dover, August 25, 26 (Match drawn)

run out	1	375-8d	24	9	25	2	L.P.Hedges c A.Dolphin	168	
							J.C.Hubble c R.Kilner		
			11	7	8	0		78-2	

705. Yorkshire v Hampshire, Southampton, August 27, (28) (Match drawn)

not out	7	242-3	18	2	60	3	E.L.Armitage lbw	201	
							G.N.Bignell lbw		
							F.P.Ryan b		

706. Yorkshire v Sussex, Hove, August (29), 30 (Match drawn)

lbw b G.R.Cox	26	187-6d	10	0	29	3	R.A.Young c and b	100	1
							M.W.Tate b		
							A.H.H.Gilligan lbw		
			4	1	10	1	R.R.Relf c E.Robinson	38-2	

707. Yorkshire v MCC, Scarborough, September 1, 2, 3 (Match drawn)

b N.E.Haig	5	175	27	7	46	1	N.E.Haig c P.Holmes	152	2
did not bat	-	95-1d	-	-	-	-		77-2	

708. Players v Gentlemen, Scarborough, September 4, 5, 6 (Players won by an innings and 110 runs)

b J.W.H.T.Douglas	52	397	21	6	42	4	R.H.Twining lbw	131	
							J.W.H.T.Douglas c A.Dolphin		
							G.E.V.Crutchley c J.W.Hearne		
							M.Falcon b		
			24.2	14	34	3	J.W.H.T.Douglas b	156	
							D.C.F.Burton c A.Dolphin		
							E.R.Wilson c G.H.Hirst		

709. Mr.C.I.Thornton's England XI v A.I.F., Scarborough, September 8, 9, 10 (Mr.C.I.Thornton's England XI won by two wickets)

lbw b. C.S.Winning	24	187	3	2	6	1	J.T.Murray b	81	
not out	23	191-8	20	5	50	1	H.L.Collins c R.H.Twining	296	2

710. Yorkshire v Rest of England, Kennington Oval, September 15, 16, 17, 18 (Rest of England won by ten wickets)

c R.H.Spooner b F.E.Woolley	19	246	30	4	112	2	J.N.Crawford c and b	493	1
							J.W.H.T.Douglas c D.C.F.Burton		
b A.S.Kennedy	65	286	-	-	-	-		40-0	

SEASON'S AVERAGES

Batting and Fielding	M	I	NO	Runs	HS	Ave	100	50	Ct
Players v Gentlemen	1	1	0	52	52	52.00	-	1	-
Championship	26	34	8	891	135	34.26	1	6	23
Other Yorkshire matches	5	9	1	247	90	30.87	-	2	5
Other matches	1	2	1	47	24	47.00	-	-	2
Season	33	46	10	1237	135	34.36	1	9	30
Career	710	1051	148	27182	201	30.10	39	134	520

Bowling	O	M	R	W	BB	Ave	5i	10m
Players v Gentlemen	45.2	20	76	7	4-42	10.85	-	-
Championship	797.3	236	1764	142	8-44	12.42	11	4
Other Yorkshire matches	182.4	42	469	13	4-69	36.07	-	-
Other matches	23	7	56	2	1-6	28.00	-	-
Season (6-ball)	1048.3	305	2365	164	8-44	14.42	11	4
Career (6-ball)	17887.4	4731 } 49725		2899	9-24	17.15	215	55
(5-ball)	2748.4	1029 }						

1920

Rhodes had another excellent season taking 161 wickets and apart from Hobbs' 17 wickets for a better average stood top of the averages again. For Yorkshire in the Championship he took 143 wickets at 12.90 and obtained more than ten wickets in a match on five occasions, his best innings performance being 8-39 against Sussex at Headingley and match performance 11-44 against Derbyshire at Derby. In effect Rhodes and Waddington carried the team on their shoulders and it is small wonder that his batting suffered once again. Although he did the 'double' again his batting was quite ordinary scoring only one century, 167* against Nottinghamshire at Headingley.

	Own Team Total	O	M	R	W		Opp Total	Ct

711. Yorkshire v Derbyshire, Bramall Lane, May 15, 17 (Yorkshire won by an innings and 223 runs)
c S.W.A.Cadman
    b T.Forester 51 419-6d | 16 | 8 | 13 | 1 | G.R.Jackson lbw 103 | 1
	8	6	2	4	A.Morton c A.Dolphin 93
					G.R.Jackson c A.Dolphin
					L.E.Flint c P.Holmes
					T.Forester b

712. Yorkshire v Lancashire, Bradford, May 22, 24, 25 (Yorkshire won by 22 runs)
b H.Dean 49 208 | 22 | 11 | 47 | 4 | J.W.H.Makepeace c and b 165 | 1
					G.E.Tyldesley lbw
					R.V.Bardsley c N.Kilner
					R.K.Tyldesley b
b H.Dean 12 144 | 17 | 5 | 27 | 0 | 165 | 1

713. Yorkshire v Warwickshire, Edgbaston, May 26, 27, 28 (Yorkshire won by 259 runs)
b F.S.G.Calthorpe 9 275 | 16.4 | 5 | 39 | 4 | C.Charlesworth b 170
					G.W.Stephens c P.Holmes
					F.R.Santall st A.Dolphin
					H.Howell c G.G.Macaulay
c E.J.Smith b H.Howell 10 247-6d	9.3	4	13	2	C.C.Smart c R.Kilner 93
					F.R.Santall c P.Holmes

714. Yorkshire v Gloucestershire, Gloucester, May 29, 31 (Yorkshire won by an innings and 55 runs)
c P.F.C.Williams
    b G.E.Dennett 64 229 | 0.3 | 0 | 1 | 1 | F.Rowlands lbw 60 | 1
| | 4 | 0 | 7 | 0 | 114 |

715. Yorkshire v Worcestershire, Worcester, June 2, 3 (Yorkshire won by an innings and 105 runs)
not out 53 472-3d | 24 | 8 | 30 | 2 | E.R.Nesfield b 162
| | | | | | F.H.Hunt c H.Sutcliffe |
| | 17 | 9 | 28 | 3 | F.H.Bowley b 205 | 1
| | | | | | A.N.Jewell b |
| | | | | | J.B.Higgins c and b |

716. Yorkshire v Nottinghamshire, Headingley, June 5, 7, 8 (Yorkshire won by ten wickets)
not out 167 324 | 13 | 3 | 30 | 1 | T.W.Oates lbw 215
did not bat - 50-0 | 16 | 6 | 21 | 0 | 157 | 1

717. Yorkshire v Cambridge University, Fenner's, June 9, 10, 11 (Yorkshire won by five wickets)
c G.E.C.Wood
    b G.A.Rotherham 17 236 | 9.3 | 0 | 44 | 3 | G.Ashton c E.Robinson 203
| | | | | | N.E.Partridge c G.G.Macaulay |
| | | | | | A.E.R.Gilligan b |
lbw b A.E.R.Gilligan 12 113-5 | 16 | 4 | 36 | 7 | G.E.C.Wood st A.Dolphin 145 | 1
					C.P.Johnstone lbw
					G.Ashton c E.Robinson
					G.Wilson b
					G.P.Brooke-Taylor c and b
					N.E.Partridge c N.Kilner
					A.P.F.Chapman b

718. Yorkshire v Middlesex, Lord's, June 12, 14, 15 (Match drawn)
c E.L.Kidd b N.E.Haig 37 303 | 32.3 | 11 | 47 | 4 | J.W.Hearne c and b 153 | 1
					P.F.Warner c E.Robinson
					E.L.Kidd lbw
					N.E.Haig lbw
					F.J.Durston lbw
	35	14	35	1	C.N.Bruce c E.Robinson 314-5	1

719. Yorkshire v Essex, Dewsbury, June 16, 17, 18 (Yorkshire won by 206 runs)
c P.Toone b J.G.Dixon 12 175 | 11 | 3 | 27 | 3 | C.A.G.Russell st A.Dolphin 159 | 1
| | | | | | N.H.Saint lbw |
| | | | | | P.Toone c P.Holmes |
c C.A.G.Russell b W.Reeves 66 347 | 21 | 11 | 20 | 5 | C.A.G.Russell b 157 | 1
					J.R.Freeman c G.G.Macaulay
					N.H.Saint lbw
					P.Toone b
					F.J.Scoulding c and b

720. Yorkshire v Surrey, Bramall Lane, June 19, 21, 22 (Surrey won by 204 runs)
```
c P.G.H.Fender b J.W.Hitch  34   199      30   11   46   6   A.Ducat c N.Kilner            305       1
                                                              A.Sandham  lbw
                                                              P.G.H.Fender  b
                                                              J.W.Hitch  lbw
                                                              H.Strudwick c A.Waddington
                                                              T.Rushby  lbw
c H.S.Harrison b J.W.Hitch   6   168      30    3   93   4   J.B.Hobbs c R.Kilner          266-9d
                                                              A.Sandham  c R.Kilner
                                                              H.S.Harrison  c A.Dolphin
                                                              G.M.Reay  c P.Holmes
```

721. Yorkshire v Leicestershire, Hull, June 23, 24 (Yorkshire won by an innings and 128 runs)
```
lbw b A.W.Shipman            4   316      13    8   10   0                                 119       1
                                           -    -    -   -                                  69
```

722. Yorkshire v Hampshire, Headingley, June 26, 28, 29 (Hampshire won by an innings and 72 runs)
```
c and b J.A.Newman           2   159      29    6   69   0                                 456-2d
run out                     64   225
```

723. Players v Gentlemen, Kennington Oval, June 30, July 1 (Players won by an innings and 87 runs)
```
c A.W.Carr b M.Falcon       28   384                                                      184       1
                                                                                          113
```

724. Yorkshire v Kent, Bramall Lane, July 3, (5), (6) (Match drawn)
```
                                                                                           36-0
```

725. Yorkshire v Northamptonshire, Bradford, July 7, 8 (Yorkshire won by 228 runs)
```
c F.I.Walden b A.E.Thomas    2   166       4    0   11   3   W.Wells c H.Sutcliffe          67
                                                              H.G.Beers c H.Sutcliffe
                                                              W.P.Walker c A.Dolphin
b W.Wells                    7   180-8d   10.5   5   16   5   R.A.Haywood c N.Kilner         51       1
                                                              W.Wells c E.Oldroyd
                                                              J.V.Murdin c P.Holmes
                                                              A.E.Thomas st A.Dolphin
                                                              W.A.Buswell b
```

726. Yorkshire v Derbyshire, Derby, July 10, 12, 13 (Yorkshire won by an innings and 71 runs)
```
did not bat                  -   219-3d   13.1   6   20   4   G.Beet lbw                     74
                                                              S.W.A.Cadman  b
                                                              W.Carter c R.Kilner
                                                              H.Wild  lbw
                                          17     7   24   7   L.Oliver  b                     74       1
                                                              A.Morton c A.Waddington
                                                              G.Beet st A.Dolphin
                                                              S.W.A.Cadman  b
                                                              H.Storer st A.Dolphin
                                                              W.Carter c D.C.F.Burton
                                                              H.Wild  c and b
```

727. Players v Gentlemen, Lord's, July 14, 15, 16 (Players won by seven wickets)
```
c H.Ashton
   b J.W.H.T.Douglas         6   225       2    0   13   0                                 230
did not bat                  -   130-3    14    2   38   2   V.W.C.Jupp c E.H.Hendren       124
                                                              J.W.H.T.Douglas  lbw
```

728. Yorkshire v Kent, Maidstone, July 17, 19, 20 (Kent won by 121 runs)
```
c J.C.Hubble
   b W.S.Cornwallis         21   358      34    3  113   5   H.T.W.Hardinge  lbw            447       1
                                                              James Seymour st A.Dolphin
                                                              F.E.Woolley c H.Sutcliffe
                                                              L.P.Hedges c D.Denton
                                                              J.C.Hubble c A.Dolphin
c J.C.Hubble b G.C.Collins  12   145       7    1   31   3   J.C.Hubble c and b             177       2
                                                              G.C.Collins c P.Holmes
                                                              W.S.Cornwallis  lbw
```

729. Yorkshire v Gloucestershire, Huddersfield, July (21), 22, (23) (Match drawn)
```
did not bat                  -   101-1
```

730. Yorkshire v Nottinghamshire, Trent Bridge, July 24, 26, (27) (Match drawn)
```
b T.L.Richmond              20   327      17    7   38   0                                  77-2
```

731. Yorkshire v Warwickshire, Harrogate, July 28, 29 (Yorkshire won by four wickets)
```
b F.S.G.Calthorpe            4    75      24    6   54   3   C.Charlesworth c E.Robinson 170
                                                              H.Venn c P.Holmes
                                                              E.J.Smith c P.Holmes
```

b C.Charlesworth 0 151-6 13.1 4 31 3 L.T.A.Bates lbw 54 2
William Quaife b
E.F.Waddy c and b

732. Yorkshire v Lancashire, Old Trafford, July 31, August 2, 3 (Match drawn)
lbw b L.Cook 15 253 22.3 3 60 4 A.W.Pewtress lbw 179 1
F.W.Musson c and b
J.D.Tyldesley c E.Robinson
C.H.Parkin st A.Dolphin
b C.H.Parkin 35 216-5d 24 7 49 3 R.H.Spooner st A.Dolphin 116-4
G.E.Tyldesley c H.Sutcliffe
J.Sharp st A.Dolphin

733. Yorkshire v Leicestershire, Aylestone Road, Leicester, August 4, 5, 6 (Match drawn)
c J.H.King b W.E.Astill 0 201-9 26 12 32 3 J.H.King lbw 202 3
S.Coe c and b
T.E.Sidwell b

734. Yorkshire v Worcestershire, Bramall Lane, August 7, 9 (Yorkshire won by an innings and 210 runs)
c E.W.Bale b C.R.Preece 78 377-5d 14 2 29 1 E.W.Bale c E.Robinson 80
  17.5 7 28 6 F.L.Bowley c H.Sutcliffe 87
J.W.C.Turner b
J.D.Abbott c D.Denton
W.H.Taylor c G.H.Hirst
E.W.Bale st A.Dolphin
J.B.Coventry c D.C.F.Burton

735. Yorkshire v Sussex, Headingley, August 11, 12, 13 (Match drawn)
b V.W.C.Jupp 5 224-9d 24 8 37 0   152
  23 9 39 8 V.W.C.Jupp lbw 91-9
J.Vine b
E.H.Bowley c H.Sutcliffe
R.A.Young lbw
M.W.Tate c R.Kilner
K.S.Ranjitsinhji c P.Holmes
A.H.H.Gilligan c A.Waddington
A.E.R.Gilligan c R.Kilner

736. Yorkshire v Middlesex, Bradford, August 14, 16, 17 (Middlesex won by 4 runs)
c E.H.Hendren b J.W.Hearne 0 169 23.4 6 53 7 C.H.L.Skeet c A.Waddington 105 1
H.W.Lee c and b
J.W.Hearne lbw
E.H.Hendren b
G.T.S.Stevens lbw
H.R.Murrell c E.Robinson
F.J.Durston c A.Waddington
b F.J.Durston 26 193 41.5 9 98 3 H.W.Lee c and b 261 2
N.E.Haig b
F.J.Durston lbw

737. Yorkshire v Essex, Southend-on-Sea, August 18, 19, 20 (Yorkshire won by 122 runs)
b G.M.Louden 1 307 26 5 60 3 P.A.Perrin c H.Sutcliffe 167
H.M.Morris c P.Holmes
J.W.H.T.Douglas c M.Leyland
did not bat - 81-2d 21 7 29 3 P.A.Perrin c A.Waddington 99
H.M.Morris c A.Waddington
J.W.H.T.Douglas lbw

738. Yorkshire v Surrey, Kennington Oval, August 21, 23, 24 (Surrey won by 31 runs)
b P.G.H.Fender 3 251 29 3 64 1 G.M.Reay c E.Robinson 325
c G.M.Reay b J.W.Hitch 0 153 18 8 28 3 A.Sandham c and b 110 1
A.Ducat st A.Dolphin
P.G.H.Fender lbw

739. Yorkshire v Sussex, Hove, August 25, 26, 27 (Sussex won by 162 runs)
lbw b V.W.C.Jupp 9 120 31 7 75 4 E.H.Bowley b 241
H.L.Wilson lbw
A.E.Relf b
M.W.Tate c A.Waddington
b V.W.C.Jupp 8 206 30 5 93 4 R.R.Relf c A.Waddington 247 1
V.W.C.Jupp st A.Dolphin
A.E.Relf c D.Denton
A.E.R.Gilligan b

740. Yorkshire v Hampshire, Portsmouth, August 28, 30, 31 (Yorkshire won by an innings and 235 runs)
not out 63 585-3d 16 4 56 5 E.I.M.Barrett b 131
J.A.Newman lbw
B.G.von B.Melle b
H.C.McDonell c G.H.Hirst
A.S.Kennedy b
25 3 73 6 H.A.W.Bowell c E.R.Wilson 219 1
E.I.M.Barrett st A.Dolphin
C.P.Mead b
L.H.Tennyson c P.Holmes
J.A.Newman st A.Dolphin
G.G.Harrison c P.Holmes

741. Yorkshire v MCC, Scarborough, September 2, 3, 4 (Yorkshire won by nine wickets)
lbw b J.W.Hearne 5 288 32 9 70 3 J.W.H.T.Douglas c P.Holmes 256-9d 1
F.T.Mann c D.Denton
C.D.McIver c P.Holmes
did not bat - 51-1 6 1 12 0 81

742. Players v Gentlemen, Scarborough, September 6, 7, 8 (Match drawn)
b E.R.Wilson 0 219 - - - - 276
c P.G.H.Fender b E.R.Wilson 6 326-7d 12 3 25 2 N.E.Haig c E.H.Hendren 131-9
P.G.H.Fender c C.A.G.Russell

743. MCC Australian Team v Mr.C.I.Thornton's XI, Scarborough, September 9, 10, 11 (MCC Australian Team won by an innings and 5 runs)
not out 71 456 3 0 10 0 261
- - - - 190

744. Rest of England v Middlesex, Kennington Oval, September 13, 14, 15 (Match drawn)
not out 29 603-5d 10 2 27 1 H.K.Longman
c C.A.G.Russell 318
6 4 2 0 192-4

SEASON'S AVERAGES

Batting and Fielding	M	I	NO	Runs	HS	Ave	100	50	Ct
Players v Gentlemen	3	4	0	40	28	10.00	-	-	1
Championship	27	36	3	949	167*	28.75	1	7	29
Other Yorkshire matches	2	3	0	34	17	11.33	-	-	2
Other matches	2	2	2	100	71*	-	-	1	-
Season	34	45	5	1123	167*	28.07	1	8	32
Career	744	1096	153	28305	201	30.01	40	142	552

Bowling	O	M	R	W	BB	Ave	5i	10m
Players v Gentlemen	28	5	76	4	2-25	19.00	-	-
Championship	918.1	276	1846	143	8-39	12.90	11	4
Other Yorkshire matches	63.3	14	162	13	7-36	12.46	1	1
Other matches	19	6	39	1	1-27	39.00	-	-
Season (6-ball)	1028.4	301	2123	161	8-39	13.18	12	5
Career (6-ball)	18916.2	5032 ⎤	51848	3060	9-24	16.94	227	60
(5-ball)	2748.4	1029 ⎦						

1920/21 - MCC in Australia

At the age of forty-three Rhodes made his last tour of Australia. His batting was not as prolific as before and his top score was only 73 in the Tests and his bowling accounted for only four wickets. Outside the Tests he was remarkably successful and the 'piece-de-resistance' was an innings of 210 in 315 minutes against South Australia at Adelaide. He added 368 with C.A.G.Russell for the second wicket which still stands as a record by an English team in Australia.

	Own Team Total	O	M	R	W		Opp Total	Ct
745. MCC v Victoria, Melbourne, November 12, 13, (15), 16 (MCC won by an innings and 59 runs)
did not bat - 418-3d - - - - 274 1

	19	4	39	6	R.E.Mayne c E.H.Hendren	85	

R.L.Park lbw
V.S.Ransford c P.G.H.Fender
J.Ryder b
A.G.Moyes st A.Dolphin
E.A.McDonald c J.W.H.T.Douglas

746. MCC v New South Wales, Sydney, November 19, 20, 22 (New South Wales won by six wickets)

b J.M.Gregory	4	236	-	-	-	-		153
lbw b C.Kelleway	26	250	3	1	6	0		335-4

747. MCC v Queensland, Exhibition Ground, Brisbane, November 27, 29, 30 (MCC won by an innings and 41 runs)

c and b S.W.Ayres	162	419	17	7	30	2	G.S.Moore c E.H.Hendren	186

F.C.Thompson c E.R.Wilson

			-	-	-	-		192

748. MCC v Australian XI, Brisbane, December 3, 4, 6 (Match drawn)

lbw b E.Trenerry	3	357	-	-	-	-		255	
			26	6	52	3	C.J.Tozer b	182	1

G.S.Moore c and b
H.Carter c F.E.Woolley

749. ENGLAND v AUSTRALIA, Sydney, December 17, 18, 20, 21, 22 (Australia won by 377 runs)

c J.M.Gregory b A.A.Mailey	3	190	-	-	-	-		267
c J.Ryder b A.A.Mailey	45	281	22	2	67	0		581

750. ENGLAND v AUSTRALIA, Melbourne, December 31, January 1, 3, 4 (Australia won by an innings and 91 runs)

b J.M.Gregory	7	251	8.3	1	26	1	W.A.S.Oldfield c and b	499	1
c H.L.Collins									
b W.W.Armstrong	28	157							

751. ENGLAND v AUSTRALIA, Adelaide, January 14, 15, 17, 18, 19, 20 (Australia won by 119 runs)

run out	16	447	5	1	23	0		354	1
lbw b E.A.McDonald	4	370	25.5	8	61	3	W.A.S.Oldfield b	582	

E.A.McDonald b
A.A.Mailey b

752. MCC v Victoria, Melbourne, February 4, 5, 7, 8 (MCC won by seven wickets)

lbw b E.A.McDonald	15	486	3.4	0	19	1	E.A.McDonald b	268
c J.L.Ellis b E.A.McDonald	5	78-3	12	4	20	2	J.L.Keating lbw	295

J.L.Ellis b

753. ENGLAND v AUSTRALIA, Melbourne, February 11, 12, 14, 15, 16 (Australia won by eight wickets)

c H.Carter b J.M.Gregory	11	284	-	-	-	-		389	1
c J.M.Gregory b A.A.Mailey	73	315	10	2	25	0		211-2	1

754. MCC v New South Wales, Sydney, February 18, 19, 21, 22 (Match drawn)

c W.A.S.Oldfield								
b A.A.Mailey	50	427	3	0	21	0		447
c A.A.Mailey								
b H.S.T.L.Hendry	17	381	7	1	23	0		151-2

755. ENGLAND v AUSTRALIA, Sydney, February 25, 26, 28, March 1 (Australia won by nine wickets)

c H.Carter b C.Kelleway	26	204	7	0	23	0		392
run out	25	280	7.2	1	20	0		93-1

756. MCC v South Australia, Adelaide, March 11, 12, 14, 15 (MCC won by an innings and 63 runs)

st A.M.Ambler b A.Smith	210	627	-	-	-	-		195
			9	3	24	0		369

SEASON'S AVERAGES

Batting and Fielding	M	I	NO	Runs	HS	Ave	100	50	Ct
Test matches	5	10	0	238	73	23.80	-	1	4
Other matches	7	9	0	492	210	54.66	2	1	2
Season	12	19	0	730	210	38.42	2	2	6
Career	756	1115	153	29035	210	30.15	42	144	558

Bowling	O	M	R	W	BB	Ave	5i	10m
Test matches	85.4	15	245	4	3-61	61.25	-	-
Other matches	99.4	26	234	14	6-39	16.71	1	-
Season (6-ball)	185.2	41	479	18	6-39	26.61	1	-
Career (6-ball)	19101.4	5073 ⎫	52327	3078	9-24	17.00	228	60
Career (5-ball)	2748.4	1029 ⎭						

1921

The all-conquering Australians arrived this year, captained by probably the largest man ever to captain a Test nation - W.W.Armstrong. Although he played in the First Test, Rhodes was dropped for the rest of the series, as England proceeded to try as many as thirty different players. Australia won the series three to nil which surprised nobody. This was Rhodes' last Test until he was recalled five years later. Once more he did the 'double' and also made his highest ever score, 267 not out against Leicestershire at Headingley. He took 7-80 in the 'Roses' match at Old Trafford in May but did not take more than nine wickets in any match.

	Own Team Total	O	M	R	W		Opp Total	Ct
757. Yorkshire v Hampshire, Southampton, May 7, 9, 10 (Match drawn)								
c A.S.Kennedy b J.A.Newman	41 220	21.4	6	42	3	B.G.von B.Melle c P.Holmes	242	
						J.A.Newman c D.C.F.Burton		
						W.H.Livsey c A.Dolphin		
not out	58 151-2	34	12	75	3	A.L.Hosie c C.T.Tyson	287	1
						L.H.Tennyson lbw		
						B.G.von B.Melle b		
758. Yorkshire v Australians, Bradford, May 11, 12, 13 (Match drawn)								
c H.L.Collins b W.W.Armstrong	63 224	23.5	3	87	5	H.L.Collins b	263	1
						C.G.Macartney c N.Kilner		
						J.M.Taylor c A.Dolphin		
						H.Carter c H.Sutcliffe		
						E.A.McDonald c D.C.F.Burton		
		6	3	13	1	W.Bardsley c E.Robinson	77-3	
759. Yorkshire v Lancashire, Old Trafford, May 14, 16, 17 (Match drawn)								
c B.Blomley b J.S.Heap	41 154	51	14	80	7	J.W.H.Makepeace		
						c A.Dolphin	239	
						J.Hallows c E.Oldroyd		
						G.E.Tyldesley c sub		
						J.Sharp c R.Kilner		
						J.D.Tyldesley c E.Oldroyd		
						J.S.Heap c G.G.Macaulay		
						R.K.Tyldesley c A.Waddington		
not out	0 116-2	25	11	36	2	J.Sharp st A.Dolphin	178-7d	
						J.S.Heap b		
760. Yorkshire v Warwickshire, Edgbaston, May 18, 19, 20 (Yorkshire won by 308 runs)								
c F.S.G.Calthorpe b A.L.Howell	14 89	8	2	15	2	William Quaife lbw	72	1
						B.W.Quaife lbw		
lbw b H.Howell	23 420	20.4	2	40	6	C.Charlesworth		
						c D.C.F.Burton	129	
						G.W.Stephens c A.Dolphin		
						B.W.Quaife c A.Dolphin		
						G.A.Rotherham c A.Dolphin		
						H.Howell st A.Dolphin		
						A.L.Howell lbw		
761. Yorkshire v Gloucestershire, Gloucester, May 12, 13, 14 (Yorkshire won by 258 runs)								
c P.T.Mills b C.W.L.Parker	9 213	33	26	19	3	A.E.Dipper c E.Oldroyd	165	1
						P.F.C.Williams c D.C.F.Burton		
						P.T.Mills c and b		
c and b F.E.Ellis	45 316-6d	6	3	14	3	F.Rowlands c E.Oldroyd	106	
						B.H.Lyon lbw		
						P.T.Mills b		
762. ENGLAND v AUSTRALIA, Trent Bridge, May 28, 30 (Australia won by ten wickets)								
c H.Carter b J.M.Gregory	19 112	13	3	33	2	C.E.Pellew c and b	232	2
						T.J.E.Andrews c and b		
c H.Carter b E.A.McDonald	10 147	-	-	-	-		30-0	

763. Yorkshire v Derbyshire, Hull, June 1, 2 (Yorkshire won by an innings and 112 runs)
  c G.A.Buckley b A.Morton   3   240   14   7   22   2   S.W.A.Cadman
                                                           c A.Waddington   105
                                                           H.Elliott lbw
                              2   0   9   0   23   2
764. Yorkshire v Kent, Bradford, June 4, 6 (Kent won by nine wickets)
  b A.P.Freeman   18   211   19   4   49   2   L.H.W.Troughton
                                                           c E.Robinson   274   1
                                                           A.C.Wright c and b
  lbw b F.E.Woolley   0   111   -   -   -   -   49-1
765. Yorkshire v Middlesex, Lord's, June 8, 9, 10 (Middlesex won by an innings and 72 runs)
  lbw b N.E.Haig   17   221   42   11 108   5   H.W.Lee c P.Holmes   432
                                                           E.H.Hendren c A.Waddington
                                                           E.L.Kidd b
                                                           G.E.V.Crutchley b
                                                           A.R.Tanner st A.Dolphin
  b A.R.Tanner   0   139
766. Yorkshire v Leicestershire, Headingley, June 11, 13, 14 (Yorkshire won by an innings and 242 runs)
  not out   267   560-6d   18.1 5   37   3   J.H.King b   154
                                                           S.Coe b
                                                           H.C.Snary b
                                        16.4 6   29   4   J.W.Middleton
                                                           c G.G.Macaulay   164   2
                                                           A.S.Matts b
                                                           H.C.Snary st W.R.Allen
                                                           F.Bale b
767. Yorkshire v Warwickshire, Bramall Lane, June 18, 20 (Yorkshire won by an innings and 140 runs)
  b F.S.G.Calthorpe   46   373   18.4 10 24   3   F.S.G.Calthorpe b   97
                                                           F.R.Santall lbw
                                                           A.L.Howell b
                                        12.2 3   33   4   F.R.Santall st W.R.Allen   136   1
                                                           R.I.Scorer c and b
                                                           G.A.Rotherham c G.G.Macaulay
                                                           T.W.Durnell b
768. Yorkshire v Surrey, Headingley, June 25, 27, 28 (Surrey won by 179 runs)
  c H.Strudwick b T.Rushby 12   228   29   11 47   2   H.A.Peach c R.Kilner   266
                                                           H.Strudwick c E.Oldroyd
  c H.Strudwick
    b P.G.H.Fender   0   153   28   5   77   2   J.W.Hitch c and b   294   1
                                                           W.J.Abel c H.Sutcliffe
769. Yorkshire v Gloucestershire, Bradford, June 29, 30 (Yorkshire won by an innings and 51 runs)
  c A.W.Roper
    b C.W.L.Parker   30   306   10   5   21   1   P.T.Mills c A.Waddington   136
                                        20.2 7   37   3   B.H.Lyon lbw   119   1
                                                           E.G.Dennett c E.Robinson
                                                           W.R.Gouldsworthy c and b
770. Yorkshire v Northamptonshire, Northampton, July 6, 7 (Yorkshire won by an innings and 194 runs)
  not out   104   383-6d   15   6   19   4   W.W.Timms c W.R.Allen   81
                                                           B.W.Bellamy c N.Kilner
                                                           K.J.Ball c W.R.Allen
                                                           J.V.Murdin c A.Waddington
                                        3.5   1   7   2   C.N.Woolley st W.R.Allen   108
                                                           A.E.Thomas c D.C.F.Burton
771. Yorkshire v Kent, Tunbridge Wells, July 9, 11, 12 (Yorkshire won by 31 runs)
  st J.C.Hubble b F.E.Woolley 23 190   14   5   44   2   G.N.Foster lbw   157   2
                                                           W.H.Ashdown b
  c J.C.Hubble b A.P.Freeman 12   231   16   3   43   1   J.L.Bryan c R.Kilner   233
772. Players v Gentlemen, Lord's, July 13, 14, 15 (Players won by nine wickets)
  c L.H.Tennyson
    b V.W.C.Jupp   30   360   -   -   -   -   129
  did not bat   -   42-1   2   0   14   0   272   1
773. Yorkshire v Sussex, Dewsbury, July 16, 18, 19 (Yorkshire won by nine wickets)
  c G.B.Street b R.R.Relf   46   394   11   6   11   2   V.W.C.Jupp c G.G.Macaulay 132
                                                           M.W.Tate c N.Kilner
  did not bat   -   34-1   13   2   29   3   E.H.Bowley c G.G.Macaulay 295   2
                                                           M.W.Tate c and b
                                                           W.L.Cornford st W.R.Allen

91

774. Yorkshire v Australians, Bramall Lane, July 20, 21, 22 (Australians won by 175 runs)
  lbw b J.M.Gregory   3   126   11   1   27   1   W.A.S.Oldfield lbw   251
  c W.A.S.Oldfield
        b J.M.Gregory   6   113   10   4   12   3   T.J.E.Andrews b   163   2
                                                           C.E.Pellew c E.R.Wilson
                                                           J.M.Gregory c and b

775. Yorkshire v Nottinghamshire, Trent Bridge, July 23, 25, 26 (Yorkshire won by an innings and 48 runs)
  c T.W.Oates b F.Barratt 24   438-9d 11.4 4   14   2   J.Hardstaff, sen. b   174   2
                                                           W.W.Whysall b
                                        21   6   49   3   G.Gunn c E.Robinson   216
                                                           G.M.Lee c R.Kilner
                                                           A.W.Carr b

776. Yorkshire v Northamptonshire, Harrogate, July 27, 28 (Yorkshire won by an innings and 397 runs)
  not out   6   548-4d   58
                                                                                       93

777. Yorkshire v Lancashire, Headingley, July 30, August 1, 2 (Match drawn)
  b L.W.Cook   9   489   21.3 12 24   3   J.W.H.Makepeace
                                                                c E.Robinson   153
                                                           J.R.Barnes b
                                                           M.N.Kenyon c P.Holmes
                                        14   2   36   0   144-3

778. Yorkshire v Leicestershire, Aylestone Road, Leicester, August 3, 4, 5 (Match drawn)
  c J.H.King b A.W.Shipman 55 452-8d 26.3 12 46   6   A.T.Sharp c G.H.Hirst   120
                                                           S.Coe lbw
                                                           G.B.F.Rudd b
                                                           G.Geary lbw
                                                           T.E.Sidwell c R.Kilner
                                                           A.W.Shipman c D.C.F.Burton
                                        10   2   11   1   W.E.Astill b   72-6

779. Yorkshire v Nottinghamshire, Huddersfield, August 6, 8, 9 (Yorkshire won by 113 runs)
  c A.W.Carr b T.L.Richmond 22 205   17   2   30   4   J.Hardstaff, sen. lbw   136
                                                           W.E.G.Payton b
                                                           S.J.Staples c G.Wilson
                                                           T.L.Richmond c R.Kilner
  b G.M.Lee   15   173   25   8   74   5   G.Gunn c E.Robinson   129
                                                           A.W.Carr c D.C.F.Burton
                                                           J.Hardstaff, sen. c P.Holmes
                                                           W.E.G.Payton b
                                                           T.W.Oates c H.Sutcliffe

780. Yorkshire v Middlesex, Bramall Lane, August 10, (11), (12) (Match drawn)
  did not bat   -   0-0   10   7   5   2   G.T.S.Stevens lbw   82
                                                           H.R.Murrell b

781. Yorkshire v Essex, Bradford, August 13, 15, 16 (Yorkshire won by an innings and 80 runs)
  b H.W.Smith   30   292-7d 13   8   15   1   P.A.Perrin c A.Waddington   66
                                        11   0   37   1   J.R.Freeman c H.Sutcliffe   146

782. Yorkshire v Surrey, Kennington Oval, August 20, 22, 23 (Match drawn)
  c sub b P.G.H.Fender   65   388   24.1 7   38   6   T.F.Shepherd st W.R.Allen   129   1
                                                           D.J.Knight c and b
                                                           M.Howell st W.R.Allen
                                                           P.G.H.Fender c W.R.Allen
                                                           H.A.Peach c A.Waddington
                                                           J.H.Lockton c H.Sutcliffe
                                        24   10 44   2   T.F.Shepherd lbw   210-8
                                                           H.A.Peach c W.R.Allen

783. Yorkshire v Essex, Leyton, August 24, 25, 26 (Match drawn)
  not out   102 283-6d 27   9   45   1   C.A.G.Russell lbw   226   1
                                        4   1   6   0   202-7

784. Yorkshire v Sussex, Hove, August 27, 29, 30 (Yorkshire won by 188 runs)
  b A.E.R.Gilligan   12   332   13   4   20   1   E.H.Bowley c E.Robinson   207
  c G.R.Cox b N.J.Holloway 35   199-8d 12.2 6   27   5   R.A.Young c G.G.Macaulay   136
                                                           H.L.Wilson st W.R.Allen
                                                           M.W.Tate c E.Robinson
                                                           G.R.Cox st W.R.Allen
                                                           N.J.Holloway st W.R.Allen

785. Yorkshire v MCC, Scarborough, September 1, 2, 3 (Yorkshire won by two wickets)
  not out   54   154   9   2   14   0   143

b A.S.Kennedy   19 143-8   10   2   31   1   G.E.V.Crutchley c R.Kilner 153-8d

786. Players v Gentlemen, Scarborough, September 5, 6, 7 (Players won by 198 runs)
b N.E.Haig   6   302   16   4   28   2   N.E.Haig b   142   1
                                                     J.W.H.T.Douglas b
not out   11 207-6d 16   7   27   3   J.W.H.T.Douglas c and b 169   2
                                                     F.T.Mann b
                                                     G.T.S.Stevens c F.E.Woolley

787. Mr.C.I.Thornton's XI v Australians, Scarborough, September 8, 9, 10 (Mr.C.I.Thornton's XI won by 33 runs)
lbw b W.W.Armstrong   12 280   5   2   12   0   231
c A.A.Mailey
   b E.A.McDonald   12 146   12   5   25   1   W.W.Armstrong   162
                                                     c P.G.H.Fender

788. Rest of England v Middlesex, Kennington Oval, September 12, (13), 14, 15 (Rest of England won by nine wickets)
not out   38 345   22.4 8   41   3   J.W.Hearne   220
                                                     c J.W.H.T.Douglas
                                                     A.R.Tanner c H.Strudwick
                                                     F.J.Durston c H.Ashton
not out   7   39-1   19   9   20   2   H.W.Lee lbw   160
                                                     N.E.Haig b

SEASON'S AVERAGES

Batting and Fielding	M	I	NO	Runs	HS	Ave	100	50	Ct
Test matches	1	2	0	29	19	14.50	-	-	2
Players v Gentlemen	2	3	1	47	30	23.50	-	-	4
Championship	24	33	6	1184	267*	43.85	3	3	19
Other Yorkshire matches	3	5	1	145	63	36.25	-	2	3
Other matches	2	4	2	69	38*	34.50	-	-	-
Season	32	47	10	1474	267*	39.83	3	5	28
Career	788	1162	163	30509	267*	30.53	45	149	586

Bowling	O	M	R	W	BB	Ave	5i	10m
Test Matches	13	3	33	2	2-33	16.50	-	-
Players v Gentlemen	34	11	69	5	3-27	13.80	-	-
Championship	787.3	273	1488	117	7-80	12.71	7	-
Other Yorkshire matches	69.5	15	184	11	5-87	16.72	1	-
Other matches	58.4	24	98	6	3-41	16.33	-	-
Season (6-ball)	963	326	1872	141	7-80	13.27	8	-
Career (6-ball)	20064.4	5399 ⎫	54199	3219	9-24	16.83	236	60
(5-ball)	2748.4	1029 ⎭						

1921/22 - In India

Rhodes went to India for the first time and appeared in the European team. In two games he made two centuries and took nineteen wickets. In the first match at Bombay he made 156 and added 185 with J.H.Parsons for the third wicket and with the captain, F.G.Travers, added 106 for the fifth wicket. To add insult to injury he then took 7-56 in the Hindus first innings. Against the Parsees he made 183 in five hours and fifty minutes with one six and 12 fours. He added 107 with C.B.Fry for the sixth wicket and 157 with George Hirst for the seventh wicket. He took 12-59 in the match (5-26 and 7-33).

	Own Team Total	O	M	R	W		Opp Total	Ct
789. Europeans v Hindus, Bombay, November 14, 15, 16 (Europeans won by an innings and 108 runs)								
c J.G.Navle b M.H.Rana	156 347	27.3	16	26	7	S.M.Dalvi c J.H.Boyd	139	1
						V.A.Dalvi st W.H.Cummings		
						C.K.Nayudu c J.H.Parsons		
						D.B.Deodhar c J.H.Parsons		
						Maharaja of Patiala c and b		
						C.L.Nayudu c H.G.Garnett		
						P.Shrivram c C.B.Fry		

| | | | 11 | 7 | 18 | 0 | | 100 | |

790. Europeans v Parsees, Bombay, November 21, 22, 23 (Europeans won by an innings and 297 runs)

			O	M	R	W		Opp	Ct
c B.E.Kapadia b J.Parekh	183	482-8d	20	10	26	5	J.H.Elchidana b	102	
							B.S.Bhapoo b		
							K.M.Mistri c W.H.Cummings		
							B.E.Kapadia c F.F.Stileman		
							J.Parekh c A.L.Hosie		
			13	3	33	7	D.D.Driver c J.H.Parsons	83	
							S.N.Gandhi c F.F.Stileman		
							D.K.Kapadia c F.G.Travers		
							K.M.Mistri c J.H.Boyd		
							J.S.Warden st W.H.Cummings		
							K.K.Irani c W.H.Cummings		
							B.E.Kapadia c J.H.Boyd		

SEASON'S AVERAGES

Batting and Fielding	M	I	NO	Runs	HS	Ave	100	50	Ct
Europeans	2	2	0	339	183	169.50	2	-	1
Career	790	1164	163	30848	267*	30.81	47	149	587

Bowling		O	M	R	W	BB	Ave	5i	10m
Europeans	(6-ball)	71.3	36	103	19	7-26	5.42	3	1
Career	(6-ball)	20136.1	5435 ⎱ 54302		3238	9-24	16.77	239	61
	(5-ball)	2748.4	1029 ⎰						

1922

The Indian continent seems to have whetted Rhodes' appetite as on his return he again accomplished the 'double' as Yorkshire won the title again. He did the 'double' for Yorkshire alone in the Championship making 1,368 runs at 40.23 and taking 100 wickets at 12.32. His 6-13 against Sussex at Hove was his best bowling. *Wisden* states that he was not quite the bowling force of Macaulay, Roy Kilner or Waddington but his figures do not really bear this statement out. With the bat he made four centuries, all for Yorkshire, second only to Holmes and Oldroyd who made five each.

		Own Team Total	O	M	R	W		Opp Total	Ct
791. Yorkshire v Northamptonshire, Northampton, May 6, 8 (Yorkshire won by ten wickets)									
c B.W.Bellamy b W.Wells	14	112	11	2	39	2	C.N.Woolley b	81	2
							J.V.Murdin c H.Sutcliffe		
did not bat	-	12-0	12	7	6	4	C.Baker c R.Kilner	42	
							W.Wells st A.Dolphin		
							A.J.B.Wright b		
							T.E.Manning lbw		
792. Yorkshire v Glamorgan, Cardiff, May 10, 11 (Yorkshire won by an innings and 258 runs)									
did not bat	-	404-2d	-	-	-	-		78	1
			3	2	7	0		68	
793. Yorkshire v Worcestershire, Dudley, May 13, 15 (Yorkshire won by an innings and 220 runs)									
lbw b W.H.Taylor	13	421	19.3	9	24	5	J.B.Higgins lbw	111	
							E.L.Bunting c R.Kilner		
							C.V.Tarbox c N.Kilner		
							W.H.Taylor c A.Dolphin		
							H.A.Gilbert c A.Waddington		
			6	2	17	3	M.K.Foster lbw	90	
							J.H.Thursfield c E.Oldroyd		
							H.A.Gilbert c E.Robinson		
794. Yorkshire v Derbyshire, Derby, May 17, 18, 19 (Yorkshire won by 251 runs)									
b A.Morton	25	147	18	6	26	1	J.Bowden lbw	130	
not out	9	314-4d	-	-	-	-		80	
795. Yorkshire v Northamptonshire, Headingley, May 20, 22, 23 (Yorkshire won by an innings and 185 runs)									
run out	8	342	-	-	-	-		69	1
			4.3	1	6	2	C.N.Woolley c and b	88	1
							R.S.Venes c E.Robinson		

796. Yorkshire v Cambridge University, Fenner's, May 24, 25, 26 (Yorkshire won by nine wickets)
c C.T.Ashton b G.O.B.Allen 28 276 19.3 8 41 4 H.Ashton c R.Kilner 258
                                                          G.O.Shelmerdine c E.R.Wilson
  T.C.Lowry c.A Waddington
  F.B.R.Browne st A.Dolphin
did not bat - 55-1 12 7 12 4 A.G.Doggart lbw 72 1
  H.Ashton c and b
  G.O.Shelmerdine c N.Kilner
  T.C.Lowry b

797. Yorkshire v Leicestershire, Aylestone Road, Leicester, May 27, 29, 30 (Match drawn)
c G.B.F.Rudd b G.Geary 90 283 42 21 45 3 S.Coe b 298
  G.B.F.Rudd b
  T.E.Sidwell c E.R.Wilson
                      7 3 11 0 180-6

798. Yorkshire v Lancashire, Bramall Lane, June 3, 5, 6 (Yorkshire won by 6 wickets)
c R.K.Tyldesley
  b L.W.Cook 13 306 21 2 48 1 L.W.Cook lbw 307
not out 8 148-4 20 8 28 4 J.R.Barnes b 144
  J.D.Tyldesley c E.Robinson
  R.K.Tyldesley b
  L.W.Cook lbw

799. Yorkshire v Warwickshire, Edgbaston, June 7, 9, 10 (Yorkshire won by an innings and 152 runs)
did not bat - 453-2d 10.2 4 12 5 William Quaife b 123
  H.L.Simms c H.Sutcliffe
  N.E.Partridge c R.Kilner
  C.C.Smart c R.Kilner
  H.Howell st A.Dolphin
                        22 7 47 4 F.S.G.Calthorpe c A.Dolphin 178
  H.L.Simms b
  B.W.Quaife c A.Dolphin
  C.C.Smart b

800. Yorkshire v Surrey, Bradford, June 10, 12, 13 (Match drawn)
c H.Strudwick
  b T.F.Shepherd 2 283 34 21 40 1 A.Jeacocke c and b 317 1
                        5 2 13 0 133-2

801. Yorkshire v Middlesex, Lord's, June 14, 15, 16 (Yorkshire won by an innings and 21 runs)
lbw b N.E.Haig 19 339-7d - - - - 138 1
                       18.1 5 47 4 J.W.Hearne c A.Dolphin 180 1
  N.E.Haig c and b
  H.R.Murrell c A.Waddington
  C.H Gunasekara b

802. Yorkshire v Nottinghamshire, Bramall Lane, June 17, 19 (Nottinghamshire won by an innings and 75 runs)
lbw b F.Barratt 1 140 32 13 39 1 J.R.Gunn lbw 353
b T.L.Richmond 3 138

803. Yorkshire v Warwickshire, Huddersfield, June 21, 22 (Yorkshire won by an innings and 271 runs)
b A.L.Howell 15 495-5d 99 1
                                      125

804. Yorkshire v Kent, Headingley, June 24, 26, 27 (Yorkshire won by ten wickets)
b G.C.Collins 48 273-9d 4 1 21 0 163 1
did not bat - 24-0 - - - - 131

805. Yorkshire v Glamorgan, Headingley, July 1, 3, 4 (Yorkshire won by an innings and 103 runs)
b J.C.Clay 110 429-7d 161
                13.1 4 25 2 J.C.P.Madden-Gaskell
                                  c H.Sutcliffe 165 1
  J.Nash c E.Robinson

806. Yorkshire v Derbyshire, Bramall Lane, July 5, (6), 7 (Match drawn)
b H.Storer 13 202-6d 1 0 8 0 99
                       14 6 20 1 A.Morton c H.Sutcliffe 69-3

807. Yorkshire v Sussex, Hull, July 8, 10, 11 (Yorkshire won by an innings and 10 runs)
b A.E.R.Gilligan 2 125 12 1 43 6 G.B.Street c and b 95 1
  M.W.Tate c H.Sutcliffe
  H.E.Roberts c H.Sutcliffe
  A.H.H.Gilligan c E.Robinson
  T.E.R.Cook c H.Sutcliffe
  A.C.Watson c E.Oldroyd
                      - - - - 20 1

808. Yorkshire v Worcestershire, Bradford, July 12, (13), 14 (Match drawn)
did not bat - 214-4d 7 5 5 0 116
25 8 39 3 F.A.Pearson b 149-7
C.R.Preece c E.Oldroyd
J.P.Davies c R.Kilner

809. Yorkshire v Essex, Harrogate, July 15, 17, 18 (Match drawn)
not out 108 314-7d 22 10 43 4 C.J.H.Treglown st A.Dolphin 105 2
H.M.Morris c G.G.Macaulay
H.W.F.Franklin lbw
L.C.Eastman c E.Robinson
21 8 43 3 H.M.Morris lbw 149-9
J.O'Connor b
L.C.Eastman c E.Oldroyd

810. Yorkshire v Kent, Maidstone, July 19, 20, 21 (Yorkshire won by 166 runs)
c James Seymour
b W.H.Ashdown 24 344 14 2 28 0 259 1
b A.P.Freeman 68 228 14.5 7 20 3 L.P.Hedges c A.Waddington 147
J.C.Hubble lbw
L.H.W.Troughton lbw

811. Yorkshire v Nottinghamshire, Trent Bridge, July 22, 24, 25 (Yorkshire won by five wickets)
c W.A.Flint b J.R.Gunn 62 222 41 16 59 4 G.Gunn c E.Robinson 257
A.W.Carr c M.Leyland
S.J.Staples lbw
F.Barratt c H.Sutcliffe
not out 32 110-5 13 3 15 0 74 2

812. Yorkshire v Gloucestershire, Dewsbury, July 26, 27 (Yorkshire won by an innings and 7 runs)
c E.G.Dennett
b C.W.L.Parker 0 228 134 1
87 2

813. Yorkshire v Leicestershire, Bramall Lane, July 29, 31, August 1 (Yorkshire won by an innings and 199 runs)
c A.W.Shipman
b W.E.Astill 84 410 3.1 2 1 1 A.Skelding lbw 97
- - - - 114

814. Yorkshire v Lancashire, Old Trafford, August 5, (7), 8 (Match drawn)
lbw b D.V.Norbury 26 122 - - - - 118 1
not out 48 129-8 11 1 37 1 R.K.Tyldesley b 135

815. Yorkshire v Gloucestershire, Bristol, August 9, 10, 11 (Yorkshire won by six wickets)
lbw b P.T.Mills 12 66 8 4 15 1 P.T.Mills b 172 2
c J.G.W.T.Bessant
b C.W.L.Parker 22 167-4 20 11 24 5 C.L.Townsend b 58
A.E.Dipper b
H.Smith lbw
P.F.C.Williams st A.Dolphin
F.G.Robinson b

816. Yorkshire v Hampshire, Bradford, August (12), 14, 15 (Hampshire won by five wickets)
c C.P.Mead b A.S.Kennedy 14 56 14 3 46 1 H.A.W.Bowell lbw 113
lbw b A.S.Kennedy 21 116 4 2 5 0 60-5

817. Yorkshire v Middlesex, Headingley, August 16, 17, 18 (Match drawn)
b F.J.Durston 105 266 6 4 8 1 G.T.S.Stevens b 170
lbw b N.E.Haig 8 144-5d 8 2 15 0 85-2

818. Yorkshire v Surrey, Kennington Oval, August 19, 21, 22 (Match drawn)
not out 42 539-5d 13 3 42 1 D.J.Knight c P.Holmes 339
10 7 5 0 165-3

819. Yorkshire v Hampshire, Bournemouth, August 23, 24, 25 (Yorkshire won by ten wickets)
c J.A.Newman b G.S.Boyes 106 293 15 3 33 1 C.P.Mead lbw 272
did not bat - 25-0 - - - - 44

820. Yorkshire v Sussex, Hove, August 26, 28 (Yorkshire won by 92 runs)
lbw b M.W.Tate 0 42 - - - - 95
c K.A.Higgs b A.E.R.Gilligan 6 228 6 3 13 6 T.E.R.Cook c A.Dolphin 83 1
G.B.Street b
A.C.Watson c A.Waddington
A.H.H.Gilligan st A.Dolphin
H.E.Roberts lbw
G.A.Stannard c and b

821. Yorkshire v Essex, Leyton, August (30), (31), September 1 (Match drawn)
                       - - - -   5-1

822. Yorkshire v MCC, Scarborough, September 4, 5, 6 (Match drawn)
   b J.W.H.T.Douglas   44   337   22.5 16 16 3 M.Howell st A.Dolphin   180
                                              A.P.F.Chapman b
                                            H.D.G.Leveson-Gower c E.R.Wilson
   did not bat   - 157-2d   13   3 34 1 F.T.Mann b   130-7

823. Players v Gentlemen, Scarborough, September 7, 8, 9 (Match drawn)
   not out   71   227   22   10 31 3 J.W.H.T.Douglas lbw   325
                                              A.P.F.Chapman b
                                            A.H.Fawcett c F.E.Woolley
   did not bat   - 171-1   17   5 38 3 H.Ashton c W.H.Livsey   264-6d 1
                                              A.W.Carr c and b
                                            E.R.Wilson c F.E.Woolley

824. Mr.C.I.Thornton's XI v MCC South African XI, Scarborough, September 11, 12, (13) (Match drawn)
   not out   10 407-7d   23   7 53 1 P.G.H.Fender b   256
                              -     -   -   -   25-1

825. Yorkshire v Rest of England, Kennington Oval, September 15, 16, 18, (19) (Match drawn)
   c T.E.Sidwell b F.E.Woolley 19 233   25   6 61 4 F.E.Woolley st A.Dolphin 207 1
                                              E.H.Hendren hit wkt
                                            A.S.Kennedy lbw
                                            A.E.R.Gilligan b
   c T.E.Sidwell
       b P.G.H.Fender 96 274   -   -   -   -   27-0

826. North v South, Eastbourne, September 20, 21 (North won by seven wickets)
   b A.E.R.Gilligan   10 162   20   5 50 3 F.H.Gillingham c G.Gunn   160
                                              J.B.Hobbs c T.W.Oates
                                            H.T.W.Hardinge c C.H.Parkin
   lbw b C.W.L.Parker   0   62-3   9   4   9 2 H.T.W.Hardinge lbw   63
                                              A.H.H.Gilligan st T.W.Oates

827. Rest of England v Royal Air Force (Ex-Service), Eastbourne, September 23, 25 (Royal Air Force (Ex-Service) won by eight wickets)
   c and b F.E.Woolley   35 144   19.1 8 27 6 J.B.Hobbs lbw   196
                                              H.T.W.Hardinge lbw
                                            A.H.Gilligan b
                                            F.W.Musson c H.Strudwick
                                            G.Geary b
                                            A.Waddington b
   b C.W.L.Parker   17   76   6   2 11 1 F.E.Woolley c C.H.Parkin 25-2

SEASON'S AVERAGES

Batting and Fielding	M	I	NO	Runs	HS	Ave	100	50	Ct
Players v Gentlemen	1	1	1	71	71*	-	-	1	1
North v South	1	2	0	10	10	5.00	-	-	-
Championship	30	36	6	1181	110	39.36	4	4	25
Other Yorkshire matches	3	4	0	187	96	46.75	-	1	2
Other matches	2	3	1	62	35	31.00	-	-	-
Season	37	46	8	1511	110	39.76	4	6	28
Career	827	1210	171	32359	267*	31.14	51	155	615

Bowling	O	M	R	W	BB	Ave	5i	10m
Players v Gentlemen	39	15	69	6	3-31	11.50	-	-
North v South	29	9	59	5	3-50	11.80	-	-
Championship	605.4	231	1068	84	6-13	12.71	5	-
Other Yorkshire matches	92.2	40	164	16	4-12	10.25	-	-
Other matches	48.1	17	91	8	6-27	11.37	1	-
Season (6-ball)	814.1	312	1451	119	6-13	12.19	6	-
Career (6-ball)	20950.2	5747 }	55753	3357	9-24	16.60	245	61
(5-ball)	2748.4	1029 }						

1922/23 - In India

For the second time Rhodes visited India and he played four matches in all: two for the Europeans, one for All India (English) and one for a combined team of Muslims and Hindus (I do not remember ever seeing a photograph of Wilfred in a turban) against Europeans and Parsees. The second match was interrupted by an argument about the new ball being taken.

		Own Team Total	O	M	R	W		Opp Total	Ct
828. Muslims and Hindus v Europeans and Parsees, Bombay, November 27, 28, 29 (Europeans and Parsees won by 246 runs)									
c F.G.Travers									
b R.J.D.Jamshedji	29	163	23	5	57	2	F.E.Kapadia lbw R.J.D.Jamshedji c P.Shivram	302	
lbw b B.K.Kalapesi	79	172	26	3	99	3	A.L.Hosie lbw J.B.Higgins c M.H.Chandarana R.Kilner b	279-5d	
829. All India (English) v All India (Indians), Bombay, November 30, December 1, 2 (All India (English) won by seven wickets)									
b Abdul Aziz Khan	9	340	15	1	51	3	K.M.Mistri c F.G.Travers C.K.Nayudu c G.T.B.Harvey Abdus Salam c and b	163	2
not out	16	102-3	25	12	49	1	Abdus Salam c A.L.Hosie	277	
830. Europeans v Hindus, Lahore, March 2, 3, 4 (Europeans won by 306 runs)									
c Ramchand									
b Jagannath Mehta	71	218	8.1	5	6	3	On Karnath c M.A.Green Ramchand c F.R.S.Shaw B.N.Khanna c J.G.Smyth	51	
c Brij Lal									
b Jagannath Mehta	29	237	-	-	-	-		98	1
831. Europeans v Muslims, Lahore, March 5, 6, 7 (Europeans won by 169 runs)									
c Hassan Shah									
b Abdus Salam	8	227	14	4	31	3	Karim Baksh c G.H.Holland Iftekharuddin c G.H.Holland Nazir Hussain c G.H.Holland	80	
lbw b Saleh Mohammed	6	112	22.3	10	36	2	Iftekharuddin c J.G.Smyth Feroze Khan c M.G.Salter	90	1

SEASON'S AVERAGES

Batting and Fielding	M	I	NO	Runs	HS	Ave	100	50	Ct
Europeans	2	4	0	114	71	57.00	-	1	2
Other matches	2	4	1	133	79	44.33	-	1	2
Season	4	8	1	247	79	35.28	-	2	4
Career	831	1218	172	32606	267*	31.17	51	157	619

Bowling		O	M	R	W	BB	Ave	5i	10m
Europeans		44.4	19	73	8	3-6	9.12	-	-
Other matches		89	21	256	9	3-51	28.44	-	-
Season	(6-ball)	133.4	40	329	17	3-6	19.35	-	-
Career	(6-ball)	21084	5787	56082	3374	9-24	16.62	245	61
	(5-ball)	2748.4	1029						

1923

The fourteenth 'double' of Rhodes' career made the season noteworthy. His bowling was again exemplary and he continued the fine form he had shown since the war. He headed both batting and bowling averages although it would be true to say that Roy Kilner and Macaulay were more deadly day in and day out. He took ten wickets in a match on two occasions, his best innings performance being 7-15 against Gloucestershire at Bristol. With such good opening batsmen as Sutcliffe and Percy Holmes Rhodes dropped down the order and stood steadfast in the middle, the Yorkshire side being a model of consistency in all departments. He made two centuries: 126 against Middlesex at Bradford and 102 against Essex at Dewsbury.

	Own Team Total	O	M	R	W		Opp Total	Ct

832. Yorkshire v Glamorgan, Cardiff, May (5), 7, 8 (Yorkshire won by nine wickets)

	Own Team Total	O	M	R	W		Opp Total	Ct
b T.Arnott	34	93	-	-	-	-		63
did not bat	-	83-1	4	2	11	0		112

833. Yorkshire v Worcestershire, Worcester, May 9, 10 (Yorkshire won by an innings and 113 runs)

	Own Team Total	O	M	R	W		Opp Total	Ct
c J.F.MacLean b J.B.Coventry	20	358	-	-	-	-		76
			22	6	35	5	E.H.Bryant st.A.Dolphin	169
							C.V.Tarbox st A.Dolphin	
							J.F.Maclean c A.Waddington	
							C.F.Root c P.Holmes	
							V.W.Humpherson st A.Dolphin	

834. Yorkshire v Middlesex, Bradford, May 12, 14, 15 (Yorkshire won by an innings and 229 runs)

	Own Team Total	O	M	R	W		Opp Total	Ct
c C.B.Sharpe b J.W.Hearne	126	411-9d	15.5	5	29	5	J.W.Hearne st A.Dolphin	122
							E.H.Hendren b	
							G.E.V.Crutchley b	
							H.J.Wenyon c A.Dolphin	
							H.R.Murrell b	
			-	-	-	-		60

835. Yorkshire v Lancashire, Old Trafford, May (19), 21, 22 (Match drawn)

	Own Team Total	O	M	R	W		Opp Total	Ct
not out	10	126-5	17.4	7	22	2	L.W.Cook c M.Leyland	108
							J.W.Whewell c R.Kilner	

836. Yorkshire v Warwickshire, Edgbaston, May 23, 24, 25 (Yorkshire won by 84 runs)

	Own Team Total	O	M	R	W		Opp Total	Ct
c C.C.Smart b H.Howell	12	113	4	1	7	1	N.E.Partridge c G.Wilson	110	1
lbw b H.Howell	0	162-6d	-	-	-	-		81	1

837. Yorkshire v Kent, Bramall Lane, May 26, 28, 29 (Match drawn)

	Own Team Total	O	M	R	W		Opp Total	Ct
lbw b F.E.Woolley	2	180-6d	22.5	7	37	6	H.T.W.Hardinge c A.Waddington	136
							F.E.Woolley hit wkt	
							W.H.Ashdown lbw	
							R.T.Bryan b	
							L.H.W.Troughton c G.G.Macaulay	
							A.C.Wright b	
			5	4	1	1	F.E.Woolley c H.Sutcliffe	48-5

838. Yorkshire v Derbyshire, Derby, May 30, 31 (Yorkshire won by an innings and 126 runs)

	Own Team Total	O	M	R	W		Opp Total	Ct
run out	4	302-9d	11.4	1	19	2	J.M.Hutchinson lbw	104
							W.Bestwick c A.Dolphin	
			7	3	9	2	J.M.Hutchinson lbw	72
							H.Elliott c A.Waddington	

839. Yorkshire v Nottinghamshire, Headingley, June 2, 4, 5 (Nottinghamshire won by 3 runs)

	Own Team Total	O	M	R	W		Opp Total	Ct
c W.W.Whysall b F.C.Matthews	5	134	44	19	70	3	W.W.Whysall lbw	200
							W.E.G.Payton c A.Dolphin	
							T.W.Oates st A.Dolphin	
b S.J.Staples	36	158	12.5	2	23	6	A.W.Carr b	95	1
							J.Hardstaff, sen. c A.Waddington	
							W.E.G.Payton st A.Dolphin	
							T.W.Oates b	
							F.Barratt c H.Sutcliffe	
							T.L.Richmond c P.Holmes	

840. Yorkshire v Cambridge University, Fenner's, June 6, 7, 8 (Yorkshire won by 165 runs)

	Own Team Total	O	M	R	W		Opp Total	Ct
c C.T.Ashton b G.O.B.Allen	10	139	1	0	4	0		63
did not bat	-	238-0d	15.2	7	20	5	R.Aird c E.Oldroyd	149
							W.J.V.Tomlinson c N.Kilner	
							C.Booth lbw	
							N.B.Sherwell c A.Dolphin	
							G.O.B.Allen c G.Wilson	

841. Yorkshire v Middlesex, Lord's, June 9, 11, 12 (Yorkshire won by six wickets)

	Own Team Total	O	M	R	W		Opp Total	Ct
b H.W.Lee	24	168	31	11	47	1	E.H.Hendren c A.Dolphin	289
not out	23	225-4	5	0	13	3	R.H.Hill b	102	1
							H.J.Wenyon c and b	
							H.R.Murrell c E.Oldroyd	

842. Yorkshire v Northamptonshire, Northampton, June 13, 14 (Yorkshire won by an innings and 60 runs)
c A.E.Thomas b W.Wells   13   308   -   -   -   -   50   2
                                       4.5   1   16   1   B.Tyler st A.Dolphin   198   1

843. Yorkshire v Surrey, Bramall Lane, June 16, 18, 19 (Yorkshire won by 25 runs)
c T.F.Shepherd
   b P.G.H.Fender   6   278   18   4   39   2   W.J.Abel st A.Dolphin   224   1
                                                    H.A.Peach c A.Waddington
c A.Ducat b P.G.H.Fender   26   129   13   4   27   0   158

844. Yorkshire v Kent, Tonbridge, June 20, 21, 22 (Yorkshire won by 120 runs)
lbw b W.H.Ashdown   26   255   -   -   -   -   130
c F.E.Woolley b A.C.Wright   2   239   7   0   20   1   G.C.Collins lbw   244

845. Yorkshire v Essex, Leyton, June 23, 25, 26 (Yorkshire won by seven wickets)
lbw b C.A.G.Russell   32   152   45   20   53   4   J.R.Freeman lbw   251   1
                                                        H.M.Morris c and b
                                                        J.W.H.T.Douglas c N.Kilner
                                                        G.M.Louden b
not out   12   164-3   6.5   3   8   5   J.O'Connor c A.Drake   64
                                              J.W.H.T.Douglas c N.Kilner
                                              A.S.Moule c A.Waddington
                                              G.M.Louden b
                                              A.B.Hipkin b

846. Yorkshire v Northamptonshire, Bradford, June 27, 28 (Yorkshire won by an innings and 155 runs)
c C.N.Woolley b E.W.Clark 58   312   -   -   -   -   78   1
                                       -    -   -   -   79

847. Yorkshire v Sussex, Headingley, June 30, July 2, 3 (Yorkshire won by an innings and 33 runs)
c K.A.Higgs
   b A.E.R.Gilligan   88   412   18   6   31   4   G.B.Street c A.Dolphin   182
                                                       M.W.Tate c E.Oldroyd
                                                       G.R.Cox c G.G.Macaulay
                                                       H.E.Roberts c G.Wilson
                                    15.2 4   29   4   T.E.R.Cook c A.Waddington 197   2
                                                       M.W.Tate c E.Oldroyd
                                                       A.F.Wensley lbw
                                                       G.R.Cox lbw

848. Yorkshire v Warwickshire, Hull, July 4, 5, 6 (Yorkshire won by 96 runs)
c F.S.G.Calthorpe
   b H.Howell   1   170   26   14   33   1   F.S.G.Calthorpe b   249
c F.S.G.Calthorpe
   b H.Howell   19   311-9d   12   3   27   1   H.Howell st A.Dolphin   136   1

849. Yorkshire v Somerset, Hull, July 7, 9, 10 (Yorkshire won by an innnings and 130 runs)
st M.D.Lyon b K.G.Blaikie   3   446-6d   23   7   76   3   M.D.Lyon b   226   2
                                                              J.C.White c and b
                                                              J.Daniell b
                                           -    -   -   -   90

850. Yorkshire v Essex, Dewsbury, July 14, 16, 17 (Yorkshire won by 280 runs)
b J.W.H.T.Douglas   3   195   1   1   0   0   96
c A.S.Moule
   b C.A.G.Russell   102   332-6d   6   1   18   1   A.S.Moule c H.Sutcliffe   151

851. Yorkshire v Leicestershire, Huddersfield, July 18, 19, 20 (Yorkshire won by an innings and 173 runs)
c T.E.Sidwell b G.Geary   36   376   7   5   4   0   71   1
                                        27   14   24   4   G.H.S.Fowke c W.R.Allen 132   2
                                                           S.S.Coulson c and b
                                                           T.E.Sidwell b
                                                           A.W.Shipman lbw

852. Yorkshire v Gloucestershire, Bramall Lane, July 21, (23), 24 (Yorkshire won by ten wickets)
did not bat   -   280-3d   26.1 10   33   4   B.S.Bloodworth b   183
                                                  W.L.Neale b
                                                  W.R.Gouldsworthy b
                                                  E.G.Dennett b
did not bat   -   38-0   11.4   3   21   1   A.E.Waters lbw   133   1

853. Yorkshire v Gloucestershire, Bristol, July 25, 26, 27 (Yorkshire won by an innings and 18 runs)
b E.G.Dennett   14   352-9d   12.4   6   15   7   H.Smith   c E.Oldroyd   95
                                                     P.F.C.Williams   lbw
                                                     W.L.Neale   b
                                                     P.T.Mills   c A.Dolphin
                                                     H.J.D.Shrimpton   b
                                                     W.R.Gouldsworthy   b
                                                     J.G.W.T.Bessant   c H.Sutcliffe
                            30.2   10   62   4   A.E.Dipper   c and b   239   1
                                                     W.L.Neale   st A.Dolphin
                                                     E.G.Dennett   b
                                                     J.G.W.T.Bessant   c H.Sutcliffe

854. Yorkshire v Nottinghamshire, Trent Bridge, July (28), 30, 31 (Match drawn)
c T.W.Oates
   b F.C.L.Matthews   35   216   27.1   10   40   3   J.R.Gunn   lbw   131   1
                                                     T.L.Richmond   c G.G.Macaulay
                                                     F.C.Matthews   b
                             11.4   4   13   3   W.W.Whysall
                                                              c G.G.Macaulay   50-5
                                                     J.R.Gunn   c R.Kilner
                                                     W.E.G.Payton   b

855. Yorkshire v Worcestershire, Harrogate, August 1, (2), 3 (Yorkshire won by an innings and 37 runs)
did not bat   -   242-2d   -   -   -   -   42
                                 21   8   36   2   M.K.Foster   c N.Kilner   163
                                                     J.B.Coventry   c E.Robinson

856. Yorkshire v Lancashire, Bradford, August 4, 6, 7 (Yorkshire won by eight wickets)
c G.Duckworth
   b R.K.Tyldesley   5   213   7   4   6   0   188   1
did not bat   -   51-2   -   -   -   -   73   1

857. Yorkshire v Leicestershire, Aylestone Road, Leicester, August 8, 9, 10 (Yorkshire won by an innings and 74 runs)
b W.E.Benskin   0   311   43   20   46   4   W.E.Astill   st A.Dolphin   129
                                                     J.H.King   b
                                                     A.Mounteney   lbw
                                                     G.H.S.Fowke   c G.G.Macaulay
                                 23   10   30   4   W.E.Astill   lbw   108
                                                     A.T.Sharp   st A.Dolphin
                                                     G.H.S.Fowke   c E.Robinson
                                                     G.Geary   c E.Robinson

858. Yorkshire v Derbyshire, Bradford, August 11, 13, 14 (Yorkshire won by eight wickets)
c W.Carter b W.J.Horsley   22   196   43   20   60   7   S.W.A.Cadman   st A.Dolphin 197
                                                     H.Storer   c H.Sutcliffe
                                                     W.Carter   c P.Holmes
                                                     J.M.Hutchinson   lbw
                                                     B.S.Hill-Wood   c E.Oldroyd
                                                     W.J.Horsley   lbw
                                                     W.Bestwick   b
did not bat   -   124-2   14.5   3   28   1   B.S.Hill-Wood   lbw   121   1

859. Yorkshire v Hampshire, Headingley, August 15, 16, 17 (Match drawn)
lbw b W.R.de la C.Shirley   44   246   37   16   69   2   C.P.Mead   c H.Sutcliffe   327   1
                                                     W.R.de la C.Shirley   st A.Dolphin
c and b G.Brown   49   206-5d

860. Yorkshire v Glamorgan, Bramall Lane, August 18, 20, 21 (Yorkshire won by an innings and 34 runs)
not out   57   233   28   13   37   3   N.V.H.Riches   c A.Dolphin   110   2
                                                     J.Stone   c and b
                                                     C.F.Walters   lbw
                             21.2   6   26   5   D.Davies   c M.Leyland   89   1
                                                     F.B.Pinch   st A.Dolphin
                                                     C.F.Walters   c A.Dolphin
                                                     T.Arnott   c P.Holmes
                                                     J.Mercer   c M.Leyland

861. Yorkshire v Surrey, Kennington Oval, August 22, 23, (24) (Match drawn)
did not bat   -   88-2   43   17   103   2   A.Ducat   c E.Robinson   360   1
                                                     D.J.Knight   c P.Holmes

862. Yorkshire v Hampshire, Portsmouth, August 25, 27 (Yorkshire won by an innings and 88 runs)
c W.H.Livsey b A.S.Kennedy 1   206   66
                                                                         52

863. Yorkshire v Sussex, Hove, August (29), 30, 31 (Match drawn)
c G.R.Cox b M.W.Tate   30   135   129
not out   43   170-5d   48-5

864. Mr.H.D.G.Leveson-Gower's XI v West Indians, Scarborough, September 3, 4, 5 (Mr.H.D.G. Leveson-Gower's XI won by four wickets)
b L.N.Constantine   7   218   12   4   20   1   H.W.Ince b   110   1
c G.A.R.Dewhurst
    b G.N.Francis   0   31-6   20   4   37   4   G.Challenor b   135
                      H.B.G.Austin lbw
                      J.A.Small c F.W.Gilligan
                      L.N.Constantine c G.E.Tyldesley

865. Players v Gentlemen, Scarborough, September 6, 7, 8 (Match drawn)
b G.O.B.Allen   34   220   -   -   -   -   128   1
b G.O.B.Allen   10   297-7d   14   4   30   2   J.C.W.MacBryan
                      c H.Sutcliffe   264-7
                      G.O.B.Allen c A.Dolphin

866. Yorkshire v MCC, Scarborough, September 10, 11, 12 (Match drawn)
c and b P.G.H.Fender   1   181   16   5   46   0   348-9d   1
not out   84   322-5d

867. Yorkshire v Rest of England, Kennington Oval, September 14, 16, 17 (Match drawn)
not out   50   430-4d   17   6   37   2   E.H.Hendren
                      c G.G.Macaulay   273
                      F.E.Woolley c E.Oldroyd
did not bat   -   26-1

868. Capped v Uncapped, Hastings, September 19, 20, 21 (Uncapped won by eight wickets)
not out   79   165   315   1
lbw b R.Kilner   23   197   49-2

SEASON'S AVERAGES

Batting and Fielding	M	I	NO	Runs	HS	Ave	100	50	Ct
Players v Gentlemen	1	2	0	44	34	22.00	-	-	1
Championship	31	38	5	1023	126	31.00	2	3	29
Other Yorkshire matches	3	4	2	145	84*	72.50	-	2	1
Other matches	2	4	1	109	79*	36.33	-	1	2
Season	37	48	8	1321	126	33.02	2	6	33
Career	868	1266	180	33927	267*	31.24	53	163	652

Bowling	O	M	R	W	BB	Ave	5i	10m
Players v Gentlemen	14	4	30	2	2-30	15.00	-	-
Championship	833.4	315	1353	120	7-15	11.27	8	1
Other Yorkshire matches	49.2	18	107	7	5-20	15.28	1	-
Other matches	32	8	57	5	4-37	11.40	-	-
Season (6-ball)	929	345	1547	134	7-15	11.54	9	1
Career (6-ball)	22013	6132 } 57629	3508	9-24	16.42	254	62	
(5-ball)	2748.4	1029 }						

1924

Yorkshire won the Championship for the third year in succession and Rhodes completed his fifteenth 'double'. Although he only made one century, 100 against Somerset at Weston-super-Mare, he was quite consistent otherwise and just failed to do the 'double' in all Yorkshire matches. With the ball he took ten wickets in a match twice, the best innings analysis being 7-15 against Gloucestershire at Bristol. It would be fair to say that he was not so formidable to the best of batsmen but against all others he quite held his own.

	Own Team Total	O	M	R	W		Opp Total	Ct

869. Yorkshire v Glamorgan, Cardiff, May 7, 8 (Yorkshire won by an innings and 177 runs)
b J.Mercer   4   275   48   1
                      50

870. Yorkshire v Gloucestershire, Gloucester, May (10), 11, 12 (Yorkshire won by eight wickets)
```
b C.W.L.Parker        3    98      6    1   10   1   R.L.H.Green  lbw        68    1
did not bat           -    14-2    -    -    -   -                           42
```

871. Yorkshire v Cambridge University, Fenner's, May 14, 15 (Yorkshire won by an innings and 6 runs)
```
c and b A.H.E.White   6   234-8d  12.2   4   22   6   T.C.Lowry  c E.Oldroyd   111
                                                      T.E.S.Francis  c E.Robinson
                                                      H.M.Austin  st A.Dolphin
                                                      L.G.Crawley  c H.Sutcliffe
                                                      N.B.Sherwell  c G.G.Macaulay
                                                      A.H.E.White  b
                                  6    0   40   2   R.J.O.Meyer
                                                              c A.Waddington   117
                                                      N.B.Sherwell  b
```

872. Yorkshire v Surrey, Headingley, May 17, 19, (20) (Match drawn)
```
lbw b P.G.H.Fender   33   262     23    8   56   1   T.F.Shepherd  st A.Dolphin  169-7   2
```

873. Yorkshire v Northamptonshire, Northampton, May 21, 22, 23 (Yorkshire won by five wickets)
```
c J.V.Murdin b C.N.Woolley 28  159  -    -    -   -                           84
b W.Wells             0    49-5    5    0   11   0                           123
```

874. Yorkshire v Nottinghamshire, Bradford, May 24, 26, 27 (Yorkshire won by three wickets)
```
c W.W.Whysall b F.Barratt  1  161  13    5   37   2   W.E.G.Payton  c A.Dolphin  147
                                                      F.Barratt  c P.Holmes
c F.Barratt b S.J.Staples 15  79-7  15    2   30   5   G.Gunn  b               92
                                                      J.R.Gunn  b
                                                      A.W.Carr  st A.Dolphin
                                                      S.J.Staples  b
                                                      F.Barratt  c G.G.Macaulay
```

875. Yorkshire v Middlesex, Lord's, May 28, 29, 30 (Middlesex won by an innings and 152 runs)
```
c H.R.Murrell
    b G.T.S.Stevens  15   192     52   19  102   3   H.L.Dales  c F.I.Turner   465-8d
                                                      H.W.Lee  c G.Wilson
                                                      E.L.Kidd  lbw
c and b F.J.Durston   0   121
```

876. Yorkshire v Kent, Hull, May 31, June (2), 3 (Match drawn)
```
c James Seymour
    b F.E.Woolley    17   257     -    -    -   -                           128-9
```

877. Yorkshire v South Africans, Bramall Lane, June 4, 5, 6 (Match drawn)
```
c J.M.Blanckenberg
    b DJ.Meintjes    52   236     13    3   25   2   J.M.M.Commaille
                                                              st A.Dolphin   111
                                                      E.P.Nupen  b
not out               5   142-3d   22    9   40   2   H.G.Deane  b             141-6
                                                      J.M.Blanckenberg  st A.Dolphin
```

878. Yorkshire v Lancashire, Headingley, June 7, 9, 10 (Lancashire won by 24 runs)
```
lbw b C.H.Parkin     18   130     20    7   28   2   J.W.H.Makepeace  b       113
                                                      F.Watson  c A.Waddington
c J.W.H.Makepeace
    b R.K.Tyldesley   7    33     15    5   28   2   C.Hallows  lbw           74
                                                      J.Iddon  b
```

879. Yorkshire v Warwickshire, Edgbaston, June 11, (12), 13 (Match drawn)
```
did not bat           -   120-3    2    0    4   0                           139
```

880. Yorkshire v Derbyshire, Chesterfield, June 14, 16, 17 (Yorkshire won by 137 runs)
```
b W.J.Horsley         5   169     4    3    4   1   H.Elliott  c A.Dolphin    74
b H.Storer           22   205    22.5   6   50   4   H.Storer  lbw           163    1
                                                      J.M.Hutchinson  c A.Waddington
                                                      W.J.Horsley  c G.G.Macaulay
                                                      W.Bestwick  b
```

881. Yorkshire v Somerset, Dewsbury, June 18, 19 (Yorkshire won by an innings and 202 runs)
```
c P.R.Johnson b C.A.Winter 56  434-8d  4    2    2   2   J.C.White  c E.Oldroyd   132    1
                                                          G.E.Hunt  c A.Waddington
                                        -    -    -   -                           100
```

882. Yorkshire v Sussex, Bramall Lane, June 21, 23, 24 (Yorkshire won by 226 runs)
```
c E.H.Bowley b M.W.Tate   5   200                                            192    2
not out              19   343-3d                                            125
```

883. Mr.H.D.G.Leveson-Gower's XI v South Africans, Reigate, June 25, 26, 27 (Mr.H.D.G.Leveson-Gower's XI won by three wickets)
c E.P.Nupen
    b J.M.Blanckenberg 5   230   29.4 5   56   6 H.W.Taylor st C.D.McIver 253   2
                                                         M.J.Susskind b
                                                         A.W.Nourse c C.D.McIver
                                                         D.J.Meintjes c and b
                                                         E.P.Nupen c M.Howell
                                                         T.A.Ward lbw
    lbw b G.F.Bissett   5   196-7   22   6   39   4 R.H.Catterall st C.D.McIver 171
                                                         J.M.Blanckenberg c M.Leyland
                                                         D.J.Meintjes b
                                                         E.P.Nupen c J.L.Bryan

884. Yorkshire v Essex, Hull, June 28, 30, July 1 (Match drawn)
    b H.J.Palmer   80   299   37   14 58   1 J.G.W.Harrold st A.Dolphin 248   1
    c C.A.G.Russell
      b J.W.H.T.Douglas   6   111   11   5   16   2 C.A.G.Russell lbw   68-6
                                                         J.G.W.Harrold b

885. Yorkshire v South Africans, Bradford, July 2, 3, 4 (Match drawn)
    lbw b E.P.Nupen   54   285   17   6   40   0   279
    c E.P.Nupen b C.D.Dixon 22 147-4d   -   -   -   -   64-3

886. Yorkshire v Middlesex, Bramall Lane, July 5, 7, 8 (Match drawn)
    c and b G.T.S.Stevens 42   334   18   3   65   1 H.R.Murrell b   358
    did not bat   -   43-0   -   -   -   -   268   1

887. Yorkshire v Essex, Southend-on-Sea, July 9, 10, 11 (Yorkshire won by an innings and 131runs)
    c and b L.C.Eastman   10   471-5d   5.1 2   12   2 J.G.W.Harrold
                                                                  c G.G.Macaulay   132
                                                         G.M.Louden c A.Dolphin
                                        15.4 10 16   4 P.A.Perrin c G.G.Macaulay   208
                                                         L.C.Eastman c G.G.Macaulay
                                                         A.B.Hipkin b
                                                         G.M.Louden c E.Oldroyd

888. Yorkshire v Kent, Maidstone, July 12, 14, 15 (Match drawn)
    b A.P.Freeman   0   205   24   7   58   0   230   1
    not out   10   196-3   8   2   16   0   273

889. Yorkshire v Somerset, Weston-super-Mare, July 16, 17, 18 (Yorkshire won by an innings and 41 runs)
    c H.S.R.Critchley-Salmonson
      b J.J.Bridges   100 342   35.5 13 49   4 T.C.Lowry c E.Oldroyd   174
                                                         P.R.Johnson c E.Robinson
                                                         G.E.Hunt lbw
                                                         M.L.Hill b
                                        16   6   28   5 A.Young c G.Wilson   127
                                                         H.S.R.Critchley-Salmonson
                                                                   st A.Dolphin
                                                         J.Daniell b
                                                         G.F.Earle c L.Ryder
                                                         J.J.Bridges lbw

890. Yorkshire v Nottinghamshire, Trent Bridge, July 19, (21), 22 (Match drawn)
    st B.Lilley b T.L.Richmond 27 206-9 -   -   -   -   216

891. Yorkshire v Glamorgan, Bradford, July 23, (24), 25 (Yorkshire won by an innings and 26 runs)
    not out   9   248-3d   3   0   36   0   116
                                         -    -   -   -   106

892. Yorkshire v Gloucestershire, Headingley, July 26, (28), (29) (Match drawn)
    did not bat   -   137-2

893. Yorkshire v Derbyshire, Huddersfield, July 30, 31, August 1 (Match drawn)
    c W.J.Horsley b A.Morton 10 300-7d 10.5 3 25   6 S.W.A.Cadman c H.Sutcliffe 111
                                                         A.Morton b
                                                         J.M.Hutchinson lbw
                                                         J.S.Heath c A.Dolphin
                                                         W.J.Horsley b
                                                         J.A.Cresswell c H.Sutcliffe
                                        5   3   2   0   78-8

894. Yorkshire v Lancashire, Old Trafford, August 2, 4, 5 (Match drawn)
    b E.A.McDonald   12   359   3   2   4   0   78-2

895. Yorkshire v Leicestershire, Aylestone Road, Leicester, August 6, 7, 8 (Yorkshire won by eight wickets)
    b G.Geary   21   228   8   4   7   0   114   1

did not bat   -   54-2   8   4   6   0   166   1

896. Yorkshire v Warwickshire, Bramall Lane, August 9, 11 (Yorkshire won by ten wickets)
     c F.S.G.Calthorpe
               b H.Howell   51   275   26   10   41   3   F.R.Santall c A.Waddington 170
                                                               L.T.A.Bates st A.Dolphin
                                                               R.E.S.Wyatt c A.Waddington
     did not bat   -   4-0   15   3   27   3   William Quaife
                                                                       c A.Waddington 107
                                                               F.R.Santall b
                                                               L.T.A.Bates b G.G.Macaulay

897. Yorkshire v Northamptonshire, Dewsbury, August 13, 14, 15 (Yorkshire won by ten wickets)
     c B.Tyler b J.V.Murdin   48   328   3.2   0   14   2   F.I.Walden c and b   163   1
                                                               J.S.Nicholson c R.Kilner
     did not bat   -   23-0   12.3   6   40   6   W.H.Denton st A.Dolphin   187   1
                                                               F.I.Walden b
                                                               B.W.Bellamy c E.Robinson
                                                               B.Tyler b
                                                               J.S.Nicholson b
                                                               J.V.Murdin lbw

898. Yorkshire v Leicestershire, Bradford, August 16, 18, 19 (Yorkshire won by 92 runs)
     c F.Bale b W.E.Astill   36   119   9   4   15   2   G.Geary st A.Dolphin   71   1
                                                               A.W.Shipman lbw
     b A.W.Shipman   16   203   26.2   7   44   2   W.E.Astill lbw   159   1
                                                               F.Bale c and b

899. Yorkshire v Hampshire, Harrogate, August 20, (21), 22 (Match drawn)
     did not bat   -   291-2d   8   3   25   2   C.P.Mead lbw   137-7   1
                                                               H.L.V.Day c G.Wilson

900. Yorkshire v Surrey, Kennington Oval, August 23, 25, 26 (Surrey won by 109 runs)
     b W.C.H.Sadler   3   100   13   1   43   2   A.Sandham b   209
                                                               T.F.Shepherd b
     not out   51   202   25   11   27   4   A.Sandham st A.Dolphin   202   1
                                                               T.F.Shepherd b
                                                               A.Jeacocke st A.Dolphin
                                                               P.G.H.Fender c E.Oldroyd

901. Yorkshire v Hampshire, Portsmouth, August 27, 28 (Yorkshire won by ten wickets)
     c W.R.de la C.Shirley
               b A.S.Kennedy 11   136   -   -   -   -   74
     did not bat   -   38-0   5   1   19   1   H.A.W.Bowell c E.Oldroyd   97

902. Yorkshire v Sussex, Hove, August 30, September 1 (Yorkshire won by an innings and 110 runs)
     not out   35   253-9d   7   1   10   3   M.W.Tate c M.Leyland   60
                                                               H.L.Wilson st A.Dolphin
                                                               N.J.Holloway b
                                           10   3   20   3   G.S.Grimston c sub   83
                                                               N.J.Holloway lbw
                                                               A.F.Wensley c H.Sutcliffe

903. Yorkshire v MCC, Scarborough, September 3, 4, 5 (Yorkshire won by four wickets)
     c G.M.Louden
               b A.S.Kennedy 10   252   -   -   -   -   101
     c F.W.Gilligan b W.E.Astill 1 171-6 17   7   44   3   L.H.Tennyson c P.Holmes   321
                                                               G.E.V.Crutchley st A.Dolphin
                                                               G.M.Louden c A.Dolphin

904. Players v Gentlemen, Scarborough, September 6, 8, (9) (Match drawn)
     run out   30   144   3   1   5   0   198   1
     did not bat   -   39-1

905. Mr.C.I.Thornton's XI v South Africans, Scarborough, September 10, 11, 12 (Mr.C.I.Thornton's XI won by
     an innings and 45 runs)
     b A.W.Nourse   56   461-6d   8   4   11   1   S.J.Pegler lbw   143
                                          21   6   45   2   J.M.M.Commaille lbw   273
                                                               H.W.Taylor c J.W.H.T.Douglas

906. Yorkshire v Rest of England, Kennington Oval, September 13, 15, 16 (Rest of England won by an innings
     and 124 runs)
     b A.E.R.Gilligan   12   166   25   3 124   0   524-8d
     not out   42   234

SEASON'S AVERAGES

Batting and Fielding	M	I	NO	Runs	HS	Ave	100	50	Ct
Players v Gentlemen	1	1	0	30	30	30.00	-	-	1
Championship	30	37	5	826	100	25.81	1	4	19
Other Yorkshire matches	5	9	2	204	54	29.14	-	2	1
Other matches	2	3	0	66	56	22.00	-	1	2
Season	38	50	7	1126	100	26.18	1	7	23
Career	906	1316	187	35053	267*	31.04	54	170	675

Bowling	O	M	R	W	BB	Ave	5i	10m
Players v Gentlemen	3	1	5	0	-	-	-	-
Championship	550.3	186	1085	81	6-25	13.39	4	-
Other Yorkshire matches	112.2	32	335	15	6-22	22.33	1	-
Other matches	80.4	21	151	13	6-56	11.61	1	1
Season (6-ball)	746.3	240	1576	109	6-22	14.45	6	1
Career (6-ball)	22759.3	6372 ⎱ 59205		3617	9-24	16.36	260	63
(5-ball)	2748.4	1029 ⎰						

1925

Yorkshire won the Championship for the fourth consecutive year but Rhodes did not have a particularly good season. At the age of forty-seven it would seem it was more of a struggle to keep up his form consistently. Even so, although his wicket aggregate fell to 57, the lowest since 1912, and for the first time in his career he failed to take five wickets in an innings, his batting continued to flourish and he made over a thousand runs for the twentieth time hitting two centuries. His 157 against Derbyshire at Headingley came at an opportune time, Yorkshire being four wickets down for not very many when he and Kilner put on 170 for the fifth wicket. His other century was 108* against Glamorgan at Huddersfield.

	Own Team Total	O	M	R	W		Opp Total	Ct
907. Yorkshire v Glamorgan, Cardiff, May 6, (7), (8) (Match drawn)								
did not bat	- 134-1							
908. Yorkshire v Gloucestershire, Bristol, May 9, 11, 12 (Yorkshire won by 119 runs)								
lbw b C.W.L.Parker	39 166	11	3	22	2	D.C.Robinson		
						c G.G.Macaulay	82	1
						J.W.Burrough b		
not out	3 77-4d	-	-	-	-		42	
909. Yorkshire v Worcestershire, Worcester, May 13, 14 (Yorkshire won by an innings and 17 runs)								
c C.F.Root b H.O.Rogers	4 295	18	11	19	2	M.K.Foster c and b	213	1
						C.J.Wilson b		
		13	7	15	1	C.V.Tarbox b	65	
910. Yorkshire v Northamptonshire, Bramall Lane, May 16, 18, 19 (Yorkshire won by an innings and 137 runs)								
run out	16 412	12.5	2	40	4	W.Wells lbw	148	1
						J.M.Fitzroy b		
						S.H.G.Humfrey c E.Robinson		
						B.W.Bellamy c E.Robinson		
		11	6	20	0		127	2
911. Yorkshire v Derbyshire, Chesterfield, May 20, 21, 22 (Yorkshire won by an innings and 160 runs)								
c G.R.Jackson b A.Ackroyd 59	330-7d	13	4	14	1	L.F.Townsend c A.W.Lupton 61		
		6	0	10	1	S.W.A.Cadman b	109	
912. Yorkshire v Kent, Headingley, May (23), 25, (26) (Match drawn)								
did not bat	- 39-0							
913. Yorkshire v Cambridge University, Fenner's, May 27, 28, 29 (Match drawn)								
lbw b H.J.Enthoven	42 161	14	5	32	1	H.J.Enthoven c H.Sutcliffe	192	
not out	10 193-5	13	1	25	0		214	
914. Yorkshire v Lancashire, Old Trafford, May 30, June 1, 2 (Match drawn)								
lbw b C.H.Parkin	59 232	15	7	25	1	J.W.H.Makepeace		
						st A.Dolphin	265	

not out   54   186-6

915. Yorkshire v Warwickshire, Edgbaston, June 3, 4, 5 (Yorkshire won by 142 runs)
    b H.Howell   50   265   19   9   33   1   A.J.W.Croom   b   195
    not out   23   275-3d   12   3   21   1   L.T.A.Bates   c   E.Oldroyd   203

916. Yorkshire v Middlesex, Lord's, June 6, 8, 9 (Yorkshire won by an innings and 149 runs)
    c H.R.Murrell b F.J.Durston   0   538-6d   -   -   -   -   118
                                       5   1   7   0   271

917. Yorkshire v Gloucestershire, Bradford, June 10, 11, 12 (Yorkshire won by ten wickets)
    c J.G.W.P.Bessant
        b W.R.Hammond   30   365   137
    did not bat   -   4-0   229   1

918. Yorkshire v Nottinghamshire, Bramall Lane, June 13, 15 (Yorkshire won by five wickets)
    lbw b F.Barratt   7   157   139   1
    not out   31   148-5   165

919. Yorkshire v Glamorgan, Huddersfield, June 17, 18, 19 (Yorkshire won by an innings and 136 runs)
    lbw b F.P.Ryan   39   579-6d   9   3   11   0   246   1
                                     -    -   -   -   197

920. Yorkshire v Leicestershire, Hull, June 20, 22, 23 (Yorkshire won by an innings and 160 runs)
    not out   9   451-3d   -   -   -   -   85
                                   10   2   30   1   T.E.Sidwell   lbw   206

921. Yorkshire v Hampshire, Hull, June 24, 25, 26 (Yorkshire won by an innings and 116 runs)
    lbw b G.S.Boyes   91   408   139
                                                         153

922. Yorkshire v Surrey, Bradford, June 27, 29 (Yorkshire won by ten wickets)
    b P.G.H.Fender   28   233   105   1
    did not bat   -   49-0   175

923. Yorkshire v Derbyshire, Headingley, July 1, 2 (Yorkshire won by an innings and 159 runs)
    lbw b W.J.Horsley   157   423-8d   -   -   -   -   128
                                   13   6   29   2   W.J.Horsley   c   E.Robinson   136
                                                          H.Elliott   b

924. Yorkshire v Somerset, Harrogate, July 4, 6 (Yorkshire won by an innings and 150 runs)
    not out   114   414-9d   -   -   -   -   148
                                   1.1   1   0   1   W.T.Luckes   b   116

925. Yorkshire v Worcestershire, Harrogate, July 8, 9, 10 (Yorkshire won by ten wickets)
    lbw b H.O.Rogers   65   438   10   6   11   1   W.E.Barnie-Adshead   b   215
    did not bat   -   14-0   16   2   34   1   W.H.N.Shakespeare   b   235   1

926. Yorkshire v Kent, Maidstone, July 11, 13, 14 (Yorkshire won by 110 runs)
    lbw b A.P.Freeman   20   196   259
    c J.C.Hubble b F.E.Woolley 26   333   160

927. Yorkshire v Essex, Bramall Lane, July 15, 16, 17 (Match drawn)
    lbw b G.M.Louden   11   303   27   13   42   3   C.A.G.Russell   lbw   250
                                                        J.W.H.T.Douglas   lbw
                                                        V.E.Jarvis   b
    did not bat   -   68-2   31   16   30   1   A.B.Hipkin   c   E.Robinson   182

928. Yorkshire v Nottinghamshire, Trent Bridge, July 18, 20, 21 (Match drawn)
    c B.Lilley b T.L.Richmond   57   386   27   8   60   4   A.W.Carr   c   E.Robinson   312
                                                        B.Lilley   st   A.Dolphin
                                                        H.Larwood   st   A.Dolphin
                                                        F.Barratt   st   A.Dolphin
    not out   23   142-4d   1   1   0   0   103-9

929. Yorkshire v Northamptonshire, Kettering, July 22, 23 (Yorkshire won by an innings and 110 runs)
    b V.W.C.Jupp   55   259-4d   6   1   10   2   J.M.Fitzroy   c   H.Sutcliffe   107
                                                        PA.Wright   st   A.Dolphin   42

930. Yorkshire v Middlesex, Headingley, July 25, 27, 28 (Match drawn)
    c G.T.S.Stevens b N.E.Haig 19   528-6d   3.4   0   9   2   G.O.B.Allen   c   A.Waddington 184
                                                        N.B.Sherwell   c   P.Holmes
                                   14   3   21   0   149-4

931. Yorkshire v Lancashire, Bramall Lane, August 1, 3, 4 (Match drawn)
    lbw b E.A.McDonald   7   277   22   11   20   2   C.Hallows   lbw   320
                                                        A.W.Pewtress   lbw
                                   5   0   21   1   J.Iddon   c   A.Dolphin   74-6

932. Yorkshire v Leicestershire, Aylestone Road, Leicester, August 5, 6, 7 (Match drawn)
  c C.H.Taylor b G.Geary 0 197 25 9 58 3 A.W.Shipman c P.Holmes 222   1
                               G.Geary c E.Oldroyd
                                T.E.Sidwell c and b
               20 11 26 2 A.W.Shipman c P.Holmes 195-5
                                G.L.Berry c E.Oldroyd

933. Yorkshire v Warwickshire, Dewsbury, August 12, 13, 14 (Yorkshire won by an innings and 56 runs)
  c E.J.Smith b F.R.Santall 33 507-8d 17 4 50 1 R.E.S.Wyatt c and b 323   3
                   6 3 4 1 R.E.S.Wyatt c sub   128

934. Yorkshire v Essex, Leyton, August 12, (13), 14 (Match drawn)
  did not bat   - 80-1 30 19 31 0   218-3d

935. Yorkshire v Sussex, Bradford, August 15, 17, 18 (Yorkshire won by 23 runs)
  c E.H.Bowley
    b A.F.Wensley   15 119 - - - -   87
  b F.B.R.Browne   3 230 11 3 20 0   239

936. Yorkshire v Hampshire, Southampton, August 19, 20, 21 (Match drawn)
  run out   13 264 2 2 0   114-4

937. Yorkshire v Surrey, Kennington Oval, August 22, (24), 25 (Match drawn)
  did not bat   - 82-0 44 19 65 4 D.J.Knight lbw   246-8d
                                D.R.Jardine c A.Dolphin
                                E.R.T.Holmes c A.Dolphin
                                H.A.Peach c H.Sutcliffe

938. Yorkshire v MCC, Lord's, August 26, 27, 28 (Yorkshire won by ten wickets)
  lbw b A.S.Kennedy 4 287 19 4 37 1 D.J.Knight lbw   206
  did not bat   - 25-0 2 2 0 0   105   1

939. Yorkshire v Sussex, Hove, August 29, 31, September 1 (Yorkshire won by nine wickets)
  c W.L.Cornford b M.W.Tate 57 305 18 6 17 3 A.F.Wensley
                               c G.G.Macaulay 156
                               G.R.Cox c A.Dolphin
                               A.E.R.Gilligan b
  did not bat   - 89-1 17 5 33 0   237   1

940. Yorkshire v Somerset, Taunton, September 2, 3, 4 (Yorkshire won by ten wickets)
  lbw b J.C.White   17 362 17 9 43 2 R.A.Ingle lbw   235
                               W.T.Greswell lbw
  did not bat   - 22-0 9 4 27 1 M.D.Lyon st A.Dolphin 147

941. Mr.C.I.Thornton's XI v MCC Australian Team, Scarborough, September 5, 7, 8 (Match drawn)
  lbw b J.W.H.T.Douglas 9 179 3 1 3 0   274
  c and b H.Sutcliffe   26 179-7 - - - -   171-5d

942. Yorkshire v MCC, Scarborough, September 9, 10, 11 (Match drawn)
  b N.E.Haig   53 450-6d 16 6 19 2 W.E.Astill c A.Waddington 161 1
                               H.W.Lee c A.Waddington
  did not bat   - 53-0

943. Yorkshire v Rest of England, Kennington Oval, September 12, 14, 15, 16 (Match drawn)
  b P.G.H.Fender   3 313 11 2 32 0   430
  not out   10 112-3 11 0 58 1 F.E.Woolley c E.Oldroyd 252-4d

SEASON'S AVERAGES

Batting and Fielding	M	I	NO	Runs	HS	Ave	100	50	Ct
Championship	32	35	7	1234	157	44.07	2	9	15
Other Yorkshire matches	4	6	2	122	53	30.50	-	1	2
Other matches	1	2	0	35	26	17.50	-	-	-
Season	37	43	9	1391	157	40.91	2	10	17
Career	943	1359	196	36444	267*	31.33	56	180	692

Bowling	O	M	R	W	BB	Ave	5i	10m
Championship	547.4	220	928	52	4-40	17.84	-	-
Other Yorkshire matches	86	20	203	5	2-19	40.60	-	-
Other matches	3	1	3	0	-	-	-	-
Season (6-ball)	636.4	241	1134	57	4-40	19.89		
Career (6-ball)	23396.1	6613 }	60339	3674	9-24	16.42	260	63
(5-ball)	2748.4	1029 }						

1926

At the age of forty-eight Rhodes was recalled to the Test arena for the first time since 1921 and his performance in the final Test helped England to win back the 'Ashes' for the first time since 1911/12. This was a precedent which thirty years later was exemplified by Cyril Washbrook, recalled to the side at the age of forty-one against Australia at Headingley, who put on 187 runs with Peter May after England had been 17 for three. Finishing second to Lancashire, Yorkshire had, for them, an ordinary season. Sutcliffe missed seven matches through representative calls, Rhodes six mainly through injury which at his age was to be expected and Kilner two. Rhodes made 1000 runs and did the 'double' for Yorkshire in all matches for the last time. He made one century, 132 against Essex at Leyton and his best bowling was 14-77 against Somerset at Huddersfield. It was noticeable that even though Rhodes increased his tally with the ball the other main bowlers experienced a falling off which was very worrying for the club in so much that the famous veteran could not go on forever.

	Own Team Total	O	M	R	W		Opp Total	Ct

944. Yorkshire v Essex, Leyton, May 1, 3, 4 (Yorkshire won by ten wickets)
c C.A.G.Russell
b J.O'Connor 132 359 - - - - 110 1
did not bat - 6-0 21 7 47 2 J.V.Richardson b 254
L.C.Eastman c R.Kilner

945. Yorkshire v Cambridge University, Fenner's, May 5, 6, (7) (Match drawn)
c F.J.Seabrook b R.J.O.Meyer 1 176 1 0 5 0 176
c K.S.Duleepsinhji
b H.J.Enthoven 9 185-9

946. Yorkshire v Derbyshire, Ilkeston, May 8, (10), 11 (Match drawn)
c J.A.Cresswell
b T.S.Worthington 2 170 109
not out 7 133-5

947. Yorkshire v Worcestershire, Worcester, May (12), 13, (14) (Match drawn)
lbw b C.F.Root 4 84-6

948. Yorkshire v Leicestershire, Headingley, May 15, 17 (Yorkshire won by an innings and 95 runs)
b G.Geary 21 295-8d 14 6 28 3 L.G.Berry st A.Dolphin 82
G.Geary c R.Kilner
T.E.Sidwell c P.Holmes
17.5 4 42 4 G.H.S.Fowke st A.Dolphin 118
A.Lord c E.Oldroyd
H.A.Smith c E.Robinson
F.Bale c E.Robinson

949. Yorkshire v Essex, Headingley, May 19, 20 (Yorkshire won by an innings and 124 runs)
not out 61 398 5 1 27 0 125
149 1

950. Yorkshire v Lancashire, Bradford, May 22, 24, 25 (Yorkshire won by an innings and 94 runs)
c E.A.McDonald
b R.K.Tyldesley 21 326 20.1 12 20 4 G.E.Tyldesley c H.Sutcliffe 159
J.R.Barnes c H.Sutcliffe
E.A.McDonald c P.Holmes
C.H.Parkin b
- - - - 73

951. Yorkshire v Warwickshire, Edgbaston, May 26, 27, 28 (Yorkshire won by an innings and 99 runs)
c F.R.Santall b R.E.S.Wyatt 43 326-6d 34 19 37 5 R.E.S.Wyatt b 162
L.T.A.Bates c A.Waddington
N.Kilner c A.Waddington
J.A.Smart b
N.E.Partridge b
13 4 22 4 J.H.Parsons lbw 65 1
L.T.A.Bates c M.Leyland
N.Kilner c P.Holmes
A.J.W.Croom b

952. Yorkshire v Kent, Bramall Lane, May 29, 30, June 1 (Match drawn)
b A.C.Wright 0 242 6 0 18 1 James Seymour
c A.Waddington 206 1

did not bat   -   71-0   19   8   26   3   James Seymour b   236
                                              J.C.Hubble   c A.Waddington
                                              A.C.Wright   c M.Leyland

953. Yorkshire v Somerset, Huddersfield, June 2, 3, 4 (Yorkshire won by an innings and 39 runs)
   c G.E.Hunt b J.C.White   21   302   21   8   29   6   M.D.Lyon st A.Dolphin   144
                                              C.C.C.Case   b
                                              J.C.White   b
                                              G.E.Northway   c A.Waddington
                                              G.F.Earle   c M.Leyland
                                              F.G.Lee   c E.Robinson
                             20.5   4   48   8   A.Young c G.G.Macaulay   119
                                              M.D.Lyon st A.Dolphin
                                              C.C.C.Case   c A.Waddington
                                                G.F.Earle   c E.Oldroyd
                                                G.E.Hunt   st A.Dolphin
                                                P.C.Ewens   c A.Mitchell
                                                H.G.Pruett   c R.Kilner
                                                F.G.Lee   c E.Robinson

954. Yorkshire v Australians, Bradford, June 5, 7, 8 (Match drawn)
   st J.L.Ellis b C.V.Grimmett   6   155   5   2   11   0   177
   did not bat   -   25-0   14   4   37   0   243-3d

955. Yorkshire v Glamorgan, Hull, June 9, 10 (Yorkshire won by an innings and 118 runs)
   c W.E.Bates b D.Davies   62   265-6d   -   -   -   -   52
                                 26   10   31   4   W.E.Bates   c E.Oldroyd   95
                                              D.Davies   b
                                              V.L.Morris   c H.Sutcliffe
                                              D.Sullivan   c E.Oldroyd

956. Yorkshire v Australians, Bramall Lane, June (16), (17), 18 (Match drawn)
                                 15   3   36   2   C.G.Macartney lbw   148-6
                                              W.M.Woodfull   b

957. Yorkshire v Middlesex, Lord's, June 19, 21, 22 (Match drawn)
   b N.E.Haig   27   415   18   8   40   0   250
                                 13   1   54   0   367

958. Yorkshire v Gloucestershire, Hull, June 23, 24, 25 (Match drawn)
   b G.A.Wedel   32   198   4   1   8   1   J.G.W.P.Bessant lbw   157   1
                                 11   7   10   0   59-5

959. Yorkshire v Surrey, Bramall Lane, June 26, 28, 29 (Yorkshire won by an innings and 13 runs)
   run out   33   398   26   5   66   3   R.J.Gregory b   228   2
                                              H.A.Peach c J.S.Douglas
                                              J.H.Lockton   c and b
                               27   6   41   4   A.Jeacocke lbw   157
                                              T.F.Shepherd   c E.Oldroyd
                                              R.J.Gregory   lbw
                                              H.A.Peach   c A.Mitchell

960. Yorkshire v Kent, Blackheath, July 3, 5, 6 (Match drawn)
   b A.C.Wright   15   428-9d   18   4   40   2   W.M.Leggatt c P.Holmes   225
                                              A.P.Freeman   b
                                 -    -   -   -   42-0

961. Yorkshire v Sussex, Dewsbury, July 7, 8, 9 (Yorkshire won by an innings and 91 runs)
   b G.R.Cox   70   385-7d   37   15   58   4   A.F.Wensley b   181
                                              L.Williams   st A.Dolphin
                                              A.H.H.Gilligan   c A.Waddington
                                              L.A.Waghorn   b
                                 8   1   16   2   J.H.Parks c and b   113   1
                                              A.F.Wensley   b

962. Yorkshire v Northamptonshire, Northampton, July 10, 12, 13 (Match drawn)
   c B.W.Bellamy b E.W.Clark 88   448-7d   40   21   60   2   J.E.Timms b   224   1
                                              J.M.Fitzroy   c M.Leyland
   did not bat   -   68-6   48.3   12   102   7   C.N.Woolley c E.Oldroyd   306
                                              H.F.Bagnall   b
                                              J.E.Timms   b
                                              F,I.Walden   lbw
                                              G.W.Norris   st A.Dolphin
                                              J.M.Fitzroy   c E.Oldroyd
                                              E.W.Clark   b

963. Yorkshire v Derbyshire, Bramall Lane, July 14, 15, 16 (Match drawn)
b W.Shardlow   41 209   31   7   68 1 H.Storer b   369
not out   43 212-5

964. Yorkshire v Middlesex, Bradford, July 17, 19, 20 (Yorkshire won by ten wickets)
run out   26 371   9   4   15 0   295
did not bat   - 6-0   5   0   8 2 H.J.Enthoven lbw   80
                                               N.E.Haig c P.Holmes

965. Yorkshire v Hampshire, Bournemouth, July 21, 22, 23 (Match drawn)
b A.S.Kennedy   7 237   10.1   5   15 4 L.H.Tennyson c A.Dolphin   174
                                               A.K.Judd c M.Leyland
                                               W.H.Livsey c A.Dolphin
                                               G.S.Boyes b
did not bat   - 251-3d 6   1   18 0   151-2

966. Yorkshire v Nottinghamshire, Trent Bridge, July 24, 26, 27 (Match drawn)
c W.W.Whysall
  b H.Larwood   19 245   14.1   2   41 3 B.Lilley c A.Dolphin   265
                                               R.H.T.Turner lbw
                                               F.Barratt c G.H.Crawford
did not bat   - 53-1 35.5 19   54 3 B.Lilley c A.Waddington   155
                                               H.Larwood c A.Waddington
                                               F.Barratt c G.G.Macaulay

967. Yorkshire v Gloucestershire, Bristol, July 28, 29, 30 (Yorkshire won by an innings and 41 runs)
c D.C.Robinson
  b T.W.J.Goddard   3 279   17   3   55 1 H.Smith c A.Waddington   170
                                4   4   0 1 C.W.L.Parker c and b   68   2

968. Yorkshire v Lancashire, Old Trafford, July 31, August 2, 3 (Match drawn)
c G.Duckworth
  b F.B.Watson   12 352   42   7 116 7 J.W.H.Makepeace b   509-9d 1
                                               G.E.Tyldesley st A.Dolphin
                                               J.Iddon c A.Dolphin
                                               E.A.McDonald c M.Leyland
                                               R.K.Tyldesley c E.Oldroyd
                                               M.L.Taylor c and b
                                               F.M.Sibbles b

969. Yorkshire v Leicestershire, Aylestone Road, Leicester, August 4, 5, (6) (Match drawn)
b G.Geary   51 473-6d 41 20   64 2 E.G.Hayes c and b   220-5 1
                                               G.Geary c A.Dolphin

970. Yorkshire v Warwickshire, Bramall Lane, August 7, 9, (10) (Match drawn)
c William Quaife
  b F.R.Santall   60 382 23.1 11   29 3 N.Kilner b   182
                                               E.J.Smith c P.Holmes
                                               E.P.Hewetson lbw
                                15   7   23 2 L.T.A.Bates c G.G.Macaulay 96-3
                                               William Quaife lbw

971. Yorkshire v Northamptonshire, Headingley, August (11), 12, (13) (Match drawn)
c J.M.Fitzroy b V.W.C.Jupp 25 177 18 11 11 2 F.I.Walden b   126
                                               A.C.L.Wills c J.S.Stephenson
                              -    -   -   -   6-0

972. ENGLAND v AUSTRALIA, Kennington Oval, August 14, 15, 17, 18 (England won by 289 runs)
c W.A.S.Oldfield
  b A.A.Mailey   28 280   25 15   35 2 W.M.Woodfull b   302
                                               A.J.Richardson c G.Geary
lbw C.V.Grimmett   14 436   20   9   44 4 W.Bardsley c F.E.Woolley   125
                                               W.H.Ponsford c H.Larwood
                                               H.L.Collins c F.E.Woolley
                                               A.J.Richardson b

973. Yorkshire v Surrey, Kennington Oval, August 21, 23, 24 (Match drawn)
b P.G.H.Fender   96 274   1   0   1 0   355-9d
did not bat   - 265-0

974. Yorkshire v MCC, Scarborough, September 4, 6, 7 (Match drawn)
c G.T.S.Stevens
  b A.E.R.Gilligan 33 349   26   8   53 0   357   1
did not bat   - 226-2d -   -   -   -   138-2

975. Mr.C.I.Thornton's XI v Australians, Scarborough, September 8, 9, 10 (Match drawn)
c W.A.S.Oldfield

b A.A.Mailey	9	244	29	5	63	5	W.M.Woodfull c J.B.Hobbs 194

W.A.S.Oldfield b
J.M.Taylor lbw
J.Ryder c M.W.Tate
C.V.Grimmett c P.Holmes

did not bat   -   79-3

976. Rest of England v Lancashire, Kennington Oval, September 11, 13, 14 (Rest of England won by 374 runs)
c F.E.Woolley

b E.A.McDonald   10   217   7   2   17   2   C.Hallows lbw   177
                                       J.Iddon st H.Strudwick

did not bat   -   468-2d   10   2   20   0   134

SEASON'S AVERAGES

Batting and Fielding	M	I	NO	Runs	HS	Ave	100	50	Ct
Test matches	1	2	0	42	28	21.00	-	-	-
Championship	26	28	3	1022	132	40.88	1	7	14
Other Yorkshire matches	4	4	0	49	33	12.25	-	-	1
Other matches	2	2	0	19	10	9.50	-	-	-
Season	33	36	3	1132	132	34.30	1	7	15
Career	976	1395	199	37576	267*	31.41	57	187	707

Bowling	O	M	R	W	BB	Ave	5i	10m
Test matches	45	24	79	6	4-44	13.16	-	-
Championship	740.4	265	1388	100	8-48	13.88	5	1
Other Yorkshire matches	61	17	142	2	2-36	71.00	-	-
Other matches	46	9	100	7	5-63	14.28	1	-
Season (6-ball)	892.4	315	1709	115	8-48	14.86	6	1
Career (6-ball)	24288.5	6928 } 62048	3789	9-24	16.37	266	64
(5-ball)	2748.4	1029 }						

1926/27 - In India

Rhodes's third visit to India, as coach to the Maharajah of Patiala, saw him take part in one first-class match, for Patiala against the M.C.C. What is perhaps less well known is that he umpired in a number of matches. He stood with the other old Yorkshire player, Arthur Dolphin, in M.C.C. v The Army at Lahore, with Morris Leyland for the M.C.C. against Southern Punjab, Northern Punjab and Northern India all at Lahore and again for M.C.C. v Bombay Presidency at Bombay, the other umpire being unknown. With P.H.Davar he did the honours against All India (Indians) at Bombay and with C.M.Keddie for M.C.C. against the Europeans in the East in Calcutta. Finally he did a stint with two others against All India (Invitation side) in Calcutta. He may have officiated in other games but it is unknown at this time.

	Own Team Total	O	M	R	W		Opp Total	Ct

977. Patiala v MCC, Patiala, February 26, 27 (Match drawn)

not out   13   303-4d   24   4   73   3   J.H.Parsons c K.M.Mistri   252-9
                                                 W.E.Astill lbw
                                            G.F.Earle st A.Dolphin

SEASON'S AVERAGES

Batting and Fielding	M	I	NO	Runs	HS	Ave	100	50	Ct
Patiala	1	1	1	13	13*	-	-	-	-
Career	977	1396	200	37589	267*	31.42	57	187	707

Bowling	O	M	R	W	BB	Ave	5i	10m
Patiala (6-ball)	24	4	73	3	3-73	24.33	-	-
Career (6-ball)	24312.5	6932 } 62121	3792	9-24	16.38	266	64
(5-ball)	2748.4	1029 }						

1927

For the first time since 1902 Rhodes failed to score one thousand runs in the season. His wicket total fell to 85 with a best innings performance of 6-20 and match performance of 9-77 against Gloucestershire at Dewsbury. He had a testimonial granted this season, sixteen years after his benefit and this realized £1821. Although he fell away as a batsmen, his highest score being 73, he still played some invaluable innings at critical times and took 82 wickets in all matches for 19 runs apiece.

	Own Team / Total	O	M	R	W		Opp / Total	Ct
978. Yorkshire v Cambridge University, Fenner's, May 4, 5, 6 (Match drawn)								
b M.J.C.Allom	73 382	28	11	50	1	E.W.Dawson b	372	1
did not bat	- 205-3d	-	-	-	-		85-3	
979. Yorkshire v Gloucestershire, Gloucester, May 7, 9, 10 (Yorkshire won by an innings and 21 runs)								
c H.Smith b P.T.Mills	8 468-5d	15	9	24	2	A.E.Dipper c and b	189	1
						B.H.Lyon c G.G.Macaulay		
		25	12	33	1	B.H.Lyon lbw	258	
980. Yorkshire v Glamorgan, Cardiff, May 11, 12 (Yorkshire won by an innings and 51 runs)								
b D.E.Davies	2 236	2	0	10	0		83	1
		-	-	-	-		102	1
981. Yorkshire v Gloucestershire, Dewsbury, May 14, 16, 17 (Yorkshire won by an innings and 2 runs)								
b G.Wedel	2 318	11.5	3	20	6	W.R.Hammond st A.Dolphin	134	
						E.G.Morrison b		
						C.W.L.Parker c A.Dolphin		
						B.S.Bloodworth lbw		
						D.F.Pope c E.Oldroyd		
						T.W.J.Goddard st A.Dolphin		
		32.2	15	57	3	W.R.Hammond b	182	
						E.G.Morrison st A.Dolphin		
						T.W.J.Goddard c R.Kilner		
982. Yorkshire v Worcestershire, Headingley, May 18, 19 (Yorkshire won by an innings and 164 runs)								
c J.B.Higgins H.O.Rogers	1 291						46	
							81	
983. Yorkshire v Warwickshire, Hull, May 21, 23, 24 (Warwickshire won by eight wickets)								
c A.J.W.Croom								
b F.S.G.Calthorpe	24 272	33	15	48	1	A.J.W.Croom lbw	393	
b F.R.Santall	6 162	-	-	-	-		43-2	
984. Yorkshire v Hampshire, Bramall Lane, May 25, 26, 27 (Match drawn)								
b F.A.Gross	33 360	9	0	22	0		214	
did not bat	- 161-1d	7	5	3	0		182-3	
985. Yorkshire v Surrey, Headingley, May 28, 30, 31 (Yorkshire won by ten wickets)								
c H.Strudwick b S.Fenley	3 333	25	9	59	5	J.B.Hobbs c A.Waddington	172	
						C.E.Daily lbw		
						T.F.Shepherd lbw		
						H.G.Baldwin c H.Sutcliffe		
						H.A.Peach c A.Waddington		
did not bat	- 44-0	14	0	69	2	J.B.Hobbs c E.Robinson	203	
						H.A.Peach c H.Sutcliffe		
986. Yorkshire v Northamptonshire, Huddersfield, June 1, 2 (Yorkshire won by seven wickets)								
lbw b J.V.Murdin	28 315						89	
did not bat	- 62-3						286	
987. Yorkshire v Lancashire, Old Trafford, June 4, 6, 7 (Lancashire won by eight wickets)								
c G.Duckworth								
b E.A.McDonald	44 166	33	15	45	2	J.Iddon c G.G.Macaulay	234	
						M.L.Taylor lbw		
run out	29 153	4	3	4	0		89-2	
988. Yorkshire v Warwickshire, Edgbaston, June 8, 9, 10 (Match drawn)								
b F.R.Santall	28 358	33	9	72	4	L.T.A.Bates c A.Mitchell	362	
						William Quaife lbw		
						A.J.W.Croom lbw		
						N.E.Partridge b		
not out	17 96-4							

989. Yorkshire v Somerset, Bradford, June 15, 16, 17 (Yorkshire won by an innings and 152 runs)
   not out   33   486-7d   12   7   19   2   G.F.Earle   c E.Oldroyd   140
                                                                      G.E.Hunt   c H.Sutcliffe
                                          11.1   4   26   4   J.W.Lee   lbw   194
                                                                      J.C.White   lbw
                                                                      W.F.Luckes   c P.Holmes
                                                                      G.E.Hunt   c E.Oldroyd

990. Yorkshire v Middlesex, Lord's, June 18, 20, 21 (Middlesex won by six wickets)
   c E.H.Hendren b N.E.Haig   2   81   14   1   33   0   178
   b F.J.Durston   3   262   12   5   21   0   169-4

991. Yorkshire v Hampshire, Portsmouth, June 22, 23, (24) (Match drawn)
   did not bat   -   156-3   54   11   120   3   C.P.Mead   c H.Sutcliffe   521-8d
                                                                      J.P.Parker   c E.Robinson
                                                                      G.S.Boyes   c M.Leyland

992. Yorkshire v Kent, Tonbridge, June 25, 27, (28) (Match drawn)
   not out   31   131   9   1   36   2   B.H.Valentine c M.Leyland   243
                                                                      C.J.Capes   c G.G.Macaulay
                                              -      -   -   -   10-1

993. Yorkshire v Somerset, Bath, June 29, (30), July (1) (Match drawn)
                                               7   4   11   1   J.Daniell   c T.A.Jacques   145-7

994. Yorkshire v New Zealanders, Bradford, July 2, 4, (5) (Match drawn)
   b C.C.R.Dacre   2   377   13   5   29   4   T.C.Lowry   c M.Leyland   133-7
                                                                      M.L.Page   c H.Sutcliffe
                                                                      H.M.McGirr   st A.Dolphin
                                                                      C.C.R.Dacre c P.Holmes

995. Yorkshire v Glamorgan, Harrogate, July 6, (7), (8) (Match drawn)
   did not bat   -   27-1   36   17   44   4   J.T.Bell   hit wkt   138
                                                                      W.G.Morgan   c P.Holmes
                                                                      J.J.Hills   c G.G.Macaulay
                                                                      J.Mercer   c A.Mitchell

996. Yorkshire v Nottinghamshire, Bradford, July 9, 11, 12 (Match drawn)
   b W.A.Flint   17   320   30   9   64   1   W.Walker   b   343

997. Yorkshire v Essex, Headingley, July 13, 14, 15 (Yorkshire won by seven wickets)
   b M.S.Nichols   3   186   -   -   -   -   100
   did not bat   -   91-3   28.5   10   40   3   A.B.Hipkin   lbw   175
                                                                      A.H.Meston   st A.Dolphin
                                                                      H.J.Palmer   b

998. Yorkshire v Middlesex, Bramall Lane, July 16, 18, 19 (Match drawn)
   c E.H.Hill b H.W.Lee   2   490-9d 19   0   45   0   302
                                              13   1   35   0   218-2   1

999. Yorkshire v Worcestershire, Worcester, July 20, (21), 22 (Match drawn)
   lbw b H.O.Rogers   18   328   19   3   44   3   H.Perry   c A.Waddington   199
                                                                      G.Ashton   c G.G.Macaulay
                                                                      J.W.Greenstock st A.Dolphin
   did not bat   -   18-2

1000. Yorkshire v Nottinghamshire, Trent Bridge, July 23, 25, 26 (Match drawn)
   c S.J.Staples b W.A.Flint   6   177   23.2   8   40   4   B.Lilley   b   298
                                                                      A.Staples   b
                                                                      F.Barratt   c W.Barber
                                                                      S.J.Staples c A.W.Lupton
   did not bat   -   72-0   16   0   43   1   W.W.Whysall b   224-6d

1001. Yorkshire v Northamptonshire, Northampton, July 27, 28, 29 (Yorkshire won by five wickets)
   c J.V.Murdin b A.E.Thomas   0   67   26   11   37   4   W.W.Timms   b   164   1
                                                                      F.I.Walden   c E.Robinson
                                                                      A.E.Thomas   c P.Holmes
                                                                      J.V.Murdin   c H.Sutcliffe
   c J.V.Murdin b A.E.Thomas   3   200-5   28   9   52   4   C.N.Woolley lbw   100
                                                                      W.Adams   c T.A.Jacques
                                                                      J.E.Timms   b
                                                                      F.I.Walden   c A.W.Lupton

1002. Yorkshire v Lancashire, Headingley, July 30, August 1, 3 (Match drawn)
   c R.K.Tyldesley
          b F.M.Sibbles   18   157   28.4   8   66   3   G.E.Tyldesley c E.Oldroyd   360-9d
                                                                      J.Iddon   c E.Robinson
                                                                      R.K.Tyldesley c A.W.Lupton

lbw b F.M.Sibbles   43   314-6

1003. Yorkshire v Leicestershire, Aylestone Road, Leicester, August 3, 4, 5 (Match drawn)
   c N.F.Armstrong b G.Geary   4   282   38   13   61   1   G.H.S.Fowke c E.Robinson   276
   did not bat   -   139-4

1004. Yorkshire v Leicestershire, Bramall Lane, August 6, (8), (9) (Match drawn)
   not out   10   292-4

1005. Yorkshire v Derbyshire, Hull, August 10, 11, 12 (Match drawn)
   c L.F.Townsend
     b T.S.Worthington   16   228   1   0   5   0   81
   did not bat   -   32-0   43.2   18   63   4   G.R.Jackson lbw   252   1
                                               T.S.Worthington c R.Kilner
                                                L.F.Townsend c and b
                                                J.A.Cresswell st A.Dolphin

1006. Yorkshire v Derbyshire, Chesterfield, August 17, (18), (19) (Match drawn)
   not out   6   92-5   16   3   30   2   G.M.Lee st A.Wood   157
                                                  L.F.Townsend c P.Holmes

1007. Yorkshire v Surrey, Kennington Oval, August (20), 22, 23 (Match drawn)
   did not bat   -   143-1   29   8   72   4   T.F.Shepherd c M.Leyland   341-8d
                                                  E.R.T.Holmes c R.Kilner
                                                R.J.Gregory lbw
                                                H.A.Peach b

1008. Yorkshire v Essex, Leyton, August 24, 25, 26 (Match drawn)
   not out   41   249-5d   12   3   23   0   128-5

1009. Yorkshire v Sussex, Hove, August 27, 29, 30 (Yorkshire won by nine wickets)
   lbw b M.W.Tate   0   302   26   9   32   1   A.H.H.Gilligan c E.Robinson 221   1
   did not bat   -   43-1   15   7   18   0   120

1010. Yorkshire v MCC, Scarborough, August 31, September 1, 2 (Yorkshire won by eight wickets)
   c L.G.Crawley b N.E.Haig   2   212   5   2   9   0   199
   did not bat   -   138-2   1   0   1   0   147

1011. Players v Gentlemen, Scarborough, September 3, 5, 6 (Match drawn)
   not out   15   513-9d   20   9   19   1   H.J.Enthoven c G.Geary   271
                                      3   0   30   0   204-3

1012. Mr.C.I.Thornton's XI v MCC South African Team, Scarborough, September 7, 8, 9 (Match drawn)
   b R.E.S.Wyatt   4   364-9d   19   6   31   1   W.R.Hammond lbw   205
                                      7   0   16   1   E.W.Dawson c J.B.Hobbs   145-1

SEASON'S AVERAGES

Batting and Fielding	M	I	NO	Runs	HS	Ave	100	50	Ct
Players v Gentlemen	1	1	1	15	15*	-	-	-	-
Championship	30	32	6	481	44	18.50	-	-	7
Other Yorkshire matches	3	3	0	77	73	25.66	-	1	1
Other matches	1	1	0	4	4	4.00	-	-	-
Season	35	37	7	577	73	19.23	-	1	8
Career	1012	1433	207	38166	267*	31.13	57	188	715

Bowling	O	M	R	W	BB	Ave	5i	10m
Players v Gentlemen	23	9	49	1	1-19	49.00	-	-
Championship	811.3	265	1546	77	6-20	20.07	2	-
Other Yorkshire matches	47	18	89	5	4-29	17.80	-	-
Other matches	26	6	47	2	1-16	23.50	-	-
Seaosn (6-ball)	907.3	298	1731	85	6-20	20.36	2	-
Career (6-ball)	25220.2	7230 }	63852	3977	9-24	16.05	268	64
(5-ball)	2748.4	1029 }						

1928

Having turned fifty years of age the previous October Rhodes, owing to the death of Roy Kilner and the more or less breakdown of Macaulay, was given a great deal of work to do and rose to the occasion splendidly. Although mediocre in batting he made his last century - 100* against Worcester at

Worcester. His bowling improved and he took 115 wickets at 19.63 each. His best analysis was 10-87 against Leicestershire at Headingley.

	Own Team	O	M	R	W		Opp	Ct
	Total						Total	

1013. Yorkshire v Worcestershire, Worcester, May 9, 10, 11 (Match drawn)

	Own Team Total	O	M	R	W		Opp Total	Ct
not out	100 560-6d	43	19	59	2	J.B.Higgins lbw	402	
						C.V.Tarbox lbw		
		14	5	35	0		203-3	

1014. Yorkshire v Essex, Leyton, May 12, 14, 15 (Match drawn)

	Own Team Total	O	M	R	W		Opp Total	Ct
did not bat	- 514-6d	39	16	60	4	J.O'Connor lbw	226	
						C.A.G.Russell c E.Robinson		
						L.C.Eastman c A.Wood		
						F.E.Hugonin c E.Robinson		
		19	7	56	1	J.A.Cutmore lbw	223-2	

1015. Yorkshire v Cambridge University, Fenner's, May (16), 17, 18 (Match drawn)

	Own Team Total	O	M	R	W		Opp Total	Ct
not out	11 224-5d	-	-	-	-		30	2
		3	3	0	0		41-5	1

1016. Yorkshire v Sussex, Hull, May (19), 21, 22 (Match drawn)

	Own Team Total	O	M	R	W		Opp Total	Ct
did not bat	- 49-1	19	5	41	0		247	

1017. Yorkshire v Northamptonshire, Northampton, May (23), 24, 25 (Match drawn)

	Own Team Total	O	M	R	W		Opp Total	Ct
lbw b A.E.Thomas	10 149	13.5	5	37	5	V.W.C.Jupp c G.G.Macaulay	164	1
						J.E.Timms lbw		
						F.I.Walden c and b		
						A.E.Thomas c H.Sutcliffe		
						E.W.Clark c A.Wood		
		5	1	9	0		50-3	

1018. Yorkshire v Lancashire, Bramall Lane, May 26, 28, 29 (Match drawn)

	Own Team Total	O	M	R	W		Opp Total	Ct
st G.Duckworth								
b R.K.Tyldesley	13 473	43	20	56	4	C.Hallows b	385	
						G.E.Tyldesley c W.A.Worsley		
						M.L.Taylor lbw		
						L.Green hit wkt		
		5	0	10	0		80-1	

1019. Yorkshire v Warwickshire, Edgbaston, May 30, 31, June 1 (Match drawn)

	Own Team Total	O	M	R	W		Opp Total	Ct
not out	57 446-6d	50	18	95	2	R.E.S.Wyatt c E.Robinson	367	1
						J.H.Mayer c G.G.Macaulay		
did not bat	- 171-4							

1020. Yorkshire v Middlesex, Lord's, June 2, 4, 5 (Yorkshire won by an innings and 88 runs)

	Own Team Total	O	M	R	W		Opp Total	Ct
b F.J.Durston	4 479	21	7	67	1	F.J.Durston c M.Leyland	261	
		21.5	8	39	7	H.W.Lee b	130	
						J.W.Hearne c E.Robinson		
						G.O.B.Allen c sub		
						H.J.Enthoven c E.Robinson		
						N.E.Haig c M.Leyland		
						F.T.Mann c E.Robinson		
						W.F.F.Price c sub		

1021. Yorkshire v Hampshire, Southampton, June 6, 7, 8 (Match drawn)

	Own Team Total	O	M	R	W		Opp Total	Ct
lbw b A.S.Kennedy	32 318	31	5	79	1	J.A.Newman b	391	1
		-	-	-	-		70-3	

1022. Yorkshire v Hampshire, Bradford, June 9, 11, 12 (Match drawn)

	Own Team Total	O	M	R	W		Opp Total	Ct
b R.P.H.Utley	20 285	20.5	5	44	4	C.P.Mead c P.Holmes	204	1
						L.H.Tennyson c E.Robinson		
						C.P.Brutton b		
						G.S.Boyes st A.Wood		
		26	13	48	1	L.Harfield st A.Wood	169	

1023. Yorkshire v West Indians, Bramall Lane, June 13, (14), 15 (Match drawn)

	Own Team Total	O	M	R	W		Opp Total	Ct
lbw b H.C.Griffith	0 179	2	0	5	0		56-3	

1024. Yorkshire v Leicestershire, Headingley, June 16, 18, 19 (Yorkshire won by an innings and 28 runs)

	Own Team Total	O	M	R	W		Opp Total	Ct
run out	8 291	40	16	55	6	G.B.F.Rudd c P.Holmes	142	1
						N.F.Armstrong c W.A.Shackleton		
						A.T.Sharp st A.Wood		
						L.G.Berry b		
						W.E.Astill c K.A.Lister-Kaye		
						T.E.Sidwell c W.A.Worsley		

A.W.Shipman lbw   121   l
A.T.Sharp c K.A.Lister-Kaye
L.G.Berry b
D.S.Oscroft b

1025. Yorkshire v Worcestershire, Hull, June 20, 21, 22 (Yorkshire won by an innings and 20 runs)
did not bat   -   295-5d   12   6   15   0   169   1
                        -   -   -   -   106

1026. Yorkshire v Kent, Dover, June 23, 25, 26 (Match drawn)
c F.E.Woolley b B.Howlett 10   242   4   2   11   0   272
c L.E.G.Ames b A.C.Wright   1   283-9d   7   4   8   0   65-3

1027. Yorkshire v Glamorgan, Huddersfield, June 27, (28), (29) (Match drawn)
did not bat   -   387-2

1028. Yorkshire v Nottinghamshire, Bramall Lane, June 30, July 2, 3 (Match drawn)
lbw b H.Larwood   6   125   4   1   9   0   134   1
did not bat   -   198-4   22   6   58   1   S.J.Staples c A.Mitchell   329-9d

1029. Yorkshire v West Indians, Headingley, July 4, 5, 6 (Yorkshire won by 190 runs)
c M.P.Fernandes
   b G.N.Francis   5   284   17   7   37   4   M.P.Fernandes lbw   208
                                         G.Challenor c E.Robinson
                                         E.L.G.Hoad c C.Turner
                                         L.N.Constantine st A.Wood
did not bat   -   172-1d   -   -   -   -   58

1030. Yorkshire v Surrey, Bradford, July 7, 9, 10 (Match drawn)
c D.R.Jardine
   b P.G.H.Fender   31   406   54   17   75   3   A.Sandham lbw   458   1
                                         T.F.Shepherd b
                                         H.G.Baldwin lbw
did not bat   -   121-1

1031. Yorkshire v Derbyshire, Derby, July 11, 12, 13 (Yorkshire won by an innings and 52 runs)
c A.G.Slater b L.F.Townsend 4   485-8d   24   8   46   2   T.S.Worthington c P.Holmes 234
                                         A.G.Slater c W.Worsley
                          21   2   59   3   J.Bowden b   199
                                         L.F.Townsend st A.Wood
                                         H.Elliott c A.Wood

1032. Yorkshire v Nottinghamshire, Trent Bridge, July 14, 16, 17 (Match drawn)
b F.Barratt   0   520-7d   54.2   19   87   5   B.Lilley c P.Holmes   350
                                         F.Barratt lbw
                                         F.W.Shipston c W.A.Worsley
                                         W.A.Flint lbw
                                         T.L.Richmond c E.Robinson
did not bat   -   210-0

1033. Yorkshire v Essex, Bramall Lane, July 21, 23, 24 (Yorkshire won by an innings and 215 runs)
c A.B.Hipkin
   b J.W.H.T.Douglas 50   512-9d   22.5   11   26   4   J.A.Cutmore c A.Mitchell   193
                                         C.J.Treglown c E.Oldroyd
                                         E.C.Thompson b
                                         G.M.Locks b
                          9   6   10   4   J.O'Connor b   104
                                         A.B.Hipkin c W.A.Worsley
                                         C.J.Treglown c E.Robinson
                                         E.G.Martin st A.Wood

1034. Yorkshire v Middlesex, Headingley, July 28, 30, 31 (Match drawn)
run out   8   303   32   4   78   2   E.T.Killick lbw   488   1
                                         H.J.Enthoven st A.Wood
did not bat   -   290-1

1035. Yorkshire v Northamptonshire, Harrogate, August 1, 2, 3 (Yorkshire won by ten wickets)
c A.D.G.Matthews
   b A.E.Thomas   61   287   11   7   11   0   125   1
did not bat   -   12-0   27.5   11   57   5   C.N.Woolley c and b   172   2
                                         B.W.Bellamy c W.A.Worsley
                                         A.H.Bakewell lbw
                                         A.D.G.Matthews b
                                         A.E.Thomas c H.Fisher

1036. Yorkshire v Lancashire, Old Trafford, August 4, 6, (7) (Match drawn)
not out   45   352   40   20   42   1   G.E.Tyldesley c E.Robinson 244-3

1037. Yorkshire v Leicestershire, Aylestone Road, Leicester, August 8, 9, 10 (Match drawn)
```
lbw b H.A.Smith          7   234      69.3  18  160  6   E.W.Dawson  b                      390
                                                          N.F.Armstrong  st A.Wood
                                                          G.L.Berry  c E.Robinson
                                                          W.E.Astill  lbw
                                                          H.A.Smith  c A.Mitchell
                                                          A.Skelding  c M.Leyland
did not bat              -   273-4
```
1038. Yorkshire v Warwickshire, Bradford, August 11, 13, 14 (Match drawn)
```
not out                 52   540-7d   20    7   38   1   J.A.Smart  b                        244     1
                                      -     -   -    -                                        21-2
```
1039. Yorkshire v Derbyshire, Dewsbury, August 15, 16, 17 (Yorkshire won by an innings and 22 runs)
```
b L.F.Townsend          13   413-9d   28.2  11  55   7   J.Bowden  st A.Wood                 126     1
                                                          G.M.Lee  c A.Mitchell
                                                          G.R.Jackson  c and b
                                                          A.G.Slater  lbw
                                                          T.S.Worthington  b
                                                          A.W.Richardson  c H.Sutcliffe
                                                          T.B.Mitchell  b
                                      16    10  13   0                                        265
```
1040. Yorkshire v Kent, Headingley, August 18, (20), (21) (Match drawn)
```
did not bat              -   43-1     13    6   16   1   H.T.W.Hardinge  b                   261     1
```
1041. Yorkshire v Surrey, Kennington Oval, August 22, 23, (24) (Match drawn)
```
c and b H.A.Peach        6   325      27    8   55   2   J.B.Hobbs  st A.Wood                273-4
                                                          H.T.Barling  c H.Sutcliffe
```
1042. Yorkshire v Sussex, Eastbourne, August 25, 27, 28 (Match drawn)
```
did not bat              -   429-4d   14    7   14   0                                        131
                                      50    8   150  6   E.H.Bowley  b                        490
                                                          J.H.Parks  c W.A.Worsley
                                                          J.Langridge  c W.Barber
                                                          A.F.Wensley  lbw
                                                          A.H.H.Gilligan  lbw
                                                          W.L.Cornford  b
```
1043. Yorkshire v Glamorgan, Swansea, August 29, 30, 31 (Yorkshire won by an innings and 112 runs)
```
c J.M.Jones b F.P.Ryan   4   433      20    6   24   2   W.E.Bates  b                        167     1
                                                          M.J.L.Turnbull  st A.Wood
                                      26    8   56   6   J.T.Bell  b                          154     1
                                                          J.M.Jones  c and b
                                                          A.H.Dyson  b
                                                          W.E.Bates  c F.Dennis
                                                          D.Davies  c E.Oldroyd
                                                          T.J.Hills  c A.Wood
```
1044. Yorkshire v MCC, Scarborough, September 1, 3, 4 (Match drawn)
```
lbw b F.J.Durston        7   294      31    6   67   4   N.E.Haig  b                         373-8d
                                                          W.E.Astill  lbw
                                                          E.H.Hendren  lbw
                                                          A.E.R.Gilligan  c A.Wood
did not bat              -   263-4
```
1045. Mr.C.I.Thornton's XI v MCC Australian Team, Scarborough, September 5, 6, 7 (Match drawn)
```
not out                 14   293      23    3   83   1   M.W.Tate  b                         416
did not bat              -   189-3    13    1   71   3   J.B.Hobbs  st F.W.Gilligan           236-5   1
                                                          H.Sutcliffe  c and b
                                                          W.R.Hammond  lbw
```

SEASON'S AVERAGES

Batting and Fielding	M	I	NO	Runs	HS	Ave	100	50	Ct
Championship	28	23	4	542	100*	28.52	1	4	18
Other Yorkshire matches	4	4	1	23	11	7.66	-	-	3
Other matches	1	1	1	14	14*	-	-	-	1
Season	33	28	6	579	100*	26.31	1	4	22
Career	1045	1461	213	38745	267*	31.04	58	192	737

Bowling	O	M	R	W	BB	Ave	5i	10m
Championship	1074.2	383	1995	103	7-39	19.36	9	1
Other Yorkshire matches	53	16	109	8	4-37	13.62	-	-
Other matches	36	4	154	4	3-71	38.50	-	-
Season (6-ball)	1163.2	403	2258	115	7-39	19.63	9	1
Career (6-ball)	26383.4	7633 ⎫	66110	3992	9-24	16.56	277	65
(5-ball)	2748.4	1029 ⎭						

1929

Now in his fifty-second year Rhodes once again took over a hundred wickets, for the 23rd time in his career. He had an analysis of 9-39 against Essex at Leyton but he also had 7-38 against Nottinghamshire at Bramall Lane, 5-46 against Kent again at Bramall Lane and 5-34 against Surrey at Leeds. In all he bowled over a thousand overs, some feat when given his age. At the close of the season he was picked to go to the West Indies as senior professional in the second English team, the other was playing in New Zealand, and returned for the final time to Test cricket.

	Own Team Total	O	M	R	W		Opp Total	Ct
1046. Yorkshire v Cambridge University, Fenner's, May 1, 2, 3 (Match drawn)								
not out	15 420	17	10	27	3	S.A.Block lbw	211	1
						G.C.Grant lbw		
						L.E.Hunt c T.A.Jacques		
		24	9	71	2	S.A.Block b	425-7	
						E.T.Killick b		
1047. Yorkshire v MCC, Lord's, May 4, (6), (7) (Match drawn)								
did not bat	- 359-5							
1048. Yorkshire v Oxford University, The Parks , May 8, 9, 10 (Match drawn)								
not out	24 378-8d	13	3	27	1	A.T.Barber lbw	168	
did not bat	- 93-6	17	6	44	2	E.M.Wellings c A.Wood	313	
						C.H.Hill-Wood c M.Leyland		
1049. Yorkshire v Essex, Leyton, May 11, 13, 14 (Yorkshire won by an innings and 37 runs)								
not out	5 299-7d	20.4	5	41	3	L.C.Eastman c W.E.Bowes	195	
						A.B.Hipkin c A.Mitchell		
						A.G.Daer c A.Mitchell		
		21.4	9	39	9	J.A.Cutmore c M.Leyland	67	
						C.J.Bray st A.Wood		
						J.O'Connor b		
						C.A.G.Russell lbw		
						H.M.Morris c E.Robinson		
						L.C.Eastman c W.A.Worsley		
						A.B.Hipkin c E.Oldroyd		
						H.P.Waugh c A.Wood		
						A.G.Daer c A.Wood		
1050. Yorkshire v Lancashire, Old Trafford, May 18, 20, 21 (Match drawn)								
c P.T.Eckersley								
b R.K.Tyldesley	42 347	44.3	27	44	3	J.Iddon c C.Turner	305	
						G.Duckworth lbw		
						E.A.McDonald b		
		-	-	-	-		127-3	1
1051. Yorkshire v Warwickshire, Edgbaston, May 22, 23, 24 (Match drawn)								
not out	30 367-6	71	21	115	2	A.J.W.Croom c A.Mitchell	536-7d	
						D.G.Foster c E.Oldroyd		
1052. Yorkshire v South Africans, Bramall Lane, May 25, 27, 28 (Match drawn)								
c Q.McMillan b N.A.Quinn	0 338	37	13	80	1	R.H.Catterall lbw	441-5d	
		10	3	32	1	Q.McMillan c W.Barber	277-8	
1053. Yorkshire v Kent, Bramall Lane, June 1, 3 (Yorkshire won by eight wickets)								
not out	53 126	5	2	9	0		125	
did not bat	- 140-2	27	8	46	5	J.A.Deed lbw	140	1
						L.E.G.Ames c F.Dennis		
						H.T.W.Harding c A.Wood		
						A.P.Freeman lbw		
						A.C.Wright c and b		

1054. Yorkshire v Glamorgan, Swansea, June (5), (6), 7 (Match drawn)
did not bat   -   147-3   24   14   30   4   D.Davies lbw   146   1
  F.W.Mathias c and b
  T.Every c F.Dennis
  J.Mercer c A.Mitchell

1055. Yorkshire v Sussex, Headingley, June 8, 10, 11 (Match drawn)
not out   43   205   32   10   63   2   J.H.Parks c E.Oldroyd   261
  J.Langridge c C.Turner
not out   55   128-5   21   7   58   1   W.L.Cornford st A.Wood   285

1056. Yorkshire v Northamptonshire, Bradford, June 12, 13, 14, (Match drawn)
c A.E.Thomas
  b N.E.Partridge   7   219   5   5   0   0   102
did not bat   -   58-4d   1   0   6   0   57-1

1057. Yorkshire v Nottinghamshire, Bramall Lane, June 15, 17, 18 (Yorkshire won by five wickets)
b A.Staples   25   205   26   8   47   4   W.Walker b   157   1
  A.Staples b
  B.Lilley st A.Wood
  S.J.Staples c E.Oldroyd
c A.W.Carr b W.Voce   0   99-5   25   11   38   7   A.W.Carr lbw   144
  W.E.G.Payton c A.Wood
  A.Staples c P.Holmes
  B.Lilley c P.Holmes
  F.Barratt c A.Mitchell
  W.Voce c W.Barber
  R.D.F.Bland lbw

1058. Yorkshire v Middlesex, Lord's, June 22, 24, 25 (Match drawn)
c W.F.F.Price
  b I.A.R.Peebles   53   197   16   5   26   0   166   1
c W.F.F.Price b I.A.R.Peebles 6   227   4   2   5   0   86-3

1059. Yorkshire v Northamptonshire, Northampton, June 26, 27, 28 (Yorkshire won by an innings and 38 runs)
lbw b V.W.C.Jupp   31   409-8d   -   -   -   -   94
  19.4   4   50   3   A.H.Bakewell c P.Holmes   277
  A.G.Liddell b
  E.W.Clark b

1060. Yorkshire v Kent, Tonbridge, June 29, July 1, 2 (Kent won by an innings and 76 runs)
c W.H.Ashdown
  b A.P.Freeman   17   108   43.3   8   116   7   H.T.W.Hardinge b   471-9d
  C.P.Johnstone lbw
  F.E.Woolley c W.B.Broadhead
  W.H.Ashdown c F.Dennis
  G.B.Legge c W.A.Shackleton
  L.J.Todd lbw
  A.P.Freeman b
b A.P.Freeman   18   287

1061. Yorkshire v Derbyshire, Chesterfield, July 3, 4, 5 (Match drawn)
lbw b T.S.Worthington   8   239   18   6   24   2   J.Bowden c E.Robinson   156
  L.F.Townsend c A.Wood
did not bat   -   37-3

1062. Yorkshire v Surrey, Headingley, July (6), 8, 9 (Match drawn)
c E.W.J.Brooks
  c M.J.C.Allom   0   324-9d   22   9   34   5   T.F.Shepherd c F.Dennis   156
  H.A.Peach c E.Oldroyd
  M.J.C.Allom b
  E.W.J.Brooks c G.G.Macaulay
  A.G.Penfold c M.Leyland
  13   6   23   0   137-1

1063. Yorkshire v Worcestershire, Huddersfield, July 10, 11, 12 (Match drawn)
c M.Nichol b C.F.Root   1   238   16   6   20   0   252   1
c W.V.Fox b C.V.Tarbox   12   267-9d   15   10   16   0   118-7

1064. Yorkshire v Nottinghamshire, Trent Bridge, July 13, 15, 16 (Match drawn)
c B.Lilley b F.Barratt   79   498   35   29   11   0   190-4

1065. Yorkshire v Glamorgan, Hull, July 17, 18, 19 (Yorkshire won by an innings and 54 runs)
did not bat   -   437-4d   43   19   50   3   W.E.Bates lbw   297   2
  A.H.Dyson lbw
  D.E.Davies c A.Mitchell

```
                    21.2  10   41   5   W.E.Bates  c A.Mitchell        86
                                        A.H.Dyson  c W.Barber
                                        N.V.H.Riches  lbw
                                        D.E.Davies  c E.Oldroyd
                                        T.Arnott  b
```

1066. Yorkshire v Essex, Bradford, July 20, 22 (Yorkshire won by ten wickets)
```
did not bat        -   239-4d   20   11   23   2   T.H.Wade  lbw        143
                                                   A.B.Hipkin  c F.Dennis
did not bat        -   18-0     2.2   2    0   1   A.G.Daer  st A.Wood   113
```

1067. Yorkshire v Warwickshire, Harrogate, July 24, 25, 26 (Yorkshire won by four wickets)
```
c N.Kilner b D.G.Foster   13   182   35   14   57   2   F.R.Santall  c H.Sutcliffe   239
                                                        J.H.Parsons  c G.G.Macaulay
not out                    8   175-6   -    -    -   -                                116
```

1068. Yorkshire v Hampshire, Headingley, August 10, 12, 13 (Yorkshire won by an innings and 18 runs)
```
not out   15   369   25   5   52   3   J.A.Newman  lbw                189
                                       G.C.A.Adams  c W.A.Worsley
                                       W.H.Livsey  b
          10   4    16   0                                           162   1
```

1069. Yorkshire v Middlesex, Bradford, August 17, 19, 20 (Yorkshire won by 196 runs)
```
c H.W.Lee b F.J.Durston   1   213   4   0   25   0                    154
lbw b J.W.Hearne          7   229-7d 7   1   22   3   N.E.Haig c W.E.Bowes   92
                                                      R.W.V.Robins c G.G.Macaulay
                                                      W.F.F.Price c A.Mitchell
```

1070. Yorkshire v Hampshire, Bournemouth, August 21, 22, 23 (Match drawn)
```
did not bat        -   270-3d   15   4   43   0                       259
                                18   6   38   1   G.C.A.Adams c M.Leyland   233
```

1071. Yorkshire v Surrey, Kennington Oval, August 24, 26, 27 (Match drawn)
```
run out            5   304   32   9   71   2   A.Ducat c A.Wood         408
                                               R.J.Gregory lbw
did not bat        -   315-1
```

1072. Yorkshire v Worcestershire, Worcester, August 28, 29, 30 (Yorkshire won by ten wickets)
```
did not bat        -   307-7d   12.2   4   25   1   P.F.Jackson c M.Leyland    94
did not bat        -   26-0     17     4   35   1   H.H.I.H.Gibbons lbw       237
```

1073. Yorkshire v Sussex, Hove, August 31, September 2, 3 (Sussex won by 78 runs)
```
b A.F.Wensley             1   152   29    12   51   3   J.Langridge c and b   169   3
                                                        J.H.Parks c F.Dennis
                                                        M.W.Tate lbw
c J.H.Parks b J.Langridge  8   204   30.1  14   54   1   J.G.Wagener c and b   265   1
```

1074. Lord Hawke's XI v MCC Australian Team, Scarborough, September 7, 9, 10 (Match drawn)
```
b H.Larwood        3   319   12   2   67   0                          553-5d
did not bat        -   211-8
```

1075. Yorkshire v MCC, Scarborough, September 11, 12, 13 (Yorkshire won by four wickets)
```
c F.W.Gilligan
  b W.E.Bowes     32   355   18.2   8   20   3   W.E.Astill c R.W.V.Robins   176
                                                 F.W.Gilligan b
                                                 W.E.Bowes c F.E.Greenwood
did not bat        -   102-6   22   5   38   2   E.W.Dawson b               280-6d
                                                 V.W.C.Jupp c A.Mitchell
```

SEASON'S AVERAGES

Batting and Fielding	M	I	NO	Runs	HS	Ave	100	50	Ct
Championship	24	27	7	543	79	27.15	-	4	13
Other Yorkshire matches	5	4	2	71	32	35.50	-	-	1
Other matches	1	1	0	3	3	3.00	-	-	-
Season	30	32	9	617	79	26.82	-	4	14
Career	1075	1493	222	39362	267*	30.96	58	196	751

Bowling	O	M	R	W	BB	Ave	5i	10m
Championship	847.1	331	1464	85	9-39	17.22	6	2
Other Yorkshire matches	158.2	57	339	15	3-20	22.60	-	-
Other matches	12	2	67	0	-	-	-	-
Season (6-ball)	1017.3	390	1870	100	9-39	18.70	6	2
Career (6-ball)	27401.1	8023 ⎫	67980	4092	9-24	16.61	283	67
(5-ball)	2748.4	1029 ⎭						

1929/30 - MCC in the West Indies

Rhodes's 'swan-song' took him to the West Indies for the first time, under the captaincy of F.S.G.Calthorpe. He played in all four representative matches, subsequently given Test match status. His batting failed, no doubt due to failing eyesight and the very bright light. All told he took 39 wickets on the tour but only ten in the Test matches. His Test career had thus spanned thirty years, a record that will surely stand forever.

	Own Team Total	O	M	R	W		Opp Total	Ct
1076. MCC v Barbados, Bridgetown, January 1, 2, 3, 4 (Match drawn)								
b C.de L.Inniss	36	513	40.1	16	80	3	L.A.Walcott b	345
							J.W.Byer c G.Gunn	
							H.C.Griffith c E.H.Hendren	
1077. ENGLAND v WEST INDIES, Bridgetown, January 11, 13, 14, 15, 16 (Match drawn)								
not out	14	467	27.1	9	44	0		369	1
did not bat	-	167-3	51	10	110	3	G.A.Headley c J.O'Connor	384	1
							J.E.D.Sealy b	
							C.R.Browne c E.H.Hendren	
1078. MCC v Trinidad, Port of Spain, January 22, 23, 24, 25 (Trinidad won by 102 runs)								
c E.A.C.Hunte								
b L.N.Constantine	11	167	14	5	30	4	C.A.Merry b	150
							L.N.Constantine lbw	
							J.E.D.Sealy b	
							N.Betancourt lbw	
not out	8	214	37	14	76	5	C.A.Wiles c L.F.Townsend	333
							W.H.St.Hill c E.H.Hendren	
							J.E.D.Sealy lbw	
							E.St.Hill c R.T.Stanyforth	
							M.G.Grell c E.H.Hendren	
1079. ENGLAND v WEST INDIES, Port of Spain, February 1, 3, 4, 5, 6 (England won by 167 runs)								
lbw b H.C.Griffith	2	208	20	5	40	1	N.Betancourt lbw	254
not out	6	425-8d	22	12	31	0		212
1080. MCC v British Guiana, Georgetown, February 10, 11, 12 (MCC won by an innings and 10 runs)								
did not bat	-	605-5d	27	8	59	1	J.W.R.Phillips lbw	307	2
			23	6	52	3	J.St.P.Dare c L.F.Townsend	288
							C.V.Wight b	
							J.M.Neblett b	
1081. MCC v British Guiana, Georgetown, February 15, 17, 18, 19 (MCC won by an innings and 107 runs)								
not out	9	555-7d	23	3	46	3	F.I.de Caires st L.E.G.Ames	264
							V.Chabrol lbw	
							M.Anthony c E.H.Hendren	
			34	12	57	5	M.P.Fernandes b	184
							K.L.Wishart lbw	
							J.St.P.Dare c E.H.Hendren	
							C.V.Wight b	
							V.Chabrol st L.E.G.Ames	
1082. ENGLAND v WEST INDIES, Georgetown, February 21, 22, 24, 25, 26 (West Indies won by 289 runs)								
b G.N.Francis	0	145	40	8	96	2	M.P.Fernandes	
							c L.E.G.Ames	471	1
							J.E.D.Sealy c and b	
not out	10	327	51	23	93	2	M.P.Fernandes	
							c F.S.G.Calthorpe	290
							J.E.D.Sealy c E.H.Hendren	

1083. MCC v Jamaica, Kingston, March 22, 24, 25, 26 (Match drawn)

c J.K.Holt b O.C.Scott	14	220	28	11	57	4	W.G.Beckford lbw	248
							J.K.Holt c G.T.S.Stevens	
							L.G.Hylton b	
							F.R.Martin c L.E.G.Ames	
did not bat	-	441-6d	19	5	37	1	R.K.Nunes c E.H.Hendren	324-4

1084. ENGLAND v WEST INDIES, Kingston, April 3, 4, 5, 7, 8, 9, 10, (11), (12) (Match drawn)

not out	8	849	20.5	12	17	1	H.C.Griffith c E.H.Hendren	286
not out	11	272-9d	24	13	22	1	C.A.Roach c G.Gunn	408-5

SEASON'S AVERAGES

Batting and Fielding	M	I	NO	Runs	HS	Ave	100	50	Ct
Test matches	4	7	5	51	14	25.50	-	-	3
Other matches	5	5	2	78	36	26.00	-	-	2
Tour	9	12	7	129	36	25.80	-	-	5
Career	1084	1505	229	39431	267*	30.90	58	196	756

Bowling		O	M	R	W	BB	Ave	5i	10m
Test matches		256	92	453	10	3-110	45.30	-	-
Other matches		245.1	80	494	29	5-59	17.03	2	-
Tour	(6-ball)	501.1	172	947	39	5-59	24.28	2	-
Career	(6-ball)	27902.2	8195 ⎱ 68927		4131	9-24	16.68	285	67
	(5-ball)	2748.4	1029 ⎰						

1930

So Rhodes's career came to an end and his final season at the age of 52 saw him finish with 73 wickets and the experience of bowling to Don Bradman whose abilities he acknowledged wholeheartedly. His final match was for H.D.G.Leveson-Gower's XI in the Scarborough Festival against the Australians when he had Bradman missed three times while taking 5-95. Thus ended the career of the greatest wicket-taker of all time and a candidate for one of the truly great, if not the greatest, all-rounder. His total of 1,110 first-class appearances is the most by any player as is his total of 1,534 innings.

	Own Team Total	O	M	R	W		Opp Total	Ct

1085. Yorkshire v Australians, Bramall Lane, May 10, 12, (13) (Match drawn)

not out	6	155	31.5	5	95	3	V.Y.Richardson c A.Wood	320
							E.L:A'Beckett st A.Wood	
							P.M.Hornibrook st A.Wood	

1086. Yorkshire v Cambridge University, Fenner's, May 14, 15, 16 (Yorkshire won by ten wickets)

not out	10	258	27.4	16	35	7	E.T.Killick c A.Mitchell	127	1
							G.C.Grant lbw	
							H.E.Carris b	
							T.W.T.Baines lbw	
							J.T.Morgan b	
							H.R.W.Butterworth lbw	
							F.R.Brown c and b	
did not bat	-	127-0	30.3	7	51	3	E.T.Killick b	257
							F.R.Brown b	
							R.C.Rought-Rought lbw	

1087. Yorkshire v Essex, Leyton, May 17, 19, 20 (Yorkshire won by 132 runs)

st J.R.Sheffield b J.O'Connor	12	290	22	7	35	1	J.A.Cutmore lbw	231
did not bat	-	203-3d	21	10	34	0		130

1088. Yorkshire v Kent, Headingley, May 24, 26, 27 (Kent won by 54 runs)

b A.P.Freeman	8	198	16	5	33	2	F.E.Woolley c G.G.Macaulay	205
							L.E.G.Ames b	
lbw b A.P.Freeman	5	242	12	0	47	1	T.F.Mitchell c E.Robinson	289

1089. Yorkshire v Essex, Dewsbury, May 28, 29, 30 (Match drawn)

b T.P.B.Smith	6	365-9d	48	21	79	2	D.F.Pope b	379
							M.S.Nichols b	
did not bat	-	226-3						

1090. Yorkshire v Hampshire, Bradford, June 4, 5, 6 (Yorkshire won by an innings and 100 runs)
  not out   5 478-9   14   7   11   0   169
                                    16   7   18   0   209
1091. Yorkshire v Lancashire, Headingley, June 7, 9, 10 (Match drawn)
  b E.A.MacDonald   13 417-9d 44   32   19   1   J.Iddon st A.Wood   305   1
  did not bat   -   11-1
1092. Yorkshire v Warwickshire, Edgbaston, June 11, 12, 13 (Yorkshire won by eight wickets)
  not out   45 364-9d 16   5   20   0   148
  did not bat   - 100-2   17.4 3   50   2   J.H.Parsons c P.Holmes   314
                                                       W.Sanders lbw
1093. Yorkshire v Northamptonshire, Northampton, June 18, 19, 20 (Yorkshire won by nine wickets)
  c E.W.Clark b A.E.Thomas 35 184   1   1   0   0   88
  did not bat   -   73-1   23   10   36   3   J.E.Timms c A.T.Barber   168   1
                                                       R.J.Partridge c F.Dennis
                                                       A.E.Thomas c F.E.Greenwood
1094. Yorkshire v Nottinghamshire, Trent Bridge, June 21, 23, 24 (Match drawn)
  not out   80 324-9d   8   1   28   0   215-4   1
1095. Yorkshire v Somerset, Bradford, June 25, 26 (Yorkshire won by 328 runs)
  b A.Young   2 186   8.2 6   2   2   A.W.Wellard c and b   43   1
                                                       A.H.S.Clark c A.T.Barber
  did not bat   - 318-1d   -   -   -   -   133   1
1096. Yorkshire v Australians, Bradford, July 2, 3, 4 (Australians won by ten wickets)
  b E.L.A'Beckett   35 146   25.3 8   49   3   A.Hurwood c A.T.Barber   302
                                                       P.M.Hornibrook c A.Mitchell
                                                       C.W.Walker st A.Wood
  c and b C.V.Grimmett 17 161   -   -   -   -   7-0
1097. Yorkshire v Surrey, Bramall Lane, July 5, 7, 8 (Surrey won by an innings and 22 runs)
  lbw b M.J.C.Allom   5 206   33   7   61   1   M.J.C.Allom c M.Leyland   438-9d
  not out   19 210
1098. Yorkshire v Somerset, Bath, July 9, 10, 11 (Yorkshire won by 170 runs)
  not out   14 161   10   5   15   3   J.C.White lbw   103
                                                       F.S.Lee b
                                                       A.W.Wellard c P.Holmes
  did not bat   - 292-3d   24   8   39   4   E.F.Longrigg b   180   1
                                                       S.G.U.Considine c A.Wood
                                                       F.S.Lee c and b
                                                       A.W.Wellard c P.Holmes
1099. Yorkshire v Gloucestershire, Bristol, July 16, 17, 18 (Yorkshire won by an innings and 187 runs)
  lbw b T.W.J.Goddard   0 462   26   7   53   4   A.E.Dipper lbw   125
                                                       D.N.Moore c A.Mitchell
                                                       C.J.Barnett lbw
                                                       R.G.Ford b
                                    27   16   21   4   W.L.Neale lbw   150
                                                       C.J.Barnett c P.Holmes
                                                       H.Smith b
                                                       E.J.Stephens c G.G.Macaulay
1100. Yorkshire v Warwickshire, Bramall Lane, July 26, (28), (29) (Match drawn)
  c J.H.Mayer b G.A.E.Paine 36 203
1101. Yorkshire v Gloucestershire, Hull, July (30), 31, August 1 (Match drawn)
  b C.W.L.Parker   1 207-9d 19   7   36   3   F.J.Seabrook lbw   108
                                                       W.L.Neale st A.Wood
                                                       C.J.Barnett c A.Mitchell
                                    20   7   44   0   263-3
1102. Yorkshire v Lancashire, Old Trafford, August 2, (4), 5 (Match drawn)
  b E.A.McDonald   0 125   32.1 9   54   3   J.Iddon c and b   284-6d   1
                                                       J.L.Hopwood lbw
                                                       P.T.Eckersley c A.T.Barber
1103. Yorkshire v Leicestershire, Aylestone Road, Leicester, August 6, (7), 8 (Match drawn)
  c G.Geary b A.W.Shipman 8 189   19   12   11   2   J.C.Bradshaw c H.Sutcliffe 115-7
                                                       G.L.Berry c M.Leyland
1104. Yorkshire v Glamorgan, Bramall Lane, August 13, 14, 15 (Match drawn)
  did not bat   - 284-3d 22   9   27   2   T.J.Hills lbw   209
                                                       J.Mercer b
  did not bat   -   65-0   29   14   30   1   T.J.Hills c A.T.Barber   332-5d

1105. Yorkshire v Nottinghamshire, Bradford, August 16, 18, (19) (Match drawn)
   b R.D.F.Bland   3   451-8d   18   5   43   1   G.Gunn b   153
                                    2   1   4   0   37-5

1106. Yorkshire v Hampshire, Bournemouth, August 20, 21, 22 (Yorkshire won by ten wickets)
   c J.A.Newman
       b O.W.Herman   40 147   6   3   8   0   141
   did not bat   - 116-0   -   -   -   -   120   1

1107. Yorkshire v Sussex, Hove, August 27, 28, 29 (Match drawn)
   c J.H.Parks b A.E.R.Gilligan 9   384   23.2 8   48   3   H.W.Parks b   269
                                                  A.E.R.Gilligan c F.Dennis
                                                  W.L.Cornford b
   did not bat   - 118-6d   11   3   20   2   E.H.Bowley c A.Mitchell   129-7
                                                  M.W.Tate c A.Mitchell

1108. Yorkshire v MCC, Scarborough, September 3, 4, 5 (Match drawn)
   c F.W.Gilligan
       b W.E.Bowes 41 253   26   7   58   2   K.S.Duleepsinhji lbw   337-7d
                                               A.S.Kennedy lbw
   did not bat   - 285-3d   10   0   48   3   N.E.Haig b   130-4
                                               K.S.Duleepsinhji c F.Dennis
                                              E.H.Hendren b

1109. Lord Hawke's XI v MCC South African Team, Scarborough, September 6, 8, (9) (Match drawn)
   b M.W.Tate   4 345-9   6   0   38   0   341-4

1110. Mr.H.D.G.Leveson-Gower's XI v Australians, Scarborough, September 10, 11, 12 (Match drawn)
   not out   16 218-9d   30.5 5   95   5   A.A.Jackson b   238
                                               A.G.Fairfax st G.Duckworth
                                             A.Hurwood b
                                               C.V.Grimmett c R.E.S.Wyatt
                                             T.W.Wall c R.E.S.Wyatt
   b A.F.Kippax   3 247

SEASON'S AVERAGES

Batting and Fielding	M	I	NO	Runs	HS	Ave	100	50	Ct
Championship	20	21	5	346	80*	21.62	-	1	8
Other Yorkshire matches	4	5	2	109	41	36.33	-	-	1
Other matches	2	3	1	23	16*	11.50	-	-	-
Season	26	29	8	478	80*	22.76	-	1	9
Career	1110	1534	237	39969	267*	30.81	58	197	765

Bowling	O	M	R	W	BB	Ave	5i	10m
Championship	588.3	236	926	47	4-21	19.70	-	-
Other Yorkshire matches	151.3	43	336	21	7-35	16.00	1	1
Other matches	36.5	5	133	5	5-95	26.60	1	-
Season (6-ball)	776.5	284	1395	73	7-35	19.10	2	1
Career (6-ball)	28679.1	8479 } 70322		4204	9-24	16.72	287	68
(5-ball)	2748.4	1029 }						

Season by Season (Batting and Fielding)

Season		M	I	NO	R	HS	Ave	100	50	Ct
1898		33	41	9	557	78	17.40	-	3	18
1899		34	49	12	432	81*	11.67	-	1	23
1900		35	42	11	655	79	21.12	-	3	11
1901		37	45	13	854	105	26.68	1	1	24
1902		37	46	14	490	92*	15.31	-	1	19
1903		36	51	9	1137	98*	27.07	-	7	20
1903/04	Australia	14	18	7	239	49*	21.72	-	-	14
1904		36	47	4	1537	196	35.74	2	8	22
1905		37	52	8	1581	201	35.93	2	11	44
1906		37	62	3	1721	119	29.16	3	12	39
1907		33	47	1	1055	112	22.93	1	6	20
1907/08	Australia	17	27	8	929	119	48.89	2	5	8
1908		36	57	4	1673	146	31.56	3	5	12
1909		37	59	7	2094	199	40.26	5	10	25
1909/10	South Africa	13	20	1	499	77	26.26	-	3	12
1910		34	59	4	1465	111	26.63	1	7	17
1911		36	64	5	2261	128	38.32	5	9	27
1911/12	Australia	14	24	4	1098	179	54.90	4	5	11
1912		37	58	5	1597	176	30.13	2	7	29
1913		36	64	4	1963	152	32.71	4	9	30
1913/14	South Africa	17	24	3	731	152	34.80	1	3	29
1914		31	49	2	1377	113	29.29	2	9	36
1919		33	46	10	1237	135	34.36	1	9	30
1920		34	45	5	1123	167*	28.07	1	8	32
1920/21	Australia	12	19	0	730	210	38.42	2	2	6
1921		32	47	10	1474	267*	39.83	3	5	28
1921/22	India	2	2	0	339	183	169.50	2	-	1
1922		37	46	8	1511	110	39.76	4	6	28
1922/23	India	4	8	1	247	79	35.28	-	2	4
1923		37	48	8	1321	126	33.02	2	6	33
1924		38	50	7	1126	100	26.18	1	7	23
1925		37	43	9	1391	157	40.91	2	10	17
1926		33	36	3	1132	132	34.30	1	7	15
1926/27	India	1	1	1	13	13*	-	-	-	-
1927		35	37	7	577	73	19.23	-	1	8
1928		33	28	6	579	100*	26.31	1	4	22
1929		30	32	9	617	79	26.82	-	4	14
1929/30	West Indies	9	12	7	129	36	25.80	-	-	5
1930		26	29	8	478	80*	22.76	-	1	9
Total		**1110**	**1534**	**237**	**39969**	**267***	**30.81**	**58**	**197**	**765**

Season by Season (Bowling)

Season		O	M	R	W	BB	Ave	5i	10m	Econ	Strike
1898	(5b)	1230	482	2249	154	7/24	14.60	12	3	2.19	39.93
1899	(5b)	1518.4	547	3062	179	9/24	17.10	12	4	2.41	42.42
1900		1553	455	3606	261	8/23	13.81	24	7	2.32	35.70
1901		1565.1	505	3797	251	8/53	15.12	25	9	2.42	37.41
1902		1306.3	405	2801	213	8/26	13.15	19	5	2.14	36.80
1903		1378	425	2813	193	8/61	14.57	16	4	2.04	42.83
1903/04	Australia	444.3	115	1055	65	8/68	16.23	7	2	2.37	41.03
1904		1197.2	351	2829	131	6/27	21.59	9	3	2.36	54.83
1905		1241.3	310	3085	182	8/90	16.95	15	4	2.49	40.74
1906		979.2	177	3018	128	6/90	23.57	8	1	3.08	45.90
1907		1075.1	231	2757	177	6/22	15.57	13	2	2.56	36.44
1907/08	Australia	427.2	100	1069	31	3/73	34.48	1	-	2.50	82.70
1908		804.1	233	1855	115	6/17	16.13	6	-	2.30	41.95
1909		873.1	205	2241	141	7/68	15.89	12	2	2.56	37.15
1909/10	South Africa	202.5	45	535	21	5/43	25.47	1	-	2.63	57.95
1910		613	138	1671	88	6/38	18.98	6	1	2.72	41.79

Year		O	M	R	W	BB	Ave	5i	10m	Econ	Strike
1911		914.1	168	2817	117	8/92	24.07	7	2	3.08	46.88
1911/12	Australia	62	9	234	0	-	-	-	-	3.77	-
1912		397.5	76	1165	53	6/102	21.98	2	-	2.92	45.03
1913		723	203	1882	86	7/45	21.88	4	1	2.60	50.44
1913/14	South Africa	240.3	53	662	31	4/27	21.35	-	-	2.75	46.54
1914		840.4	214	2157	118	7/19	18.27	5	1	2.56	42.74
1919		1048.3	305	2365	164	8/44	14.42	11	4	2.25	38.35
1920		1028.4	301	2123	161	8/39	13.18	12	5	2.06	38.33
1920/21	Australia	185.2	41	479	18	6/39	26.61	1	-	2.58	61.77
1921		963	326	1872	141	7/80	13.28	8	-	1.94	40.97
1921/22	India	71.3	36	103	19	7/26	5.42	3	1	1.44	22.57
1922		814.1	312	1451	119	6/13	12.19	6	-	1.78	41.05
1922/23	India	133.4	40	329	17	3/6	19.35	-	-	2.46	47.17
1923		929	345	1547	134	7/15	11.54	9	1	1.66	41.59
1924		746.3	240	1576	109	6/22	14.45	6	1	2.11	41.09
1925		636.4	241	1134	57	4/40	19.89	-	-	1.78	67.01
1926		892.4	315	1709	115	8/48	14.86	6	1	1.91	46.57
1926/27	India	24	4	73	3	3/73	24.66	-	-	3.04	48.00
1927		907.3	298	1731	85	6/20	20.36	2	-	1.90	64.05
1928		1163.2	403	2258	115	7/39	19.63	9	1	1.94	60.69
1929		1017.3	390	1870	100	9/39	18.70	6	2	1.83	61.05
1929/30	West Indies	501.1	172	947	39	5/59	24.28	2	-	1.88	77.10
1930		776.5	284	1395	73	7/35	19.10	2	1	1.79	63.84
Total		**28679.1**	**8479**	**65011**	**3871**	**9/39**	**16.79**	**263**	**61**	**2.26**	**44.46**
Total	**(5b)**	**2748.4**	**1029**	**5311**	**333**	**9/24**	**15.94**	**24**	**7**	**1.93**	**41.27**

Career Summary (Batting and Fielding)

	M	I	NO	R	HS	Ave	100	50	Ct
Championship	763	1021	136	26868	267*	30.35	38	137	521
Other Yorkshire matches	120	175	25	4230	128	28.20	8	18	66
Test matches	58	98	21	2325	179	30.19	2	11	60
MCC abroad	62	81	20	2757	210	45.19	7	11	47
Players v Gentlemen	39	60	12	1296	82	27.00	-	5	24
North v South	8	12	2	329	93	32.90	-	3	5
Other matches	60	87	21	2164	183	32.78	3	12	42
Career	**1110**	**1534**	**237**	**39969**	**267***	**30.81**	**58**	**197**	**765**

Career Summary (Bowling)

		O	M	R	W	BB	Ave	5i	10m	Econ	Strike
Championship		20961.1	6486	45213	2862	9/39	15.71	202	50	2.15	43.94
	(5b)	2073.1	813	3766	255	9/28	14.76	20	5	1.81	40.65
Other Yorkshire matches		3047.2	802	7966	440	8/68	18.10	27	5	2.61	41.55
	(5b)	304.3	105	689	40	7/56	17.22	3	1	2.26	38.07
Test matches		1248.5	328	3084	114	8/68	27.05	6	1	2.46	65.27
	(5b)	146.2	41	341	13	4/58	26.23	0	0	2.32	56.30
MCC abroad		1228.3	317	2975	145	6/39	20.51	9	1	2.42	50.83
Players v Gentlemen		716.1	180	1866	97	6/27	19.23	4	1	2.60	44.29
	(5b)	98	26	220	6	4/27	36.66	0	0	2.24	81.66
North v South		215.2	47	673	38	6/19	17.71	4	0	3.12	34.00
Other matches		1261.5	319	3234	175	9/39	18.48	11	3	2.56	43.26
	(5b)	126.3	44	295	19	9/24	15.52	1	1	2.33	33.31
Career		**28679.1**	**8479**	**65011**	**3871**	**9/39**	**16.79**	**263**	**61**	**2.26**	**44.46**
	(5b)	**2748.4**	**1029**	**5311**	**333**	**9/24**	**15.94**	**24**	**7**	**1.93**	**41.27**

Record For Each Team (Batting and Fielding)

Team	M	I	NO	R	HS	Ave	100	50	Ct
All India (England)	1	2	1	25	16	25.00	-	-	2
Capped	1	2	1	102	79*	102.00	-	1	1
England (Test Matches)	58	98	21	2325	179	30.19	2	11	60
England XI	3	3	1	133	121	66.50	1	-	3
Europeans	4	6	0	453	183	75.50	2	1	3
C.B.Fry's XI	1	2	0	21	12	10.50	-	-	-
Lord Hawke's XI	2	2	0	7	4	3.50	-	-	-
Kent and Yorkshire	1	2	0	26	17	13.00	-	-	-
Lancashire and Yorkshire	3	3	2	110	75*	110.00	-	1	2
H.D.G.Leveson-Gower's XI	3	6	1	36	16*	7.20	-	-	3
Lord Londesborough's XI	4	7	0	117	51	16.71	-	1	3
MCC	62	81	20	2757	210	45.19	7	11	47
MCC Australian Team	7	11	4	295	85	42.14	-	3	5
MCC South African Team	2	4	0	62	52	15.50	-	1	-
Muslims and Hindus	1	2	0	108	79	54.00	-	1	-
North v South	8	12	2	329	93	32.90	-	3	5
Patiala	1	1	1	13	13*	-	-	-	-
Players v Gentlemen	39	60	12	1296	82	27.00	-	5	24
Players of England	1	1	1	11	11*	-	-	-	2
Rest of England	12	16	4	330	78	27.50	-	1	11
C.I.Thornton's XI	12	16	4	310	81	25.83	-	2	5
Under 30s	1	1	1	5	5*	-	-	-	1
Yorkshire	883	1196	161	31098	267*	30.04	46	155	587
Total	**1110**	**1534**	**237**	**39969**	**267***	**30.81**	**58**	**197**	**765**

Record for Each Team (Bowling)

Team	O	M	R	W	BB	Ave	5i	10m	Econ	Strike
All India (England)	40	13	100	4	3/51	25.00	-	-	2.50	60.00
England (Test Matches)	1248.5	328	3084	114	8/68	27.05	6	1	2.46	65.72
(5b)	146.2	41	341	13	4/58	26.23	-	-	2.32	56.30
England	26.3	7	74	5	4/14	14.80	-	-	2.79	31.80
Europeans	116.1	55	176	27	7/26	6.51	3	1	1.51	25.81
Lord Hawke's XI	18	2	105	0	-	-	-	-	5.83	-
Kent and Yorkshire	7	0	26	0	-	-	-	-	3.71	-
Lancashire and Yorkshire	72	18	179	16	7/46	11.18	2	1	2.48	27.00
H.D.G.Leveson-Gower's XI	114.3	24	247	20	6/22	12.35	2	1	2.15	34.35
Lord Londesborough's XI	41.4	5	129	10	4/29	12.90	-	-	3.09	25.00
MCC	1228.3	317	2975	145	6/39	20.51	9	1	2.42	50.83
MCC Australian Team	147.5	37	389	18	5/78	21.61	1	-	2.63	49.27
MCC South African Team	18	5	49	1	1/37	49.00	-	-	2.72	108.00
Muslims and Hindus	49	8	156	5	3/99	31.20	-	-	3.18	58.80
North v South	215.2	47	673	38	6/19	17.71	4	-	3.12	34.00
Patiala	24	4	73	3	3/73	24.33	-	-	3.04	48.00
Players v Gentlemen	716.1	180	1866	97	6/27	19.23	4	1	2.60	44.29
(5b)	98	26	220	6	4/72	36.66	-	-	2.24	81.66
Players of England	36.4	3	115	5	5/115	23.00	1	-	3.13	44.00
Rest of England	223.1	69	521	27	6/27	19.29	1	-	2.33	49.59
(5b)	88.4	25	244	9	4/50	27.11	-	-	2.74	49.33
C.I.Thornton's XI	291	60	805	28	5/63	28.75	1	-	2.76	62.35
(5b)	37.4	19	51	10	9/24	5.10	1	1	1.34	18.90
Under 30s	36.2	9	90	6	3/38	15.00	-	-	2.47	36.33
Yorkshire	24008.3	7288	53179	3302	9/38	16.10	229	55	2.21	43.62
(5b)	2377.4	918	4455	295	7/56	15.10	23	6	1.87	40.30
Total	28679.1	8479	65011	3871	9/39	16.79	263	61	2.26	44.45
Total (5b)	2748.4	1029	5311	333	9/24	15.94	24	7	1.93	41.27

Career by Country (Batting and Fielding)

	M	I	NO	R	HS	Ave	100	50	Ct
Australia	57	88	19	2996	210	43.42	8	12	39
England	1007	1379	205	35015	267*	29.82	47	177	675
India	7	11	2	599	183	66.55	2	2	5
South Africa	30	44	4	1230	152	30.75	1	6	41
West Indies	9	12	7	129	36	25.80	-	-	5
Career	**1110**	**1534**	**237**	**39969**	**267***	**30.81**	**58**	**197**	**765**

Career by Country (Bowling)

		O	M	R	W	BB	Ave	5i	10m	Econ	Strike
Australia		1119.1	273	2837	114	8/68	24.88	9	2	2.53	58.90
England		26386.2	7856	59525	3627	9/39	16.41	248	58	2.24	43.94
England	(5b)	2748.4	1029	5311	333	9/24	15.94	24	7	1.93	41.27
India		229.1	80	505	39	7/26	12.94	3	1	2.20	35.25
South Africa		443.2	98	1197	52	5/43	23.01	1	-	2.70	51.15
West Indies		501.1	172	947	39	5/57	24.28	2	-	1.88	77.10
Career		**28679.1**	**8479**	**65011**	**3871**	**9/39**	**16.79**	**263**	**61**	**2.26**	**44.45**
Career	**(5b)**	**2748.4**	**1029**	**5311**	**333**	**9/24**	**15.94**	**24**	**7**	**1.93**	**41.27**

Career by Month in England (Batting and Fielding)

	M	I	NO	R	HS	Ave	100	50	Ct
May	202	263	37	6296	201	27.85	9	25	124
June	234	334	40	8546	267*	29.06	9	46	168
July	233	316	51	8647	157	32.63	14	42	172
August	237	312	43	8187	199	30.43	14	46	150
September	101	154	34	3339	101*	27.82	1	18	61
Career	**1007**	**1379**	**205**	**35015**	**267***	**29.82**	**47**	**177**	**675**

Career by Month in England (Bowling)

		O	M	R	W	BB	Ave	5i	10m	Econ	Strike
May		5148.4	1629	11367	740	9/39	15.36	53	12	2.20	41.70
May	(5b)	441.4	167	838	81	9/28	10.34	8	2	1.89	51.72
June		6538.5	1971	13979	857	8/23	16.31	58	17	2.13	45.77
June	(5b)	725.4	275	1343	96	7/24	13.98	7	2	1.85	37.80
July		6060.3	1854	13475	861	8/72	15.65	54	12	2.22	42.23
July	(5b)	580.4	205	1196	56	6/71	21.35	2	-	2.05	51.85
August		6271.5	1812	14295	856	8/26	16.69	64	14	2.27	43.96
August	(5b)	823.1	328	1488	81	9/24	18.37	6	2	1.80	50.81
September		2366.3	590	6409	313	7/46	20.47	19	3	2.43	50.48
September	(5b)	177.1	54	446	19	7/56	23.47	1	1	2.51	46.63
Career		**26386.2**	**7856**	**59525**	**3627**	**9/39**	**16.41**	**248**	**58**	**2.24**	**43.94**
Career	**(5b)**	**2748.4**	**1029**	**5311**	**333**	**9/24**	**15.94**	**24**	**7**	**1.93**	**41.26**

Career by Month Overseas (Batting and Fielding)

	M	I	NO	R	HS	Ave	100	50	Ct
January	25	38	8	1130	119	37.66	2	7	29
February	26	43	8	1235	179*	35.28	3	4	22
March/April	12	20	6	643	210	45.92	1	3	10
October/November	22	27	7	1074	183*	53.70	3	4	19
December	18	27	3	872	152*	36.33	2	2	10
Career	**103**	**155**	**32**	**4954**	**210**	**40.27**	**11**	**20**	**90**

Career by Month Overseas (Bowling)

	O	M	R	W	BB	Ave	5i	10m	Econ	Strike
January	586.5	163	1434	60	8/68	23.90	4	1	2.43	58.95
February	655.5	173	1568	60	6/62	26.13	4	1	2.39	65.58
March/April	268.3	88	574	28	4/51	20.50	-	-	2.13	57.53
October/November	469.3	137	1066	67	7/26	15.91	6	1	2.27	42.04
December	312.1	62	844	29	5/94	29.10	1	-	2.70	64.62
Career **(6b)**	**2292.5**	**623**	**5486**	**244**	**8/68**	**22.48**	**15**	**3**	**2.38**	**56.45**

For Yorkshire in the County Championship Season by Season (Batting and Fielding)

Season	M	I	NO	R	HS	Ave	100	50	Ct
1898	26	30	8	472	78	21.45	-	3	14
1899	23	35	9	359	81*	13.80	-	1	17
1900	26	29	7	400	79	18.18	-	2	6
1901	27	31	7	522	53	21.75	-	1	20
1902	22	24	5	299	92*	15.73	-	1	7
1903	26	37	6	751	79*	24.22	-	5	12
1904	26	35	2	1082	196	32.78	2	4	16
1905	25	35	4	1117	201	36.03	2	9	35
1906	28	46	3	1431	119	33.27	2	11	32
1907	25	34	1	890	112	26.96	1	5	14
1908	27	43	1	1412	146	33.61	3	5	5
1909	24	40	2	1351	199	35.55	3	5	19
1910	28	49	4	1282	111	28.48	1	7	9
1911	27	48	3	1606	125	35.68	2	7	20
1912	20	32	4	965	176	34.46	2	3	17
1913	28	49	4	1531	152	34.02	3	8	24
1914	27	44	1	1176	113	27.34	1	8	35
1919	26	34	8	891	135	34.26	1	6	23
1920	27	36	3	949	167*	28.75	1	7	29
1921	24	33	6	1184	267*	43.85	3	3	19
1922	30	36	6	1181	110	39.36	4	4	25
1923	31	38	5	1023	126	31.00	2	3	29
1924	30	37	5	826	100	25.81	1	4	19
1925	32	35	7	1234	157	44.07	2	9	15
1926	26	28	3	1022	132	40.88	1	7	14
1927	30	32	6	481	44	18.50	-	-	7
1928	28	23	4	542	100*	28.52	1	4	18
1929	24	27	7	543	79	27.15	-	4	13
1930	20	21	5	346	80*	21.62	-	1	8
Total	**763**	**1021**	**136**	**26868**	**267***	**30.35**	**38**	**137**	**521**

For Yorkshire in the County Championship Season by Season (Bowling)

Season		O	M	R	W	BB	Ave	5i	10m	Econ	Strike
1898	(5b)	990	393	1745	126	7/24	13.84	11	3	1.76	39.28
1899	(5b)	1083.1	420	2021	129	9/28	15.66	9	2	1.86	41.98
1900		1165.1	359	2532	206	8/23	12.29	20	6	2.17	33.93
1901		1155.4	389	2664	196	8/53	13.59	20	8	2.30	35.37
1902		876.4	291	1748	140	8/26	12.48	12	5	1.99	37.57
1903		1061.4	333	2105	143	8/61	14.72	12	3	1.98	44.54
1904		917.3	276	2070	104	6/27	19.90	8	3	2.25	52.93
1905		842.5	232	1986	126	8/90	15.76	10	3	2.37	39.89
1906		729	141	2036	91	6/90	22.37	6	1	2.79	48.06
1907		893.2	196	2314	141	6/22	16.41	12	2	2.59	38.01
1908		593.1	183	1295	78	6/17	16.60	3	-	2.18	45.62
1909		670.5	176	1635	107	7/68	15.28	11	2	2.43	37.61

1910	522.5	121	1384	77	6/38	17.97	6	1	2.64	40.74
1911	758	141	2260	93	8/92	24.30	6	2	2.98	48.90
1912	292.5	62	808	37	5/68	21.83	1	-	2.75	47.48
1913	603.1	169	1560	62	7/45	25.16	2	-	2.58	58.37
1914	775.4	200	1965	110	7/19	17.86	5	1	2.53	42.30
1919	797.3	236	1764	142	8/44	12.42	11	4	2.21	33.69
1920	918.1	276	1846	143	8/39	12.90	11	4	2.01	38.52
1921	787.3	273	1488	117	7/80	12.71	7	-	1.88	40.38
1922	605.4	231	1068	84	6/13	12.71	5	-	1.76	43.26
1923	833.4	315	1353	120	7/15	11.27	8	1	1.62	41.68
1924	550.3	186	1085	81	6/25	13.39	4	-	1.97	40.77
1925	547.4	220	928	52	4/40	17.84	-	-	1.69	63.19
1926	740.4	265	1388	100	8/48	13.88	5	1	1.87	44.44
1927	811.3	265	1546	77	6/20	20.07	2	-	1.90	63.23
1928	1074.2	383	1995	103	7/39	19.36	9	1	1.85	62.54
1929	847.1	331	1464	85	9/39	17.22	6	2	1.72	59.80
1930	588.3	236	926	47	4/21	19.70	-	-	1.57	75.12
Total	20961.1	6486	45213	2862	9/39	15.79	202	50	2.15	43.94
Total (5b)	2073.1	813	3766	255	9/28	14.76	20	5	1.81	40.65

For Yorkshire in the County Championship
Against Each Opponent (Batting and Fielding)

Opponent	M	I	NO	R	HS	Ave	100	50	Ct
Derbyshire	46	55	8	1299	157	27.63	2	6	35
Essex	58	70	12	2048	132	35.31	5	10	28
Glamorgan	16	9	2	321	110	45.85	1	2	14
Gloucestershire	47	57	3	1227	110	22.72	1	6	33
Hampshire	45	56	8	1599	135	33.31	2	7	26
Kent	54	83	8	1574	101	20.98	1	8	33
Lancashire	57	86	15	1892	107	26.64	1	8	30
Leicestershire	50	62	10	2253	267*	43.32	5	12	44
Middlesex	55	85	9	1970	126	25.92	2	10	33
Northamptonshire	34	45	5	1436	140	35.90	3	7	42
Nottinghamshire	55	80	8	2039	176	28.31	2	12	36
Somerset	43	55	10	1737	201	38.60	5	5	34
Surrey	55	80	12	1663	107	24.45	1	10	34
Sussex	52	73	11	2316	199	37.35	4	15	31
Warwickshire	58	79	11	1988	81	29.23	-	12	45
Worcestershire	38	46	4	1506	196	35.85	3	7	23
Total	763	1021	136	26868	267*	30.35	38	137	521

For Yorkshire in the County Championship
Against Each Opponent (Bowling)

Opponent		O	M	R	W	BB	Ave	5i	10m	Econ	Strike
Derbyshire		981.4	342	1865	167	7/16	11.16	10	2	1.89	35.26
	(5b)	156.2	58	356	22	5/65	16.18	1	-	2.27	35.54
Essex		1609.1	528	3280	228	9/28	14.38	14	5	2.03	42.34
	(5b)	197.2	84	315	36	9/39	8.75	4	2	1.59	27.41
Glamorgan		330.5	137	496	41	6/56	12.09	3	-	1.49	48.41
Gloucestershire		1133	404	2510	221	8/72	11.35	20	8	2.21	30.76
	(5b)	80.4	30	159	19	6/16	8.35	2	-	1.96	21.26
Hampshire		1086.5	303	2546	134	8/23	19.00	8	3	2.34	48.66
	(5b)	61	31	85	10	4/35	8.50	-	-	1.39	30.50
Kent		1155	321	2690	148	8/26	18.17	12	2	2.32	46.82
	(5b)	184	77	281	16	4/36	17.56	-	-	1.52	57.50
Lancashire		1759.2	570	3582	210	8/43	17.05	14	3	2.03	50.26
	(5b)	214	87	355	18	4/50	19.72	-	-	1.65	59.44
Leicestershire		1611.1	563	3154	211	7/55	14.94	12	3	1.95	45.81
	(5b)	80.4	33	120	16	5/25	7.50	2	-	1.48	25.25

Middlesex	1763.1	448	4094	208	8/153	19.68	17	5	2.32	50.86
(5b)	154.3	40	353	15	7/147	23.53	1	-	2.28	51.53
Northamptonshire	785	254	1729	141	8/92	12.26	10	2	2.20	33.40
Nottinghamshire	1627.2	508	3531	211	8/38	16.73	15	1	2.18	45.95
(5b)	183	76	326	20	8/38	16.30	2	1	1.78	45.75
Somerset	999	284	2337	174	8/48	13.43	12	4	2.33	34.44
(5b)	96.3	42	173	22	7/24	7.96	3	1	1.79	21.95
Surrey	1702	473	4106	215	6/29	19/09	14	6	2.41	47.49
(5b)	163.4	61	319	16	7/24	19.93	2	1	1.94	51.18
Sussex	1538.4	382	3703	178	8/39	20.87	13	1	2.40	51.86
(5b)	244.4	94	514	24	6/64	21.41	2	-	2.09	51.00
Warwickshire	1822.3	600	3606	242	8/44	14.90	17	3	1.98	45.06
(5b)	175	69	268	14	5/69	19.14	1	-	1.53	62.50
Worcestershire	1056.3	369	1984	133	8/81	14.91	11	2	1.87	46.66
(5b)	81	31	142	7	3/32	20.28	-	-	1.75	57.85
Total	20961.1	6486	45213	2862	9/39	15.79	202	50	2.15	43.94
Total (5b)	2073.1	813	3766	255	9/28	14.76	20	5	1.81	40.65

For Yorkshire Against Other Opponents (Batting and Fielding)

Opponent	M	I	NO	R	HS	Ave	100	50	Ct
All Ireland	1	1	0	13	13	13.00	-	-	2
Australians	14	18	2	467	108	29.18	1	2	9
Australian Imperial Forces	1	2	0	95	90	47.50	-	1	-
Cambridge University	25	35	6	752	102	25.93	1	2	22
An England XI	2	3	1	62	36	31.00	-	-	-
Gentlemen of Ireland	1	1	0	10	10	10.00	-	-	1
Lancashire	2	3	1	163	105*	81.50	1	1	1
MCC	43	63	5	1707	128	29.43	5	7	21
New Zealanders	1	1	0	2	2	2.00	-	-	-
Oxford University	3	3	1	32	24*	16.00	-	-	-
Rest of England	10	18	3	480	96	32.00	-	3	5
South Africans	8	13	2	258	54	23.45	-	2	4
Surrey	1	1	1	41	41*	-	-	-	-
C.I.Thornton's XI	5	9	3	129	35*	21.50	-	-	1
West Indies	3	4	0	19	13	4.75	-	-	-
Total	120	175	25	4230	128	28.20	8	18	66

For Yorkshire Against Other Opponents (Bowling)

Opponent	O	M	R	W	BB	Ave	5i	10m	Econ	Strike
All Ireland	27	7	88	9	5/77	9.77	1	-	3.25	18.00
Australians	292.3	61	810	43	5/49	18.83	2	-	2.76	40.81
Australian Imperial Forces	42	12	106	6	4/169	17.66	-	-	2.52	42.00
Cambridge University	726	230	1626	125	8/68	13.00	9	4	2.23	34.84
(5b)	72.1	28	158	12	4/18	13.16	-	-	2.18	30.08
An England XI	66	19	160	6	5/92	26.66	1	-	2.42	66.00
Gentlemen of Ireland	31	11	64	4	4/47	13.02	-	-	2.06	46.50
Lancashire	47.4	15	116	9	5/35	12.88	1	-	2.43	31.77
MCC	953.4	237	2542	139	6/15	18.28	8	-	2.66	41.16
(5b)	144	48	329	18	5/59	18.27	2	-	2.28	40.00
New Zealanders	13	5	29	4	4/29	7.25	-	-	2.23	19.50
Oxford University	69.4	12	221	7	4/129	31.57	-	-	3.17	59.71
Rest of England	268.1	45	909	27	6/49	33.66	2	1	3.38	59.59
South Africans	288.4	93	679	32	6/102	21.21	1	-	2.35	54.12
Surrey	48.3	16	120	7	6/110	17.14	1	-	2.47	41.57
C.I.Thornton's XI	122.3	26	374	15	5/35	24.93	1	-	3.05	49.00
(5b)	88.2	29	202	10	7/56	20.20	1	1	2.28	44.20
West Indians	51	13	122	7	4/37	17.42	-	-	2.39	43.71
Total	3047.2	802	7966	440	8/68	18.10	27	5	2.61	41.55
Total (5b)	304.3	105	689	40	7/56	17.22	3	1	2.26	38.07

For England against Each Opponent (Batting and Fielding)

Opponent	M	I	NO	R	HS	Ave	100	50	Ct
Australia	41	69	14	1706	179	31.01	1	9	36
South Africa	13	22	2	568	152	28.40	1	2	21
West Indies	4	7	5	51	14	25.50	-	-	3
Total	58	98	21	2325	179	30.19	2	11	60

For England against Each Opponent (Bowling)

Opponent		O	M	R	W	BB	Ave	5i	10m	Econ	Strike
Australia		843	197	2275	96	8/68	23.69	6	1	2.69	52.68
Australia	(5b)	146.2	41	341	13	4/58	26.33	-	-	2.32	56.30
South Africa		149.5	39	356	8	3/33	44.50	-	-	2.37	112.37
West Indies		256	92	453	10	3/110	45.30	-	-	1.76	15.36
Total		1248.5	328	3084	114	8/68	27.05	6	1	2.46	65.27
Total	(5b)	146.2	41	341	13	4/58	26.33	-	-	2.32	56.30

For England Season by Season (Batting and Fielding)

Opponent	M	I	NO	R	HS	Ave	100	50	Ct
1899	3	4	1	18	8	6.00	-	-	1
1902	5	7	6	67	38	67.00	-	-	4
1903/04	5	9	2	126	40	18.00	-	-	5
1905	4	5	2	146	39	48.66	-	-	6
1907/08	5	10	0	205	69	20.50	-	1	1
1909	4	7	2	168	66	33.60	-	2	6
1909/10	5	10	1	226	77	25.11	-	2	10
1911/12	5	9	1	463	179	57.87	1	3	5
1912	6	8	0	257	92	32.12	-	2	3
1913/14	5	8	1	289	152	41.28	1	-	10
1920/21	5	10	0	238	73	23.80	-	1	4
1921	1	2	0	29	19	14.50	-	-	2
1926	1	2	0	42	28	21.00	-	-	-
1929/30	4	7	5	51	14	25.50	-	-	3
Total	58	98	21	2325	179	30.19	2	11	60

For England Season by Season (Bowling)

Season		O	M	R	W	BB	Ave	5i	10m	Econ	Strike
1899	(5b)	146.2	41	341	13	26.33	4/58	-	-	2.32	56.30
1902		140.5	38	336	22	15.27	7/17	2	-	2.38	38.40
1903/04		172	36	488	31	15.74	8/68	3	1	2.83	33.29
1905		110.3	21	314	10	31.40	3/36	-	-	2.84	66.30
1907/08		157.4	42	421	7	60.14	4/102	-	-	2.67	135.14
1909		79	9	242	11	22.00	5/83	1	-	3.06	43.09
1909/10		57	14	147	2	73.50	1/4	-	-	2.57	171.00
1911/12		18	3	57	0	-	-	-	-	3.16	0/00
1912		25.2	7	74	3	24.66	3/59	-	-	2.92	50.66
1913/14		88.5	24	195	6	32.50	3/33	-	-	2.19	88.83
1920/21		85.4	15	245	4	61.25	3/61	-	-	2.85	128.50
1921		13	3	33	2	16.50	2/33	-	-	2.53	39.00
1926		45	24	79	6	13.16	4/44	-	-	1.75	45.00
1929/30		256	92	453	10	45.30	3/110	-	-	1.76	153.60
Total		1248.5	328	3084	114	27.05	8/68	6	1	2.46	65.72
Total	(5b)	146.2	41	341	13	26.33	4/58	-	-	2.32	56.30

For England on Each Ground (Batting and Fielding)

Ground	M	I	NO	R	HS	Ave	100	50	Ct
Adelaide	4	8	1	200	59	28.57	-	2	4
Bramall Lane	1	2	2	14	7*	-	-	-	1
Bridgetown	1	1	1	14	14*	-	-	-	2
Cape Town	2	4	1	82	77	27.33	-	1	4
Durban	3	5	0	136	44	27.20	-	-	5
Edgbaston	2	2	2	53	38*	-	-	-	2
Georgetown	1	2	1	10	10	10.00	-	-	1
Headingley	2	4	0	45	16	11.25	-	-	1
Johannesburg	4	7	0	270	152	38.57	1	1	9
Kennington Oval	7	11	3	265	66	33.12	-	2	9
Kingston	1	2	2	19	11*	-	-	-	-
Lord's	5	5	0	114	59	22.80	-	1	-
Melbourne	8	15	1	466	179	33.28	1	2	9
Old Trafford	4	6	3	133	92	44.33	-	1	7
Port Elizabeth	1	2	1	27	27	27.00	-	-	2
Port of Spain	1	2	1	8	6	8.00	-	-	-
Sydney	8	15	1	366	69	26.14	-	1	2
Trent Bridge	3	5	1	103	39	25.75	-	-	2
Total	**58**	**98**	**21**	**2325**	**179**	**30.19**	**2**	**11**	**60**

For England on Each Ground (Bowling)

Ground	O	M	R	W	BB	Ave	5i	10m	Econ	Strike
Adelaide	108.5	30	297	5	3/61	59.40	-	-	2.75	130.60
Bramall Lane	30.1	6	96	6	5/63	16.00	1	-	3.18	30.16
Bridgetown	78.1	19	154	3	3/110	51.33	-	-	1.97	156.33
Cape Town	10	2	24	0	-	-	-	-	2.40	-
Durban	71	18	166	4	3/33	41.50	-	-	2.33	106.50
Edgbaston	22	8	34	8	7/17	4.25	1	-	1.54	16.50
Georgetown	91	31	189	4	2/93	47.25	-	-	2.07	136.50
Headingley	31	6	96	6	4/38	16.00	-	-	3.09	31.00
Johannesburg	54.5	14	138	4	3/93	34.50	-	-	2.51	82.25
Kennington Oval	152	47	321	7	4/44	45.85	-	-	2.11	130.28
(5b)	47	10	106	3	3/27	35.33	-	-	2.25	78.33
Kingston	44.5	25	39	2	1/17	19.50	-	-	0.86	134.50
Lord's	35.3	6	129	6	3/59	21.50	-	-	3.63	35.50
(5b)	44	15	117	3	3/108	39.00	-	-	2.65	73.33
Melbourne	135.5	22	434	21	8/68	20.66	2	1	3.20	38.80
Old Trafford	82	12	274	17	5/83	16.11	1	-	3.34	28.94
Port Elizabeth	10	4	14	0	-	-	-	-	1.40	-
Port of Spain	42	17	71	1	1/40	71.00	-	-	1.69	252.00
Sydney	188.4	44	480	16	5/94	30.00	1	-	2.54	70.75
Trent Bridge	61	17	128	4	2/33	32.00	-	-	2.09	91.50
(5b)	55.2	16	118	7	4/58	16.85	-	-	2.12	39.57
Total	**1248.5**	**328**	**3084**	**114**	**8/68**	**27.05**	**6**	**1**	**2.46**	**65.72**
Total (5b)	**146.2**	**41**	**341**	**13**	**4/58**	**26.23**	**-**	**-**	**2.32**	**56.30**

For MCC Overseas Season by Season (Batting and Fielding)

Season	M	I	NO	R	HS	Ave	100	50	Ct
1903/04	9	9	5	113	49	28.25	-	-	9
1907/08	12	17	8	724	119	80.44	2	4	7
1909/10	8	10	0	273	64	27.30	-	1	2
1911/12	9	15	3	635	119	52.91	3	2	6
1913/14	12	16	2	442	76	31.57	-	3	19
1920/21	7	9	0	492	210	54.66	2	1	2
1929/30	5	5	2	78	36	26.00	-	-	2
Total	**62**	**81**	**20**	**2757**	**210**	**45.19**	**7**	**11**	**47**

For MCC Overseas Season by Season (Bowling)

Season	O	M	R	W	BB	Ave	5i	10m	Econ	Strike
1903/04	272.3	79	567	34	16.67	6/55	4	1	2.08	48.08
1907/08	269.4	66	648	24	27.00	5/73	1	-	2.40	67.41
1909/10	145.5	31	388	19	20.42	5/43	1	-	2.66	46.05
1911/12	44	6	177	0	-	-	-	-	4.02	0.00
1913/14	151.4	29	467	25	18.68	4/27	-	-	3.07	36.40
1920/21	99.4	26	234	14	16.71	6/39	1	-	2.34	42.71
1929/30	245.1	80	494	29	17.03	5/57	2	-	2.01	50.72
Total	1228.3	317	2975	145	20.51	6/39	9	1	2.42	50.83

For Players v Gentlemen Season by Season (Batting and Fielding)

Season	M	I	NO	R	HS	Ave	100	50	Ct
1898	1	2	0	23	21	11.50	-	-	-
1899	1	2	1	38	31	38.00	-	-	-
1900	2	3	2	48	40	48.00	-	-	1
1901	2	2	2	8	6*	-	-	-	-
1902	2	3	1	52	19*	26.00	-	-	2
1903	3	4	1	123	82	41.00	-	1	3
1904	1	2	0	81	50	40.50	-	1	-
1905	1	1	0	22	22	22.00	-	-	-
1906	2	4	0	42	19	10.50	-	-	1
1907	1	2	0	8	6	4.00	-	-	-
1908	1	1	0	15	15	15.00	-	-	1
1909	2	2	1	97	61*	97.00	-	1	-
1910	3	5	0	100	40	20.00	-	-	5
1911	3	6	1	94	24	18.80	-	-	1
1912	2	4	0	139	43	34.75	-	-	1
1913	2	4	0	107	49	26.75	-	-	1
1919	1	1	0	52	52	52.00	-	1	-
1920	3	4	0	40	28	10.00	-	-	1
1921	2	3	1	47	30	23.50	-	-	4
1922	1	1	1	71	71*	-	-	1	1
1923	1	2	0	44	34	22.00	-	-	1
1924	1	1	0	30	30	30.00	-	-	1
1927	1	1	1	15	15*	-	-	-	-
Total	39	60	12	1296	82	27.00	-	5	24

For Players v Gentlemen Season by Season (Bowling)

Season		O	M	R	W	BB	Ave	5i	10m	Econ	Strike
1898	(5b)	43	15	89	4	4/72	22.25	-	-	2.06	53.75
1899	(5b)	55	11	131	2	2/131	65.50	-	-	2.38	137.50
1900		90	14	267	10	4/93	26.70	-	-	2.96	54.00
1901		73.2	22	210	12	6/27	17.50	2	1	2.86	36.66
1902		61.3	21	103	8	5/71	12.87	1	-	1.67	46.12
1903		84.3	18	190	7	2/31	27.14	-	-	2.24	72.42
1904		16	3	40	0	-	-	-	-	2.50	-
1905		52	14	119	8	5/71	14.87	1	-	2.28	39.37
1906		50.1	6	213	7	4/122	30.42	-	-	4.24	43.00
1907		1	0	1	1	1/1	1.00	-	-	1.00	6.00
1908		5	2	10	1	1/10	10.00	-	-	2.00	30.00
1909		16	1	49	6	4/17	8.16	-	-	3.06	16.00
1910		21	5	70	1	1/15	70.00	-	-	3.33	126.00
1911		49	5	191	7	3/39	27.28	-	-	3.89	42.00
1912		0.2	0	0	1	1/0	0.00	-	-	0.00	2.00
1913		10	4	29	3	3/29	9.66	-	-	2.90	20.00
1919		45.2	20	76	7	4/42	10.85	-	-	1.67	38.85

1920		28	5	76	4	2/25	19.00	-	-	2.71	42.00
1921		34	11	69	5	3/27	13.80	-	-	2.02	40.80
1922		39	15	69	6	3/31	11.50	-	-	1.76	39.00
1923		14	4	30	2	2/30	15.00	-	-	2.14	42.00
1924		3	1	5	0	-	-	-	-	1.66	
1927		23	9	49	1	1/19	49.00	-	-	2.13	138.00
Total	**(6b)**	**716.1**	**180**	**1866**	**97**	**6/27**	**19.23**	**4**	**1**	**2.60**	**44.29**
Total	**(5b)**	**98**	**26**	**220**	**6**	**4/72**	**36.66**	**-**	**-**	**2.24**	**81.66**

For North v South Season by Season (Batting and Fielding)

Season	M	I	NO	R	HS	Ave	100	50	Ct
1900	2	3	1	30	30*	15.00	-	-	2
1904	2	3	1	176	93	88.00	-	2	2
1905	1	1	0	56	56	56.00	-	1	-
1906	1	1	0	45	45	45.00	-	-	-
1907	1	2	0	12	12	6.00	-	-	1
1922	1	2	0	10	10	5.00	-	-	-
Total	8	12	2	329	93	32.90	-	3	5

For North v South Season by Season (Bowling)

Season	O	M	R	W	BB	Ave	5i	10m	Econ	Strike
1900	49	16	132	5	5/120	26.40	1	-	2.69	58.80
1904	42.1	6	161	8	5/88	20.12	1	-	3.81	31.62
1905	28	6	88	4	4/88	22.00	-	-	3.14	42.00
1906	42.4	6	185	8	5/124	23.12	1	-	4.33	32.00
1907	24.3	4	48	8	6/19	6.00	1	-	1.95	18.37
1922	29	9	59	5	3/50	11.80	-	-	2.03	34.80
Total	215.2	47	673	38	6/19	17.71	4	-	3.12	34.00

For other Teams in England (Batting and Fielding)

Opponent	M	I	NO	R	HS	Ave	100	50	Ct
C.B.Fry's XI	1	2	0	21	12	10.50	-	-	-
C.I.Thornton's XI	12	16	4	310	81	25.83	-	2	5
Capped	1	2	1	102	79	102.00	-	1	1
An England XI	3	3	1	133	121	66.50	1	-	3
Lord Hawke's XI	2	2	0	7	4	3.50	-	-	-
H.D.G.Leveson-Gower's XI	3	6	1	36	16	7.20	-	-	3
Lord Londesborough's XI	4	7	0	117	51	16.71	-	1	3
MCC Australian Team	7	11	4	295	85	42.14	-	3	5
MCC South African Team	2	4	0	62	52	15.50	-	1	1
Players of England	1	1	1	11	11*	-	-	-	2
Rest of England	12	16	4	330	78	27.50	-	1	11
Under 30s	1	1	1	5	5*	-	-	-	1
Yorkshire & Kent	1	2	0	26	17	13.00	-	-	-
Yorkshire & Lancashire	3	3	2	110	75	110.00	-	1	2
Total	53	76	19	1565	121	27.45	1	10	37

For other Teams in England (Bowling)

Opponent	O	M	R	W	BB	Ave	5i	10m	Econ	Strike
An England XI	26.3	7	74	5	4/14	14.80	-	-	2.79	31.80
Lord Hawke's XI	18	2	105	0	0/00	0.00	-	-	5.83	0.00
H.D.G.Leveson-Gower's XI	114.3	24	247	20	6/56	12.35	2	1	2.15	34.35
Lord Londesborough's XI	41.4	5	129	10	4/29	12.90	-	-	3.09	25.00
MCC Australian Team	147.5	37	389	18	5/78	21.61	1	-	2.63	49.27
MCC South African Team	18	5	49	1	1/37	49.00	-	-	2.72	108.00
Players of England	36.4	3	115	5	5/115	23.00	1	-	3.13	44.00

Rest of England	223.1	69	521	27	6/27	19.29	1	-	2.33	49.59
(5b)	88.4	25	244	9	4/50	27.11	-	-	2.34	49.33
C.I.Thornton's XI	291	60	805	28	5/63	28.75	1	-	2.76	62.35
(5b)	37.4	19	51	10	9/24	5.10	1	1	1.34	18.90
Under 30s	36.2	9	90	6	3/38	15.00	1	-	2.47	36.33
Yorkshire & Kent	7	0	26	0	0/00	0.00	-	-	3.71	0.00
Yorkshire & Lancashire	72	18	179	16	7/46	11.18	2	1	2.48	27.00
Total	**1032.4**	**239**	**2729**	**136**	**7/46**	**20.06**	**8**	**2**	**2.64**	**39.96**
Total (5b)	**126.3**	**44**	**295**	**19**	**9/24**	**15.52**	**1**	**1**	**2.33**	**33.31**

Record against Other Opponents (Batting and Fielding)

Opponent	M	I	NO	R	HS	Ave	100	50	Ct
In England									
Australians	11	16	4	256	75	21.33	-	2	4
Australian Imperial Forces	1	2	1	47	24	47.00	-	-	2
Mr.J.Bamford's XI	1	2	1	56	33	56.00	-	-	1
An England XI	1	2	1	23	23	23.00	-	-	1
Home Counties	1	1	0	0	0	0.00	-	-	3
Kent	3	5	0	119	78	23.80	-	1	3
Lancashire	2	2	0	39	29	19.50	-	-	1
Lord Londesborough's XI	3	6	1	100	85	20.00	-	1	3
MCC Australian Team	3	4	1	52	26	17.33	-	-	1
MCC South African Team	3	3	1	18	10	9.00	-	-	-
Middlesex	3	4	3	110	38	110.00	-	-	2
Over 30s	1	1	1	5	5*	-	-	-	1
The Rest	3	3	0	188	121	62.66	1	1	3
Rest of England	5	8	1	134	52	19.14	-	1	2
Royal Air Force	1	2	0	52	35	26.00	-	-	-
South Africans	4	5	0	151	81	30.20	-	2	4
A.E.Stoddart's XI	1	2	1	3	2	3.00	-	-	1
Surrey & Sussex	2	2	0	32	16	16.00	-	-	2
C.I.Thornton's XI	1	1	1	71	71*	-	-	1	-
Uncapped	1	2	1	102	79	102.00	-	1	1
Warwickshire	1	1	1	0	0*	-	-	-	1
West Indians	1	2	0	7	7	3.50	-	-	1
Total	**53**	**76**	**19**	**1565**	**121**	**27.45**	**1**	**10**	**37**
In Australia									
Australia	20	38	3	1032	179	29.48	1	5	15
Australians XI	3	4	0	45	34	11.25	-	-	2
New South Wales	8	14	3	567	119	51.54	2	3	4
Queensland	4	5	2	328	162	109.33	1	2	4
South Australia	6	6	2	349	210	87.25	1	1	3
Tasmania	6	8	4	308	119	77.00	2	-	6
Victoria	7	10	3	226	66	32.28	-	1	5
Victorian XI	1	1	1	105	105*	-	1	-	-
Western Australia	2	2	1	36	32	36.00	-	-	-
Total	**57**	**88**	**19**	**2996**	**210**	**43.42**	**8**	**12**	**39**
In South Africa									
Border	3	5	0	146	38	29.20	-	-	4
Cape Province	1	1	0	5	5	5.00	-	-	2
Eastern Province	1	1	0	31	31	31.00	-	-	-
Natal	4	5	0	114	64	22.80	-	1	2
Orange River Colony	1	1	0	68	68	68.00	-	1	4
South Africa	10	18	2	515	152	32.18	1	2	20
Transvaal	7	8	1	278	76	39.71	-	2	6
Western Province	3	5	1	73	35	18.25	-	-	3
Total	**30**	**44**	**4**	**1230**	**152**	**30.75**	**1**	**6**	**41**

In West Indies

	M	I	NO	Runs	HS	Ave	100	50	Ct
Barbados	1	1	0	36	36	36.00	-	-	-
British Guiana	2	1	1	9	9*	-	-	-	2
Jamaica	1	1	0	14	14	14.00	-	-	-
Trinidad	1	2	1	19	11	19.00	-	-	-
West Indies	4	7	5	51	14	25.50	-	-	3
Total	**9**	**12**	**7**	**129**	**36**	**25.80**	**-**	**-**	**5**

In India

	M	I	NO	Runs	HS	Ave	100	50	Ct
All India (Indians)	1	2	1	25	16	25.00	-	-	2
Europeans and Parsees	1	2	0	108	79	54.00	-	1	-
Hindus	2	3	0	256	156	85.33	1	1	2
MCC	1	1	1	13	13*	-	-	-	-
Muslims	1	2	0	14	8	7.00	-	-	1
Parsees	1	1	0	183	183	183.00	1	-	-
Total	**7**	**11**	**2**	**599**	**183**	**66.55**	**2**	**2**	**5**

Record against Other Opponents (Bowling)

Opponent	O	M	R	W	BB	Ave	5i	10m	Econ	Strike
In England										
Australians	198.5	27	577	29	5/63	19.89	3	-	2.90	41.13
(5b)	37.4	19	51	10	9/24	5.10	1	1	1.34	18.90
Australian Imperial Forces	23	7	56	2	1/6	28.00	-	-	2.43	69.00
Mr.J.Bamford's XI	32.5	8	77	4	2/14	19.25	-	-	2.34	49.25
An England XI	44	5	132	9	5/78	14.66	1	-	3.00	29.33
Home Counties (5b)	27	6	66	1	1/35	66.00	-	-	2.44	135.00
Kent	30.2	8	87	2	2/9	43.50	-	-	2.86	91.00
Lancashire	34	8	77	4	2/17	19.25	-	-	2.26	51.00
Lord Londesborough's XI	39	11	120	2	1/35	60.00	-	-	3.07	97.50
MCC Australian Team	51	7	224	4	3/71	56.00	-	-	4.39	76.50
MCC South African Team	55	13	138	3	1/16	46.00	-	-	3.01	91.66
Middlesex	87.4	29	175	10	4/58	17.50	-	-	1.99	52.60
Over 30s	36.2	9	90	6	3/38	15.00	-	-	2.47	36.33
The Rest	16	2	60	1	1/14	60.00	-	-	3.75	96.00
Rest of England	151	43	372	21	7/46	17.71	2	1	2.46	43.14
Royal Air Force	25.1	10	38	7	6/27	5.42	1	-	1.50	21.57
South Africans	115.4	25	272	17	6/56	16.00	1	1	2.35	40.82
Surrey & Sussex	47.2	14	153	6	3/55	25.50	-	-	3.23	47.33
(5b)	22.4	6	74	4	4/50	18.50	-	-	3.24	28.50
A.E.Stoddart's XI (5b)	39	13	104	4	4/64	26.00	-	-	2.66	48.75
C.I.Thornton's XI	3	0	10	0	-	-	-	-	3.33	-
Warwickshire	10.3	5	14	4	4/14	3.50	-	-	1.33	15.75
West Indians	32	8	57	5	4/37	11.40	-	-	1.78	38.40
Total	**1032.4**	**239**	**2729**	**136**	**7/46**	**20.06**	**8**	**2**	**2.64**	**39.96**
Total (5b)	**126.3**	**44**	**295**	**19**	**9/24**	**15.52**	**1**	**1**	**2.33**	**33.31**
In Australia										
Australia	433.2	96	1211	42	8/68	28.83	3	1	2.79	61.90
Australian XI	47	9	129	3	3/52	43.00	-	-	2.74	94.00
New South Wales	137	31	373	14	6/55	26.64	2	-	2.72	58.71
Queensland	53	13	132	6	3/58	22.00	-	-	2.49	53.00
South Australia	97	23	240	5	2/78	48.00	-	-	2.47	116.40
Tasmania	98	34	208	5	3/29	41.60	-	-	2.12	117.60
Victoria	158.1	40	339	29	6/39	11.68	4	1	2.14	32.72
Victorian XI	40	9	90	3	3/90	30.00	-	-	2.25	80.00
Western Australia	55.4	18	115	7	2/4	16.42	-	-	2.06	47.71
Total	**1119.1**	**273**	**2837**	**114**	**8/68**	**24.88**	**9**	**2**	**2.53**	**58.90**
In South Africa										
Border	33	9	82	6	4/27	13.66	-	-	2.48	33.00
Cape Province	15	2	54	4	4/54	13.50	-	-	3.60	22.50

Natal	64.5	20	116	12	5/43	9.66	1	-	1.78	32.41
Orange River Colony	4	0	24	0	-	-	-	-	6.00	-
South Africa	145.5	38	342	8	3/33	42.75	-	-	2.34	109.37
Transvaal	132.4	18	454	16	3/46	28.37	-	-	3.42	49.75
Western Province	48	11	125	6	4/51	20.83	-	-	2.60	48.00
Total	**443.2**	**98**	**1197**	**52**	**5/43**	**23.01**	**1**	**-**	**2.70**	**51.15**
In West Indies										
Barbados	40.1	16	80	3	3/80	26.66	-	-	1.99	80.33
British Guiana	107	29	214	12	5/57	17.83	1	-	2.00	53.50
Jamaica	47	16	94	5	4/57	18.80	-	-	2.00	56.40
Trinidad	51	19	106	9	5/76	11.77	1	-	2.07	34.00
West Indies	256	92	453	10	3/110	45.30	-	-	1.76	153.60
Total	**501.1**	**172**	**947**	**39**	**5/57**	**24.28**	**2**	**-**	**1.88**	**77.10**
In India										
All India (Indians)	40	13	100	4	3/51	25.00	-	-	2.50	60.00
Europeans and Parsees	49	8	156	5	3/99	31.20	-	-	3.18	58.80
Hindus	46.4	28	50	10	7/26	5.00	1	-	1.07	28.00
MCC	24	4	73	3	3/73	24.33	-	-	3.04	48.00
Muslims	36.3	14	67	5	3/31	13.40	-	-	1.83	43.80
Parsees	33	13	59	12	7/33	4.91	2	1	1.78	16.50
Total	**229.1**	**80**	**505**	**39**	**7/26**	**12.94**	**3**	**1**	**2.20**	**35.25**

Record on Each Ground (Batting and Fielding)

Ground	M	I	NO	R	HS	Ave	100	50	Ct
In England									
Bath	7	8	3	270	115*	54.00	1	1	6
Blackheath	1	1	0	15	15	15.00	-	-	-
Bournemouth	8	9	1	325	106	40.62	1	1	4
Bradford	90	124	17	3028	126	28.29	4	13	56
Bramall Lane	105	149	22	3508	146	27.62	3	23	70
Bray	2	3	0	31	12	10.33	-	-	1
Bristol	14	18	1	406	110	23.88	1	1	12
Canterbury	4	8	1	173	95	24.71	-	1	5
Cardiff	5	3	0	40	34	13.33	-	-	4
Catford	3	5	0	36	18	7.20	-	-	1
Cheltenham	4	6	0	58	25	9.66	-	-	1
Chesterfield	12	16	2	365	82*	26.07	-	2	8
Derby	9	9	1	228	69	28.50	-	2	4
Dewsbury	29	41	2	1310	135	33.58	2	7	32
Dover	4	6	0	105	53	17.50	-	1	2
Dublin	1	1	0	13	13	13.00	-	-	2
Dudley	1	1	0	13	13	13.00	-	-	-
Eastbourne	3	4	0	62	35	15.50	-	-	-
Edgbaston	31	37	10	1015	81	37.59	-	4	18
Fenner's	24	33	6	738	102	27.33	1	2	22
Glossop	2	2	0	1	1	0.50	-	-	1
Gloucester	5	6	0	201	72	33.50	-	2	4
Harrogate	29	37	9	1403	176	50.10	5	7	23
Hastings	14	18	6	379	93	31.58	-	2	13
Headingley	88	124	14	3096	267*	28.14	7	8	50
Hove	24	35	4	1078	199	34.77	2	6	17
Huddersfield	29	33	3	1081	140	36.03	2	6	28
Hull	37	44	4	1054	105*	26.35	1	7	24
Ilkeston	1	2	1	9	7*	9.00	-	-	-
Kennington Oval	58	84	20	1937	96	30.26	-	12	42
Kettering	1	1	0	55	55	55.00	-	1	-
Leicester (Aylestone Road)	24	29	2	1114	152	40.89	3	8	18
Leicester (Grace Road)	2	2	1	31	27	31.00	-	-	3
Leyton	27	34	7	882	132	32.66	2	2	15

Liverpool	1	2	0	58	58	29.00	-	1	1
Lord's	72	107	11	2439	121	25.40	1	15	33
Maidstone	6	12	2	239	68	23.90	-	1	5
Northampton	16	22	3	734	110	38.63	2	2	19
Old Trafford	34	51	12	1160	94*	29.74	-	6	22
The Parks	3	3	1	32	24*	16.00	-	-	-
Portsmouth	7	8	1	279	98	39.85	-	3	2
Reigate	1	2	0	10	5	5.00	-	-	2
Scarborough	83	124	22	2825	128	27.69	5	14	43
Southampton	8	11	3	250	58*	31.25	-	1	6
Southend-on-Sea	2	2	0	11	10	5.50	-	-	-
Stourbridge	1	1	0	51	51	51.00	-	1	2
Swansea	2	1	0	4	4	4.00	-	-	3
Taunton	12	16	2	503	201	35.92	1	1	11
Tonbridge	5	9	2	126	31*	18.00	-	-	2
Trent Bridge	31	41	6	1192	83	34.05	-	9	22
Tunbridge Wells	4	6	0	145	53	24.16	-	1	4
Uttoxeter	1	2	1	56	33	56.00	-	-	1
Weston-super-Mare	2	3	0	126	100	42.00	1	-	1
Worcester	18	23	2	715	196	34.04	2	3	10
Total	**1007**	**1379**	**205**	**35015**	**267***	**29.82**	**47**	**177**	**675**

In Australia

Adelaide	10	14	3	549	210	49.90	1	3	7
Brisbane (Exhibition)	1	1	0	162	162	162.00	1	-	-
Brisbane (Woolloongabba)	6	8	2	211	70*	35.16	-	2	6
Hobart	3	3	1	227	119	113.50	2	-	4
Launceston	3	5	3	81	39	40.50	-	-	2
Melbourne	15	25	4	692	179	32.95	1	3	14
Perth	2	2	1	36	32*	36.00	-	-	-
South Melbourne	1	1	1	105	105*	-	1	-	-
Sydney	16	29	4	933	119	37.32	2	4	6
Total	**57**	**88**	**19**	**2996**	**210**	**43.42**	**8**	**12**	**39**

In South Africa

Bloemfontein	1	1	0	68	68	68.00	-	1	4
Cape Town	5	9	2	155	77	22.14	-	1	7
Durban	5	8	0	235	64	29.37	-	1	7
East London	2	3	0	79	35	26.33	-	-	3
Johannesburg	8	14	1	547	152	42.07	1	3	12
Kingwilliamstown	1	2	0	67	38	33.50	-	-	1
Pietermaritzburg	2	2	0	15	14	7.50	-	-	-
Port Elizabeth	3	4	1	63	31	21.00	-	-	4
Pretoria	2	1	0	1	1	1.00	-	-	2
Vogelfontein	1	-	-	-	-	-	-	-	1
Total	**30**	**44**	**4**	**1230**	**152**	**30.75**	**1**	**6**	**41**

In West Indies

Bridgetown	2	2	1	50	36	50.00	-	-	2
Georgetown	3	3	2	19	10*	19.00	-	-	3
Kingston	2	3	2	33	14	33.00	-	-	-
Port of Spain	2	4	2	27	11	13.50	-	-	-
Total	**9**	**12**	**7**	**129**	**36**	**25.80**	**-**	**-**	**5**

In India

Bombay	4	6	1	472	183	94.40	2	1	3
Lahore	2	4	0	114	71	28.50	-	1	2
Patiala	1	1	1	13	13*	-	-	-	-
Total	**7**	**11**	**2**	**599**	**183**	**66.55**	**2**	**2**	**5**

Record on Each Ground (Bowling)

Ground	O	M	R	W	BB	Ave	5i	10m	Econ	Strike
In England										
Bath	118	32	279	18	6/109	15.50	1	-	2.36	39.33
(5b)	54.3	26	78	18	7/24	4.33	3	1	1.42	15.16
Blackheath	18	4	40	2	2/40	20.00	-	-	2.22	54.00
Bournemouth	163.3	47	442	18	4/32	24.55	-	-	2.70	54.50
Bradford	2341.1	675	5622	374	8/43	15.03	30	11	2.40	37.55
(5b)	228.2	88	433	31	7/24	13.96	4	2	1.89	36.83
Bramall Lane	2835.4	819	6286	385	7/38	16.32	20	2	2.21	44.19
(5b)	293.2	117	516	30	6/71	17.20	1	-	1.75	48.90
Bray	31	11	64	4	4/47	16.00	-	-	2.06	46.50
Bristol	391.2	131	861	72	7/15	11.95	6	2	2.20	32.61
(5b)	28.4	14	31	9	6/16	3.44	1	-	1.07	16.00
Canterbury	110.4	26	279	18	8/55	15.50	1	1	2.52	36.88
Cardiff	9	4	28	0	-	-	-	-	3.11	-
Catford	95.2	29	189	19	8/26	9.94	1	1	1.98	30.10
Cheltenham	118	40	247	32	7/67	7.71	4	2	2.09	22.12
Chesterfield	213.4	66	428	37	7/16	11.56	1	-	2.00	34.64
(5b)	30	14	47	4	3/47	11.75	-	-	1.56	37.50
Derby	206.2	61	389	38	7/24	10.23	2	2	1.88	32.57
(5b)	42	21	62	5	3/36	12.40	-	-	1.47	42.00
Dewsbury	783.3	235	1780	136	7/55	13.08	11	2	2.27	34.56
(5b)	94.2	39	168	16	5/25	10.50	2	-	1.77	29.50
Dover	72	30	90	3	2/25	30.00	-	-	1.25	144.00
Dublin	27	7	88	9	5/77	9.77	1	-	3.25	18.00
Dudley	25.3	11	41	8	5/24	5.12	1	-	1.60	19.12
Eastbourne	118.1	34	261	18	6/27	14.50	2	-	2.20	39.38
Edgbaston	945.5	319	1817	130	8/90	13.97	11	1	1.92	43.65
(5b)	83	37	109	5	3/25	21.80	-	-	1.31	83.00
Fenner's	697	219	1571	118	8/68	13.31	9	4	2.25	35.44
(5b)	72.1	28	158	12	4/18	13.16	-	-	2.18	30.08
Glossop	66.3	24	155	15	6/22	10.33	1	-	2.33	26.60
Gloucester	108.4	57	160	22	7/47	7.27	1	1	1.47	29.63
Harrogate	670.1	212	1523	97	8/28	15.70	7	1	2.27	41.45
(5b)	100	24	290	11	5/57	26.36	1	-	2.90	45.45
Hastings	356.5	91	1057	57	7/46	18.54	8	2	2.96	37.56
(5b)	88.4	25	244	9	4/50	27.11	-	-	2.74	49.33
Headingley	2506.2	801	5218	343	8/39	15.21	28	9	2.08	43.84
(5b)	220	83	374	18	5/69	20.77	1	-	1.70	61.11
Hove	730	194	1727	80	7/115	21.58	6	1	2.36	54.75
(5b)	133.4	63	244	14	6/64	17.42	1	-	1.82	47.78
Huddersfield	598.5	203	1230	99	8/48	12.42	8	1	2.05	36.29
(5b)	44	22	70	9	4/35	7.77	-	-	1.59	24.44
Hull	908.3	345	1633	97	8/23	16.83	6	2	1.79	56.19
Kennington Oval	1418.2	369	3702	152	6/38	24.35	6	2	2.61	55.98
(5b)	111	30	253	4	3/27	63.25	-	-	2.27	138.75
Kettering	6	1	10	2	2/10	5.00	-	-	1.66	18.00
Leicester (Aylestone Road)	854.4	299	1676	103	7/55	16.27	7	1	1.96	49.78
Leicester (Grace Road)	51.3	21	78	6	4/63	13.00	-	-	1.52	51.50
(Grace Road) (5b)	32.4	10	67	9	5/33	7.44	1	-	2.04	18.22
Leyton	752.4	232	1574	97	9/39	16.22	6	2	2.09	46.55
(5b)	63	24	103	20	9/28	5.15	2	1	1.63	15.75
Liverpool	27.4	7	78	8	5/35	9.75	1	-	2.81	20.75
Lord's	1773.3	445	4354	195	8/53	22.32	11	1	2.45	54.56
(5b)	281.1	88	633	22	7/147	28.77	1	-	2.25	63.90
Maidstone	122.4	24	334	17	4/35	19.64	2	-	2.72	43.29
(5b)	40	15	56	2	2/39	28.00	-	-	1.40	100.00
Northampton	450.1	151	920	75	8/92	12.26	5	2	2.04	36.01
Old Trafford	946.4	281	2074	107	7/80	19.38	7	-	2.19	53.08
(5b)	105	46	161	7	3/98	23.00	-	-	1.53	75.00

The Parks	69.4	12	221	7	4/129	31.57	-	-	3.17	59.71
Portsmouth	183	36	507	25	6/73	20.28	2	1	2.77	43.92
Reigate	51.4	11	95	10	6/56	9.50	1	1	1.83	31.00
Scarborough	1854.3	449	4973	257	6/19	19.35	12	-	2.68	43.29
(5b)	314.1	107	683	42	9/24	16.26	4	2	2.17	37.40
Southampton	203.5	48	490	20	3/42	24.50	-	-	2.40	61.15
(5b)	22	11	30	3	2/20	10.00	-	-	1.36	36.66
Southend-on-Sea	67.5	24	117	12	4/16	9.75	-	-	1.72	33.91
Swansea	70	28	110	12	6/56	9.16	1	-	1.57	35.00
Taunton	378.4	95	978	70	6/52	13.97	6	2	2.58	32.45
Tonbridge	101	22	265	15	7/116	17.66	2	-	2.62	40.40
(5b)	61.4	23	117	4	3/90	29.25	-	-	1.89	77.25
Trent Bridge	945.3	309	1920	103	7/40	18.64	6	-	2.03	55.07
(5b)	170.2	69	288	25	8/38	11.52	2	1	1.69	34.08
Tunbridge Wells	104.4	33	242	10	5/42	24.20	1	-	2.31	62.80
Uttoxeter	32.5	8	77	4	2/14	19.25	-	-	2.34	49.25
Weston-super-Mare	51.5	19	77	9	5/28	8.55	1	-	1.48	34.35
Worcester	601	205	1148	62	8/87	18.51	5	1	1.91	58.16
(5b)	34	5	96	4	2/45	24.00	-	-	2.82	42.50
Total	**26386.2**	**7856**	**59525**	**3627**	**9/39**	**16.41**	**248**	**58**	**2.25**	**43.64**
Total (5b)	**2748.4**	**1029**	**5311**	**333**	**9/24**	**15.94**	**24**	**7**	**1.93**	**41.27**

In Australia

Adelaide	205.5	53	537	10	3/61	53.70	-	-	2.16	123.50
Brisbane (Exhibition)	17	7	30	2	2/30	15.00	-	-	2.05	51.00
Brisbane (Woolloongabba)	83	15	231	7	3/52	33.00	-	-	2.79	71.14
Hobart	53	23	81	5	3/29	16.20	-	-	1.52	63.60
Launceston	45	11	127	0	-	-	-	-	2.82	-
Melbourne	294	62	773	50	8/68	15.46	6	2	2.62	35.28
Perth	55.4	18	115	7	2/4	16.42	-	-	2.06	47.71
South Melbourne	40	9	90	3	3/90	30.00	-	-	2.25	80.00
Sydney	325.4	75	853	30	6/55	28.43	3	-	2.61	65.13
Total	**1119.1**	**273**	**2837**	**114**	**8/68**	**24.88**	**9**	**2**	**2.53**	**58.90**

In South Africa

Bloemfontein	4	0	24	0	-	-	-	-	6.00	-
Cape Town	58	13	149	6	4/51	24.83	-	-	2.56	58.00
Durban	112.5	30	243	11	5/43	22.09	1	-	2.15	61.54
East London	18	5	41	1	1/28	41.00	-	-	2.27	108.00
Johannesburg	151.5	26	461	16	3/46	28.81	-	-	3.03	56.93
Kingwilliamstown	15	4	41	5	4/27	8.20	-	-	2.73	18.00
Pietermaritzburg	23	8	39	5	4/34	7.80	-	-	1.69	27.60
Port Elizabeth	25	6	68	4	4/54	17.00	-	-	2.72	37.52
Pretoria	33	5	124	2	2/100	62.00	-	-	3.75	99.00
Vogelfontein	2.4	1	7	2	2/7	3.50	-	-	2.62	8.00
Total	**443.2**	**98**	**1197**	**52**	**5/43**	**23.01**	**1**	**-**	**2.70**	**51.15**

In West Indies

Bridgetown	118.2	35	234	6	3/80	39.00	-	-	1.97	118.33
Georgetown	198	60	403	16	5/57	25.18	1	-	2.03	74.25
Kingston	91.5	41	133	7	4/57	41.00	-	-	1.44	78.71
Port of Spain	93	36	177	10	5/76	17.70	1	-	1.90	55.80
Total	**501.1**	**172**	**947**	**39**	**5/57**	**24.28**	**2**	**-**	**1.88**	**77.10**

In India

Bombay	160.3	57	359	28	7/26	12.82	3	1	2.23	34.39
Lahore	44.4	19	73	8	3/6	9.12	-	-	1.63	33.52
Patiala	24.0	4	73	3	3/73	24.33	-	-	3.04	48.00
Total	**229.1**	**80**	**505**	**39**	**7/26**	**12.94**	**3**	**1**	**2.20**	**35.25**

How He Scored His Runs

0	135
1-9	442
10-19	307
20-29	174
30-39	129
40-49	92
50-59	79
60-69	44
70-79	30
80-89	22
90-99	22
100+	58
Total	**1534**

How His Innings Ended

b	*c*	*c&b*	*hw*	*lbw*	*ro*	*st*	*no*	*total*
408	631	58	1	142	37	20	237	1534

Bowlers Who Dismissed Rhodes

392 bowlers dismissed W.Rhodes during his career. The following dismissed him most times:

25	J.W.H.T.Douglas
19	W.Brearley
18	J.T.Hearne
17	C.Blythe, A.Fielder
15	C.P.Buckenham, E.G.Dennett
14	J.W.Hitch, A.S.Kennedy
13	P.G.H.Fender, F.A.Tarrant
12	H.Dean, N.E.Haig, W.Mead, C.W.L.Parker, W.C.Smith
11	G.R.Cox, E.F.Field. G.Geary, E.A.McDonald, E.Robson, S.Santall, A.E.Trott, F.E.Woolley
10	W.B.Short, G.H.T.Simpson-Hayward, A.E.R.Gilligan, H.Howell, G.J.Thompson
9	F.R.Foster, A.P.Freeman, S.Hargreave, J.W.Hearne, F.J.Laver
8	W.W.Armstrong, W.E.Astill, R.D.Burrows, F.J.Durston, A.W.Hallam, A.E.Relf, A.E.E.Vogler, T.G.Wass, W.Wells
7	L.C.Braund, J.M.Gregory, J.R.Gunn, V.W.C.Jupp, J.A.Newman, T.Richardson, S.G.Smith, M.W.Tate, A.Warren
6	W.Bestwick, G.L.Jessop, N.A.Knox, A.A.Mailey, A.Morton, T.L.Richmond, A.E.Thomas
5	E.G.Arnold, W.B.Burns, C.P.Carter, B.Cranfield, J.A.Cuffe, W.J.Fairservice, M.Falcon, J.S.Heap, J.Iremonger, T.Jayes, A.W.Lewis, C.G.Macartney, J.R.Mason, A.W.Nourse, W.W.Odell, S.J.Pegler, F.W.Tate, H.Trumble, R.K.Tyldesley, W.J.Whitty, H.I.Young

Fieldsmen Who Dismissed Rhodes

397 fielders and wicket-keepers were responsible for dismissing W.Rhodes during his career. The following dismissed him most times:

15	James Seymour
13	H.Carter (12 ct, 1 st)
11	T.W.Oates
8	L.C.Braund, G.R.Cox
7	W.S.Bird, B.J.T.Bosanquet, A.O.Jones, A.F.A.Lilley (6 ct, 1 st), J.C.Hubble (6 ct, 1 st), H.Strudwick
6	F.H.Huish, J.Humphries, H.R.Murrell (4 st, 2 st), F.E.Woolley
5	H.Board, F.S.G.Calthorpe, H.A.Carpenter, G.Duckworth (4ct, 1st), A.C.MacLaren, M.A.Noble, A.E.Relf, F.A.Tarrant

How He Dismissed His Victims

b	c	c&b	hw	lbw	st	total
899	2231	190	20	496	368	4204

Batsmen Who Were Dismissed by Rhodes

1224 different batsmen were dismissed by W.Rhodes during his career. The following were his victims most often:

34	G.L.Jessop
26	J.W.H.T.Douglas, A.O.Jones
25	T.W.Hayward, William Quaife
24	A.E.Relf, J.T.Tyldesley
23	C.Charlesworth, J.H.King, C.P.McGahey
22	P.F.Warner
21	J.Hardstaff, sen., G.J.Thompson
20	P.A.Perrin
19	W.W.Armstrong, L.C.Braund
18	J.H.Board, V.T.Trumper
17	M.A.Noble, W.Reeves
16	H.A.Carpenter, J.R.Gunn, E.G.Hayes, A.E.Trott
15	W.E.Astill, C.B.Fry, G.Gunn, J.B.Hobbs, W.S.Lees, M.W.Tate
14	E.G.Arnold, S.Coe, G.R.Cox, E.H.Hendren, A.E.Knight, H.D.G.Leveson-Gower, H.R.Murrell, W.E.G.Payton, G.E.Tyldesley
13	F.Barratt, N.E.Haig, J.W.Hearne, R.H.Spooner, J.Vine, W.Wells, S.M.J.Woods, F.E.Woolley, H.Wrathall
12	W.Bestwick, C.P.Buckenham, S.W.A.Cadman, A.Hearne, J.T.Hearne, F.H.Huish, S.P.Kinneir, A.E.Lewis, A.F.A.Lilley, A.C.MacLaren, W.Mead, A.Morton, K.S.Ranjitsinhji, E.Robson, F.I.Walden, H.Whitehead
11	B.J.T.Bosanquet, C.E.De Trafford, S.E.Gregory, J.Iremonger, J.W.H.Makepeace, T.W.Oates, H.A.Peach, S.Santall, James Seymour, J.Sharp, H.Strudwick, C.J.B.Wood
10	F.L.Bowley, J.Daniell, R.A.Duff, E.F.Field, T.S.Fishwick, H.K.Foster, G.C.Gill, J.S.Heap, E.Humphreys, K.L.Hutchings, J.J.Kelly, E.H.Killick, G.MacGregor, J.A.Newman, T.M.Russell, John Seymour, T.F.Shepherd, F.A.Tarrant

Fieldsmen and Wicket-Keepers Who Caught Rhodes' Victims

190 fielders and wicket-keepers were responsible for catching W.Rhodes' dismissals during his career. The following took most catches from Rhodes' bowling:

201	J.Tunnicliffe
189	W.Rhodes
154	D.Denton
148	G.H.Hirst
143	D.Hunter
92	S.Haigh
87	A.Dolphin
68	E.Robinson
64	P.Holmes
57	H.Sutcliffe
56	A.Waddington
52	E.Oldroyd
50	J.T.Brown, sen.
44	R.Kilner
42	F.Wainwright
39	G.G.Macaulay
36	E.Smith
35	M.W.Booth, W.H.Wilkinson
33	Lord Hawke

30	H.Myers
27	A.Drake, F.S.Jackson, M.Leyland
23	A.Mitchell, J.T.Newstead
22	W.E.Bates
21	L.Whitehead
20	J.W.Rothery
19	W.L.Taylor
17	F.Mitchell
15	D.C.F.Burton, B.B.Wilson
14	N.Kilner, A.Wood
13	L.C.Braund, E.H.Hendren, A.F.A.Lilley, F.E.Woolley
12	C.H.Grimshaw
11	T.W.Hayward, J.T.Tyldesley
10	F.Dennis, E.R.Wilson

Wicket-Keepers Who Stumped Rhodes' Victims

21 wicket-keepers were responsible for stumping W.Rhodes' dismissals during his career. Those who stumped most were:

164	D.Hunter
124	A.Dolphin
21	A.Wood
11	A.F.A.Lilley
9	W.R.Allen
7	H.Strudwick
6	A.Bairstow

Centuries (58)

105	Yorkshire	v MCC & Ground	Scarborough	1901
196	Yorkshire	v Worcestershire	Worcester	1904
107	Yorkshire	v Surrey	Bradford	1904
201	Yorkshire	v Somerset	Taunton	1905
108	Yorkshire	v Somerset	Harrogate	1905
119	Yorkshire	v Leicestershire	Leicester (AR)	1906
115*	Yorkshire	v Somerset	Bath	1906
109	Yorkshire	v MCC & Ground	Scarborough	1906
112	Yorkshire	v Leicestershire	Leicester (AR)	1907
119	MCC	v Tasmania	Hobart	1907/08
105*	MCC	v Victorian XI	South Melbourne	1907/08
146	Yorkshire	v Worcestershire	Bramall lane	1908
140	Yorkshire	v Northamptonshire	Huddersfield	1908
122	Yorkshire	v Leicestershire	Harrogate	1908
199	Yorkshire	v Sussex	Hove	1909
114	Yorkshire	v Essex	Headingley	1909
108	Yorkshire	v Australians	Bramall Lane	1909
101	Yorkshire	v Kent	Huddersfield	1909
101	Yorkshire	v MCC	Scarborough	1909
111	Yorkshire	v Sussex	Hove	1910
128 } 115	Yorkshire	v MCC	Scarborough	1911
125	Yorkshire	v Sussex	Headingley	1911
121	England	v Rest of England	Lord's	1911
100	Yorkshire	v Derbyshire	Bramall Lane	1911
179	ENGLAND	v AUSTRALIA	Melbourne	1911/12
119	MCC	v New South Wales	Sydney	1911/12
109	MCC	v New South Wales	Sydney	1911/12
102	MCC	v Tasmania	Hobart	1911/12
176	Yorkshire	v Nottinghamshire	Harrogate	1912

107		Yorkshire	v Lancashire	Bradford	1912
152		Yorkshire	v Leicestershire	Leicester (AR)	1913
110		Yorkshire	v Gloucestershire	Bristol	1913
110		Yorkshire	v Northamptonshire	Northampton	1913
102		Yorkshire	v Cambridge University	Fenner's	1913
152		ENGLAND	v SOUTH AFRICA	Johannesburg	1913/14
113		Yorkshire	v Sussex	Bradford	1914
105*		Yorkshire	v Lancashire	Hull	1914
135		Yorkshire	v Hampshire	Dewsbury	1919
167*		Yorkshire	v Nottinghamshire	Headingley	1920
210		MCC	v South Australia	Adelaide	1920/21
162		MCC	v Queensland	Brisbane	1920/21
267*		Yorkshire	v Leicestershire	Headingley	1921
104*		Yorkshire	v Northamptonshire	Northampton	1921
102*		Yorkshire	v Essex	Leyton	1921
183		Europeans	v Parsees	Bombay	1921/22
156		Europeans	v Hindus	Bombay	1921/22
110		Yorkshire	v Glamorgan	Headingley	1922
108*		Yorkshire	v Essex	Harrogate	1922
106		Yorkshire	v Hampshire	Bournemouth	1922
105		Yorkshire	v Middlesex	Headingley	1922
126		Yorkshire	v Middlesex	Bradford	1923
102		Yorkshire	v Essex	Dewsbury	1923
100		Yorkshire	v Somerset	Weston-super-Mare	1924
157		Yorkshire	v Derbyshire	Headingley	1925
114*		Yorkshire	v Somerset	Harrogate	1925
132		Yorkshire	v Essex	Leyton	1926
100*		Yorkshire	v Worcestershire	Worcester	1928

Century Wicket Partnerships (131)

109	9th	L.Whitehead	Yorkshire	v Sussex	Harrogate	1899
161	9th	E.Smith	Yorkshire	v Sussex	Bramall Lane	1900
159	8th	E.Smith	Yorkshire	v MCC & Ground	Scarborough	1901
118	9th	S.Haigh	Yorkshire	v Somerset	Headingley	1901
146	9th	G.H.Hirst	Yorkshire	v Worcestershire	Worcester	1901
173	5th	S.Haigh	Yorkshire	v Sussex	Hove	1902
100	5th	J.T.Brown	Yorkshire	v Gloucestershire	Bristol	1903
105*	5th	G.H.Hirst	Yorkshire	v C.I.Thornton's XI	Scarborough	1903
130	10th	R.E.Foster	ENGLAND	v AUSTRALIA	Sydney	1903/04
129	3rd	D.Denton	Yorkshire	v Worcestershire	Worcester	1904
114	5th	G.H.Hirst	Yorkshire	v Essex	Headingley	1904
132	5th	S.Haigh	Yorkshire	v Worcestershire	Worcester	1904
151	5th	D.Denton	Yorkshire	v Middlesex	Bramall Lane	1904
108	6th	G.H.Hirst	North	v South	Scarborough	1904
123	7th	G.H.Hirst	North	v South	Scarborough	1904
146	7th	J.H.King	North	v South	Hastings	1904
152	8th	J.W.Rothery	Yorkshire	v Hampshire	Portsmouth	1904
162	9th	S.Haigh	Yorkshire	v Lancashire	Manchester	1904
105	2nd	D.Denton	Yorkshire	v Middlesex	Lord's	1905
107	6th	D.Denton	Yorkshire	v Hampshire	Bournemouth	1905
108	6th	G.H.Hirst	North	v South	Scarborough	1905
111	6th	S.Haigh	Yorkshire	v Essex	Huddersfield	1905
117	6th	S.Haigh	Yorkshire	v Somerset	Harrogate	1905
151	8th	Lord Hawke	Yorkshire	v Somerset	Taunton	1905
105	1st	J.W.Rothery	Yorkshire	v Essex	Bradford	1906
106	1st	R.H.Spooner	North	v South	Scarborough	1906
107	1st	J.Tunnicliffe	Yorkshire	v Surrey	Kennington Oval	1906
108	1st	J.Tunnicliffe	Yorkshire	v Leicestershire	Leicester (AR)	1906
105	2nd	D.Denton	Yorkshire	v Middlesex	Lord's	1906
124*	2nd	G.H.Hirst	Yorkshire	v Somerset	Bath	1906
131	2nd	D.Denton	Yorkshire	v Somerset	Huddersfield	1906

170	2nd	D.Denton	Yorkshire	v Nottinghamshire	Trent Bridge	1906
130	1st	J.Tunnicliffe	Yorkshire	v Leicestershire	Leicester (AR)	1907
123	2nd	D.Denton	Yorkshire	v Somerset	Headingley	1907
101	6th	L.C.Braund	MCC	v New South Wales	Sydney	1907/08
210	6th	J.Hardstaff, sen.				
			MCC	v Tasmania	Hobart	1907/08
141	3rd	W.H.Wilkinson				
			Yorkshire	v Gloucestershire	Bramall Lane	1908
102	4th	G.H.Hirst	Yorkshire	v Leicestershire	Harrogate	1908
156	4th	G.H.Hirst	Yorkshire	v Worcestershire	Bramall Lane	1908
103	4th	D.Denton	Yorkshire	v Warwickshire	Edgbaston	1908
122	2nd	D.Denton	Yorkshire	v Nottinghamshire	Trent Bridge	1909
104	3rd	C.B.Fry	ENGLAND	v AUSTRALIA	Kennington Oval	1909
149	3rd	J.W.Rothery	Yorkshire	v Sussex	Hove	1909
104	5th	J.W.H.Makepeace				
			Yorkshire & Lancashire	v Australians	Hull	1909
149	5th	G.H.Hirst	Yorkshire	v Kent	Huddersfield	1909
102	1st	J.B.Hobbs	MCC	v Eastern Province	Port Elizabeth	1909/10
159	1st	J.B.Hobbs	ENGLAND	v SOUTH AFRICA	Johannesburg	1909/10
207	1st	J.B.Hobbs	MCC	v Natal	Durban	1909/10
221	1st	J.B.Hobbs	ENGLAND	v SOUTH AFRICA	Cape Town	1909/10
117	1st	J.W.Rothery	Yorkshire	v Kent	Dewsbury	1910
135	2nd	D.Denton	Yorkshire	v Northamptonshire	Bramall Lane	1910
182	5th	B.B.Wilson	Yorkshire	v Sussex	Hove	1910
122	1st	B.B.Wilson	Yorkshire	v Nottinghamshire	Hull	1911
134	1st	B.B.Wilson	Yorkshire	v MCC	Lord's	1911
124	2nd	D.Denton	Yorkshire	v Warwickshire	Edgbaston	1911
142	2nd	D.Denton	Yorkshire	v Derbyshire	Bramall Lane	1911
159	2nd	D.Denton	Yorkshire	v MCC	Scarborough	1911
119	3rd	A.Drake	Yorkshire	v Worcestershire	Bradford	1911
138	3rd	W.E.Bates	Yorkshire	v Kent	Bramall Lane	1911
125	4th	H.Wilson	Yorkshire	v Essex	Bramall Lane	1911
170	7th	J.Iremonger	England	v The Rest	Lord's	1911
147	1st	J.B.Hobbs	ENGLAND	v AUSTRALIA	Adelaide	1911/12
323	1st	J.B.Hobbs	ENGLAND	v AUSTRALIA	Melbourne	1911/12
102	2nd	G.Gunn	ENGLAND	v AUSTRALIA	Melbourne	1911/12
123	2nd	J.B.Hobbs	MCC	v Victoria	Melbourne	1911/12
127	2nd	J.W.Hearne	ENGLAND	v AUSTRALIA	Melbourne	1911/12
138	2nd	G.Gunn	MCC	v New South Wales	Sydney	1911/12
206	2nd	F.E.Woolley	MCC	v Tasmania	Hobart	1911/12
124	1st	J.B.Hobbs	Players	v Gentlemen	Lord's	1912
108	1st	B.B.Wilson	Yorkshire	v Essex	Leyton	1913
109	1st	B.B.Wilson	Yorkshire	v Surrey	Kennington Oval	1913
131	1st	B.B.Wilson	Yorkshire	v Sussex	Bramall Lane	1913
180	1st	B.B.Wilson	Yorkshire	v Leicestershire	Leicester (AR)	1913
197	1st	B.B.Wilson	Yorkshire	v Gloucestershire	Bristol	1913
115	2nd	S.Haigh	Yorkshire	v Warwickshire	Edgbaston	1913
106	3rd	R.Kilner	Yorkshire	v Middlesex	Bramall Lane	1913
100	1st	J.B.Hobbs	ENGLAND	v SOUTH AFRICA	Johannesburg	1913/14
133	1st	J.B.Hobbs	ENGLAND	v SOUTH AFRICA	Durban	1913/14
141	1st	A.E.Relf	ENGLAND	v SOUTH AFRICA	Johannesburg	1913/14
211*	1st	J.B.Hobbs	MCC	v Transvaal	Johannesburg	1913/14
152	3rd	C.P.Mead	ENGLAND	v SOUTH AFRICA	Johannesburg	1913/14
102	3rd	R.Kilner	Yorkshire	v Northamptonshire	Huddersfield	1914
114	3rd	G.H.Hirst	Yorkshire	v Surrey	Bradford	1914
104	4th	G.H.Hirst	Yorkshire	v Nottinghamshire	Trent Bridge	1914
271	4th	B.B.Wilson	Yorkshire	v Sussex	Bradford	1914
103	5th	G.H.Hirst	Yorkshire	v Worcestershire	Hull	1914
150	1st	P.Holmes	Yorkshire	v Australian Imperial Forces		
					Bramall Lane	1919
106	4th	D.Denton	Yorkshire	v Leicestershire	Huddersfield	1919
156	6th	E.Robinson	Yorkshire	v Derbyshire	Chesterfield	1919
254	7th	D.C.F.Burton	Yorkshire	v Hampshire	Dewsbury	1919
119*	4th	D.Denton	Yorkshire	v Worcestershire	Worcester	1920

128*	4th	P.Holmes	Yorkshire	v Hampshire	Portsmouth	1920
133	4th	R.Kilner	Yorkshire	v Worcestershire	Bramall Lane	1920
149	4th	R.Kilner	Yorkshire	v Derbyshire	Bramall Lane	1920
368	2nd	C.A.G.Russell	MCC	v South Australia	Adelaide	1920/21
184	4th	J.W.H.T.Douglas MCC		v Queensland	Brisbane	1920/21
105*	3rd	C.Tyson	Yorkshire	v Hampshire	Southampton	1921
116	5th	E.Robinson	Yorkshire	v Essex	Leyton	1921
276	5th	R.Kilner	Yorkshire	v Northamptonshire	Northampton	1921
229	6th	N.Kilner	Yorkshire	v Leicestershire	Headingley	1921
185	3rd	J.H.Parsons	Europeans	v Hindus	Bombay	1921/22
106	5th	F.G.Travers	Europeans	v Hindus	Bombay	1921/22
107	6th	G.H.Hirst	Europeans	v Parsees	Bombay	1921/22
157	7th	C.W.Beart	Europeans	v Parsees	Bombay	1921/22
107	4th	H.Sutcliffe	Yorkshire	v Nottinghamshire	Trent Bridge	1922
114	4th	H.Sutcliffe	Yorkshire	v Hampshire	Bournemouth	1922
129	4th	R.Kilner	Yorkshire	v Middlesex	Headingley	1922
160	4th	E.Oldroyd	Yorkshire	v Leicestershire	Bramall Lane	1922
165	5th	E.Oldroyd	Yorkshire	v Glamorgan	Headingley	1922
103	8th	A.Dolphin	Yorkshire	v Rest of England	Kennington Oval	1922
192*	8th	G.G.Macaulay	Yorkshire	v Essex	Harrogate	1922
153	4th	E.Oldroyd	Yorkshire	v Sussex	Headingley	1923
111*	5th	R.Kilner	Yorkshire	v Rest of England	Kennington Oval	1923
113	5th	R.Kilner	Yorkshire	v MCC	Scarborough	1923
117	5th	R.Kilner	Yorkshire	v Essex	Dewsbury	1923
190	6th	M.Leyland	Yorkshire	v Middlesex	Bradford	1923
117	4th	E.Oldroyd	Yorkshire	v South Africans	Bramall Lane	1924
103	4th	M.Leyland	Yorkshire	v Warwickshire	Edgbaston	1925
132	4th	M.Leyland	Yorkshire	v Worcestershire	Harrogate	1925
151	5th	R.Kilner	Yorkshire	v Nottinghamshire	Trent Bridge	1925
170	5th	R.Kilner	Yorkshire	v Derbyshire	Headingley	1925
108	5th	R.Kilner	Yorkshire	v Middlesex	Lord's	1926
110	5th	E.Robinson	Yorkshire	v Glamorgan	Hull	1926
141	5th	E.Oldroyd	Yorkshire	v Essex	Leyton	1926
193	5th	A.Mitchell	Yorkshire	v Northamptonshire	Northampton	1926
100*	6th	M.Leyland	Yorkshire	v Derbyshire	Bramall Lane	1926
198	6th	M.Leyland	Yorkshire	v Worcestershire	Worcester	1928
117	7th	A.Mitchell	Yorkshire	v Northamptonshire	Harrogate	1928
117	5th	H.Sutcliffe	Yorkshire	v Middlesex	Lord's	1929
116*	6th	E.Robinson	Yorkshire	v Sussex	Headingley	1929
247	7th	P.Holmes	Yorkshire	v Nottinghamshire	Trent Bridge	1929

Five Wickets in an Innings (287)

18.4	10	24	9	C.I.Thornton's England XI	v Australians	Scarborough	1899
15.2	6	28	9	Yorkshire	v Essex	Leyton	1899
21.4	9	39	9	Yorkshire	v Essex	Leyton	1929
12.5	5	23	8	Yorkshire	v Hampshire	Hull	1900
14.5	4	26	8	Yorkshire	v Kent	Catford	1902
12.5	4	28	8	Yorkshire	v Essex	Harrogate	1900
25.3	14	38	8	Yorkshire	v Nottinghamshire	Trent Bridge	1899
23	9	39	8	Yorkshire	v Sussex	Headingley	1920
19	4	43	8	Yorkshire	v Lancashire	Bradford	1900
12.2	1	44	8	Yorkshire	v Warwickshire	Bradford	1919
20.5	4	48	8	Yorkshire	v Somerset	Huddersfield	1926
26.2	9	53	8	Yorkshire	v Middlesex	Lord's	1901
31.4	11	55	8	Yorkshire	v Kent	Canterbury	1901
30	8	61	8	Yorkshire	v Lancashire	Bradford	1903
28.1	9	68	8	Yorkshire	v Cambridge University	Fenner's	1900
15	0	68	8	ENGLAND	v AUSTRALIA	Melbourne	1903/04
20.5	6	72	8	Yorkshire	v Gloucestershire	Bradford	1900

46	17	87	8	Yorkshire	v Worcestershire	Worcester	1903
52.5	21	90	8	Yorkshire	v Warwickshire	Edgbaston	1905
38	10	92	8	Yorkshire	v Northamptonshire	Northampton	1911
12.4	6	15	7	Yorkshire	v Gloucestershire	Bristol	1923
13.5	4	16	7	Yorkshire	v Derbyshire	Chesterfield	1911
11	3	17	7	ENGLAND	v AUSTRALIA	Edgbaston	1902
15.5	7	19	7	Yorkshire	v Derbyshire	Headingley	1914
11.1	4	20	7	Yorkshire	v Worcestershire	Bradford	1900
20.2	12	20	7	Yorkshire	v Gloucestershire	Hull	1901
19.1	9	24	7	Yorkshire	v Surrey	Bradford	1898
13.4	4	24	7	Yorkshire	v Somerset	Bath	1898
22	11	24	7	Yorkshire	v Middlesex	Bradford	1902
17	7	24	7	Yorkshire	v Derbyshire	Derby	1920
27.3	16	26	7	Europeans	v Hindus	Bombay	1921/22
20.4	6	32	7	Yorkshire	v Derbyshire	Derby	1900
13	3	33	7	Europeans	v Parsees	Bombay	1921/22
27.4	16	35	7	Yorkshire	v Cambridge University	Fenner's	1930
19	8	36	7	Yorkshire	v Gloucestershire	Headingley	1902
16	4	36	7	Yorkshire	v Cambridge University	Fenner's	1920
25	11	38	7	Yorkshire	v Nottinghamshire	Bramall Lane	1929
21.5	8	39	7	Yorkshire	v Middlesex	Lord's	1928
29.3	11	40	7	Yorkshire	v Nottinghamshire	Trent Bridge	1903
16	3	45	7	Yorkshire	v Middlesex	Bradford	1905
15.1	4	45	7	Yorkshire	v Northamptonshire	Headingley	1913
19	4	46	7	Yorkshire	v Essex	Leyton	1900
22	6	46	7	Lancashire & Yorkshire	v Rest of England	Hastings	1903
15.4	5	47	7	Yorkshire	v Gloucestershire	Gloucester	1919
23.4	6	53	7	Yorkshire	v Middlesex	Bradford	1920
21	4	55	7	Yorkshire	v Leicestershire	Leicester (AR)	1901
28.2	11	55	7	Yorkshire	v Derbyshire	Dewsbury	1928
24.2	10	56	7	Yorkshire	v C.I.Thornton's XI	Scarborough	1899
15.2	3	56	7	ENGLAND	v AUSTRALIA	Melbourne	1903/04
28	4	59	7	Yorkshire	v Sussex	Bramall Lane	1900
43	20	60	7	Yorkshire	v Derbyshire	Bradford	1923
16	3	63	7	Yorkshire	v Gloucestershire	Bristol	1901
27.4	7	67	7	Yorkshire	v Gloucestershire	Cheltenham	1900
16.4	2	68	7	Yorkshire	v Lancashire	Bradford	1909
31	11	72	7	Yorkshire	v Derbyshire	Bramall Lane	1900
21.5	7	74	7	Yorkshire	v Nottinghamshire	Bramall Lane	1919
21.2	2	78	7	Yorkshire	v Gloucestershire	Bristol	1901
51	4	80	7	Yorkshire	v Lancashire	Old Trafford	1921
48	17	83	7	Yorkshire	v Warwickshire	Edgbaston	1909
25.5	3	87	7	Yorkshire	v Nottinghamshire	Bradford	1909
37.5	13	98	7	Yorkshire	v Cambridge University	Fenner's	1913
48.3	12	102	7	Yorkshire	v Northamptonshire	Northampton	1926
42.3	7	115	7	Yorkshire	v Sussex	Hove	1900
42	7	116	7	Yorkshire	v Lancashire	Old Trafford	1926
43.3	8	116	7	Yorkshire	v Kent	Tonbridge	1929
32	4	123	7	Yorkshire	v Essex	Bradford	1902
65.1	21	147	7	Yorkshire	v Middlesex	Lord's	1899
7.5	4	4	6	Yorkshire	v Nottinghamshire	Trent Bridge	1901
8.2	4	9	6	Yorkshire	v Essex	Huddersfield	1905
6	3	13	6	Yorkshire	v Sussex	Hove	1922
11	5	15	6	Yorkshire	v MCC & Ground	Lord's	1902
14.4	5	16	6	Yorkshire	v Gloucestershire	Bristol	1899
14	4	16	6	Yorkshire	v Cambridge University	Fenner's	1905
15	7	17	6	Yorkshire	v Leicestershire	Leicester (AR)	1908
9	1	19	6	North	v South	Scarborough	1907
11.5	3	20	6	Yorkshire	v Gloucestershire	Dewsbury	1927
13	6	21	6	Yorkshire	v Somerset	Bath	1898
10	1	22	6	Yorkshire	v Derbyshire	Glossop	1907
12.2	4	22	6	Yorkshire	v Cambridge University	Fenner's	1924
12.5	2	23	6	Yorkshire	v Nottinghamshire	Headingley	1923

20.4	9	24	6	Yorkshire	v Essex	Bradford	1898
12.4	5	24	6	Yorkshire	v MCC	Scarborough	1903
10.5	3	25	6	Yorkshire	v Derbyshire	Huddersfield	1924
12	4	27	6	Players	v Gentlemen	Hastings	1901
16	7	27	6	Yorkshire	v Hampshire	Headingley	1904
19.1	8	27	6	Rest of England	v R.A.F. (Ex-Servicemen)		
						Eastbourne	1922
16.3	4	28	6	Yorkshire	v Essex	Leyton	1899
17.5	7	28	6	Yorkshire	v Warwickshire	Bramall Lane	1920
23	9	29	6	Yorkshire	v Essex	Leyton	1909
15	6	29	6	Yorkshire	v Surrey	Headingley	1911
21	8	29	6	Yorkshire	v Somerset	Huddersfield	1926
30	13	32	6	Yorkshire	v Nottinghamshire	Trent Bridge	1898
18	5	32	6	Yorkshire	v Somerset	Taunton	1902
22.3	9	33	6	Yorkshire	v Warwickshire	Bramall Lane	1902
16	7	33	6	Yorkshire	v Warwickshire	Edgbaston	1904
18	7	33	6	Yorkshire	v Nottinghamshire	Headingley	1908
20	6	33	6	Yorkshire	v Northamptonshire	Northampton	1919
15	4	34	6	Yorkshire	v Gloucestershire	Cheltenham	1902
21.2	11	36	6	Yorkshire	v Gloucestershire	Cheltenham	1900
15	5	36	6	Yorkshire	v Middlesex	Lord's	1909
22.3	7	37	6	Yorkshire	v Middlesex	Headingley	1903
22.5	7	37	6	Yorkshire	v Kent	Bramall Lane	1923
12	1	38	6	Yorkshire	v Surrey	Kennington Oval	1903
16.2	6	38	6	Yorkshire	v Surrey	Bradford	1910
24.1	7	38	6	Yorkshire	v Surrey	Kennington Oval	1921
19	4	39	6	MCC	v Victoria	Melbourne	1920/21
16.2	5	40	6	Yorkshire	v Essex	Harrogate	1900
15.4	1	40	6	Yorkshire	v Gloucestershire	Cheltenham	1904
16	4	40	6	Yorkshire	v Lancashire	Bradford	1909
20.4	2	40	6	Yorkshire	v Warwickshire	Edgbaston	1921
12.3	6	40	6	Yorkshire	v Northamptonshire	Dewsbury	1924
15	5	41	6	Yorkshire	v Leicestershire	Leicester (AR)	1901
23	9	42	6	Yorkshire	v Kent	Bradford	1902
30.3	9	43	6	Yorkshire	v Hampshire	Hull	1900
12	1	43	6	Yorkshire	v Sussex	Hull	1922
18.5	5	45	6	Yorkshire	v Essex	Headingley	1901
31	10	46	6	Yorkshire	v Leicestershire	Scarborough	1901
20	10	46	6	Yorkshire	v Lancashire	Old Trafford	1907
30	11	46	6	Yorkshire	v Surrey	Bramall Lane	1920
26.3	12	46	6	Yorkshire	v Leicestershire	Leicester (AR)	1921
29.5	11	47	6	Yorkshire	v Warwickshire	Edgbaston	1900
18.1	3	47	6	Yorkshire	v MCC & Ground	Scarborough	1901
19.1	4	47	6	Yorkshire	v Leicestershire	Dewsbury	1909
18	6	47	6	Yorkshire	v Northamptonshire	Northampton	1911
45	23	49	6	Yorkshire	v Warwickshire	Headingley	1902
18.5	3	49	6	Yorkshire	v MCC & Ground	Scarborough	1902
24	8	52	6	Yorkshire	v Leicestershire	Huddersfield	1900
15	3	53	6	Yorkshire	v MCC	Scarborough	1905
24.3	7	54	6	Yorkshire	v Worcestershire	Dewsbury	1901
17	2	55	6	MCC	v New South Wales	Sydney	1903/04
40	16	55	6	Yorkshire	v Leicestershire	Headingley	1928
29.4	5	56	6	H.D.G.Leveson-Gower's XI			
					v South Africans	Reigate	1924
26	8	56	6	Yorkshire	v Glamorgan	Swansea	1928
24	8	57	6	Yorkshire	v Leicestershire	Leicester (AR)	1909
24.3	6	58	6	Yorkshire	v Surrey	Bramall Lane	1900
26.1	10	59	6	Yorkshire	v Somerset	Taunton	1900
32.1	10	59	6	Yorkshire	v Warwickshire	Headingley	1909
20	2	59	6	Yorkshire	v Cambridge University	Fenner's	1911
27.2	7	61	6	Yorkshire	v Somerset	Taunton	1907
30	6	62	6	MCC	v Victoria	Melbourne	1903/04
41	22	64	6	Yorkshire	v Sussex	Hove	1899
24	4	66	6	Yorkshire	v Hampshire	Dewsbury	1919

28	7	67	6	Yorkshire	v Somerset	Taunton	1901
22.5	6	68	6	Yorkshire	v Leicestershire	Dewsbury	1909
24	6	68	6	Yorkshire	v Middlesex	Bramall Lane	1914
26.1	2	69	6	Yorkshire	v Somerset	Taunton	1907
30	8	71	6	Yorkshire	v Gloucestershire	Bramall Lane	1898
28	8	71	6	Yorkshire	v Lancashire	Headingley	1907
32	12	72	6	Lancashire & Yorkshire	v Rest of England	Hastings	1903
26.2	3	73	6	Yorkshire	v Surrey	Headingley	1905
25	3	73	6	Yorkshire	v Hampshire	Portsmouth	1920
26.5	6	76	6	Yorkshire	v MCC & Ground	Lord's	1900
52.6	21	87	6	Yorkshire	v Worcestershire	Worcester	1905
26	3	90	6	Yorkshire	v Sussex	Hove	1906
41	18	95	6	Yorkshire	v Warwickshire	Edgbaston	1904
37.2	9	95	6	Yorkshire	v Nottinghamshire	Trent Bridge	1906
34.1	7	99	6	Yorkshire	v Rest of England	Kennington Oval	1905
29.1	4	101	6	Yorkshire	v Hampshire	Bradford	1907
29	2	102	6	Yorkshire	v South Africans	Huddersfield	1912
29	3	109	6	Yorkshire	v Somerset	Bath	1909
24	0	109	6	Yorkshire	v Surrey	Bradford	1914
42.3	15	110	6	Yorkshire	v Surrey	Kennington Oval	1901
38.2	10	115	6	Yorkshire	v Somerset	Taunton	1901
48.4	13	124	6	Yorkshire	v Worcestershire	Worcester	1903
24.4	5	120	6	Yorkshire	v Gloucestershire	Bradford	1900
36.2	10	132	6	Players	v Gentlemen	Hastings	1901
52.3	15	132	6	Yorkshire	v Warwickshire	Edgbaston	1907
44.4	2	141	6	Yorkshire	v Northamptonshire	Dewsbury	1911
46.5	12	145	6	Yorkshire	v Somerset	Headingley	1901
50	8	150	6	Yorkshire	v Sussex	Eastbourne	1928
69.3	18	160	6	Yorkshire	v Leicestershire	Leicester (AR)	1928
9	6	4	5	Yorkshire	v Worcestershire	Huddersfield	1903
4.4	2	5	5	Yorkshire	v Derbyshire	Bradford	1910
6.1	3	6	5	MCC	v Victoria	Melbourne	1903/04
6.5	3	8	5	Yorkshire	v Essex	Leyton	1923
9.4	5	11	5	Yorkshire	v Somerset	Bath	1899
10.2	4	12	5	Yorkshire	v Warwickshire	Edgbaston	1922
6.3	0	16	5	Yorkshire	v Warwickshire	Edgbaston	1919
10.5	5	16	5	Yorkshire	v Northamptonshire	Bradford	1920
10.5	4	20	5	Yorkshire	v Gloucestershire	Bramall Lane	1903
21	11	20	5	Yorkshire	v Essex	Dewsbury	1920
15.2	7	20	5	Yorkshire	v Cambridge University	Fenner's	1923
9	2	21	5	Yorkshire	v Essex	Bramall Lane	1903
10	1	22	5	Yorkshire	v Gloucestershire	Headingley	1902
19.3	9	24	5	Yorkshire	v Worcestershire	Dudley	1922
20	11	24	5	Yorkshire	v Gloucestershire	Bristol	1922
30	16	25	5	Yorkshire	v Leicestershire	Dewsbury	1898
20.2	8	26	5	MCC	v Victoria	Melbourne	1903/04
13	4	26	5	Yorkshire	v Warwickshire	Dewsbury	1905
20	10	26	5	Europeans	v Parsees	Bombay	1921/22
21.2	6	26	5	Yorkshire	v Glamorgan	Bramall Lane	1923
12.2	6	27	5	Yorkshire	v Sussex	Hove	1921
16	6	28	5	Yorkshire	v Somerset	Weston-super-Mare	1924
15.5	5	29	5	Yorkshire	v Middlesex	Bradford	1923
15	2	30	5	Yorkshire	v Nottinghamshire	Bradford	1924
20	9	33	5	Yorkshire	v Leicestershire	Leicester (GR)	1898
15.3	1	34	5	Yorkshire	v Kent	Bramall Lane	1901
11.3	3	34	5	Yorkshire	v Nottinghamshire	Trent Bridge	1905
11.2	1	34	5	Yorkshire	v Surrey	Bradford	1910
22	9	34	5	Yorkshire	v Surrey	Headingley	1929
11	2	35	5	Yorkshire	v Lancashire	Liverpool	1913
26.4	10	35	5	Yorkshire	v Kent	Headingley	1919
22	6	35	5	Yorkshire	v Worcestershire	Worcester	1923
14.5	3	36	5	Yorkshire	v Sussex	Bradford	1901
19.2	6	36	5	Yorkshire	v Gloucestershire	Bristol	1905

18	5	36	5	Yorkshire	v MCC	Scarborough	1908
34	19	37	5	Yorkshire	v Warwickshire	Edgbaston	1926
13.5	5	37	5	Yorkshire	v Northamptonshire	Northampton	1928
16	8	39	5	Yorkshire	v Somerset	Headingley	1901
17	2	40	5	Yorkshire	v Warwickshire	Harrogate	1906
21.2	10	41	5	Yorkshire	v Glamorgan	Hull	1929
13.4	3	42	5	Yorkshire	v Kent	Tunbridge Wells	1913
18.3	2	42	5	Yorkshire	v Middlesex	Headingley	1919
18.5	4	43	5	MCC	v Natal	Durban	1909/10
10.5	0	43	5	Yorkshire	v Kent	Maidstone	1910
30.3	12	46	5	Yorkshire	v Surrey	Bradford	1898
20	3	46	5	Yorkshire	v Sussex	Harrogate	1919
27	8	46	5	Yorkshire	v Kent	Bramall Lane	1929
32.3	11	47	5	Yorkshire	v Middlesex	Lord's	1920
30	9	48	5	Yorkshire	v Warwickshire	Dewsbury	1905
11	2	49	5	Yorkshire	v Australians	Bradford	1902
16	3	49	5	Yorkshire	v Lancashire	Old Trafford	1906
18.4	6	49	5	Yorkshire	v Middlesex	Bradford	1908
22	8	51	5	Yorkshire	v Hampshire	Harrogate	1901
17.3	3	53	5	Yorkshire	v C.I.Thornton's XI	Scarborough	1900
26	6	54	5	Yorkshire	v Surrey	Headingley	1911
24	3	56	5	Yorkshire	v Surrey	Bradford	1914
16	4	56	5	Yorkshire	v Hampshire	Portsmouth	1920
32	12	57	5	Yorkshire	v Sussex	Harrogate	1899
33	9	57	5	Yorkshire	v Nottinghamshire	Headingley	1903
23.1	4	57	5	Yorkshire	v Middlesex	Lord's	1910
27.5	11	57	5	Yorkshire	v Northamptonshire	Harrogate	1928
34	12	57	5	MCC	v British Guiana	Georgetown	1929/30
23.3	4	58	5	Yorkshire	v Worcestershire	Worcester	1907
26	7	59	5	Yorkshire	v MCC & Ground	Scarborough	1898
25	3	59	5	Yorkshire	v Rest of England	Kennington Oval	1905
25	9	59	5	Yorkshire	v Surrey	Headingley	1927
33	8	60	5	Yorkshire	v Sussex	Hove	1903
42	16	61	5	Yorkshire	v Worcestershire	Bramall Lane	1904
20.4	4	62	5	Yorkshire	v Gloucestershire	Headingley	1906
17.1	3	63	5	ENGLAND	v AUSTRALIA	Bramall Lane	1902
29	5	63	5	C.I.Thornton's XI	v Australians	Scarborough	1926
32	12	65	5	Yorkshire	v Derbyshire	Dewsbury	1899
29	9	66	5	Yorkshire	v Gloucestershire	Hull	1901
22	3	66	5	Yorkshire	v Lancashire	Bramall Lane	1905
24.1	7	67	5	Yorkshire	v Lancashire	Old Trafford	1901
27.3	4	67	5	Yorkshire	v Lancashire	Headingley	1907
46.1	26	68	5	Yorkshire	v Essex	Bradford	1898
32.3	13	68	5	Yorkshire	v Essex	Leyton	1904
21	3	68	5	Yorkshire	v Essex	Leyton	1904
23.3	6	68	5	Yorkshire	v Nottinghamshire	Harrogate	1912
49	20	69	5	Yorkshire	v Warwickshire	Headingley	1898
38.4	18	71	5	Players	v Gentlemen	Scarborough	1902
33	12	71	5	Players	v Gentlemen	Lord's	1905
31	8	72	5	Yorkshire	v Essex	Bradford	1902
20	1	72	5	Yorkshire	v Gloucestershire	Bristol	1907
40	11	73	5	MCC	v New South Wales	Sydney	1907/08
24.5	7	73	5	Yorkshire	v Middlesex	Bramall Lane	1910
24.5	4	74	5	Yorkshire	v Lancashire	Old Trafford	1919
25	8	74	5	Yorkshire	v Nottinghamshire	Huddersfield	1921
29	7	76	5	Yorkshire	v Surrey	Headingley	1902
34	4	76	5	Yorkshire	v Sussex	Bramall Lane	1907
37	14	76	5	MCC	v Trinidad	Port of Spain	1929/30
22	5	77	5	Yorkshire	v All Ireland	Dublin	1908
32	5	78	5	MCC Australian Team			
					v An England XI	Hastings	1908
24.1	5	80	5	Yorkshire	v Middlesex	Headingley	1919
25	0	83	5	ENGLAND	v AUSTRALIA	Old Trafford	1909
26.1	7	84	5	Yorkshire	v Cambridge University	Fenner's	1903

30	5	84	5	Yorkshire	v Leicestershire	Leicester (AR)	1904
23.5	3	87	5	Yorkshire	v Australians	Bradford	1921
54.2	19	87	5	Yorkshire	v Nottinghamshire	Trent Bridge	1928
21.1	3	88	5	North	v South	Hastings	1904
33	5	91	5	Yorkshire	v Nottinghamshire	Trent Bridge	1902
34.4	6	91	5	Yorkshire	v Lancashire	Bradford	1903
42	15	92	5	Yorkshire	v An England XI	Hastings	1901
41.3	13	93	5	Yorkshire	v Kent	Tonbridge	1914
40.2	10	94	5	ENGLAND	v AUSTRALIA	Sydney	1903/04
24	4	94	5	Yorkshire	v Sussex	Hove	1906
30.5	5	95	5	H.D.G.Leveson-Gower's XI			
					v Australians	Scarborough	1930
39	5	97	5	Yorkshire	v Middlesex	Lord's	1907
42	11	108	5	Yorkshire	v Middlesex	Lord's	1921
38	9	111	5	Yorkshire	v MCC & Ground	Scarborough	1899
34	3	113	5	Yorkshire	v Kent	Maidstone	1920
36.4	3	115	5	Players of England	v Australians	Kennington Oval	1902
24	2	118	5	Yorkshire	v MCC & Ground	Lord's	1906
36	9	120	5	North	v South	Hastings	1900
29.4	4	124	5	North	v South	Scarborough	1906

Ten Wickets in a Match (68)

32	10	56	15	Yorkshire	v Essex	Leyton	1899
30.2	3	124	15	ENGLAND	v AUSTRALIA	Melbourne	1903/04
43.2	14	66	14	Yorkshire	v Hampshire	Hull	1900
29.1	9	68	14	Yorkshire	v Essex	Harrogate	1900
41.5	12	77	14	Yorkshire	v Somerset	Huddersfield	1926
56	16	139	14	Yorkshire	v Northamptonshire	Northampton	1911
37.2	5	141	14	Yorkshire	v Gloucestershire	Bristol	1901
45.3	11	192	14	Yorkshire	v Gloucestershire	Bradford	1900
94.4	30	211	14	Yorkshire	v Worcestershire	Worcester	1902
26.4	10	45	13	Yorkshire	v Somerset	Bath	1898
36	9	96	13	Yorkshire	v Leicestershire	Leicester (AR)	1901
49	18	103	13	Yorkshire	v Gloucestershire	Cheltenham	1900
32.4	6	108	13	Yorkshire	v Lancashire	Bradford	1909
54	18	118	13	Lancashire & Yorkshire			
					v Rest of England	Hastings	1903
64.4	14	152	13	Yorkshire	v Lancashire	Bradford	1903
40.3	15	52	12	Yorkshire	v Kent	Catford	1902
29	9	58	12	Yorkshire	v Gloucestershire	Headingley	1902
33	13	59	12	Europeans	v Parsees	Bombay	1921/22
49.4	21	70	12	Yorkshire	v Surrey	Bradford	1898
42.2	14	80	12	Yorkshire	v Essex	Leyton	1929
49.2	21	86	12	Yorkshire	v Gloucestershire	Hull	1901
42	10	115	12	Yorkshire	v Leicestershire	Dewsbury	1909
57	25	128	12	Yorkshire	v Warwickshire	Edgbaston	1904
53.3	9	130	12	Yorkshire	v Somerset	Taunton	1907
62.2	20	134	12	Yorkshire	v Middlesex	Lord's	1901
48.2	14	159	12	Players	v Gentlemen	Hastings	1901
66.2	17	182	12	Yorkshire	v Somerset	Taunton	1901
63	12	195	12	Yorkshire	v Essex	Bradford	1902
24.1	10	36	11	Yorkshire	v Worcestershire	Bradford	1900
30.1	13	44	11	Yorkshire	v Derbyshire	Derby	1920
19.1	6	52	11	Yorkshire	v Gloucestershire	Gloucester	1919
36.1	9	68	11	MCC	v Victoria	Melbourne	1903/04
27.4	7	72	11	Yorkshire	v Surrey	Bradford	1910
41.4	11	77	11	Yorkshire	v Derbyshire	Derby	1900
43	16	77	11	Yorkshire	v Gloucestershire	Bristol	1923
41	12	83	11	Yorkshire	v Surrey	Headingley	1911
51	19	85	11	Yorkshire	v Nottinghamshire	Bramall Lane	1929
40.4	12	90	11	Yorkshire	v Kent	Canterbury	1901

66.5	35	92	11	Yorkshire	v Essex	Bradford	1898
66	28	112	11	Yorkshire	v Nottinghamshire	Trent Bridge	1899
41	7	129	11	Yorkshire	v Hampshire	Portsmouth	1920
55.3	12	138	11	Yorkshire	v Lancashire	Headingley	1907
60.1	20	141	11	Yorkshire	v Cambridge University	Fenner's	1900
59.1	10	158	11	Yorkshire	v Rest of England	Kennington Oval	1905
48	3	165	11	Yorkshire	v Surrey	Bradford	1914
62.2	20	184	11	Yorkshire	v Somerset	Headingley	1901
50	7	184	11	Yorkshire	v Sussex	Hove	1906
23	10	39	10	Yorkshire	v Hampshire	Headingley	1904
37.4	19	51	10	C.I.Thornton's England XI			
					v Australians	Scarborough	1899
38	14	56	10	Yorkshire	v Middlesex	Bradford	1902
32.3	13	60	10	Yorkshire	v Gloucestershire	Cheltenham	1902
40	11	67	10	Yorkshire	v Northamptonshire	Northampton	1919
43	13	74	10	Yorkshire	v Warwickshire	Dewsbury	1905
21.4	2	75	10	Yorkshire	v Warwickshire	Bradford	1919
43.5	18	78	10	Yorkshire	v Essex	Headingley	1901
25.3	4	80	10	Yorkshire	v Cambridge University	Fenner's	1920
29	4	81	10	Yorkshire	v Surrey	Kennington Oval	1903
58.1	23	86	10	Yorkshire	v Cambridge University	Fenner's	1930
74	36	87	10	Yorkshire	v Leicestershire	Headingley	1928
51.4	11	95	10	H.D.G.Leveson-Gower's XI			
					v South Africans	Reigate	1924
47.5	19	112	10	Yorkshire	v Cambridge University	Fenner's	1913
40.4	5	115	10	Yorkshire	v Surrey	Headingley	1905
42.4	7	122	10	Yorkshire	v Middlesex	Headingley	1919
53.3	16	136	10	Yorkshire	v Essex	Leyton	1904
60	14	139	10	Yorkshire	v Surrey	Bramall Lane	1920
42	8	145	10	Yorkshire	v Middlesex	Bradford	1905
51.2	14	147	10	Yorkshire	v C.I.Thornton's XI	Scarborough	1899
65.3	15	151	10	Yorkshire	v Middlesex	Bradford	1920

Corrections to *Wisden*

1899	v Worcestershire	4th May	1st inns: 4 maidens (not 3)
	v Middlesex	29th May	1st inns: 20 maidens (not 21)
	v Warwickshire	22nd June	1st inns: H.W.Bainbridge c W.Rhodes (not F.Mitchell)
	v Sussex	6th July	2nd inns: E.H.Killick c D.Hunter (not B.B.Wilson)
1900	v Derbyshire	6th June	1st inns: W.Rhodes c J.Humphries (not J.J.Hulme)
	v Essex	14th July	1st inns: C.P.Buckenham lbw (not c&b)
1904	v Somerset	23rd July	1st inns: 8 maidens (not 3)
1905	v Warwickshire	25th May	2nd inns: 10 overs (not 12)
1906	v MCC	2nd August	2nd inns: T.W.Leather 14 W.Rhodes 13 (not vice-versa)
1907	v Somerset	24th June	1st inns: 3 maidens (not 8)
	v Kent	22nd August	1st inns: 18 overs (not 10)
1908	v Nottinghamshire	13th July	1st inns: W.Rhodes c A.O.Jones (not bowled)
1909	v Derbyshire	12th August	2nd inns: A.Morton c&b W.Rhodes
1910	v Lancashire	16th May	1st inns: 20 overs (not 21)
	v Northamptonshire	20th June	2nd inns: 19 overs (not 10)
1913	v Somerset	30th June	1st inns: J.C.White c W.Rhodes (not M.W.Booth)
1914	v Kent	6th July	2nd inns: 1.4 overs (not 1.1)
1919	v Lancashire	9th June	1st inns: W.Rhodes 37, P.Holmes 43, R.Kilner 45, D.C.F.Burton 11
	v A.I.F.	16th June	2nd inns: W.Rhodes 17-6-37-2 (not 9-2-18-2) G.H.Hirst (vice-versa)
	v Nottinghamshire	27th June	2nd inns: W.S.Lee st A.Dolphin (not J.R.Gunn)
	v Surrey	21st July	1st inns: T.Rushby and E.C.Kirk dismissals should be reversed - thus it is E.C.Kirk st A.Dolphin b W.Rhodes
	v Sussex	1st August	2nd inns: 8 overs (not 5)
	v Kent	25th August	2nd inns: E.Humphreys c Hirst (not Rhodes)
1920	v Lancashire	22nd May	1st inns: 11 maidens (not 1)
1921	v Lancashire	14th May	1st inns: 14 maidens (not 4)
	v Gentlemen	5th September	2nd inns: V.W.C.Jupp c W.Rhodes (not bowled)
1922	v Gloucestershire	26th July	1st inns: W.Rhodes c E.G.Dennett (not P.T. Mills)
1923	v Leicestershire	18th July	1st inns: J.H.King c P.Holmes (not W.Rhodes)
	v Lancashire	4th August	2nd inns: R.K.Tyldesley c P.Holmes (not W.Rhodes)
1925	v Gloucestershire	10th June	2nd inns: H.Smith c W.Rhodes (not P.Holmes)
1926	v Warwickshire	7th August	1st inns: 23.1 overs (not 23)
1929	v Hampshire	21st August	2nd inns: W.H.Livsey c A.W.Worsley (not W.Rhodes)
1930	v Gloucestershire	30th July	1st inns: W.Rhodes lbw (not bowled)